JONATHAN GATHORNE-HARDY was born in 1933 in Edinburgh, the son of a doctor. He was educated at Bryanston and Cambridge, where he edited the university magazine *Granta*. After living in Berlin and in Spain, he returned to England, where he was variously a teacher, bookseller, publisher, reviewer and advertising copywriter.

Since the publication in 1972 of *The Rise and Fall of the British Nanny*, Jonathan Gathorne-Hardy has been a full-time writer of fiction, non-fiction and children's books. He is married, and has two children.

JONATHAN GATHORNE-HARDY

The Rise and Fall of the British Nanny

**WITH A NEW INTRODUCTION
BY THE AUTHOR**

WEIDENFELD · LONDON

First published in Weidenfeld paperback in 1993
by Weidenfeld & Nicolson,
a division of the Orion Publishing Group,
Orion House, 5 Upper St Martin's Lane,
London WC2H 9EA

A catalogue record for this book is
available from the British Library.

ISBN 0 297 81395 1

Printed in Great Britain by
Butler & Tanner Ltd,
Frome and London

CONTENTS

Contents

ILLUSTRATIONS

Mrs Everest, Nanny to Winston Churchill (reprinted by kind permission of Curtis Brown Ltd on behalf of Winston Churchill, M.P.)

Nurse with children, circa 1860 (BBC Hulton Picture Library)

Park scene, 1890 (Mansell Collection)

Children in their nursery, 1884 (Mary Evans Picture Library)

Mrs Fanny Clamp (Martin Llewellyn)

Illustrated London News, 11 September 1920 (*Illustrated London News* Picture Library)

Edward Sackville-West, aged 11 months

Heatwave in Hyde Park, 1917 (BBC Hulton Picture Library)

Nannies at society wedding, 1938 (BBC Hulton Picture Library)

Nanny Marks outside Longleat (by courtesy of John Chillingworth)

Nanny Marks with Lady Caroline Somerset and her children (by courtesy of the Duchess of Beaufort)

Pram parade in Kensington Gardens, 1933 (BBC Hulton Picture Library)

The Parade Ground at the Norland Nursery Training College (by courtesy of Brian Long)

Lord Curzon

PREFACE TO
1993 EDITION

Dr Johnson considered that for a book to be regarded seriously it must last a hundred years. Cyril Connolly suggested a benchmark of ten years. A publisher today is pleased if a book is still alive after six months.

The Rise and Fall of the British Nanny was first published in 1972. The fact that it is being reissued now does not necessarily imply any particular quality. Books can survive for, or reappear after, many years not because of some outstanding intrinsic merit but because they strike some chord of peculiar resonance at the time (*The Diary of an Edwardian Lady* was an example of this). But since I think the chord, or chords, that this book seemed to strike are still resounding, it might be interesting to look briefly at them now.

The first is obvious: nostalgia. But there are unobvious aspects to this. It is perhaps no longer generally realised what an enormous part domestic service played until fairly recently in the economies of Western Europe—and particularly in Britain. In the 1890s, for instance, at nearly two million, there were nearly twice as many people employed in domestic service as were employed on the land. Only industry, with just over seven million, employed more.

The great change came in 1939. In my view the significant divide in twentieth-century social history was not the First but the Second World War. The number of domestic servants plummeted after the Second World War—and with them plummeted the Nanny. (I deal with precise figures in the body of the book.) This meant that by 1972 the last sizeable generation of children brought up by Nannies (those born between 1930 and 1939) were in their forties—the age at which nostalgia begins to bite. They formed a considerable proportion of the first readership, solidly backed up by their parents and grandparents (and old Nannies).

Today, one assumes, interest in the subject will be nostalgia for a curious part of a past age, pure and simple. Nostalgia is often despised today. In Americans, for instance, it is seen (by us) as an attempt to manufacture what, in European terms, they barely have—a history and a tradition. Among the British it is seen (by others and ourselves) as a desperate effort to return, if only in imagination, to the days when we were great and powerful and more civilised.

No doubt there is some limited truth in these strictures. In general terms, however, they are nonsense. Consider the past. From one angle, Sir Walter Scott's vast *oeuvre* (and much of Dickens) is a sustained exercise in nostalgia. In the late 1780s there was a sudden fashion for imitating the Jacobean in architecture. During the very century that our Empire got under way in earnest, all educated men and women looked admiringly to the civilisations of classical Rome and Greece for their models. Britain was not alone in this: the same feelings about the classical past were found all over Europe. Nor was it just the eighteenth century: during Spain's *siglo d'ora*, her golden age, the *hidalgos* (gentlemen) turned back to an invented age of chivalry—a fact exploited by Cervantes. Indeed, you could argue that for some 2,000 years the whole of Western culture has rested on a base of nostalgia—on a religion which looked back to a time of perfection before the Fall, and to the precepts of a teacher and God which would reverse the effects of that terrible event. Could so argue—until you find exactly the same sort of attitude to the past in China and India and Japan.

The fact is, of course, that 'nostalgia'—by which I mean a longing to return to (and belief in) an imagined ideal past—is an important and fundamental aspect of human nature. (As such it probably has its roots, as I later suggest, in the principle subject of this book—that is, in babyhood and early childhood.)

Any work of history benefits from the simple pleasure of imagining oneself for a moment in the past (even if that work upsets some idealised and artificial picture). Nothing is more alive in this respect than oral history, and by a lucky coincidence first-hand accounts provided the bulk—and the most interesting and entertaining part—of this book. Lucky, because the book appeared when a return to narrative and 'what-it-was-like-at-the-time' history was just beginning. Barbara Tuchman's *A Distant Mirror*, for instance, was published not long afterwards. The movement has continued, and increased, reaching an apogee quite recently in the work of Simon Schama. His books, especially the extraordinary and brilliant *Citizens*, are likely to have a profound effect, not just on academic historiography, but on the writers of popular history too—increasing the use of contemporary testimony and writing and, where possible, surviving oral report as well.

Other factors which helped the book's reception had nothing to do with nostalgia or a love of history. By the 1950s the discoveries and ideas of what can loosely be called the psychoanalytic school of thought had spread sufficiently widely and deeply for books and articles on child-upbringing to be published in large numbers. For a hundred years the majority of middle-class mothers had had virtually nothing important to do with the upbringing of their small children. Now they were compelled to take charge of it themselves. It is hardly surprising if they devoured instruction manuals on the subject with feverish anxiety. This book caught the continuing and hypnotised interest in the subject, which is one of its central themes (to the extent that it was used widely in courses for social workers to impart in palatable form essential information about the dynamics of child-upbringing).

At the same time—and in some ways in contradiction to this—increasing numbers of middle-class women did *not* want to be burdened with looking after their little children full-time. They wanted to work, and the most obvious solution was (whatever you called her) some version of the Nanny. It was not until the late 1960s that American writers like Betty Friedan began to be widely known here; nor was the work of people like Germaine Greer and Kate Millett influential before then. By 1972, when *The Rise and Fall of the British Nanny* appeared, the problem was acute and noticeable.

It remains so today. Hard statistics seem not to exist, but Nursery Training Colleges and advertising departments of magazines such as *The Lady* and *Nursery World* say that a considerable proportion of their enquiries come from mothers who want someone to look after their young children while they work. I suspect that these now make up the largest proportion of people employing Nannies or Nanny-substitutes. Articles are written about this, including an excellent recent one by Madeleine Marsh (*Independent on Sunday*, 21st March 1993). I was fascinated to see things I had discovered again and again, from 1850 onwards, surfacing once more as sharp, poignant and tangled as ever. The nubile young Nanny seducing the husband. The battle between mother and Nanny: 'Interfering mums, they're the worst,' said Rachel, one of Madeleine Marsh's informants. 'The best thing is just let the Nanny get on with the job she's paid to do. If they interfere, they shouldn't have a Nanny at all—they should be looking after the kids themselves.' Or the Nanny leaving: I know one busy young woman whose unfortunate little child has had ten Nannies in four years —with completely predictable results.

Here, nothing I had written needed to be changed. Indeed, the only significant alteration I have made to this edition is to update the table in Appendix B giving comparative values of the pound. It is perplexing, in fact often meaningless, to read about prices and wages in the past without some idea of what they would be worth today. Apart from this, though there have been advances and alterations in areas I researched earlier, none, as far as I could see, warranted any fundamental change in the conclusions I reached then.

In the most important area of all—the effects on further development and behaviour of the first five to ten years of life—there has been some change of emphasis in recent years. There is more optimism about efforts to offset the damaging effects of early upbringing. More especially, much is made of the possibilities of personality development and 'growth' in later life. Nevertheless, these are relatively minor modifications to the view which was generally accepted when I was writing. That view is accepted still: namely, that the first five to ten years are of overwhelming importance, and in precisely those ways that I describe.

Aside from correcting some minor errors, this book is therefore essentially the same as it was in 1972. But even such a short time as twenty years has given some details a period flavour—for instance when I refer to Nanny Franco, or the power wielded by the old Nanny of the Shah of Persia, or make admiring and wondering references to motorways about to be constructed which have not only long since been completed but have started to crumble away or else, under a wrong-headed transport policy, are being widened to seven lanes or even eight. I have unashamedly left all these in. A book about Nannies *should* have a period flavour.

PREFACE

I estimate that the conclusions in this book are based on a sample of 296 Nannies. This includes Nannies I interviewed, Nannies who wrote to me or whom I read about and Nannies I had described to me. Now I understand that for a subject of this magnitude a sample of nearly three hundred should be extremely reliable. Unfortunately, it is not nearly as impressive as it sounds.

The reason is that the quality of my sample was very uneven. People frequently exaggerated the importance of books they advised me to read. For example, someone said I should read a novel by Gissing, *The Odd Women*; "I seem to remember a first-rate Nanny figure there." At that time I wanted to read Gissing. He was one of many examples of upper and upper-middle class men of that period who preferred lower class girls to those of their own class, a phenomenon I was interested in. *The Odd Women* is a long book and took me nearly two days to read. There was only one reference to a Nurse or Nanny and it occurred three pages from the end, on page 493: "They engaged a good nurse for the child." Another person said there was a wonderful old colonel figure in one of Evelyn Waugh's early novels who borrowed some money from his Nanny in order to go to a brothel. The Nanny as Bank is a slender but recurring theme, so once again I doggedly set to. I located the fiction after four novels–in *Scoop*. There are numerous Nannies in Waugh's books, kindly if conventional portraits on the whole; the main one here is Nanny Bloggs (one might call her Nanny Scoop), and it is true she does lend a colonel figure, Uncle Theodore Boot, some money and that he does seem to be planning a visit to a brothel. But as the entire action of the novel, taking place over several months, separates the two events, a direct connection seems unlikely.

The same poverty sometimes applied to my interviews. A long and rambling discourse would end with my having only corroborated again the sort of way a Nanny learnt her trade or having recaptured once more the 'feel' of a particular Edwardian nursery.

It will be evident from the text which books I found most fruitful. As far as personal interviews go, I have relied chiefly on eighteen 'in-depth', discussions with Nannies, and sixteen similar interviews with people about their Nannies. By 'in-depth' I mean useful interviews of two or three hours, usually repeated.

Now, although these interviews were backed up on many individual points by dozens of less valuable discussions, by reading, and by a great number of letters, an effective live sample of thirty-four is a considerable reduction on 296. At the outset, therefore, I must emphasise that any conclusions I have drawn can only be tentative. Any one of them—the average age, for example, at which children were left by their Nannies, plainly a significant factor—could be entirely upset by a more thorough statistical survey. And there is still just time to make such a survey. Because of the nature of their training, and the accidents of longevity, it is still possible to find quite large numbers of Nannies whose experience of conditions in the latter half of the nineteenth century and Edwardian days is as good as first hand, or sometimes actually is first hand. There are still more who were actively Nannying in the '20s and '30s. In ten or fifteen years it will be too late.

All my conclusions, therefore, are inherently tentative; it is arguable that I am not justified in drawing some of them at all. A number of anthropologists and sociologists would certainly think so. In *The People of Great Russia*, for instance, Geoffrey Gorer makes the observation that you cannot say that a particular type of individual upbringing, because it causes a certain individual to behave in a certain way, is the cause of more general social behaviour. I do not agree with this. At the least, I think you can say that if a behaviour pattern in a culture is very marked and if it relates strongly to the method of upbringing, then that correlation must be suggestive. You are entitled to ask a critic, how else do you explain the phenomenon? Sometimes it is *only* possible to understand certain social patterns by the way the children in that society were reared. The violent group loyalty and extreme social cohesion of Kibbutzniks, along with other characteristics of Kibbutz society, are inexplicable without reference to their upbringing.

The lives of Nannies, anecdotes about their employers, their charges, their battles with other servants, are sometimes moving, frequently interesting, quite often the intense trivia of long vanished nurseries are still amusing; but I also think that in a study of this sort it would show a lack of courage not to attempt some more profound conclusions. Speculation about the deeper impulses at work in society is exciting. Certainly it is not a courage Gorer lacks. *The People of Great Russia* is an attempt, on a scale I do not think I would dare, to relate entire chunks of Russian behaviour to the fact that they were all severely swaddled as babies. I do not actually agree with this thesis; I do not see, for instance, how he can explain why those very wide ranging characteristics he attributes directly to swaddling were not general in Europe during the many centuries that severe swaddling was the universal practice. But there can be no question that it is a very brilliant, stimulating and illuminating book; there can also be no question that it is based on the idea that you *can* draw conclusions about general social behaviour from a study of individual upbringing. There must be a suspicion that when Gorer says you can't he is trying to have his cake and eat it.

How you make up your mind affects this book, but less seriously. I think you can draw conclusions from Nannies and I have drawn them. If you do not agree with them then they remain as a thread which guides us into and allows us to explore certain aspects of English society. The book remains quite simply as their history; a study of a unique and curious way of bringing up children, which evolved among the upper and upper-middle classes during the nineteenth century, flourished for approximately eighty years and then, with the Second World War, disappeared for ever.

ACKNOWLEDGEMENTS

During the course of my researches I received some 250 letters, a number of which resulted in a good deal of correspondence. These letters were invaluable, particularly those of Lady Anne Hill, Mrs. Frances Partridge, Miss Bridget Tisdall, and a correspondent who wished to remain anonymous, but who will be recognisable as the one who had eleven Nannies in eleven years. Some of those who wrote to me may feel I have not made sufficient use of the information they gave me; I can only say that without their letters this book would have been much harder, if not impossible, to write. I owe a large debt to everyone who wrote to me; and an equal one to all those who allowed me to talk to them.

A number of other people helped me in different ways. Although I take him to task somewhat for his neglect of Mrs. Everest, a neglect which I am sure he would acknowledge, Dr. Anthony Storr was generous with his time and fruitful in his comments. I am grateful to Anne Wolley Dod and Juliet Brightmore who assisted me with some reading. The book could barely have appeared but for Jenny Scott's sometimes clairvoyant skill at deciphering my handwriting and translating it into perfect typescript. I am very grateful to Richard King, who for an entire year put at my disposal a large, empty, luxuriously furnished and permanently centrally heated London house. I would like to thank Mr. Douglas Matthews of the London Library. For me, as for all authors who use that fine institution, the depth of his encyclopaedic reading, the pertinence of his suggestions, and his continuing interest, were extremely helpful and encouraging. My thanks are due to Ogilvy, Benson and Mather for their generosity with time; to Robin Denniston for his encouragement, and to him and Hodder and Stoughton for their financial generosity; and to Kyle Cathie for her skill in collecting the illustrations. Finally I would like to thank Diana Crawfurd for her never-failing enthusiasm and support and for a friendship and kindness which sustained me more than anything else.

Two books I would like to single out since it is not clear from the text, as it is with all other written sources, how much I relied on them. These are two of my predecessors in this little-explored field: *The Years of the Nannies* by

Mary Ann Gibbs and, to a slightly lesser extent, *The Story of the Nursery* by Magdalen King-Hall. Although the way it is interpreted and the use to which I put it are my own, a great deal of the material in Chapter 2 came from these books. I must also formally acknowledge the following publishers, institutions and people for their permission, often after substantial payment, to quote from the books whose copyright they control: William Heinemann Ltd. for extracts from *Winston S. Churchill*, Vol. I: *Youth 1874–1900* by Randolph Churchill and Houghton Mifflin Company for permission to reprint this material in the U.S.A.; the Estate of Sir Alan Herbert and Ernest Benn Ltd., for permission to quote from the former's 'Other People's Babies', included in *Ballads for Broadbrows*, and also his poem 'Nanny'; B.P.C. Publishing Ltd. and Sir Compton Mackenzie for permission to quote from the latter's *Sinister Street*, and him and Chatto and Windus Ltd. for permission to quote from *My Life and Times—Octave 1*; Curtis Brown Ltd. and the Estate of Edward Sackville-West for permission to quote from *Simpson*, and Curtis Brown Ltd. for permission to quote from the play *All for Mary* by Kay Bannerman and Harold Brooke; Jonathan Cape Ltd. for permission to quote from *The Kandy Kolored Tangerine-Flake Streamline Baby* by Tom Wolfe, and Farrar, Straus and Giroux, Inc. for use of the same material in the U.S.A.; the B.B.C. for permission to quote from the *Man Alive* television programme made by Desmond Wilcox called 'Who'll be Mother?'; the *Sunday Times* and Laurens van der Post for a review he wrote in that paper; *Harpers & Queen* for quotations from interviews given to Francis Wyndham; *Nursery World* for permission to quote the poem on page 223; and J. P. Donleavy for permission to quote from *The Beastly Beatitudes of Balthazar B*.

NANNY

I sing a long neglected dame
Let plays and poets all proclaim
The wonder of the mother's name,
And even that of granny;
Let others tell with loud hurrahs
The general praises of papas—
I hymn the mother of mamas,
I sing the British Nanny.
Not every pink and girlish thing
That pushes round a pram,
The ancient rock-like NURSE I sing,
Britannia's virgin dam,
That, old as mountains and as stout,
From child to child is passed about,
Till childless yet, she passes out,
The lonely British Nanny.

A. P. Herbert

CHAPTER ONE

The Nanny Phenomenon and the Case of Winston Churchill

Some years ago I read two books, by chance one after the other, in each of which a Nanny briefly figured. The first was a biography of Lord George Curzon by Kenneth Rose. In this he quotes some notes about the Nanny, Miss Paraman—the very name is like some flagellant's fantasy—which Curzon made years later.

> In her savage moments she was a brutal and vindictive tyrant; and I have often thought since that she must have been insane. She persecuted and beat us in the most cruel way and established over us a system of terrorism so complete that not one of us ever mustered up the courage to walk upstairs and tell our father or mother. She spanked us with the sole of her slipper on the bare back, beat us with her brushes, tied us for long hours to chairs in uncomfortable positions with our hands holding a pole or a blackboard behind our backs, shut us up in darkness, practised on us every kind of petty persecution, wounded our pride by dressing us (one in particular) in red shining calico petticoats (I was obliged to make my own) with an immense conical cap on our heads round which, as well as on our breasts and backs, were sewn strips of paper bearing in enormous characters, written by ourselves, the words Liar, Sneak, Coward, Lubber and the like. In this guise she compelled us to go out in the pleasure ground and show ourselves to the gardeners. She forced us to walk through the park at even distances, never communicating with each other, to the village and show ourselves to the villagers. It never occurred to us that these good folk sympathised intensely with us and regarded her as a fiend. Our pride was much too deeply hurt . . . She made us trundle our hoops as young children, all alone, up and down a place in the grounds near the hermitage where were tall black fir trees and a general air of gloom and of which we were intensely afraid. She forced us to confess to lies which we had never told, to sins which we had never committed, and then punished us savagely, as being self-condemned. For weeks we were not allowed to speak to each other or to a human soul.

Immediately after this, I read *Churchill—Four Faces and the Man*, a collection of essays about Churchill, among which there was one, and it was the best, by Anthony Storr. At one point he quotes part of a passage (which I here give in full) from Churchill's only novel *Savrola*.

> Savrola's thoughts were interrupted by the entrance of the old woman with a tray. He was tired, but the decencies of life had to be; he rose, and passed into the inner room to change his clothes and make his toilet. When he returned the table was laid; the soup he had asked for had been expanded by the care of his housekeeper into a more elaborate meal. She waited on him, plying him the while with questions and watching his appetite with anxious pleasure. She had nursed him from his birth up with a devotion and care which knew no break. It is a strange thing, the love of these women. Perhaps it is the only disinterested affection in the world. The mother loves her child; that is maternal nature. The youth loves his sweetheart; that too may be explained. The dog loves his master; he feeds him; a man loves his friend; he has stood by him perhaps at doubtful moments. In all there are reasons; but the love of a foster-mother for her charge appears absolutely irrational. It is one of the few proofs, not to be explained even by the association of ideas, that the nature of mankind is superior to mere utilitarianising and that his destinies are high.

It was not the passage itself which struck me particularly. It is quite a celebrated one and I vaguely remembered reading it before. Nor was it the contrast between Churchill's feelings towards his Nurse and the understandable bitterness which Curzon felt towards the monster who had ruled him. But it was the use that Dr. Storr made of it. His comment on it was that what was surprising was Churchill's surprise that a Nurse should love her charges. It is almost as though he expected a Nurse to dislike them. Yet, Dr. Storr argued, Nannies and Nurses have no children or husbands. It is natural they should love the children put under them.

Now, leaving aside for the moment that Churchill is not saying this love is unnatural, but that it is not based on any obvious, rational self-interested motive, and that he, as Savrola, is expressing not so much surprise as gratitude, what further struck me as strange was that Dr. Storr never once referred to Churchill's Nurse again. Yet I seemed to remember from somewhere, probably where I had originally read the passage Storr quoted, that Churchill's Nurse had played an important, even crucial, role in his life.

Certainly Miss Paraman had dictated the general shape of Curzon's future career; her savagery both whipping him on and, it could be argued, creating those difficulties of temperament which finally prevented him becoming Prime Minister. If the same dominance could be attributed to the person who looked after Churchill, then these were two extremely important and influential women. Curzon, among a great many other posts, was Viceroy of India from 1898 to 1905, governing three hundred million people for seven years, and Foreign Secretary in the Governments of Lloyd George, Bonar Law and Baldwin. Churchill's position needs no explanation. It next occurred to me, in the process which led to this book, that an entirely new view, and a very much more accurate one, might be obtained of a large number of our past rulers if they were studied with reference to their Nannies. Indeed, it might well lead one to a new interpretation of British history—the Nanny View of History. Because, as well as Curzon and (if I was right) Churchill, probably the vast majority of those, in all spheres, who had governed or influenced our lives during the last hundred or hundred and fifty years (Curzon was born in 1850, Churchill in 1874) had been brought up by a Nanny. These devoted or docile or savage women—their temperaments as various as human nature—might be expected to have played an infinitely greater part in the upbringing and character-formation of our great men than had their own parents.

And not only great men; thousands, even perhaps millions, of lesser men too. For surely it had been an army, a great host of Nannies that had swept Britain some time in the nineteenth and early twentieth centuries, engulfing not just the aristocracy and upper ranks of society, but reaching far down into the middle classes as well. It was, when I thought about it, a remarkable phenomenon. How was it that hundreds of thousands of mothers, apparently normal, could simply abandon all loving and disciplining and company of their little children, sometimes almost from birth, to the absolute care of other women, total strangers, nearly always uneducated, about whose characters they must usually have had no real idea at all? It was a practice, as far as I knew, unparalleled on such a vast scale in any other culture which had ever existed. How had it arisen? When and under what circumstances? How did it progress and, as it had certainly now done, decline? Above all, what effects did it have?

So began my long and often perplexing pursuit of that unique, sometimes saint-like, sometimes horrifying, sometimes baffling figure—the British Nanny.

SCOPE OF THE BOOK

Churchill and Curzon aroused my curiosity, but of course number is the point. A cultural pattern of this sort is of no significance unless it is statistically large enough to affect the society in which it operates. Ten Nannies may be interesting, and, if they are the Nannies of Prime Ministers, will have had influence. Two thousand or five thousand Nannies, as perhaps we have now, makes an interesting study in survival in a specialised area of privilege. But one million Nannies, two million Nannies (I shall deal later with the accuracy of Nanny figures), and this continuing for a great number of years, is a situation worth studying to see (however tentatively) if it had any recognisable and large-scale social effects. For this reason it is important that I define precisely the limits of this book, who I will and will not count as a British Nanny.

Early on, when I was still reading and interviewing, I received an extremely sharp letter from an old ex-Nanny called Mrs. Wake. She said that it was impossible for me to have had a Nanny myself (indeed impossible for me to know or write about Nannies) because the real Nanny, the true Victorian Nanny, disappeared in 1914. This old Nanny would have started, she said, as a nursery-maid at twelve, worked long and arduous hours under a draconian R.S.M. Nanny, painfully worked her way up to Under-Nurse, or even Second Under-Nurse, and finally have achieved Nanny-dom herself, with a nursery far removed from the rest of the house, nursery-maids under her, and numerous charges. Over these charges she would have wielded despotic power, to use benevolently or not according to her temperament. Nor would the parents have had anything to do with the children until they were at least seven—if then. They might have seen their mother for ten minutes in the morning; then, some time between four-thirty and six, they would have spent an hour or so in the drawing-room before returning to the nursery. This pattern would have been inflexible.

Now this figure, the Classic Nanny, will of course occupy an important position in this book; she marks the point at which our subject reached her apogee. (Accurately placed by Mrs. Wake between 1895 and 1914, the Classic Nanny would probably not, incidentally, have been called Nanny —at least by the adults. The origins of the word are extremely obscure, but it seems not to have become universal until the 1920s; before the First World War it was used by children and not adults, and in the nineteenth century she was called Nurse or Mrs. Nor did the Classic Nanny disappear in 1914; on the contrary she flourished until 1939, and even now, in some distant wealthy spot in a remote county you can occasionally find single, usually very ancient, but still vigorous specimens, wrinkled relics of the pre-plasticine age.) The Classic Nanny is in a sense the centre of this book; she is not its whole subject.

Because, as I have said, the unusual and interesting thing about large segments of English Society, at various times but particularly from somewhere round the mid-nineteenth century on, has been their willingness to allow other people to bring up their children. It is this situation in its entirety that I want to study. I want to include all the women who looked after other people's children. I shall examine all forms of delegation—from the most absolute, when the child was given to foster-parents, through the infinitely various and often subtle degrees of control accorded to, or shared with, the Nanny, down to the reverse situation, where the mother is dominant and only helped by a maid.

And our study will sometimes include women who appear to have the role of, or are even called, Governess. This is partly because in the sixteenth, seventeenth and, to a degree, still in the eighteenth centuries, the Nurse in larger, grander households, was also expected to teach a child to read and write—but at the age of two or three, when her chief role was still nursing. Jack Verney in the sixteenth century was taught to sing at the age of three. John Evelyn, the seventeenth-century diarist wrote that "I was not instructed in my rudiments until I was four"; evidently late. In the nineteenth century this practice of Nurse/Governess continued with the nursery governess, but as it became fashionable to have a governess the nursery prefix would often get dropped. Where the charges are six or under and where her duties are not so much to instruct as to look after and 'bring up' the children, then she is in effect a Nanny and I have included her. But where the children are older and where education is the prime object, then she falls outside my scope.

CHURCHILL AND NANNY EVEREST

"We shall go on till the end, we shall fight in France, we shall fight on the seas and oceans, we shall fight with growing confidence and growing strength in the air, we shall defend our island, whatever the cost may be, we shall fight on the beaches, we shall fight on the landing grounds, we shall fight in the fields and in the streets, we shall fight in the hills; we shall never surrender . . ."

House of Commons, June 4, 1940

This is a famous speech. It has supplanted the words which Shakespeare gave Henry V before Agincourt. Before delving into the historical background of the Nanny, necessary and fascinating as this was, I decided first to satisfy my curiosity about Winston Churchill.

In his essay on the subject, though he has used several subsidiary factors as buttresses to the line of argument, Anthony Storr bases his main case on parental neglect. This he has no difficulty in establishing. There can be no doubt that Churchill was neglected by both parents: his father Lord Randolph was an obsessed politician, absorbed in the machinations of politics; his mother was extremely young, extremely beautiful and completely caught up in the whirl of fashionable society. They entertained, and were entertained, constantly. Sometimes whole weeks passed when they barely saw Winston at all.

Now the consequences of a deprived and neglected childhood have been well charted. Dr. Storr charts them again and then sees how they fit Churchill. Their aptness is, at times, quite uncanny.

If a child's emotional needs are not fulfilled, or are only partially fulfilled by his parents, he will feel frustrated. Frustration leads to feelings of hostility, but hostility which cannot be expressed against those who have caused it because the child needs the love they are denying him. A number of things, therefore, happen. The first is that he creates, in his imagination, a picture of the parents he would like to have had and pretends he did have that love.

> Psychiatrists have often observed [writes Dr. Storr], that delinquent and emotionally disturbed children, who have parents who are actually neglectful or cruel, still maintain that these 'bad' parents are really 'good', and blame themselves for their parents' faults. A small child being weak and defenceless, finds it unbearable to believe that there are no adults who love, support and guide him; and if there are not, he invents them.

But this idealisation is of course very much easier if the parents are never there. They can then, in effect, become idols as well. Both processes took place in Churchill. All his life he expressed his admiration and love of his parents, particularly of his mother. "She shone for me," he wrote, "like the Evening Star. I loved her dearly—but at a distance." Later, he transferred this conception of romantic perfection on to women in general. Violet Bonham-Carter, among others, commented on this.

> This inner circle of friends contained no women. They had their own place in his life. His approach to women was essentially romantic. He had a lively susceptibility to beauty, glamour, radiance, and those who possessed these qualities were not subjected to analysis. This possession of all the cardinal virtues was assumed as a matter of course. I remember him taking umbrage when I once commented on the 'innocence' of his approach to women. He was

affronted by this epithet as applied to himself. Yet to me he would certainly have applied it as a term of praise.

And, of course, since women were perfect, a woman Queen must be the quintessence of perfection. Once, after staring raptly at a photograph of her for some time, he murmured, "Lovely! Inspiring! All the film people in the world, if they had scoured the globe could not have found anyone so suited to the part."

Another aspect of deprived children is that they often continue to make the demands in adult life which were not met when they were young. They are selfish and querulous, they insist on little services, appear incapable of looking after themselves; they behave like big spoilt babies. Churchill certainly had this side to his character and when he was able to obtain the attentions he wanted he revelled in them. Whenever he was ill he tried to get at least two nurses to look after him. Lady Churchill once said to Churchill's doctor, Lord Moran, "Winston is a pasha. If he cannot clap his hands for a servant he calls for Walter as he enters the house. If it were left to him he'd have two nurses for the rest of his life. He would like two in the room, two in the passage. He is never so happy, Charles, as he is when one of the nurses is doing something for him while Walter puts on his socks."

But the repressed hostility engendered by neglect has to go somewhere. Frequently it turns itself against authority in general. The worst behaved children are the least loved, and all his life Churchill was to regard anyone in authority with potential dislike. His hostility also found expression in a general aggressiveness and pugnacity, which used to burst out with startling force and for whose victims Churchill was often afterwards sorry.

But above all it led Churchill to compensate by ambition. If the world is unkind then I will take it on at its own game and beat it. This ambition appeared in Churchill at an extremely early age and took the form of dreams that he had been chosen by destiny for some great purpose. This fantasy was to pursue him until he was sixty-five. And although, coming from a political family, politics was the career in which he would most likely choose to shine, it is interesting that political success depends in part on being accepted, admired, even, in a sense, loved, by a great number of people. But parental neglect not only explains the fury of Churchill's ambition; it also explains the form of its final demise. Storr is perceptive about the genesis of this development.

In the ordinary course of events, a child takes in love with his mother's milk.

A child who is wanted, loved, played with, cuddled, will incorporate within himself a lively sense of his own value; and will therefore surmount the inevitable setbacks and disappointments of childhood with no more than temporary sorrow, secure in the belief that the world is predominantly a happy place, and that he has a favoured place in it. A child, on the other hand, who is unwanted, rejected, or disapproved of will gain no such conviction. Although such a child may experience periods of both success and happiness, these will neither convince him that he is lovable, nor finally prove to him that life is worthwhile. A whole career may be dedicated to the pursuit of power, the conquest of women, or the gaining of wealth, only, in the end, to leave the person face to face with despair and a sense of futility, since he has never incorporated within himself a sense of his value as a person; and no amount of external success can ultimately compensate him for this.

One of the most tragic pictures, which can be sensed in Lord Moran's account of Churchill's last years, though it is scarcely mentioned, veiled over with tact, is of his ultimate unhappiness. He would sit for days, weeks, months it seems, silent and crushed, convinced of failure and of the uselessness of his life. His old enemy 'Black Dog', kept at bay so long, conquered him in the end.

For this was the final fruit of parental neglect; it brought forth in Churchill an inherited tendency to depression. This is a perfectly well attested phenomenon. Manic/depressive phases, which often run in families, can lie latent, sometimes for a lifetime; but should circumstances be particularly adverse, like an unhappy childhood or a series of crippling blows from fortune, then they will become manifest. Certainly these moods of depression, his 'Black Dog' moods, recurred throughout his life, usually when out of office (and so symbolically once again unloved). He conquered them by activity—writing, painting, bricklaying. The feeling of abasement and failure alternating or combined with self-glorification is precisely expressed in Churchill's remark to Violet Bonham-Carter, "We are all worms. But I do believe that I am a glow worm."

This complex series of deep-seated reactions to his early childhood not only, says Dr. Storr, explains Churchill's character; in particular it explains the events of 1940, when he was sixty-five. Then, miraculously, reality and fantasy blended; at last the sense of destiny was fulfilled. The release of passion and energy, as sometimes happens when a man falls in love with a woman who incarnates some deep subconscious wish, was immediate and immense. The force that filled him flowed from the most profound springs of his nature. At last his hostility, his rage, his aggressiveness could find complete and legitimate outlet. Not only that, but

England was in a desperate state. Despair was everywhere. It was national. But Churchill had met despair—and defeated it. Only a man who had done that could carry conviction. It was this knowledge, that deep despair and depression could be overcome, which gave him his great strength, his certainty. It is this combination that accounts for the messianic force of his leadership, the heroic, almost visionary glow which surrounded him at that time and which inspired England and led her to victory.

There is, actually, something almost messianic and visionary about Dr. Storr's portrait itself. And it is more convincing even than this. It is supported by ingenious and penetrating side analyses. For instance there is Churchill's puny physique. As a boy he was small and delicate. He grew up, according to Moran, "into a man, small in stature, with thin, un-muscular limbs, and the white delicate hands of a woman; there was no hair on his chest and he spoke with a lisp and a slight stutter." He was five feet six inches tall and his chest, when he was at Sandhurst, measured thirty-one inches. Very young, he trained his will so that he could force himself to be brave and physically strong and active. Brendan Bracken said to Moran, "You and I think of Winston as self-indulgent; he has never denied himself anything, but when a mere boy he deliberately set out to change his nature, to be tough and full of male spirits." Plainly, this is another good reason for that aggressiveness already explained by parental neglect. And there are other suggestions of a similar cogency.

True, Dr. Storr does give a modest disclaimer at the end of his discourse.

> It is at this point that psycho-analytic insight reveals its inadequacy. For although I believe that the evidence shows that the conclusions reached in this essay are justified, we are still at loss to explain Churchill's remarkable courage. In the course of his life he experienced many reverses: disappointments which might have embittered and defeated a man who was not afflicted by the 'Black Dog'. Yet his dogged determination, his resilience, and his courage enabled him, until old age, to conquer his own inner enemy, just as he defeated the foes of the country he loved so well.

But of course he isn't at a loss at all. This is just the routine genu-flexion obligatory for anyone writing about 'genius' (especially if that genius is Churchill). No amount of explaining can 'really' explain, one says, the wonder of man. In fact Dr. Storr feels quite confident that he has done just this. And so do we, or at least so did I until, to put at rest that vague doubt which had stirred in me when I read the quotation from his novel *Savrola*, I read further into Churchill's early life. There to my astonishment I found a quite different picture of his childhood; so far from being neglected, his early years were remarkable for their security and love, but it was security and love received after the fashion of the time —from the arms of a Nanny. For some reason, perhaps because it destroys the neatness of his portrait, in a study devoted to Churchill's childhood, Dr. Storr has more or less ignored one fact, a mountain of a fact if you like, namely the most important person in it.

Mrs. Everest was engaged as Nanny by the Randolph Churchills very soon after Winston was born in 1874. From then on, wrote his son, "until her death in 1895, when Winston was twenty, [she] was destined to be the principal confidante of his joys, his troubles, and his hopes." She was, in effect, far more than this. For the first eight years of his life he was virtually never separated from her. He slept in her room, was washed, changed, dressed and fed by her. A calm, loving, warm character, whose gentle exterior hid reserves of considerable strength and determination, she adored Winston and, if the evidence of her giving him presents is anything to go by, often over-indulged him. Instead of neglect or lack of love, he had for the first five years of his life, until his brother Jack was born, the total love and undiluted attention of this good woman concentrated entirely on his well-being. It is right that with unconscious, indeed anachronistic Freudian accuracy his nickname for her was 'Woomany'.

Like so many Nannies, she peopled his life with her past charges. "Before she came to us," he wrote, "she had brought up for twelve years a little girl called Ella, the daughter of a clergyman, who lived in Cumberland. 'Little Ella', though I never saw her, became a feature in my early life. I knew all about her; what she liked to eat; how she used to say her prayers; in what ways she was naughty and in what ways good. I had a vivid picture in my mind of her house in the North Country."

The depth of Winston's love for Mrs. Everest, and hers for him, is shown by how long it continued. Its simple strength shines forth in their letters to each other. "Winny dear, do try to keep the new suit expressly for visiting, the brown one will do for every day wear, please do this to please me. I hope you will not take cold my darling take care not to get damp or wet." Or, "Thank you so much dearest for getting me a present, it has not yet arrived. It is very kind of you but you know my Lamb I would rather you did not spend your money on me." When he has to go to France one holiday: "If you have to go to France without coming home I will send or bring your big tweed coat and some fine flannel shirts for you to sleep in, those you wore at Banstead."

Winston's schoolboy letters to his mother (his letters to Mrs. Everest do not survive) are always full of questions about his Nanny and requests to see her. "Has Everest gone for her holiday yet?"—"Darling, I hope you will come down to see me when you come home and bring Everest"—"My best love to Everest." Whenever he was ill at school, he wrote at once and pleaded to be allowed to see 'Woomany'. While any illness of hers immediately worried him. "Dearest Mother, I suppose you have heard about Everest's illness [Winston is thirteen]. I and Jack at present (Sat 30th) are staying at Dr. Roose's. It is very hard to bear—we feel so destitute. Dr. Gordon says that Everest has two patches down her throat but that is more Quinzy than Diptheria."

But Mrs. Everest's love was not just immensely valuable emotionally and psychologically; twice at least it saved him in more immediate and decisive ways. When he was eleven he caught pneumonia and only her devoted nursing saved his life.

But earlier than that she had saved him from what, when he was old, he described as 'penal servitude', the horrific prep school he was sent to when he was eight. Roger Fry, who was at St. George's a few terms before Winston, wrote this description of the headmaster:

Mr. Sneyd-Kynnersley explained to us with solemn gusto the first morning we were all gathered together before him, that he reserved to himself the right to a good sound flogging with the birch rod. . . . But as I was from the first and all thro' either first or second in the school I was bound *ex officio* to assist at the executions and hold down the culprit. The ritual was very precise and solemn—every Monday morning the whole school assembled in the Hall and every boy's report was read aloud.

After reading a bad report from a form master Mr. Sneyd-Kynnersley would stop and after a moment's awful silence say, "Harrison minor, you will come up to my study afterwards." And so afterwards the culprits were led up by the two top boys. In the middle of the room was a large box draped in black cloth and in austere tones the culprit was told to take down his trousers and kneel before the block over which I and the other head boy held him down. The swishing was given with the master's full strength and it took only two or three strokes for drops of blood to form everywhere and it continued for fifteen or twenty strokes when the wretched boy's bottom was a mass of blood. Generally, of course, the boys bore it with fortitude but sometimes there were scenes of screaming, howling and struggling which made me almost sick with disgust. Nor did the horrors even stop there. There was a wild red-haired Irish boy, himself rather a cruel brute, who whether deliberately or as a result of pain or whether he had diarrhoea, let fly. The irate clergyman instead of stopping at once went on with increased fury until the whole ceiling and walls of his study were spattered with filth. I suppose he was afterwards somewhat ashamed of this for he did not call in the servants to clean up but spent hours doing it him-self with the assistance of a boy who was his special favourite.

This was not Winston. He was hopeless at work and beaten frequently. It was Mrs. Everest, seeing the weals from those senseless blows, who told his mother and had him removed. (Incidentally, Winston's attitude at this school has been adduced as evidence of his 'hostility towards authority'. A saint could not be blamed for feeling hostile towards Mr. Sneyd-Kynnersley.)

By 1893, extravagance had led Randolph Churchill and his wife into serious financial trouble. By the standards of the time and their past position they were broke. Plans were set in motion to retrench, and one of the victims of these plans was Mrs. Everest. (Though paid for by Lord Randolph, she was ostensibly employed by the Duchess of Marlborough.) Winston, now aged eighteen and up at Sandhurst, immediately sprang to her defence.

My dear Mamma,
I have felt very uncomfortable since I got here about Everest. I fear that at the time you told me—I was so occupied with Jack and Harrow that I did not think about it seriously. Now however—I have a very uneasy conscience on the subject. . . .
In the first place if I allowed Everest to be cut adrift without protest in the manner which is proposed I should be extremely ungrateful—besides I should be sorry not to have her at Grosvenor Square—because she is in my mind associated—more than anything else with *home*.
She is an old woman—who has been your devoted servant for nearly twenty years—she is more fond of Jack and I than of any other people in the world, so to be packed off in the way the Duchess suggests would possibly, if not probably, break her down altogether.
Look too at the manner in which it would be done. She is sent away—nominally for a holiday as there is no room at Grosvenor Square for her. Then her board wages are refused her—quite an unusual thing. Finally she is to be given her congé by letter—without having properly made up her mind where to go or what to do.
At her age she is invited to find a place and so practically begin over again. Of course I am extremely fond of Everest so it is perhaps for this reason that I think such proceedings cruel and rather mean.
I know you have no choice in the matter and that the Duchess has every right to discharge a servant for whom she has 'no further use'. But I do think that you ought *to arrange that she remains at Grosvenor Square—until I go* back to Sandhurst and Jack to school. In the meantime she will have ample time to make up her mind where to go—to find a place and resign herself to a change. Then when a *good* place *has been* secured for her she could leave and be

given a pension—which would be sufficient to keep her from want—and which should continue during her life.

The letter ends:

> Dearest Mamma—I know you are angry with me for writing—I am very sorry but I cannot bear to think of Everest not coming back much less being got rid of in such a manner. If you can arrange with the Duchess or persuade her to let Everest stay till after Christmas—I should feel extremely relieved. If you can't, I will write and explain things to papa, who will I am sure forgive me troubling him. . . .

Sometime after this, however, she moved back to an old employer. There she broke her arm and had to go and stay with her sister. She used to write long loving letters to Winston, which were found among his papers when he died. It was at this time Lord Randolph died. Churchill, aged twenty, became head of a family in ever worsening financial straits. But it was now he began to support her.

"My darling Precious Boy", she wrote to him in April 1895, "I have just received £2 10s from Cox and the Charing Cross on your account." She continues, over several pages, an endearing, tender letter, which ends, "I hope you will take care of yourself, my darling. I hear of your exploits at steeple-chasing. I do so dread to hear of it. Remember Count Kinsky broke his nose once at that . . ."

The payments were not to continue for long. Soon after this, as he describes in *My Early Life*, she fell seriously ill. The moment he heard, he writes,

> I travelled up to London to see her. She lived with her sister's family in North London. She knew she was in danger, but her only anxiety was for me. There had been a heavy shower of rain. My jacket was wet. When she felt it with her hands she was greatly alarmed for fear I should catch cold. The jacket had to be taken off and thoroughly dried before she was calm again. Her only desire was to see my brother Jack, and this unhappily could not be arranged. I set out for London to get a good specialist; and the two doctors consulted together upon the case, which was one of peritonitis. I had to return to Aldershot by the midnight train for a very early morning parade. As soon as it was over I returned to her bedside. She still knew me, but she gradually became unconscious. Death came very easily to her. She had lived such an innocent and loving life of service to others and held such a simple faith, that she had no fears at all, and did not seem to mind very much. She had been my dearest and most intimate friend during the whole of the twenty years I had lived.

He at once telephoned the clergyman in Cumberland, and when they gathered at the grave the old man was there, 'without little Ella' Churchill sadly noted.

He never forgot Mrs. Everest. Even in extreme old age, in lucid moments, he would suddenly refer to his love for her; and for many years after she died he paid an annual sum to the local florist for the upkeep of her grave.

Erected in Memory
of
Elizabeth Anne Everest
who died 3rd July 1895
by
Winston Spencer Churchill
Jack Spencer Churchill

THE CASE FOR NANNY EVEREST

In one sense, of course, speculation about the early life of anyone dead is quite fruitless. We cannot possibly know for certain, perhaps even remotely, what went on in the mind of the baby Churchill and what effect it had later on. The biographies of our great men, like our history, have to be continually rewritten so that they conform to whatever view of man's nature is currently fashionable. Then we understand them again, and can gain pleasure and inspiration from them. It is, if you like, a sort of game, and a fascinating one; but there are certain rules. One of them is that you don't suppress the evidence.

Accordingly, when I had finished reading about Churchill, I wrote to Dr. Storr to put my views on Mrs. Everest and to see if he had any reason for neglecting her. He answered at once that he agreed she saved his life. But that a Nanny's love never made up for a hostile or neglectful mother because a child always knew the mother was the authority and therefore thought the Nanny was somehow on the mother's side. He quoted a cruel mother/kind Nanny case of his, suitably anonymous, as an example.

Now it is quite true, as we shall see, that this is not an uncommon type of Nanny set-up, but in my experience it can only arise if certain conditions are also present. The mother has to be around a certain amount, vaguely there, demanding and expecting an obedience and a love when she has done nothing to deserve it. Then, either the mother is actually unkind or hostile. Or else the Nanny is unkind and the idealised mother is also blamed ("Why won't she save me?"). In these cases, certainly, the tensions, resentments, repressed anger are quite obvious.

But none of these factors exist in Churchill's case. The Nanny was not cruel; she was kind. Nor was the mother hostile. Indeed during these crucial years 'neglect' is a loaded word. A 'neglected' childhood is one with insufficient love or care. Churchill's was the reverse of this. It is not so much that Lady Randolph was neglectful as that she was never there at all. "The lack of interest shown in him by his parents," wrote Churchill's son in his biography, "[was] remarkable even judged by the standards of late Victorian and Edwardian days . . ." Even when he was twelve Winston didn't know what schools his father had been to. The fact is that for the first important years it is quite probable that the baby Winston didn't know he had any other mother than Mrs. Everest.

Aspects of his early development bear this out. That formidable will and dominance which Moran says made even to wake him from his afternoon sleep something of an adventure, developed very early, and in a way which suggests it sprang from a completely secure and unneglected background. Clement Attlee, for instance, in his somewhat laconic account of his own early childhood (no reference to a Nanny, though clearly from his circumstances he had one) gives an example when Winston was about seven. Curiously enough, Attlee, who was born in 1883, had the same nursery governess as Churchill, "whom she described," he writes, "as a very determined little boy. She could never have thought that the two little boys were destined in turn to be Prime Minister. A story was current in our family that one day a maid came into the room and asked Miss Hutchinson if she had rung the bell, whereupon young Winston said, 'I rang. Take away Miss Hutchinson, she is very cross'."

There is a point in his study where, without mentioning her, Dr. Storr seems about to give Mrs. Everest her due. He is discussing Churchill's childhood fantasy of glory, and because I am sure what he says, before he suddenly withdraws, is true of Churchill, I shall quote it.

The conviction of being 'special' is, in psycho-analytic jargon, a reflection of what is called 'infantile omnipotence'. Psychoanalysis postulates, with good reason, that the infant has little appreciation of his realistic status in the world into which he is born. Although a human infant embarks on life in a notably helpless state, requiring constant care and attention in order to preserve him, his very helplessness creates the illusion that he is powerful. For the demands of a baby are imperious. A baby must be fed, cleaned, clothed, and preserved from injury, and, in the normal course of events these demands are met by a number of willing slaves who hasten to fulfil them. As the child matures, he will gradually learn that his desires are not always paramount, and that the needs of others must sometimes take precedence. This is specially so in a family where there are other children. The hard lesson that one is not the centre of the universe is more quickly learned in the rough and tumble of competition with brothers and sisters. Only children may fail to outgrow this early stage of emotional development, and, although Winston Churchill was not an only child, his brother Jack, born in 1880, was sufficiently younger for Winston to have retained his solitary position during five crucial years.

Suddenly, however, Dr. Storr remembers that it is the consequences of *neglect* he is supposed to be describing. Hastily he adds that, as well as this, a child who is *deprived* of love can continue in this state, striving all his life to get the attention denied when he was young.

It is clear from this, and other passages, what happened. Studying Churchill's character Dr. Storr found what looked like a classic case of someone deprived of love and who therefore might be supposed to have repressed hostility to his parents. (In fact, quite often what he describes in his psychological exegesis are the consequences of love deprivation which, as we have seen, are irrelevant to Churchill's childhood.) Then he looked at the parental background and found 'neglect'. Eureka! Intoxicated with the completeness and perfection of his portrait (quite a number of psychiatrists are artists manqué) he swept into his study of Churchill which, let me reiterate, he has executed with a brilliance to which I'm afraid my précis did little justice. In the exhilaration of composition, Mrs. Everest got forgotten.

In a way, of course, Churchill would have agreed with him. Not in ignoring Mrs. Everest, but in the effect the undoubted difficulties of his early life had on him. In his biography of Marlborough he wrote, "It is said that famous men are usually the product of an unhappy childhood. The stern compression of circumstances, the twinges of adversity, the spur of slights and taunts in early years, are needed to evoke that ruthless fixity of purpose and tenacious motherwit without which great actions are seldom accomplished."

This can be quite true. But it is also true that that very early confidence and security, so deep that their roots become indiscernible, merging into the very bone of the character, and which can only come from the strong and continuous love of a mother or mother-substitute, are still more necessary. In my view, Everest was that mother.

CHAPTER TWO

Childhood up to 1850—How the Nanny evolved

". . . a sort of little Bastille, in every closet of which was to be found a culprit, some were sobbing and repeating verbs, others eating their bread and water, some preparing themselves to be whipped."
Lady Anne Lindsey on her eighteenth-century home

Nevertheless the question remains—how did Mrs. Everest ever reach such a position of dominance in Churchill's young life? Why did his mother feel no need to intervene in any but the most spasmodic way in his early upbringing? The British Nanny evolved out of, and held her sway in, a particular society with very definite views about the nature and upbringing of little children. To understand how she could behave as she did, to discover from whence she drew her immense power, it is necessary to go briefly into the history of those views and the history of that society in so far as it affected her. We shall find during this fairly brief survey that many of the themes we shall afterwards study in some detail often have roots which go back hundreds of years.

People forget their childhood; and people with unhappy childhoods forget, or repress them, more thoroughly than most. From the fourteenth century right up to the nineteenth there appears to have been an almost complete, large-scale, collective act of forgetfulness on the part of the British people about their infancy. Nevertheless, from this deep and melancholy gloom—not for nothing was it said that childhood wasn't invented till the eighteenth century—some pertinent factors can be singled out.

The first is summed up in an Italian text, *A Relation of the Island of England*, of the late fifteenth century, describing customs in the reign of Henry VII.

The want of affection in the English is strongly manifested towards their children; for after having kept them at home till they arrive at the age of seven or nine years at the utmost, they put them out, both males and females, to hard service in the houses of other people, binding them generally for another seven or nine years . . . during that time they perform all the most menial offices; and few are born who are exempted from this fate, for everyone, however rich he may be, sends away his children into the houses of others, whilst he, in return, receives those of strangers into his own.

A number of points should be noticed about this. In the first place, it was a custom which extended far back into the thirteenth and possibly twelfth centuries, and forward into the sixteenth century. Nor were the children necessarily as old as seven; it was not unusual for them, boys especially, to be sent away when they were six or even five.

This practice also illustrates the medieval idea—but an idea that lingered on in subterranean ways into Tudor and Stuart times—that you had to learn to *serve* others before you could be expected to lead them or even conduct your life among them. And you had to learn to serve no matter what station you eventually filled. The first sphere of learning was in domestic service. Nor was this thought degrading. Virtually no distinction was drawn between domestic service and any other sort; the boy and girl would wait at table, and at the same time he would learn to be his master's secretary, she her mistress's seamstress or help in the nursery. There was not so much confusion as identification between all the various sorts of service to be performed by servants and taught to children, and an identification also, therefore, between servants and children. So much so that the books (and there were vast numbers of them) specifically written to teach 'servants' manners were called 'babees' books'. This teaching took place in other people's houses, partly because it was thought to be easier to learn, or rather easier to teach, in a house where the child wasn't already known and established. Also because if possible children were always sent to grander households than their own, where they could be expected to better themselves in various ways.

Now this attitude to service is important to our subject for a simple reason. While it remained, no mother would think it below her to perform even the most menial task in the nursery, no matter how high born she might be. The 1605 conversation, which I shall quote a little later on, shows into what detail mothers went. It is not until this attitude has disappeared—as it did gradually through the sixteenth, seventeenth and eighteenth centuries—and not until a domestic servant 'class' has grown up, whose 'place in life' is accepted by both sides to be waiting, serving and performing all the unpleasant physical functions in a household, that the way is open in our sphere of interest, psychologically even more than physically, for the Nanny.

It is an illustration, incidentally, of the enormous tenacity of ideas about education and bringing-up generally, that this ancient practice of sending children away at a cruelly early age persists to this day. In no other Continental country does the prep school play the part it does here. And an Italian seeing the droves of whey-faced, tearful, seven-year-old upper-class little English boys, clutching the hands of their mothers—or even, still, their Nannies—at Waterloo or Paddington or Euston Stations at the start of another term, might well write home in exactly the same vein today as his countryman did five hundred years ago.

The second practice which has bearing on our subject during these early centuries is fostering. This is the farming out of little babies, more or less from birth, for almost any length of time from when they are weaned until they are properly 'trained' at five or six.

In Scotland this was very common indeed. Lady Antonia Fraser describes in her biography of Mary Queen of Scots how the family of the Earls of Mar had become the hereditary foster-parents of the Royal children of Scotland. But farming out was a universal custom among the rich families of that country.

In England, it is very difficult to discover how common it was. It was quite a usual custom for the parish to pay money to women to take babies belonging to the unwanted poor; middling well-off families would sometimes do this with illegitimate children. Since the money paid was usually a lump sum, and since the continued existence of the children was therefore a drain on capital, they frequently did not continue to exist for very long. But the appalling death rate which resulted—amounting at times, in effect, to mass murder—together with other facets of this practice, did not take place at the level of social life with which we are concerned.

Here, the use of foster-parents was also not uncommon. Juliet, Shakespeare makes plain, was suckled and looked after by foster-parents when her mother and father were away at Mantua. Mary Verney, because it was the Civil War, could only find to foster her child "Raff Rodes' wife . . . I feare but poore and looks like a slatterne . . . but she sayeth if she takes the child she will have mighty care of it, and truly she hathe two as fine children of her owne as ever I sawe."

And the custom of farming out children continued well into the nineteenth century. An analysis of advertisements appearing in *The Times* from 1822 onwards shows that practically every day there were requests, or offers, to take one or two children. Only gradually do these advertisements fall off towards the end of the century. Those asking for foster-parents quite often seem to have been those who were going out to one of our colonies, usually India, and it is possible that the growth of Empire led to a revival of this practice in the nineteenth century. Kipling and his sister were two children treated in this way, and their appalling sufferings, particularly his, I shall deal with later.

Nevertheless, it does not seem possible to ascertain with any accuracy just how common a practice fostering was. The most one can say is that it is another example of, another contributory strand to, the English ability to allow others to look after their young.

THE WET NURSE

From very early times (at what point precisely, or even vaguely, no one seems to know) until well into the eighteenth century, it was extremely common all over Europe for wealthy, and often just quite well-off women to have their children suckled by poor women to whom they paid money.

Evidence for this is plentiful. Laws were made about them for example. In 1235 Henry III passed a law against Christian wet nurses suckling Jews. A whole literature grew up, some of it devoted to advice on how to choose wet nurses, some of it containing instructions for the rich on how to cope with their overflowing bosoms. Andrew Boorde, a doctor in the middle of the fifteenth century, wrote in his *Fyrst Book of The Introduction of Knowledge* some advice on 'curdling of milk in women's breasts'. He dismisses an old-fashioned remedy—'Repercussions'—and goes on, "I wolde not do so, I do thus: I do take Dragavant and gomme Arabycke, and do compounde them with the whyte of rare egges, and the oyle of violettes and do make a playster. Or else I do take pytch and do liquifye it in Oyle of Roses, puttinge a lytle doves dinge to it, and dregges of wyne or ale, and make playsters."

But, as usual with a custom universally established, the extent of it is as often revealed negatively; that is by the surprise expressed at its absence or by the attacks on it. In the fourteenth century, for instance, the Countess Yde of Boulogne was noted and wondered at for the ferocity with which she determined to feed her own children.

The attacks on wet nurses were continuous throughout the period, and these attacks sometimes suggest the possible reasons for the custom. Breast-feeding is tiring and it causes the breasts to lose their shape (it also makes the uterus contract, so restoring a woman more quickly to her figure, but no one at the time seems to have been aware of this). A theologian inveighing against wet nurses in the fourteenth century (theologians and priests were particularly against them) said that the reasons for their existence were that women were afraid of losing their figures, that they wished to frolic with their husbands and that the practice of feeding your own children was not fashionable.

Sir Walter Raleigh, writing on the subject, said, "Unnatural curiosity has taught all women, but the beggar, to find out nurses, which necessity only ought to command." He is using 'curiosity' here, I think, in the sense it sometimes had in Elizabethan times of delicacy. It is possible that he was being ironic, and for delicacy one should read 'laziness'.

As well as theologians, doctors led the attack on wet nurses. An example, out of many, is a French doctor writing in the sixteenth century. Why, he asks, did God give women breasts—as decorations or for feeding children? If women realised the pleasure they'd get by suckling they wouldn't give it to wet nurses. And the child's love for its wet nurse ravishes the heart. Women say that their husbands say that feeding a child would spoil their figures. In point of fact these fastidious husbands are usually making love to the wet nurses all the time. Feed your own child and you gain in every way.

It seems to have been the custom during the Middle Ages and even later, and especially during winter when food was scarce, to keep babies at the breast for as long as possible. The Nurse in Romeo and Juliet says that she fed Juliet for three years (Act I, Scene III). The argument, employed by a number of the historians of our subject, is that these wet nurses, once their feeding had been done, stayed on and became the Nurse/Nanny figure for the rest of the child's infanthood.

Now, it is quite true that examples of this can be found. Juliet's Nurse is presumably one. Another is to be found in the family of Princess Anne, the daughter of James II. In 1689 she had already had twelve miscarriages and three little girls had died. She was not surprisingly a semi-invalid, but despite this continued to do her duty and in this year a son was born—the Duke of Gloucester. Since he was the heir to the throne, great care was taken: doctors were in constant attendance, almost continuous prayers were said; and a highly considered, proven wet nurse, Mrs. Sharman, engaged to feed the little prince.

Nevertheless, the baby did not thrive and after a while developed convulsions. Immediately the court began to panic; wet nurse after wet nurse was thrust upon the prince (each being given five guineas consolation) and when they all failed a large reward was publicly announced. At this, newly-delivered countrywomen converged on the palace in droves and soon the ante-room, staircase and driveway were jammed with eager contestants.

Among them, already in the ante-room itself, was Mrs. Pack with her one-month-old son. She was plain and very dirty, but a large robust woman, with the deeply ruddy complexion which can come from health or alcohol or even, as in this case, both; particularly noticeable were her breasts, which were gigantic. It was these that caught the eye of Prince George hurrying through the ante-room to see his wife, and he immediately ordered Mrs. Pack in to feed his son.

Miraculously, and almost at once, the baby recovered. Mrs. Pack was now in an extremely powerful position, since the life of the heir to the throne apparently depended upon her milk. Orders were given that she was never to be contradicted, and that she was to be given as much to eat and drink as she wanted. Of all three, Mrs. Pack took full advantage. Her behaviour became gross in the extreme. She never washed, she was frequently drunk; far more fit for a pigsty, one of the doctors said, than a royal nursery.

When they moved to Craven House in Kensington her power was consolidated and increased. She was in sole charge of the nursery wing, with immediately beneath her the Chief Nurses, Mrs. Atkinson and Mrs. Fortress (each with their own footmen and various attendants) and under them again, a retinue of thirty servants, nursery-maids, footmen, seamstresses and so on. This position, however, Mrs. Pack was unable to sustain. The responsibilities, but more particularly the opportunities for unlimited and prolonged indulgence, proved too much. She died some months after they had moved in.

She had achieved, by virtue of her milk, a position as autonomous as any we shall see when we come to the Nanny proper. Yet, just as this was exceptional, so was the result it brought. Nor, despite her position, was she in any real sense a Nurse. Her interest was in food and drink. She never won the affection of the little Duke of Gloucester. When Mrs. Pack died, the Queen asked him if he was sorry. "No, Madam," he said. The person he loved was Mrs. Atkinson, whom he called Atty, and she in fact is far more of a Nanny figure than ever Mrs. Pack was. She spoilt the little prince so much that it was commented on and she is one of the first of that type we will meet somewhat rarely in this book, the over-indulgent Nanny.

The example of Mrs. Pack could be multiplied. Mrs. Cheveley in the family of George III is another wet nurse who achieved power—but I want to reserve her till a little later because she illustrates an early appearance of two major themes: the extraordinary duplication by the Nanny of classic, almost mythological, family relationships and situations (in this case Mrs. Cheveley was a Step-Nanny); and second, the ease with which an unkind Nanny could hide her cruelties both from parents and outside observers.

But the fact is that until the nineteenth century examples are nearly meaningless. The numbers are too few. It is true some Nurses were at first wet nurses; it is equally true that a great many (actually in terms of numbers it would seem more) were not. Katherine Ashley, Queen Elizabeth I's Nurse was not, nor was Nan Fudd of the Verneys, or Hetty Yallop who appears in Parson Woodford's Journal in the eighteenth century. Again, though there is evidence that children were kept at the breast for a long time (a fundamental factor, since this would establish the wet nurse and child together), there is as much evidence that children were weaned quite early. Because of bad water, for instance, children of one and two were often fed on wine or small beer (a narcotic thread which we will see re-emerge with the discovery of gas in the nineteenth century). In 1512, in the Earl of Northumberland's household accounts, there is the item: "Breakfast for the Nurcery, for my Lady Margaret and Mr. Ingram Percy [aged three and one and a half], a manchet [fine bread], one quart of beer, 3 mutton bones boiled." Pap boats, from which a mixture of water, milk and bread was taken, were recommended from the age of seven or eight months.

There are, however, a number of more positive reasons why I think it unlikely that the wet nurse had very much to do with the evolution of the Nanny/Nurse. A minor one is linguistic. From quite early times the word 'dry nurse' was used to differentiate a child's nurse who looked after it from one which fed it—thus recognising a difference in function. (Though in Shakespeare a dry nurse also means a medical nurse.) Again—the wet nurse had a child of her own. It is true that great poverty and a more easy acceptance of childhood death might lead a poor mother to neglect her own child in preference for that of another. An appalling instance of this occurred in the life of Benjamin Haydon, the painter of monumental historical paintings. Five of his children died, including his beloved daughter.

Her whole life span, 2 years, 7 months, 12 days, was one continual torture. One day when she was reduced to a skeleton, and her mother ill, I kissed her and she sucked my cheek violently. I visited a wet nurse instantly and found her, her husband, and a fine fat pink baby living in great poverty. "Is it just," I thought, "to risk the life of another child to save my darling Fanny?" I went home tortured about what I should do, but the desire to save her predominated. She seized the bosom like a tigress and was saved, but the fine baby sank and perished. I was never easy and Fanny soon followed.

Quite often the wet nurse had several children, as did Raff Rodes's wife, foster-mother to another of the Verney family, and this too would make it difficult, if not impossible, to continue as a Nurse after weaning.

The most cogent reason, however, why the wet nurse and the Nurse proper were different people is because the wet nurse had to give milk and the Nurse/Nanny had to look after children. The qualities required were quite different. Those of the wet nurse were worked out in enormous detail, and carefully set down in books of instruction. Jacques Guillemean, *chirurgien* to the French Kings, Charles IX, Henri III and Henri IV, wrote that she must have an agreeable face, clear eyes, well-made nose, red mouth, white teeth, strong round neck and a deep chest. The shape of her breasts was immensely important and minute particulars were given as to their size, shape and colour, and on how they were to be prodded and felt for firmness and resilience. The wet nurse should not be pregnant; she should speak well and should be neither a drinker nor a glutton. She should feed the baby whenever it likes, and frequently unswaddle it and wash it. She should not desire the company of her own husband; as to her employer's husband, if possible she should have an actual aversion to him. She should be able to sing pleasantly.

The reason for all this care, which continued throughout the period up to the eighteenth century and all over Europe, was, of course, that breast milk was magic. With it, the baby imbibed something both of the physical appearance and character of the nurse. As a result, a mystique attached itself to the wet nurse which gave her great power; but it also sharply defined her position and dictated its duration.

Just how strong and deep this belief was—and it must have originated in the primitive days of sympathetic magic—is illustrated by the behaviour of the Countess Yde of Boulogne in the fourteenth century. She fed all her children herself, and in fact forbade anyone else to do so. One day, when she was at Mass, her new son, Eustace, woke up and cried. The maid attending him, unable to make him quiet, called a wet nurse and made her suckle the child. However, the Countess noticed something had happened, questioned the maid, and discovered someone else had been suckling her child. Her reaction was dramatic.

Her heart shook . . . she fell back upon a seat . . . sore gasped her heart under her breast . . . she called herself a poor leper. Swiftly she flew all trembling with rage and caught the child under the arms; the child of tender flesh she caught him in her hands, her face was black as coal with the wrath that seethed within. . . . There on a mighty table she bade them spread out a purple quilt and hold the child; then she rolled him and caught him by the shoulders that he delayed not to give up the milk which he had sucked . . . the maiden stood more benumbed than worm in winter time . . . she fled before the bursting of the storm and absented herself from the Countess's presence, several months.

Then the saintly and devoted Countess laid the child in the place where he should be, and suckled him so long until she had laid him to rest, and all three (the first child too) were covered with her ermine mantle.

Rooted deep in the past, the belief in the transference of characteristics by breast milk continued almost up to the present day. Margot Asquith who was born in 1864, wrote in her autobiography, "My second sister, Charlotte . . . was the only member of the family . . . who was tall. My mother attributed this—and her good looks—to her wet nurse, Janet Mercer, a mill-girl at Innerleithen, noted for her height and beauty."

Nurses and Nannies had their own mystique—their medical and superstitious lore, their stories, their almost Roman authority—but it was far removed from, and had nothing to do with, the primitive magic of the wet nurse. And the final proof of this is that just as conditions became right for the evolution of the Nanny, and by the time she was almost ready to emerge, strict, starched, completely formed, the wet nurse disappeared.

The chorus of disapproval against wet nurses reached its height in the eighteenth century. Rousseau argued against it in *Emile*. Doctors became almost unanimous (much as they are today) in favour of mothers feeding their own children. Dr. Cadogan, for example, wrote in 1747 that the children of the poor had a better chance of survival because their own mothers suckled them. A Dr. Buchan knew that breast milk protected against disease (actually, this had been noticed in the Middle Ages). As a result, it became rapidly more common for mothers to suckle their children and by the end of the century it was taken as a matter of course. Letters redolent of the pleasures of suckling are usual. "My dear little girl sleeps in bed with me after her first sucking," Georgiana, Duchess of Devonshire wrote to her mother Lady Spencer in 1783. It was only when his wife was ill that Haydon, who was born in 1786, went to a wet nurse. By 1865 Lord Amberley can write about the subject like this. His child wouldn't suck, which irritated him. "It seems very badly managed by nature that little babies should not find it as easy to suck as little puppies; but if that is one of the arrangements that was made in consequence of Original Sin, we must not complain of it." With enormous difficulty they managed to find a wet nurse, but, and this is the point, it was "a terrible disappointment to her, for we both care very much about ladies nursing."

In the nineteenth century wet nurses finally disappear. An analysis of advertisements in *The Times* shows that in 1822 a wet nurse was wanted once every four days, between 1845 and 1865 it is one every five days, 1873 one every six days, 1882 one every twelve days and from then on wet nurses are neither asked for nor offer themselves. And these were the very years when the Nanny at last appeared.

Nevertheless, it was in terms of attitude a very recent disappearance. (Isolated examples, of course, lingered on. Churchill had a wet nurse.) And the attitude is the same one we have met before, the attitude that another woman should take over the functions of the mother; in this case in an area which, as we shall see, a number of psychiatrists consider to be fundamental both to the mother/child relationship and to the psychological development of the child itself.

EARLY ATTITUDES TO INFANTS AND CHILDREN; THE EXTENDED FAMILY; PURITANISM

One of the reasons history is an art is that the historian has to re-create the character of the past, which in effect means to re-create the people of the past. Using such information about them as he can get, and his knowledge of himself, he must create a world. Just so, from the rag-bag of his acquaintance and himself, does a writer create a novel. Both require the ability to identify with and reconstruct figures which, no matter how many 'facts' the creator uses, must essentially be of the imagination. So strong are most people's feelings about childhood and ways of bringing up children, that here it is particularly difficult to understand the attitudes of the remote past. Nevertheless, an attempt must be made, and it is possible, so tenacious is custom in this sphere, that we may find that some of those distant attitudes set up echoes in the Nannies we shall later study, and even in ourselves.

It is often said that children up to, and into, the eighteenth century were regarded with far less concern than they are today. One reason for this is that so many of them died young. It was rare for even a quarter of the children born to survive. They died of everything: croup (inflammation of lungs and larynx), fevers, colds, whooping cough, all aggravated by poor diet and by the standard medical treatment of bleeding. In fact medical treatment quite often killed them. In the eighteenth century smallpox inoculation was carried out by a thread dipped in cow's pustules and then drawn through the skin of the patient. The patient was often dirty and infected, the thread would then be drawn through another patient and another and another . . . early inoculation was nearly as risky as the disease itself. So much early death, it is said, not only inured parents to it (even in the eighteenth century court mourning was not expected for a child under seven), but led them to feel less about their children in the first place.

Another and more subtle reason for this supposed indifference to children, or at least relative lack of status given them, has been advanced by, among others, Philippe Ariès in his book *Centuries of Childhood*. His thesis is that the modern idea of the family did not exist in the Middle Ages; his evidence being that the family unit is never shown in the 'iconographic' material of the time, in the pictures, illuminated manuscripts, church decorations etc., which are our principal sources for discovering the social customs and ideas of the past. Households of this period, and on into Stuart times, were enormous. A household of sixty was not considered large. They were composed, apart from servants, of the ramifications of entire families: uncles, aunts, grandparents, in-laws, cousins. But these 'families' weren't considered as units for producing and bringing up children, as they are today; they were considered as a line, a dynasty, a group, related by blood and marriage, whose function was to get property, power, patronage and, by marriage, ally themselves with other dynasties who were seeking, and who possessed, these same things.

A family was an economic and defensive/offensive unit—like the village, the manor, the castle. Children were not important to this sort of family nor was the family important to the children. Other units—peer group units, servant units—were of far more consequence to children.

The modern 'idea' of a family slowly grew during the sixteenth and seventeenth centuries, says Ariès, and this is shown by the growth of its depiction in art until, during the seventeenth century, we get family scenes of as close and familiar an intimacy as *La Femme en mariage* by Guerand which shows a mother wiping the bottom of a naked child. Not until this intimate idea of a family grew, the idea that it was a father, a mother and children set apart from the world, could you get that concentration on children which leads, ultimately, to the position they hold in our lives today.

Now this is certainly fruitful, but in my view Ariès, and others who push this concept of the 'extended' family, have got their emphasis wrong. After all, they were wiping bottoms long before the seventeenth Century. Sir Thomas More adored his daughters and used to lure them into his study by showing them his collection of coins and oddments. "I have given you kisses enough," he writes to one, "but stripes hardly ever." The Paston letters of the fifteenth century show strong parental concern. St. Bernadino of Siena (1388–1444) sees that the natural helper of the wife with child is the husband. And it would not be difficult to produce further evidence that in a sense—that is from the point of view of a child from birth to five years—the 'family' consisted of its mother, nurse, helpers, brothers and sisters and the presence, rare but positive, of an interested father. This is much as it was in the eighteenth century—indeed much as it can be today.

The fact that this isn't depicted in the iconography is a subject for the history of art; it is to do with the function of the artist in a religious age. It doesn't mean there wasn't, in the sense I have used it above, a family. The family isn't particularly emphasised in the iconography of today either. But though in some respects it is going through a rocky period, no one would seriously deny its central role in child-rearing. (I am not an expert in this field at all, but actually I think, when the artists got a chance in earlier centuries, they did show family scenes. There are things called *misericordes*, coverings on benches and choir stalls in churches which, when turned back, the monks could lean against. Because these normally remained hidden, the sculptors could let themselves go. Here you quite often get family situations—there are some in the churches of the Ile de France for instance or, in England, in Westminster Abbey. There is a charming *Wife beating husband* at the end of Westminster Abbey.)

It is not lack of concern we find at this time, but a particular type of concern. Because the fact is that the dynastic family did not diminish the importance of children but increased it. They were not only the essential pawns in the complex marriage alliances which formed such a feature of its aggrandisement, but they were also, after all, provided they lived, going to *be* the family. Thus the sending away of children at the age of six is not only an example of allowing others the care of their children—it is also an example of how this different sort of concern worked in practice. The more important and powerful the family the happier its members would be. Therefore they were sent away when young to gain influence and marry people who would enhance the family, and so ultimately improve their own lot.

Similarly, the frequency with which children died increased the importance of those that lived. Nor am I convinced that this frequency did a great deal to accustom parents to their despair. Throughout this period one is struck just as, or more, often by the depth and poignancy of their grief as by the lack of it.

But children were no good to the dynastic family unless they were adults, and so we come upon the theme which I regard as a far more significant result of the extended family and a theme which is fundamental to this book: that children are really little adults, but adults with defects who must be trained and taught as quickly as possible to be true adults. The images are always of forcing, restraining, disciplining, cutting back, pruning (it is highly significant that English is the only language which has the same word, nursery, for the place where children are brought up and where plants are grown). It is fundamental because it lasted so long. It is an attitude which was still widespread in 1950 when Geoffrey Gorer did his enormous survey *Exploring English Character*.

It was also an attitude which went far into the past. To accustom little Saxon babies as fast as possible to the sights and sounds of war, Tacitus describes how the camps for women and children were deliberately pitched close to the battlefield. And Galen says that new-born babies were plunged into icy water to harden them.

As the centuries progressed the instructions on how to bring up infants were laid down in a great number of *Babees' Bokes, Bookes of Urbanity, Bokes of Vertue* and so on. These instructions are extremely detailed; they are also very familiar. One of the things that always fascinated me about Nannies was the vast repertoire of often, it seemed to me, almost pointless little prohibitions and laws they enforced. And what was stranger still was the way this repertoire was shared, even though they can't all have met each other, nor had they undergone some strict training at a common college of Nannies. It was as though there was a collective Nanny Unconscious to which they all had access. And in a way that is what there was. Because here, in the fourteenth and fifteenth centuries, we find those Nanny maxims written down. Take these rules, from a book of 1475: little children (from three onwards) must not speak till spoken to, they must not chatter or stare about, they must stand till they are told to sit, they must not look sulky, they mustn't pick their noses or scratch their ears, pick their nails or teeth, they mustn't drink with their mouths full, mustn't lean against post or door, mustn't put their elbows on the table, nor wink or roll their eyes. . . . The list is almost endless, and could be duplicated in dozens of books of the same sort. It is tempting to speculate that in many respects upper and upper-middle class children of the nineteenth and early twentieth centuries were brought up according to rules developed during the later Middle Ages—for where else can they have come from?—and preserved in the folk memories of their lower-class Nurses and Nannies.

The idea that childhood was not a separate state, but a period of defective adulthood out of which children had to be trained as fast as possible, persisted, as I have said, for a very long time. It is indicative that not until well into the twentieth century were children dressed as children; before that they were dressed as tiny adults. But during the sixteenth, seventeenth and eighteenth centuries an element was added to this training which is also important to a full understanding of Nannies. That element was religion.

Throughout the sixteenth and early seventeenth centuries the books of instruction became increasingly moralistic. Seager's *School of Vertue,* for instance, first published in 1557, and reprinted in 1626, gives lists of psalms to be learnt at an early age, advice is given on how to behave in church, fierce warnings are thundered against every conceivable immorality or backsliding—gambling, swearing, drinking, lying, anger, malice, over-sleeping, to give but a few; while lists of virtues—charity, love, patience, kindliness, meekness—are similarly pressed.

It was during this period that most of the Protestant middle class, but particularly the Puritans, evolved the equation that moral rectitude led to social and economic success; that if you were good, you would work hard and your work would flourish. It is a simple step from here to assume that hard work is in itself a moral good; and an equally simple step to reverse the formula and say that anything that interferes or is opposed to work— i.e. anything pleasurable—is a moral evil. Pleasure itself is evil. Without appreciating this very considerable strand in the English character much Nanny behaviour becomes perplexing. Take the Nanny in Compton Mackenzie's *Sinister Street,* an unkind, vicious, wrinkled, alcoholic little woman, based on his own Nanny.

Treats were important factors in Michael's life. Apparently anything even mildly pleasant came under the category of treats. It was a treat to walk on the grass in the Gardens; it was a treat to help push Stella's perambulator; it was a treat to have a sponge floating beside him in the bath, to hum, to laugh, to read, to stay up one minute after half-past six, to accompany Nanny on her marketing, and most of all to roll the slabs of unbaked dough down in the kitchen. The great principle of a treat was its rarity. As anything that had to be asked for became a treat automatically and as the mere fact of asking was made a reason for refusing to grant a treat, the sacred infrequency of the treat was secured.

Now Compton Mackenzie's Nanny—or rather Michael Fane's in *Sinister Street*—had, apart from gin, virtually only one form of pleasure, and that was in thwarting and denying Michael Fane. But the form this denying took, and the fact that she could feel as she did it that she was 'doing him good', derive directly from the Protestant/Puritan attitudes developed in the sixteenth and seventeenth centuries and already, in that period, being applied to children. The final phrase I quoted, "the sacred infrequency of the treat was secured", is, remarkably, though probably unconsciously, accurate: infrequency, of everything, was sacred indeed. We shall find many Nannies, infinitely kinder, gentler and in every way more admirable than Compton Mackenzie's, acting in a similar way and from similar motives.

One more step took place in the attitudes to moral behaviour. Because hard work, prayer and good behaviour were not only morally good for you, but led to business success, it was natural to assume you *enjoyed* behaving well. Parodoxically, the stern duties and obligations and disciplines which on the one hand were meant to be opposed to the transitory indulgent pleasures of life, were now also supposed to be pleasurable themselves. Isaac Watts, in one of his *Divine and Moral Songs for Children* wrote:

> Let children that would fear the Lord
> Hear what their teachers say:
> With reverence meet their parents word,
> And with delight obey.

"And with delight obey"—that note, that sanctimonious mixture of strictness towards children, disguised by a thin sugary coating of assumed and expected enjoyment, is one we shall find frequently in Victorian nurseries.

An appreciation of these Protestant, but more particularly Puritan, ideas and ideals is essential for a proper understanding of English or American national character. Especially American—where material success, which used to prove religious faith, has retained all its fanatic religious fervour while losing any qualities of compassion it may once have had. These ideas, still more important when they are implemented in a sphere connected with the bringing-up of children, were of course sometimes more and sometimes less powerful. They reached a height during the rule of Cromwell and then, from the Restoration of Charles II till the end of the seventeenth century became less influential. After this, despite the moderate, sophisticated and on the whole tolerant main stream of eighteenth-century rationalism, the religious revivals associated with Wesley had considerable success. By the end of the century even quite ordinary, worldly households barred toys on Sundays. Little William Goodwin was told off because he stroked a cat on the Sabbath. Sermons frequently lasted three hours. During Victorian times and thereafter, Puritanism and all its related attitudes must always be born in mind; even today, despite appearances, they cannot be ignored.

BEATING

There is a more sinister aspect of the long persisting aim to make children adults as soon as possible—that is, the methods used.

In the fourteenth century, a book, *The Goodwife* (but similar advice is found in every book of this sort), said this about misbehaving children.

> And if thy children be rebel and will not them bow,
> But if any of them misdoeth, neither ban nor blow [don't curse or cuff]
> But take a smart rod and beat them in a row
> Till they cry for mercy and be of their guild aknow.

So we hear for the second time in this book the thud of that cane which is to beat its cruel and pointless way through too many of its pages. It was universally accepted until well into the nineteenth century that the most effective, indeed the only effective way in which to discipline even tiny children was to beat them. But there was more to it than effectiveness. "Marriage fills the earth, virginity fills heaven," wrote St. Jerome. To be born at all meant one was full of original sin. It had to be forced out by baptism—and by beating. Beating was a way of *saving* children, not just correcting them; a child that was spared the rod would not only be spoilt, it might lose its soul. It is from this view that that unpleasant word 'naughty' derives its powerful undertones. Naughty, naught, nothing—a child who was naughty was nothing, worthless, soulless, evil.

And this view, though consciously it gradually receded into the background, is the reason beating was started so young and continued so vigorously. The Earl of Warwick, guardian to Henry VI, complains that the King grew "more and more to grucche with chastysing and to loth it". Henry VI was at this time eight months old and used to preside at Council sitting on his mother's knee. His infanthood is punctuated, as far as his caretakers are concerned, with incitements to violence.

Beating is universal in these early centuries. When Agnes Paston sent her little son to school in the late fifteenth century he took with him a request to the master to "well belashe him". In the sixteenth century one of the little Verneys (Edmund, aged three) is beaten for shyness. He is sent to his great-great-grandmother. She had heard "he is disliked, he is so strange", but after having him to stay she writes pleading for him to be beaten less. "He is too young to be strudgeled in any forcing way. I had intelligence your father was troubled to see him so strange . . . he knows the child was fellow-good-enough at my house. I pray show him what I have written about him, and be sure that he be not frightened by no means: he is of gentle sweet nature, soon corrected."

John Wesley's mother, writing to him on the principal rules she observed when educating her family, had this to say on the subject, "When turned a year old (and some before) they were taught to fear the rod, and to cry softly; by which means they escaped abundance of correction they might otherwise have had; and that most odious noise of the crying of children was rarely heard in the house; but the family usually lived in as much quietness as if there had not been a child among them."

Such examples could be endlessly multiplied right until, indeed, the present day. Dr. Johnson, helping Boswell with a case about a schoolmaster who was accused of beating his pupils too hard, puts the eighteenth-century view with his usual force and concision. "The charge is, that he has used immoderate and cruel correction. Correction, in itself, is not cruel; children, being not reasonable, can be governed only by fear. To impress this fear is therefore one of the first duties of those who have care of children. It is the duty of a parent, and has never been thought inconsistent with parental tenderness. . . ." At another time, discussing with Boswell the lashings he himself had received, he says, "No attention can be obtained from children without the infliction of pain, and pain is never remembered without resentment."

Resentment—there is a key word on this subject. The effect of beating on young children is to fill them with rage. But since the person beating them is usually the person who is looking after them, the person in fact they love and depend on for love, they often find it difficult to express or even admit this rage and the murderous, vengeful fantasies it gives rise to. They suppress them, suppress their burning, frustrated resentment, and the aggression does not surface until adolescence or adulthood. It is scarcely surprising that the Middle Ages were a period of such brutality and violence, a period notorious for men of terrible rages. Henry II, whose anger led to the murder of Becket, would at times become completely beside himself and like another king, King John, lie on the floor foaming at the mouth and gnashing his teeth in the rushes. And this long-repressed resentment not infrequently found expression on the person who had caused it. There are numbers of cases in legal records of parents being assaulted by their children. The Earl of Warwick, fearful that when he came of age Henry VI might revenge himself by having him murdered for having done his duty, always asked the Council to sanction his 'chastysings'.

And one cannot help feeling that this resentment, which is inevitable in very young children, however justified a beating may seem to be, must have been compounded by the fact that, under the guise of 'doing them good', parents, tutors, Nurses and later Nannies, were sometimes just indulging impulses that were quite simply cruel and sadistic. From the accepted (religious) position of hating the sin and loving the sinner they moved imperceptibly to hating the sinner because of his sin and so justified the utmost excesses of violence the real motives of which were often deeper and more sinister.

We have met Curzon's Miss Paraman; we shall find Nannies almost as bad. In the seventeenth century Lady Wentworth wrote, "Hear is a strange unatural reporte of Lady Abergane that she had in a pation killed her own child about seven years old, she having been a great while whiping it, my Lord being grieved to hear it crye so terryably, went into the roome to beg for it, and she threw it with such forse to the ground she break the skul; the girl lived but fourer howers after it."

Another instance, among a great many, concerns a rather curious ghost story. In Elizabethan times, the mistress of Bisham Abbey was a Lady Hoby. She was a clever woman and a scholar, but given to furious outbursts of rage and brutality which were particularly fired by stupidity or slowness. The story was that she used to beat her little son, William, and eventually beat him so cruelly that he died. Her ghost used to be seen coming from a bedroom, washing its hands. Now, oddly enough, Lady Hoby's life is quite well documented. We know when she was born and died and when she was at Bisham Abbey. But there is no record of her ever having had a son William. No record, that is, until comparatively recently. Then, when alterations were made to the house, some very old and badly blotted copybooks were found hidden behind the original Elizabethan skirting boards, as though hurriedly stuffed there. They bore the name William Hoby in a childish hand.

Sadism certainly plays its part in the story of the Nanny, as we shall see. But it is the exception. And, though the treatment of children right up to and including the nineteenth century was often brutal by our standards, one thing must be realised: it does not mean that parents and Nurses did not love their charges. Beating was the accepted method of discipline. Indeed it is of immense importance throughout this book to remember that the vast majority of parents and Nannies loved their children. They wished to do the best they could for them and frequently did so. Mistakes, when they were made, were usually caused by ignorance.

And during the late seventeenth and the eighteenth century people were becoming a little less ignorant about the nature of children. It is time now to look briefly at the more enlightened ideas which were also around as the Nanny slowly emerged.

GROWTH OF ENLIGHTENED IDEAS ABOUT CHILDHOOD

In the sixteenth century they invented something called the Black Pudding. This was a huge round hat, like a puff-ball, of thickly wadded black velvet which little children wore so that they wouldn't bump their heads when they fell over. St. Austin preached against children being hemmed in "on every side with terrors, threats and stripes [that is, beatings] so that they can get no liberty whatsoever". Elizabeth I's Counsellor Lord Burleigh wrote, "Bring up children in learning and obedience; yet without austerity; the foolish cockering [over-indulgence] of some parents and the overstern carriage of others causeth more men and women to take ill causes than their own inclinations." Breast-feeding, even if it was someone else's breasts, appears always to have been given when babies cried.

These instances of kindness, and I have given others, men and women who understood the need for moderation and gentleness, sprinkle our period. Towards the end of the seventeenth century they start to increase. The Restoration, which brought a relaxation in manners, and a near collapse in morals, was reflected in a more indulgent attitude to children. The Frenchman Maison wrote in 1698; "On a une extraordinaire complaisance en Angleterre pour les jeunes Enfants, toujour caresser, toujour applaudie, a ce qu'ils fait." In 1707 Madame de Maintenon wrote about an English custom of letting babies out of swaddling bands at three months, and swaddling declined quite quickly through the century. In the mid-eighteenth century Sir Roger Newdigate, obviously kindly if still rough, wrote to his daughter suggesting that her baby should be "tossed about by a stout nimble nurse from morning to evening". One or two books appeared, like Bishop Earle's _The Child Microcosmography_, which not only took the world of little children as important and worthy of rational enquiry, but began to see that little children were _different_.

The most important of these was John Locke's _Some Thoughts Concerning Education_ published in 1692. It was originally a series of letters written by Locke to his friend Edward Clarke in 1684 advising him on how to educate and bring up his son. It was subsequently expanded by other letters and additions. Although Locke uses the word 'Education', he in fact saw this as the entire process of upbringing from the earliest years, and in the original letters the learning part came last—and least.

One of the principal targets of the _Thoughts_ was over rigorous use of the rod. Locke wrote:

> I would have children very seldom beaten. 'Tis to make slaves and not virtuous men to use them to be governed by the fear of the scourge and to know no other motive of their actions, no other rule of right and wrong, but the cudgel. . . . A gentle persuasion and reasoning will most times do much better. You will perhaps wonder to find me mention reasoning with children, and yet I cannot but think that the true way of dealing with them. They understand it as early as they do language, and if I misobserve not they love to be treated as rational creatures sooner than is imagined.

'Rational creatures'—it might be thought that these are just the little adults of before, upon whom Locke is grafting the Reason of the eighteenth century. But it is clearly more than this. He has a genuine knowledge and love, this bachelor, of small children: "The little, or almost insensible impressions on our tender infancies have very important and lasting consequences. . . . Innocent Folly, Playing and Childish Actions are to be left perfectly free and unrestrained. . . . Inadvertancy, Carelessness and Gaiety is the character of that age." And he writes elsewhere, "If the Faults of their Age rather than the Children themselves, were as they should be left only to Time and Imitation, and riper years to cure, children would escape a great deal of misapply'd and useless correction." He also urged that children should see as much of their parents as possible, and not be left with servants.

Although this was because he believed servants would corrupt children with their lewdness and dishonesty, it was a step, like most of Locke's advice, in the right direction, even if sometimes for peripheral reasons. The direction, that is, first towards closer family relations—which we have already seen in the advocation that mothers should do their own breast-feeding. Next, towards a more humane and gentle attitude to children, which did very gradually grow during the next two centuries. And finally towards the conception of children as different, as living in a world which was separate and which should be seen and concentrated on as separate. This idea is plainly of prime importance when one considers the emergence of the Nanny in the nineteenth century, when just that separation and concentration took place, but a concentration which, paradoxically, was obtained by banishing the mother from the care of her children instead of enlisting her help.

Another book which had a certain influence around this time was Rousseau's *Emile*, published in 1762. When you examine this book, and the rest of Rousseau's thought as it might be applied to children, he is not in fact nearly so revolutionary as Locke. Man was born free and everywhere was in chains, it is true, but this meant there should be no unnecessary restriction and he does not seem to advocate nearly as much or as specific a freedom as Locke does. He advocates mothers breast-feeding. He believes that children should be brought up like savages, but this only meant they should be trained in hunger, thirst, cold, etc. (This ancient Saxon idea was echoed again in Locke, too. He said that children should wear leaky shoes to toughen their feet.) Rousseau also felt strongly that the mother should nurse and bring up the children; the father should tutor them. Or wrote strongly, rather. His own children were put in a foundling hospital.

Yet his influence was probably more liberalising than these rather meagre proposals of his would suggest. For one thing he believed that the early years were by far the most important in a person's life; and the more important they were felt to be the more attention would be paid to them. For another, as time passed, there occurred a process common among influential writers. The less he became read the simpler, more general and more influential Rousseau's message became. It came simply to mean 'freedom', and the child was a 'noble savage' who, forced to be less virtuous by adult restrictions, must be set free.

There is other, anecdotal, evidence that the end of the eighteenth century and beginning of the nineteenth century saw the growth of a more indulgent attitude to children, paralleling the general laxity which characterised the Regency. A Miss Weeton, for instance, had an appalling time being Nanny/Governess to the Armitage family in Huddersfield. The children were extremely spoilt, "screaming dreadfully whenever she tried to teach them, and flying into violent fits of passion". The eldest girl, aged seven, went on strike and refused to do anything. Miss Weeton says she tried persuading and requesting in vain. "The maddening child only smiled and tossed her head." In the end—"not withstanding it is so repugnant to the present mild system of education"—she had to resort to the rod. But even this was no good. The children screamed as though they were being killed. (Miss Weeton said she was only hitting their clothes, but since they were inside them the effect must have been much the same.) They all went on strike and any semblance of discipline collapsed.

Nonetheless, how widespread and how influential these tendencies were must remain extremely debatable. Though Locke considered the very early years important, when his treatise was republished in the late seventeenth century, with the addition of several relevant chapters, it came to be considered primarily as an educational document, and this is where its chief influence lies. (It is still remarkably modern in this sphere. He argued against the value of the classics and against public schools. Learning should be more like play, etc.) And though he and Rousseau and thinkers like them did to some extent affect the climate of infant care, it must be doubtful if any of their ideas reached the ears of the slowly emerging Nanny.

Nor does Miss Weeton prove a great deal. Here—indeed at all times in this book—the anecdotal material is statistically far too meagre to do anything more than illustrate a point. It can never establish a trend or a custom. Against Miss Weeton, for instance, one could set the formidable figure of Mrs. Crabtree. Mrs. Crabtree is interesting to our story because not only is she an early example of something like a full-blown Nanny (although too vulgar) but she is one of the first, if not the first, Nanny-figure to play a leading part in a book.* She appears in *Holiday House*, written by Catherine Sinclair in 1835. This is the story of three children, Frank (the eldest), Harry and Laura Graham whose father goes on a trip to Rome, Naples and Paris to forget the death of his wife (it is perhaps significant that this death appears to affect the children not a jot). They are left in charge of their indulgent aunt and uncle, Major and Lady Graham—and Mrs. Crabtree. I shall come again to Mrs. Crabtree; at the moment only one aspect of her fairly rough-hewn character need concern us. The children's father is afraid the children will be spoilt. "Not if you leave that old vixen, Mrs. Crabtree, as Governess of the

*Mrs. Crabtree is of additional interest to me because I discovered while writing this book that she was based, by a curious coincidence, on the Nurse of my great-great-grandmother, Lady Elizabeth Hunter Blair.

Nursery," answered Major Graham, laughing. "She ought to have been the drummer of a regiment, she is so fond of beating. I believe there never was such a tyrant since the time when nursery-maids were invented." Mrs. Crabtree more than lives up to her reputation. All the children are beaten every morning; and the book is regularly punctuated by her eruptions. When they ask some friends to tea she is immediately put into a passion. "I never heard of such things in all my life, Master Harry!" (Mrs. Crabtree has loud, raucous tones.) "But, sure as eggs is eggs, you shall repent of this, for not one morsel of cake or anything else shall you have to give any of the party; no! not so much as a crust of bread or a thimbleful of tea!" A few pages and incidents later she comes storming into the nursery, "so flaming with fury, she might have blown up a powder mill". She threatens to whip them round the room—and does so. She shouts until her face became red and her voice hoarse. Another time she is described as a thrashing machine, and in fact her entire behaviour goes to show, as Harry remarks at one point, that there is no law against beating boys.

The point is, of course, that throughout history the one area of human life that has changed least and changes slowest is the bringing up of children. We bring up very small children as we were brought up ourselves —and so instinctive is this that psychiatrists quite often discover how patients were treated as infants by the way they react to their own very young children.

Also for centuries (still indeed) in the perplexing business of rearing infants, mothers and Nurses relied on the experience of those who had already done it. Nothing is so tenacious or so resistant to education as knowledge passed down by word of mouth.

Just how tenacious, in the particular sphere of disciplining children we have been examining, is shown by Geoffrey Gorer's *Exploring English Character*. (This survey, which I have referred to before and will again, was carried out in 1950 and 1951. The sample was fourteen thousand, and the results based on five thousand of this. It was slightly overweighted towards the young. It was published in 1955.) Gorer found overruling evidence that most English parents were still obsessed with the need to punish children and the pleasure they got from its severity. On the whole, spanking was approved of, and twenty-one per cent of the fathers and fourteen per cent of mothers still thought beating or a harsh caning a good thing. On this subject people spoke with gusto especially—though the viewpoint went across class barriers—the lower class informants. "A boy should have his 'seat' slapped until he screams for mercy and make him promise never to do the same thing again." A great many people, as one would hope and expect, were of course against violent beating. But Gorer says that the vehemence of the answers against it was so strong and they poured onto the questionnaire in such quantities as to suggest there were powerful unconscious temptations against which defences had to be erected.

I should like to make three final observations on this subject. First, little children can be maddening. Even the most humane and permissive of modern child psychiatrists don't deny they sometimes provoke one to blows—and should be given one, though if possible not too violent, if only to relieve the feelings of the parent or Nanny and prevent the build-up of frustrated anger ultimately just as harmful. Second, when you couple this with the fact that a reign of terror *works*, it is hardly surprising an over-violent system of disciplining children evolved. For the fact is that you can frighten children into obedience. They submit to violence. It may do them serious damage, and as a result of their subsequent behaviour damage or diminish society as a whole. But not until fundamental advances had been made in the study of human nature could this be understood. And, the third point, these advances had not been made by the late eighteenth century. The child is father to the man is not a Freudian statement, it is a medieval one. "In short, he [Dr. Johnson] is a memorable instance of what has often been observed," writes Boswell, "that the boy is the man in miniature: and that the distinguishing characteristics of each individual are the same through the whole course of his life." Not until the modern ideas of history— i.e. that man's present was the product of his past; and of evolution— that man had evolved from his past—had been worked out, would it be possible for people to appreciate the importance of the early years of childhood. And when I go briefly into the very interesting history of this development later in the book, I shall hope to show that not until the Second World War did ideas of this sort gain sufficiently wide and deep a currency to be of relevance to the upbringing of children. Until then, Boswell's view of man was still much more like the one accepted by most people, and particularly perhaps by Nannies.

In fact here, as in most things pertaining to Nannies (and I suspect our social history generally), it is 1939 that is the significant watershed, not 1914. On the whole, childhood in the eighteenth century and on into the nineteenth century must have been by our standards unpleasant and sad, and more often than not houses resembled the little Bastilles described in the quotation with which I headed this chapter—with tiny children cringing and weeping in every closet, learning verbs, eating bread and water and preparing themselves to be thrashed.

EVOLUTION OF THE NURSERY IN THE EIGHTEENTH AND NINETEENTH CENTURIES; CENTRAL POSITION OF THE MOTHER

During the Middle Ages and onwards living conditions were crude, un-private and undifferentiated. In large draughty castles, people mixed indiscriminately, living mostly in great halls with their narrow, unglazed windows and smoke streaming through *louvres* in the roof. Above this was the chamber set aside for women and children. Everyone slept in the chamber, disturbed during the long melancholy medieval nights by gross snoring and the crying of children. "There cameth from the child a wailing and weeping that at midnight maketh thee to waken."

Slowly, separate rooms developed. The Solar, or private room for the husband and wife was situated on the first floor (in medieval tales this is where the lover hides). In the fifteenth century the winter parlour evolved; this became the dining-room. It is plain that a room, or rooms, would be set aside for the children, and from these the nursery developed.

There is some doubt as to the speed with which this happened, though this need not concern us overmuch. Ariès talks about the end of the seventeenth century and early eighteenth century. Certainly, even in Tudor and Stuart times, though there was considerable differentiation between rooms, they often tended to lead one into another and were more like wide spaces, bulges, in a continuously winding corridor than separate, shut-off rooms. But in fact there were 'nurcerys' in the thirteenth century. What it amounts to is that the dukes and great lords, the rich, had always had something very like nurseries. Gradually, as more people became wealthy and building became more sophisticated, more and more people had them. As far as we are concerned, number is as important as architectural development.

During the eighteenth century the nursery became increasingly common. It also began to double as the schoolroom. During the Regency and afterwards, however, one usually reads of these two being separate, though even then Elizabeth Ham can write, describing the utter loneliness of her life as a Governess, "The dreary winter day and still more dreary evening, confined to the dull schoolroom . . . with the noisy young children—for those who were too young to be my pupils were not thought too young to be turned into the schoolroom to play."

But it would seem likely that it was during the first thirty or forty years of the nineteenth century that the Victorian nursery as it is often pictured finally crystallised—an austere area, furnished with furniture not needed elsewhere. Austere, and remote—situated at the top or in far-flung parts of the house, among the servants. When there was a fire it was the children or servants who burnt, as in the fire at Lady Molesworth's house described by Horace Walpole.

This was the physical factor in the emergence of the Nanny. Plainly, until her kingdom had been firmly marked out, until her territories were sufficiently numerous for her to become a force in the land, the Nanny could not come into her own. It was during this period that these conditions were established.

One consequence of the physical proximity of women and children in earlier centuries was that mothers played a much more significant role in the up-bringing of their children. Nor, of course, is this any contradiction to what I said earlier about a tradition of allowing others to do this. It was the mother in 1350, after all, who quite voluntarily made the decision to send her daughter aged five to be educated at the house of Lady X.

Even in grand households, where there were numerous Nurses and maids the mother would supervise and check continually and down to the minutest details. Sometimes one detects an almost modern note of neurotic anxiety. Here is a conversation written in 1605:

Lady: Good morrow, Nurse.
Nurse: God give you good morrow, Madame.
Lady: How now, how doth the child?
Nurse: He is fayre and plump, and doth very wel, thanks be to God, saving that he hath been somewhat waiward the last night. . . .
Lady: Unswaddle him, undoe his swaddling bands, give him his breakfast while I am here, make his pappe, take away that fier-wand that smoketh for it will taste of the smoke, where is his little spoone? Wash him before me, have you clean water?

Instructions, observations, reprimands, endearments begin to stream from her in swift succession; she becomes a machine-gun. She tells the Nurse to wash his ears, face, lift up his hair a little in search of some dirt she thinks she sees on his forehead. She notices his eyelid.

What hath he upon his eyelid? Methinks his eyes are somewhat watish, make them clene; how quick is his eyebal, hath he not a pimple upon his nose? His little cheeks are wet, I believe you did leave him alone to cry and weepe; picke his nostrils, wipe his mouth and his lips. How many teethe hath he? His gummes be sore. Showe me his tongue, let me see the pallet of his mouth, he hath a prettie chin. What a fair necke he hath! Pull off his shirt, thou art pretty and fat my little darling, wash his arme-pits; what ayleth his elboe? O what an arme he hath! His hand wrist is very small; open his right hand; the palme of his left hand is all on water, did he sweat? How he spreadeth his small fingers.

This pattern continues. Nurses and maids assist and do much work; it is the mother who has absolute power, who supervises. In the late seventeenth century, Lord North and his wife brought up a large family. Their son Roger wrote, "Our childhood passed as usual under mother's government. We were taught to reverence our father, whose care consisted chiefly in the Gravity and Decorum of his Comportment, Order and Sobriety of Life. . . ." This, incidentally, was more usually the role of the father until almost our own time. Not till now has the father consented, or been forced, to descend into the turmoil of the nursery. Lady North, though tender, was entirely of her age as regards punishment. She "thanked God for the Good Rail [rod] which she said was to break our spirits, which it did effectively." And it might have been noticed that in the two examples I gave earlier of excessive beatings, it was the mothers, Lady Abergane and Lady Hoby, who administered them.

Finally, there still lingered that lack of specialisation in domestic service—as well as the feeling that there was nothing unjustified or unworthy about doing it—which I noted in earlier centuries. Mrs. Boscawen, a prolific writer of nursery letters in the eighteenth century, had some difficulty with an immoral Nurse. "On Nurse Smith wishing to leave me and having for some time perceived her increase of size, I had some suspicions and now find she is with child, has neither friend nor money and must remain upon this parish." But Mrs. Boscawen herself now looks after the children, changing a housemaid into a nurserymaid, while cook helps out.

EARLY EMERGENCE OF SOME NANNY THEMES

Nevertheless, throughout this period, Nurse and Nanny examples continually appear. Before examining the reason for the eventual appearance of the Nanny as an institution, I think it would be useful to look briefly at some of these early examples, because they often prefigure, sometimes closely, sometimes more remotely, some of the themes we shall later study in detail. They are as follows: the Nanny as mother, the ease of hiding cruelty, the decline of the mother, the Nanny in retirement, the Nanny and medicine, medicine as a weapon, food as a weapon, the Nanny as Bard, the Nanny and snobbery.

The Nanny could duplicate every possible position a mother could have: the ordinary Nanny, bringing up the children; Grand-Nannies and Great-Grand-Nannies (and called this); the equivalent of Nannies-in-law. And you get Step-Nannies. An example of this last is found in the household of George III, a Mrs. Cheveley, who I have already mentioned.

The court of George III, as far as the children were concerned, was bourgeois, homely and German. One or two of the children of Queen Charlotte's attendants were brought up with the royal children, sharing their apartments and Nurses. One of these was Charlotte Albert who years later wrote her memoirs.

In these she describes the first royal Nurse, a Mrs. Chapman whom they all loved and admired, and who ran the nursery with great sweetness and efficiency. But unfortunately the Queen had a baby a year. Mrs. Chapman became unable to cope. Now enters the Step-Nanny—Mrs. Cheveley. She is soon hated. She "blinds the just discernment of the Queen . . . gain and favour were her idols. Every judicious arrangement hitherto followed for the benefit and happiness of the nursery and the Royal Children . . . was now broken into. Confusion, want of confidence and respect ensued." Mrs. Cheveley denigrates Mrs. Chapman, manoeuvres and plots like a politician, and eventually ousts her, installing instead her own sister, a Miss Nevin. "This was a person," remembers Charlotte Albert, "ill-bred, ill-looking, ill-natured, puffed with pride and arrogance, the only redeeming point in her character being that she retired more within herself than her sister and therefore only those who had business with her were so fully subjected to her revolting manner."

How the wounds of childhood sting, as fresh still in middle-age as they were in the nursery. They can raise the humblest prose to new heights. And how easy it was for Mrs. Cheveley to conceal what she did from outside eyes, however observant. Fanny Burney, who was at the court at the same time as Mrs. Cheveley, wrote in her Journal that she was "rather handsome, and of a starry appearance, and a woman of exceeding good sense, whose admirable management of the young Princess has secured her affection without spoiling her."

Sometimes the Nanny actually became the mother. An early instance of this occurred in the fourteenth century. As we have seen, it was the custom then and later for ducal and royal households to appoint some high-born lady to run the 'nurcery'. Catherine Swynford, born in 1350 and married to Sir Hugh Swynford in 1368, was given this position in the household of the Duke of Lancaster. Her husband was complaisant and quite soon, as well as looking after his daughter, Catherine became the Duke's mistress. In 1396, Sir Hugh being dead, she married the Duke and from her children, the Beaufort family, sprang three successive kings of England: Edward IV, Richard III, Henry VII. The hand that had rocked the royal cradle came, eventually, to fill it. This is a small theme but a vivid one, and though it is stretching it a bit to call Catherine Swynford a Nanny, or even a Nurse, I have found four instances of Nannies bearing the children of their masters, all in the twentieth century.

Although, as I have described, mothers on the whole played a dominant role in the upbringing of their children up to the eighteenth century, it was during that century that their position began to decline. Increasingly, one comes across that situation, possibly the most important that we shall study in this book in terms of its effects, where the children only see their mother for a short, stated period every day. A figure of the mid-eighteenth century for example, the Duchess of Portland, was very involved with the accomplishments of her time. She devoted herself to collecting strange plants and flowers, exotic birds, scarlet Japan. Turning on a lathe particularly obsessed her, and she became adept at turning jet, ivory, wood, even amber. And as the chips flew, her children were forgotten. She saw them once a day for 'an hour's jumping', after which they returned—as so many were to return—to the nursery. Outside interests, as we shall see in a moment, were not the main influence on this separation. It progressed swiftly for another reason, and reached, in many families, a pitch where Jane Austen's niece, though speaking about her aunt's childhood could generalise, "Children were kept in the nursery, out of the way not only of visitors, but of their parents; they were trusted to hired attendants, they were allowed a great deal of exercise, were kept on plain food, forced to give way to the comfort of others, accustomed to be overlooked, slightly regarded, considered of trifling importance."

If you leave your children to 'hired attendants' you must take the consequences if those attendants are negligent. John Evelyn, the seventeenth-century diarist, though a sweet and conscientious father who loved his children, had a Nurse who by mistake suffocated one of his sons, Richard aged five. His brother had a daughter aged two, who was literally crushed to death by an iron bodice put on her so that she would grow into, and present, the requisite little-adult appearance.

Many other minor themes appear early on. One of the warming things about Nannies is their retirement. Governesses had an appalling time when they retired. No one seemed to care about them. But Nannies have their children much younger; the love they inspire is therefore more fundamental. In later years they are supported by those they once looked after. Henry V gave his Nurse Joanna Waring a pension of twenty pounds a year (say fifteen hundred today) when he came to the throne. Henry VIII did the same for Anne Luke. The Verney letters describe how Nan Fudd helped to bring up eleven children of Sir Edmund and Dame Margery, brought up numerous of their children's children, and was then, albeit somewhat reluctantly, pensioned off.

The *tone* of the Nanny appears early; that tone compounded of love and discipline, of control exercised down to the smallest, minute detail, that complete absorption in the world of the nursery. Here is Luce Shepherd (Verneys again) on the children in her charge. After saying that Miss Mary is merry and good humoured and that she and Miss Margreat love French *potage*, she writes, "as for Miss Margreat she is, thanks be to God, a very healthy and wholesom child, and in my opinion will make a hansum woman. . . . Mr John and Miss Margreat wareth fur gloves, not that shee hath any chilblains this yeare on her hands at all, but shee hath chilblains on her feet but no great matter." (For a complete demonstration of the Nanny tone see the appendix of Nanny sayings and practices.)

That concentration on the world of the nursery, incidentally, seems to be what protects Nannies in time of war. It protected the Verney Nurses in the Civil War. And much later, as though surrounded by the impenetrable bars of some celestial play-pen, we shall see Nannies pass unmoved and unharmed through the most appalling cataclysms of two World Wars, Russian Revolution and the Spanish Civil War.

The importance of the Nurse was enhanced by her knowledge of medicine. For centuries remedies remained very chancy. In the seventeenth century rocks and semi-precious stones still had curative powers ascribed to them. Coral, for instance, was medicinal, which is why we still have coral teethers. For teething in those days you had to rub the gums with a mixture of fresh butter, the milk of a bitch and the brains of a pig. In the eighteenth century a popular remedy was to put a sheep in bed with someone "because these creatures are easily infected and draw the venom to themselves by which means some ease may happen to the sick person". A Nurse who knew remedies that worked not only saved lives, but also time, trouble, and much rather revolting mucking about.

This prerogative of the Nanny continued well into the twentieth century—and many other people owed their lives to their Nannies. Apart from Churchill, Edward Sackville-West did, one of the major novelists of the Nanny. But at the end of the nineteenth century a curious perversion takes place. As doctors usurped their ancient function, and the remedies they were left with became more and more trivial, so cruel or vindictive Nannies began to use their medicines as weapons and punishments. Castor oil, mixtures of every kind, enemas, suppositories—powerful aperients were particularly seized on and childhoods echo to the sound of the dreaded Gregory Powders detonating in little bowels.

Curiously enough, the same thing happened with food. As we shall see in a later chapter, the milk we imbibe from the breast or bottle is the first and most powerful manifestation we receive of love. For that reason food remains immensely important psychologically throughout childhood, and indeed all our lives. People who love their children want them to eat heartily. It pleases them; it is a way of showing their love. Similarly, those who do not particularly care for their children and are guilty about it, feel that by filling them with food they can somehow compensate for their lack of love. It is hardly surprising that in later life adults who are not loved, or not loved enough, will often eat instead.

Nannies recognised the love-power of food and were early using it for the diametrically opposite purpose. Mrs. Crabtree naturally employed it. "If Laura and Harry left any breakfast, Mrs. Crabtree kept it carefully till dinner time, when they were obliged to finish the whole before tasting meat; and if they refused it at dinner the remains were kept for supper. Mrs. Crabtree always informed them that she did it for their good!"

'Their good'; therein lies the complexity. Nannies believed, many people still believe, that children should be made to 'eat up', that unless they 'eat up' they will starve or get the wrong diet, or become sloppy and slack and fail to learn manners. I shall deal with this subject later, but whatever the merits of 'eating up', we shall find there can be little doubt that some unpleasant Nannies used food as a weapon.

The Nanny as Bard: the records of Tom Thumb, Robin Goodfellow, Humpty-Dumpty and many others go back before the Norman Conquest. They were almost certainly preserved by, among others, Nurses telling them to their charges. For many centuries the Nurse was books, television, wireless all in one—and frequently as frightening. Charlotte M. Yonge's nursery in the early nineteenth century was a gloomy passage room, its narrow windows darkened by great trees. One of her nursemaids used to take her here and then repeat John Taylor's tragic poem the *Melancholy*

Adventures of Poor Puss because she enjoyed seeing Charlotte roll about on the floor in agony.

The Nanny as snob: nearly all servants are outrageous snobs, partly out of sycophancy, partly because their own status depends upon that of their master or mistress. Nannies seem to me to have been more snobbish than most. This may be because they often identified very closely with their charges and families; or it may be because they came into close proximity with other Nannies, so making competition and comparison direct, in a way which didn't often happen to other servants. Whatever the reason, their snobbism was considerable and they will demonstrate it frequently and sometimes ludicrously throughout this book. One early example will suffice. When the Duke of Wellington asked whether Queen Victoria's new child was a girl or boy, Mrs. Lilly replied—"It is a *Prince*, your Grace."

GROWTH OF WEALTH AND POPULATION— THE NANNY APPEARS

I should like now to come to the final crucial factors in the evolution and emergence of the Nanny.

We can approach this obliquely through the appearance during the early history of another theme—the Nanny as specialist.

Traces of this specialisation can be found, as can the beginnings of so much Nanny material, in the eighteenth century. For instance, there had evolved in grand houses a type of servant known as a Rocker. These were lower even than nursery-maids. Their job was to do the most menial tasks like cleaning the baby and rocking the cradle. Georgiana, Duchess of Devonshire writing to her mother Lady Spencer in September 1783, describes one:

> You know I would bring the Rocker with me, meaning, as she was poor, to keep her while I suckled. She was only rather dirty till last night, when she was quite drunk. My dear little girl sleeps now in bed with me after her first suck-ing, as it is cold to move, the Rocker was to turn her dry and lay her down to sleep. I perceived that she made the bed stink of wine and strong drink when-ever she came near it. . . . This morning I learnt she had been so drunk as to fall down and vomit. . . . I have therefore paid her ten guineas and told her I would pay her journey up to town. . . .

Not surprisingly, her mother rebuked her for being too generous to such a slattern. Perhaps it is because it attracted people of rather low calibre that the position (of which there are traces as far back as the Middle Ages) seems to have died out by the nineteenth century.

Nevertheless, this seemingly small item of information is in fact more important than any of the other examples I have given before. Because Rockers were a result of two developments crucial in the evolution of the Nanny: the increase in wealth and the growth in population.

Specialisation depends on number; if there are few people in a community, only essential functions can be performed, several, often, by one person; as numbers rise, the number of different things that can be done each by one person increases proportionally. During the eighteenth century the population increased steadily, and with it the supply of domestic servants. This accompanied (and no doubt intensified) a concept of man's relationship to society which became very rigid in that century. This view—a Platonic one in essence—was that everyone had been given their place in society by God. This place had a function and was permanent. If everyone kept their place and performed their function then society would work harmoniously. Servants were to look after the rich and they were to look after everything: clothes, food, house, horses, garden, and children. To put it another way, if the rich had anything that needed looking after—whether it was a coat or a child—then there was a servant to do it. Plainly this view of society is very different, its concept of service is very different, from the one we found in medieval Europe. It is also one much more conducive to the acceptance of Nannies; indeed it could be said to dictate them.

During the eighteenth century, medicine improved and infant mortality decreased. From the beginning of the nineteenth century the population began to explode. For a hundred years—from 1801 to 1911—it grew by *over eleven per cent every single year*. The effects of this fantastic growth can scarcely be exaggerated. Families grew larger and larger. In 1830 the *average* family had six or seven children; but probably among the wealthy the average family was even larger, since conditions were better. Edward Lear had twenty-one brothers and sisters. It is scarcely surprising that when his mother died, at a relatively early age, the cause was said to be 'general decay'. These teeming hordes of children on their own would very rapidly have produced some regularised method of looking after and controlling them.

The second crucial factor that produced the Nanny (and the Rocker) was of course the increase in wealth. During the eighteenth century the Industrial Revolution gathered the momentum which, accelerating by a sort of compound increase in speed, was to make Britain easily the richest country in the world during the nineteenth century. But this wealth was concentrated in few hands. In 1870, for instance, 400 peers were estimated to own one sixth of the entire country. And in 1901, out of a population of 32·5 million, only 400,000 had an income of over £400 a year (though in fact you could employ domestic servants on well under £400 a year).

A very large number of poor seeking employment; a relatively smaller number of rich, with vast families of children whom they expected servants to look after: it is scarcely surprising Nursemaids, Nurses, Nannies multiplied with prodigious speed. I don't want to go into the absolute numbers of Nannies at the moment, but the rate at which they grew is neatly illustrated by a study of the advertisements in *The Times*. From 1822 to 1882 this shows a steep rise both in the demand for Nurses, and the number offering themselves as Nurses. Thereafter, for various reasons, the numbers of both drop abruptly away. In 1822, for instance, there was an average of one advertisement for a Nurse a day, in 1838 an average of 2·3 advertisements a day, 1856, 5·1 advertisements a day, until by the '70s and '80s the demand had become what one can only call raging; 10·4 advertisements a day in 1873, 12·4 a day in 1882. The same picture is true of Nurses asking for places—by 1882 this had risen to 13·3 advertisements a day from one a day in 1822. (And it is interesting, incidentally, as a measure of their importance, that Nurses were always put at the head of any list of positions vacant or wanted.)

Now a number of things can be gleaned from these advertisements. Their number does of course partly reflect the growth of *The Times* itself. But it didn't grow that fast (especially after 1861), and there can be no denying the soaring upward curve of the Nanny/Nurse advertising. Also the number of these advertisements grows both faster and greater in proportion to the other advertisements.

What did baffle me at first is why they fell off in the late '80s, the very moment one would expect them to reach their peak. Closer study showed that, paradoxically, this was an effect of the success and vigour of the Nanny/Nurse situation. In the early 1860s, agencies for the employment of domestic servants began to appear. By the late '70s and early '80s these agencies were dealing with increasing numbers of Nurses. In the '90s agencies grew up devoted entirely to Nurses. These became very precise in their advertising. For instance, on November 2, 1902, an agency asking for Nannies, detailed six—one in Bournemouth, a nursery-maid in London, and so on through the list. They also became very large. 1912 saw the rise of the great Norah Beresford Agency.

Not only did agencies syphon much work away from *The Times*, but the growth of the domestic servant market meant that other papers grew up to cater for it. In 1850 *The Times* was actually rejecting advertisements, but from then on the competition grew rapidly fiercer. Nor was this just from other daily newspapers like *The Sketch* or *Telegraph*. Special papers and fiction magazines grew up: *The Family Herald*, as early as 1842; later, *The Family Herald Supplement, Family Pocket Stories* and *Family Reader* (combined circulation of 300,000). These fiction magazines—which so stimulated and tempted Robert Louis Stevenson's puritanical Nurse—were very popular. *The Magazine of Fiction* claimed a circulation of one million. And they all carried advertising.

But undoubtedly it was the vast numbers of Nannies which made advertising redundant. When everyone you knew had one, or generally more than one, you obtained your Nanny from a friend or relation who no longer had need of her, or who had a Second Nurse who was due for promotion. The great bulk of Nannies were obtained in this way.

The Times advertisements also show that Nannies were by no means confined to the gentry. From 1850 on it is quite common for a "thorough nurse in a genteel tradesman's family" to be asked for. This bears out what someone I interviewed told me, that by the end of the century you were barely considered middle class if you didn't have at least a nurse-maid for the children. *Ayahs* (that is, Indian Nurses) gradually appear in the 1830s. They are common by the 1860s. And by this time Nurses frequently state that they are willing to travel anywhere. Both facts will be relevant when we come to consider the mobility of the Nanny.

Finally, *The Times* suggests a biological law: the more propitious an environment is for life, the more life-forms will evolve to fill it. The environment, as we have seen, was extremely propitious for domestic servants; therefore a great number of different species evolved. *The Times* of Tuesday January 3, 1832, has nineteen servants asked for or requesting positions in seven different categories: 2 Upper Nurses, 2 Cook Housekeepers, 7 Cooks, 3 Housemaids, 3 Footmen, 1 Coachman, 1 Groom.

The Times of January 10, 1870 (and it is by no means untypical) has this formidable list: 2 Head Nurses, 5 Upper Nurses, 8 Nurses, 2 Under Nurses, 1 Nursemaid, 13 Ladies' Maids, 4 Under Ladies Maids, 2 Maids, 7 Parlourmaids, 2 Needlewomen, 2 Housekeepers, 5 Cook Housekeepers, 29 Cooks, 2 Upper Housemaids, 16 Housemaids, 2 Under Housemaids, 4 Chambermaids, 4 Kitchen Maids, 2 Laundry Maids, 1 Stillroom Maid, 1 Scullery Maid, 10 Butlers, 2 Travelling Servants, 3 Valets, 12 Indoor Servants, 3 Footmen, 2 Pages, 22 Coachmen,

1 Second Coachman, 5 Grooms, 1 Head Gardener, 1 Gardener, 1 Boots.

Just to skim is to get the message. A hundred and seventy-seven offers and requests have evolved now into thirty-three separate species. (Note that in each case children's Nurses form approximately a tenth of the total servants asked for.) This elaboration is important to the Nanny for a simple reason. To prevent anarchy among the armies of their domestic servants, the Victorians imposed a rigid system of rules, hierarchies, uniforms, functions, promotions and so on; a code of discipline which was almost military both in strictness and in its multifarious subdivision. It was in this context that the institution of the Nanny grew firm. Between 1850 and 1880 her place in the household, her power, her duties, her clothes, her training, were all defined.

It is possible that her very title first became general now. One historian of the subject has said the word Nanny first appears in print in early editions of Mrs. Beeton, around 1860. I failed to find it there. The earliest record I found was in a letter of January 1711 which Lady Mary Wortley Montagu wrote to her old Nurse and which began 'Dear Nanny'.

In fact the origins of the word are extremely obscure. There was a report in the papers a few years ago of Prince Charles talking to two children in a pit village in Wales. After a while he turned to a matronly woman standing nearby and said pleasantly, "And I suppose you're their Nanny?" The paper was fairly caustic about this, but in fact Charles may have been correct. Grandmothers are still often called Nanny in Wales, as they are in several places in the North and Midlands of England. In many fairly primitive societies, grandmothers and the older women of the family play a major part in the bringing up of the children. In Russia, for instance, they used to do it exclusively and were called *babushka*. It is possible that Nanny for Granny spread east from Wales and south from the Midlands, meaning someone who cared for children. Dictionaries are of little help. Webster gives Nana as a short version of Anne (not much shorter). So does Fowler, and both suggest that Nanny came from this. But were so many Nurses called Anne? It seems an odd coincidence. Several of my correspondents had Nans and Nanas— just as in the seventeenth century—whose Christian names were anything but Anne. As an alternative to Anne, Webster says Nanny is just elliptical for Nanny Goat, which might suggest a somewhat coarse derivation from the wet nurse. But, as we have seen, by the end of the nineteenth century wet nurses had been declining for two hundred years and it would be odd if some ancient nickname for them suddenly surfaced at this time. In the sixteenth and seventeenth centuries a Nanny-house was a brothel—this was a rare use and can surely have little to do with our subject. Nanny might have developed from 'Nursie' which was a common diminutive in the early nineteenth century.

But though interesting, the derivation and development of the word are not of vital importance. Plainly, Nursie, Nana, Nanny are, like Mummy, Mama, Ma, just typical childish utterances which could well have various roots. By the 1920s it was the universal word, more common than Nurse, and was used in advertisements (though it was still not included in the 1933 Oxford Dictionary). Before 1914 it was fairly common among children (and must, therefore, have existed before 1900); but adults on the whole did not use it. They either said Nurse, or used the surname of the person, or used the surname with the honorary 'Mrs' which her position, like that of Cook, entitled her to. (This was a very old custom going back far beyond Mrs. Crabtree—who, I need hardly say, was unmarried—into the eighteenth century.) Once established, the title of Nanny was used in a variety of ways. Frequently, the Nanny takes on the surname of the family, as it might be Nanny Gathorne-Hardy. But this was not invariable. Nanny could be used before her own surname. Or, at some point in her career, perhaps the first family she stayed with for a long time, her assumed surname became fixed. So, Nanny Gathorne-Hardy moving to the Hills after fifteen years would continue to be known as Nanny Gathorne-Hardy and not as Nanny Hill. Nanny snobbism might play a part here. I heard of one Nanny whose charge, though her surname was Laurence, was a relative of Quintin Hogg. The Nanny by rights should have been called Nanny Laurence but insisted on being called Nanny Hailsham. But it is true this occurred in a very competitive situation where six Nannies were helping to run a girls' prep school during the Second World War.

CONCLUSIONS

What conclusions can one draw from this brief and therefore I'm afraid sometimes sketchy survey of the various historical influences and developments which went into the making of the British Nanny?

Let me try and summarise. The Nanny emerged into a society and a class where, though now remote, there was a definite tradition of mothers allowing other people to look after their children. She emerged at a time when, partly owing to the rise of a servant class and partly owing to changes in attitude towards service, the position of the mother was already to a certain extent in decline. She came when children were still widely regarded as little, defective adults, sodden with original sin. Their sin was to be squeezed out of them by cramping disciplines; an accepted method was by beating, applied even to small children. There had been some progress towards a more kindly and enlightened view of childhood, but it is doubtful how deeply it had penetrated. We have seen the appearance of certain themes: the Nanny taking the place of the mother, the Nanny as snob, the cruel Nanny, the Nanny as specialist and so on. We have seen that the most important reasons for the Nanny's appearance were the growth in population and the increase in wealth among, and its concentration in, the upper and upper-middle classes. Let us now see what happened when all these strands and the others we have discussed, these subterranean currents, these frequently massive historical movements, finally contrived to form a moment propitious for our subject; let us proceed to a full examination of the British Nanny from 1850 to 1939.

CHAPTER THREE

Class and Position of the Nanny—First Sexual Detour

"I am happy now that Charles calls on my bedchamber less frequently than of old. As it is, I now endure but two calls a week and when I hear his steps outside my door I lie down on my bed, close my eyes, open my legs and think of England."
Lady Hillingham, Journal, 1912

Although Mrs. Everest was neglected in Storr's version of Churchill's story, perhaps conveniently, she has, like most Nannies, much in common with many other Nannies. She furnishes therefore an appropriate springboard from which to plunge into the aspects which I want to study first.

The first of these is class. Class divisions in England go back many centuries and have complex roots—feudal, religious, material, philosophical (we saw the influence of Plato in the eighteenth century). It is enough here to say that they were still immensely important in Victorian and Edwardian England, and of only slightly less importance up to the Second World War. The Victorians minded very much about the class of people looking after their children. Governesses, for instance, *had* to be upper class, or at least genteel—which was why the financial collapse of a grand or well-bred house meant the surrounding families fell upon the unmarried and now impoverished daughters like flocks of ravening vultures.

> We need the impudences, extravagancies, mistakes, and crimes of a certain amount of fathers, to sow the seed from which *WE* reap the harvest of governesses. The daughters of tradespeople, however well-educated, must necessarily be underbred and as such unfit to be the inmates of *OUR* dwellings, or guardians of *OUR* children's minds and persons. We shall never prefer to place those about *OUR* offspring who have not been born and bred with somewhat of the same refinement as *OURSELVES*.

This comes from Charlotte Brontë's *Shirley*, and she knew about it. She had suffered as a governess herself and records elsewhere, among other humiliations, how when one of her little pupils put his hand in hers and said he loved her, the mother cried out, "Love the *governess*, dear?" as though that were impossible.

But for Nannies and Nurses coarser grain was allowed. They were invariably working class, the daughters of plasterers, builders, farmers, carpenters and so on. A number of people writing about Nannies have suggested that a majority of them were farmers' daughters. Curiously enough, Miss Keymer, the Principal of the Norland Nursery Training College when I visited it, said that though she had not tested this she felt about sixty per cent of her students were farmers' daughters. Yet there is no reason why this should be so generally or even at Norland which, though situated deep in rural Berkshire, has a reputation all over Britain. As I noted in the introduction, including Nannies people have told me about (and I have always asked for their backgrounds), Nannies I have interviewed and Nannies I have read about, I calculate this book is based on a sample of 296 Nannies. This is statistically valuable; but from it there comes no bias towards farmers' daughters. My own feeling is that commentators think Nannies *ought* to be farmers' daughters. They like the idea of rosy-cheeked, apple-bosomed country girls, glowing with rude health from churns of fresh milk, looking after children with all the easy naturalness which comes from seeing calves and pigs born, eggs laid, kittens suckled. There is no evidence for it.

In fact there is no bias towards anything. They are just working class. I thought at one time that I was finding a disproportionate amount of Baptist, Methodist and Presbyterian Nannies. I should have liked this because it would have made a neat pattern of stricter religious and moral training. But I was forced to the conclusion that there only seemed more because people with Baptist and so on Nannies, who certainly did have a stricter moral and religious upbringing, mentioned the religion of their Nannies because it impinged on their lives. Those with, say, an Anglican Nanny didn't mention it. There was no statistical significance.

But the fact that they were almost without exception working class (I only found one who was not) is important enough in itself. A psychiatrist I consulted about this book suggested I should watch out for signs of strain between the lower class language ('pardon'), values, etc., of the Nanny and upper class language ('what'), values, etc., of the parents. But of course there was no strain. On the contrary, as I have already indicated, Nannies nearly always identified completely with the *mores* and values of the class they served—which was practical and sensible of them. They knew which side their bread was buttered. If they had any effect at all in this sphere it was, by drawing the attention of their charges to them continually and from the beginning, to accentuate and preserve class distinctions more sharply and for longer than would otherwise have been the case. Nanny Marks, Nanny to the children of the Marquis of Bath and his first wife Daphne when they were Lord and Lady Weymouth, refused to allow the evacuees in the Second World War to cross the front garden, though no one else minded what they did. She would rush from the house and personally chase them off the lawns. She impressed their inferiority on the Thynne children. In Hyde Park there were children they could play with and children who were 'rough' and could not be played with. Alexander, the eldest son, remembers how they all looked the same and that he could never understand how Nanny Marks instantaneously recognised who was rough and who not. Nanny Ellis—a Nanny in the 1920s, but pre-1914 trained—said it was 'common' to eat out of doors (especially sweets and ices), common to stare and common to mix with 'trade' children, however rich.

Nanny snobbery was by no means always as clear-cut and coarse as this, however. When they went abroad, for instance, it was really enough just to be British. Count Frederich Ledebur, then seventy, told me that if you were a member of the Austrian upper classes before the First World War it was quite inevitable that you would have a British Nanny. (There are in fact some hundred very ancient retired British Nannies in and around Vienna to this day.) Their own Nanny was called Nanny MacEliot. She used to complain that there were no gentlemen in Austria. A great many—indeed too many—princes and counts, but no *gentlemen*. Sometimes she would admit that Frederich's father, Count Adolph, was a gentleman. One day Frederich's brother complained to her that she didn't give him his title. My title is Count, he said, Count Ledebur. Nanny at once said why didn't you give me my title? I didn't know you had a title. Certainly, said Nanny; my title is *Mac*. *Mac*Eliot. In Scotland, Mac is a title.

But even in England the identification of Nannies with the family and class they had joined often became so complete that the very word snobbery seems somehow inappropriate. Nanny Buckles, aged seventy, was, when I saw her, Nanny to the child of Edwina and Pierson Dixon. Edwina is the daughter of Duncan Sandys, and Nanny Buckles had also Nannied her (she had met Mrs. Sandys at Mrs. Boucher's famous agency in Basil Street). Talking to her, I felt not so much that she admired the distinguished people she had met as a result of those she served, but almost as

though she were related to them too. She referred with ease and pleasant-
ness to Churchill and Chartwell and how well Nanny Soames was doing
in Paris. Her conversation reminded me of my grandmother's—"Didn't
he marry one of the Warcups? I think it was Betsy Warcup and of course
she was a cousin of the Suffolk Campbells, rather a difficult family"—
I've forgotten all the names, just as I did with my grandmother; these
are inventions—"Then they bought a place in Wales I think." In fact
when Mrs. Dixon showed me into the drawing-room, where Nanny
Buckles was sitting, gave me a whisky, offered Nanny one (refused)
and then deferentially melted away, it was far more as though she,
Mrs. Dixon, were the Nanny, and that Nanny Buckles were the mistress
of the house.

This, of course, has something to do with an aspect I want to deal with
later—how the post-war scarcity of Nannies has led to a great increase
in their power and status. In certain important respects Nanny Buckles
was the mistress of the house. Ellen Stevens—known to her children as
Diddy—was Nanny at one time to the Jarvis family, and then, during
which time she 'retired', to the family of the Duke of Devonshire.
When Harold Macmillan resigned, Diddy was put next to him at a lunch
party given for Devonshire's twenty-one-year-old son Peregrine. "Ex-
Nanny sitting next to ex-Prime Minister," she said. It was clear that
she believed herself at least his equal.

POWER OF THE NANNY

Nanny Everest chose Churchill's clothes, his books, his presents, his
food, his companions; she regulated his life from the largest down to the
smallest particulars. For weeks at a time she was alone with him. She
had him removed from his school; and there are numerous instances of
Nannies choosing the schools, particularly the prep schools, their charges
went to. In her sphere, the Nanny's power was absolute; and this power
is continuous through our period—from around 1850, that is, until 1939.
Mrs. Crabtree, in *Holiday House*, not only beats and thrashes the children,
her whole aspect is that of a gaoler in sole charge of a gaol. Their life
is hedged with petty restrictions. They can have no pets. And she wears
a huge bunch of keys which ring and jangle "like a rattlesnake giving
warning of her approach" so that everybody has time to put on a look
of good behaviour before she arrives. In a desperate attempt to mollify
her, Frank the elder boy saves up his money to buy her a gown and Mrs.
Crabtree "looks almost good-humoured for the space of five minutes"

(actually a surprisingly long time, considering the gown is bright apple-green covered in huge spots of red, yellow, blue, orange, black and violet).

Mrs. Crabtree is a tyrant, and in effect a farcical one. Absolute power by no means always corrupted so absolutely, but power—the sole control of the nursery, its staff and the children in it—was in a great many cases the *sine qua non* of Nannydom. In interview after interview, book upon book, Nannies state that they had to be in charge and describe how, even if they occasionally seemed to give way to the mother, they always preserved the substance of power. And in interviews, books and letters, their now adult charges describe the exercise of that power, mothers their usually unavailing attempts to curb it, share it, or their delighted or feeble acquiescence in its existence. "In my day, the nursery was a Kingdom and the Nanny had complete control"—Nanny Marks again. Nanny Hopkins, in an interview with Francis Wyndham in the *Queen* magazine some years ago, describes how Lady Radziwill used to say she was terrified of her. "And do you know the reason she gave? Because I wouldn't let her wake the child at night and cuddle it! Certainly I wouldn't—not only for my sake, but for the baby's too."

British Nannies abroad often furnish particularly clear examples of certain aspects of the Nanny. Partly this is because their isolation in a foreign country leads to defensive exaggeration (for instance the Nanny in Nancy Mitford's *The Blessing* who becomes obsessed with the smell of French drains). But it is also because the foreign mother, seeing the Nanny from a distance, can only discern a single characteristic, imagines it is the only one and fosters its exaggeration herself. (I found an instance of this while researching for this book, though in another sphere, when I read a mid-nineteenth century French advertisement asking for "*Une Gouvernante Anglais—methodes drastique*".)

The Empress of Russia for example had clearly been very much struck by the immense authority of the British Nanny. When Nanny Eager arrived in 1899, carefully chosen by a member of the British Royal family, she was at once given totalitarian powers in the Imperial nurseries. As well as running all the usual things, including embroidery (a kettle-holder for the Tzar—"Polly put the kettle on"), riding, story-telling, etc., she organised the nursery side of festivals in which the whole court had to play a part, like Easter and Christmas. Her influence extended to religion. The favourite hymn of Grand Duchess Olga (aged three) and Grand Duchess Tatiana (one and a half) was *Rock of Ages*. And in fact her rank can be measured in military terms. When the girls grew older, tutors were engaged to teach them. These were called 'Your Excellency' and given the rank of general. But Nanny Eager came above the tutors. She was in effect (though the distinction was never conferred) a field-marshal.

It was her power which led to her downfall. It was noticed, resented, and feared. When on August 12, 1904 (her birthday), the much-wanted heir to the throne was born, her days were numbered. The court officials could allow a Nanny to influence a few grand duchesses. There could be no question of the same influence over their future ruler. Soon after he was born she was sent home with a pension of a hundred pounds a year.

But the subject of the power of the Nanny is not nearly as straight-forward as this. Mothers often resented not being allowed to play a part in looking after their children. Sometimes a partnership was worked out. But more often there were long jealous battles, some lasting years and resulting in tensions and divided loyalties, some ending swiftly in a clean sacking and the engagement of a new Nanny (one mother in the 1920s had eighteen Nannies in four years). After 1914, as the influence of Freud and other investigators very very slowly filtered down into not particularly receptive upper class English minds, the pressure to know at least something about how their children were being brought up increased. This was reinforced by the movements towards greater freedom and greater participation by women, movements which were at least partly caused by the sense of uselessness, the loss of role, that the Nanny's power had brought about. There were material pressures—the slow decline in the number of domestic servants, for instance. At the same time, contrary to these pressures, as the Nanny system continued, it became not just accepted, but regarded by the upper classes as inevitable; the only sensible or desirable way to bring up children.

Nevertheless, despite these complex interactions, the power of the Nanny is one of the first instances of what I call the Nanny Block. By this I mean that, though there were changes in the power and position of Nannies between 1850 and 1939, it is far more accurate to regard Nannies as a block existing during this entire period essentially unchanged. That is not to say there were not differences between, for example, Nanny Marks in 1933 and Nanny Everest in 1874. Lady Weymouth certainly saw much more of her children than Lady Churchill. You could probably have shocked Nanny Everest; Nanny Marks was quite difficult to shock (of an acquaintance who was in gaol she said cosily "At least he's not a *dull* character"). And there were differences in other fields. It would be harder (though not impossible) to match a Mrs. Crabtree or Nurse Pratt for coarse brutality in 1935 than in 1895. But in terms of their power over their charges I do not think such differences one can detect are nearly as large or nearly as significant as the similarities.

It is of course impossible to prove this. Though I will give a number of examples which suggest it, it is still really no more than an impression I am left with after research. But for the purposes of this chapter and the next, that doesn't matter. For the moment it is only necessary, as with class, to hold in the mind a fairly simple, familiar and early stereotype of the Nanny which might be described as follows:

Her kingdom—where she sits, all-powerful and fairly beneficent, sewing, chiding, comforting, watchful, rocking in her rocking chair in front of a coal fire—consists of a day nursery, a night nursery (where she may sleep herself), a still-room or pantry and possibly the room of her servants. These consist of an Under-Nurse, nursery-maids (probably one to each child), and possibly a French *bonne*. Her other subjects are inanimate—toys, continually strewn about and tidied up, medicines, clothes, hairbrushes, chamber pots. The parents are hardly seen at all. Mother may look in for ten minutes around ten o'clock in the morning. Then all the children go down to the drawing-room for an hour around tea-time, very clean and very well-behaved. That is all.

Above all, the feeling of the nursery is that it is separate. Nanny is separate, suspended half-way between the mother and the rest of the staff, half-parent, half-servant. The children may see other adults, but there is always the sense of venturing out. The other servants look on the nursery as a separate and almost alien world. The footman dislikes having to carry the food up to it. Nursery-maids leave it in the role of ambassadors. And this psychic separation is expressed physically. It may have its own staircase, its own door out into the grounds, it may be in a separate wing, a separate corridor, a separate floor, cut off and even silenced from the rest of the house by a muffling, brass-studded, green baize door.

IDEALISATION OF THE MOTHER

Separation—particularly separation from the parents, and even more particularly from the mother—is the central element in the Nanny situation. It has already been demonstrated by Nanny Everest, and it will form a major theme of this book. At the moment, I want to study one aspect of it.

As a matter of fact this too has been demonstrated by Churchill.

"She shone for me like the Evening Star"—I have already quoted what he wrote about his mother—"I loved her dearly—but at a distance." The idealisation of the mother, the turning of her into a remote, beautiful, untouchable goddess, is so common between 1850 and 1939 that I was at first tempted to think of it as inevitable. Bernard Shaw and his two elder sisters (he was born in 1856), were almost entirely brought up by Nurses and servants. Talking about food, he wrote; "I hated the servants and liked my mother because on the one or two rare and delightful occasions when she buttered my bread for me, she buttered it thickly instead of merely wiping a knife on it. Her almost complete neglect of me had the advantage that I could idolise her to the utmost pitch of my imagination and had no sordid or disillusioning contacts with her. It was a privilege to be taken for a walk or a visit with her, or on an excursion."

The remoteness of these idols, these 'mothers', is hardly surprising; they were remote. Their canonisation, for the aura about them is frequently religious, was augmented by a number of factors. One of these was a paradoxical element in the power and position of the Nanny. Children are very quick to sense the realities of power, and nearly always they realised that, though the Nanny's power was absolute, she derived it from the mother. "I shall tell your mother/father" was always the ultimate threat. The climax of each day, the moment towards which frenzies of brushing and washing and dressing moved, was the visit to the drawing-room. If the Nanny was cruel, then the one moment she was not cruel was when the mother was present. Eleanor Acland, in her book *Goodbye for the Present*, describes how her extremely unpleasant Nurse Barley retired into a background of 'obsequious gentility' whenever her mother came into the nursery. Though Nanny was the one to be reckoned with, the mother, as the fountainhead of power, was the one to be worshipped. Just so, a medieval subject obeyed (and was terrified of) the king, but reserved his prayers and adoration for God.

This paradoxical element extended to class. Plainly the Nanny's total acceptance, indeed intensification, of the class structure could, in one sense, only result in lowering her in the eyes of her charges and raising their mother. Children, very early trained to be hierarchical, always recognised the servant status of Nannies as compared to them and their parents. And they could use it as a weapon. In *Sinister Street* by Compton Mackenzie, the little boy Michael Fane, totally dominated by his cruel Nanny, has only one victory over her. They go out to buy Valentines and he wishes to buy one for his governess.

"Come along now," said Nanny.

"Oh, but can't I get one for Miss Carthew? No, let me."

"Tut-tut-tut. What nonsense. I do declare. Whatever do you want to give her a Valentine for?" Nurse demanded, as she tried to hustle Michael from the shop.

"Oh let me, Nanny."

"Well come along, and don't be all day choosing. Here, this will do," said Nurse, as she picked one from the penny tray.

But Michael has other ideas. He wants one of those huge satiny cushion ones. They argue. He stands up to her and insists on the nice ones.

"You will, will you, naughty boy? You won't then. Go now! You dare defy me. I never heard of such a thing. No, nothing more this morning, thank you," Nurse added, turning to the stationer. "The little boy has got all he wants. Say 'thank you' to the gentleman and 'good-morning'," Nurse commanded Michael.

He refuses. On the way back he says his mother would have let him buy it. And now Nanny, thinking she is revealing the root of her power, lays herself open to the one attack to which she is vulnerable.

"Your mother isn't here. And when she isn't here, I'm your mother," said Nanny, looking more old and wrinkled and monkey-like than ever.

"How dare you say you're my mother," gasped the outraged son. "You're not. You're not. Why, you're not a lady, so you couldn't ever be my mother."

And at this lightning, deadly shaft, Nanny, the unkind, omnipotent always victorious Nanny, collapses entirely and bursts into uncontrollable tears.

Nannies frequently contributed to the idealisation of the mother directly—whether to produce an example for the children to emulate, or to suck up ("Nanny says you're the most wonderful person in the world, Mummy"), or because they genuinely believed it. Numerous correspondents described this and said how grateful they were to their Nannies for preserving in them, or perhaps creating would be a more accurate word, such pleasant pictures of their mothers, even though they never saw them.

And of course the mothers frequently were, or must have seemed, angelic. After all, it was not so difficult for them. They had none of the wear and tear of bringing up children or indeed of anything else—there was nothing to make them tired and irritable. And many of them, most of them, did love their children. It may have been rather an unreal love sometimes. Lucy Lyttleton writing of her childhood in the 1840s, describes the great moment of the day when her parents put their heads into the nursery on their way to their rooms. "You little pigs," Mama would say with a smile; and Papa, smiling as well, "Absurd little monkeys." Their children might have been pets, or curious animated dolls. But it was a genuine love all the same, and the only time it could express itself was during the afternoon visit to the drawing-room. It is hardly surprising therefore that these visits were often tremendous fun. Mary Clive in *Christmas with the Savages* describes riots and orgies of sweets and games and spoilt behaviour. Lady Anne Hill (both these are pre-1911 childhoods) wrote in a letter to me: "The after-tea hour with my mother and brothers in the drawing-room was magical, a different realm and state of existence to the drab nursery life. When Nannie came to fetch me to bed, my brothers would point at her and say 'Whooooo's this?' to me, to tease me. I was then easy to tease; it always worked and I was always carried screaming and struggling from the drawing-room." Over these Edens, reigned the gentle, indulgent, loving, angelic mother.

But quite often the mother did, as it were, actually become ethereal, scarcely any longer seeming to take part in the world of the living. The complex process of bringing up children, tending, teaching, feeding and loving them is immensely satisfying to many women. It is fascinating, creative, and fulfilling at deep levels. This is especially so if the *mores* of their society expect them to do it and praise them for doing it well. This was certainly so in England among the vast majority of people up to 1939. Yet, expecting and needing to conform, many upper and upper-middle class English mothers were in fact, by the accident of domestic service development which we have traced, largely denied any chance of looking after their children at all. Apart from running their homes, which they could always delegate, they had really nothing to occupy them except the trivia of social life. It is scarcely surprising that many of them suffered from a profound sense of uselessness and often retired, neurotic, fainting and depressed to be 'ill' on couches or in their bedrooms for years and years and years. The figure of the sick mother appears in several autobiographical novels about the Nanny, notably in Sackville-West's *Simpson* and Julian Fane's *Morning*.

Indeed so common is she in Victorian and Edwardian literature, where her main appearance usually ends in an affecting death, that I think here she is more than just an illustration of an existing type. The frequency of her appearance, particularly in novels for children, is a fact of the Nanny situation itself. That is to say, so faint and distant were many mothers because of Nurses and Nannies that it was more realistic to picture them as ill and near the world of the dead than it was to have them healthy in the world of the living. After 1914, partly for reasons of critical taste, this figure becomes less common in literature; it is possible she became less common in life. Nevertheless during my interviews I came across many figures like Nanny Williams's employer Mrs. F (this is mid-1920s) who was so weak and fragile, beset with such a jangling and twinge-ing of nerves, that even when she only saw her children for ten minutes a day she complained that it 'tired her'.

In all these areas—where the Nanny was kind and also held the mother up for praise, where the mother was herself spoiling and loving (if only for an hour or so a day), and where the mother, neurotically languishing, became like some distant, scarcely alive being, already an angel—then the idolised and remote mother is very common indeed. It became accepted as normal. In a deeply sentimental autobiography called *Being Little in Cambridge when Everyone Else was Big*, Eleanor Hallowell Abbott (b. 1872) wrote, "But of our mother we knew practically nothing—except we loved her!" Mrs. Hallowell has an irritating habit of referring to her past self as 'it'. Later in the book she says, "It was not, I think, so much the custom to tell its parents much of anything. No slightest lack of personal friendliness or affection was evidenced by this hiatus, I believe. The hiatus was simply there! That was all!"

But there is one other area where the mother is idolised, and to illus-trate this I should like to quote again from *Sinister Street*. This early and, in my view, best book of Compton Mackenzie's is very important for the study of the Nanny. It is interesting, for example, how writing in 1912 about the years of his childhood from 1883 to 1888 (the early part of the book is entirely autobiographical as the *Octaves* make clear) he uses the words Nurse and Nanny interchangeably. In this instance he makes very real the agony of that passionate and adoring love the children of Nannies felt for their absent mothers.

The Fanes have just moved into a new house, 64, Carlington Road, West Kensington. Michael Fane is aged about four, his sister Stella is younger. Soon it becomes clear that Mrs. Fane is going away.

> "Isn't Mrs. Fane coming at all then?" enquired Cook.
> "For a few minutes—for a few minutes," said Nurse quickly, and Michael would not have been suspicious had he not observed the nodding of her head long after there was any need to nod it.
> "Is mother going to stay with us?" he asked.

"Stay? Stay? Of course, she'll stay. Stay for ever," asserted Nurse in her bristling voice.

However, a few minutes later Mrs. Fane comes into the nursery.

"How cosy you all look," said Mother. "Darling Stella, are you enjoying your rice pudding? And, darling Michael," she added, "I hope you're being very good."

"Oh yes," said Nanny. "Good! Yes. He's very good. Oh, yes. Tut-tut! Tut-tut! . . ."

"There's no need to bother about any of the rooms except the night nursery and the day nursery. You're quite straight in here. I shall be back by the end of June."

His Nanny shook her head violently at this, and Michael felt tears of apprehension welling up into his eyes. Mrs. Fane paused a moment doubtfully; then she waved beautiful slim gloves and glided from the room. Michael listened to delicate footsteps on the stair, and the tinkle of small ornaments. A bleak silence followed the banging of the front door.

"She's gone away. I know she's gone away," he moaned.

"Who's She?" demanded Nurse. "She's the Cat's mother."

"Mother! Mother!" he wailed. "She always goes away from Michael."

"And no wonder," said Nurse. "Dear, dear! Yes—tut-tut—goodness gracious, she won't be gone long. She'll be back in June."

"What's June?" Michael asked.

"If you ask any more silly questions, you'll go to bed, young man; but if you're a good boy, I'll tell you a story."

"A real story? A nice long story?" asked Michael.

"I'll tell you a story about Jack o' my Nory
And now my story's begun.
I'll tell you another about Jack and his brother
And now my story's done."

Nurse twiddled her thumbs with a complacent look, as she smacked her palate upon the final line.

"That isn't a story," said Michael sullenly. "When will mother be back?"

"In June. That's enough,"said Nurse. . . .

Michael went to sleep that night trying to materialise this mysterious June. It came to mean a distant warmth of orange light towards which he walked very slowly. He lay awake thinking of June in the luminousness of a bright light shielded from his direct vision by a basin. His hands were muffled in fingerless gloves to prevent thumb-sucking. Suddenly upon the quiet came a blaze of light. Had he reached June? His sleepy eyelids uncurled to the scented vision of his beautiful mother. But it was only gaslight playing and fluttering over the figure of the anaemic Nanny taking hairpin after hairpin from her hair.

Then at long last—she returns "in the richness of a midsummer twilight". They all go to the seaside. Disciplines are relaxed.

> Michael was often allowed to sit up an extra half hour and even when he went to bed his mother would come and hear him say his prayers. She would sit by him, her lovely face flushed by the rose-red August sunsets that floated in through the open window on a sound of sea-waves. As it grew darker and, over the noise of happy people walking about in the cool evening, a distant band played music, his mother would lean over and kiss him goodnight. He would be loath to let her go, and just as she was closing the door quietly he would call her back and whisper "One more kiss" and because that goodnight kiss was the most enchanting moment in his day, he would whisper as he held her to him very close "Only one more, but much, much, much the longest kiss in all the world."

It occurs to me, incidentally, reading this passage again, that the Nanny situation is one reason why Proust is so deeply appreciated in England. But there are several other observations to make about Compton Mackenzie. The first is that, following the principle of behavioural generalisation we will look at later, he created a whole class of idealised women who derived from this mother. In *Sinister Street* they are called princesses, and 'the first princess' is his governess Miss Carthew, who closely resembles his mother in her slimness, her beauty and her curious quality of unreality. Churchill, as we saw, went even further and idolised all women as a sex, upper class women at any rate. We shall see soon that it is likely this was a typical reaction.

But the most important point about Michael Fane/Compton Mackenzie's Nanny is, of course, that she is not in the least pleasant. This aspect— the cruelty of the Nanny—will have to be studied in full, the degrees and types of cruelty, the reasons for it, its effects and so on. In fact, though I quote him here partly because he gets the *density* of childish feelings so well, I want to reserve my examination of Compton Mackenzie as a whole till later. For one thing, his attitude to his mother is actually far more ambiguous than it appears here or than he seems to realise. But what this passage does illustrate is that, whereas before the idealisation of the mother arose naturally as a result of the various circumstances we discussed, here in this final area where the Nanny is cruel it becomes psychologically imperative. With a cruel Nanny, children had to think they had a kind mother, even if they never saw her, to create inside themselves the feeling that they were loved at all. Or when I say had to, I mean they often did. There were several reactions to the cruel Nanny, but this was one of them and a very common one. An even more striking example is Kipling.

With Kipling we leave the Nanny for the moment and move into a related part of the general English upper class picture of letting other people take care of their children. This is the situation of foster-parents. Though not nearly as common as the Nanny (though it often gave rise to the same type of person and with the same results), the practice of boarding little children out with foster-parents was by no means unknown in the second half of the nineteenth century (Kipling was born in 1865) and, as I have already pointed out, seems to have been a familiar practice for parents returning to some part of the British Empire where they were unable to take their children. Kipling and his younger sister were left in just such circumstances; his account of the experience in a long story called *Baa Baa Black Sheep* is in almost every particular accurately auto-biographical.

Punch and Judy, aged five and three, lead an idyllic life in India. They are looked after, loved, spoilt by their attendant *ayahs;* they adore and worship their parents, particularly their mother. Then, one day, they all set out for England.

> "Punch-*baba* is going away," said the ayah. "In another week there will be no Punch-*baba* to pull my hair any more." She sighed softly for the boy of the household was very dear to her heart.

They sail across the sea and come eventually to Donne Lodge, a grim and gloomy villa by the sea. Waiting to greet them stands a woman in black, smiling largely with dry chapped lips. Behind her is a man, big, bony and grey, who is lame. This couple have a son Harry, a bit older than Punch, with black hair.

The mother and father stay six days and then leave, weeping, for India.

> "Don't forget us," pleaded Mama, "Oh my little son, don't forget us, and see that Judy remembers too."
> "I've told Judy to bemember," said Punch wriggling, for his father's beard tickled his neck. "I've told Judy ten-forty-leven thousand times. But Ju's so young—quite a baby—isn't she?"
> "Yes," said Papa, "quite a baby, and you must be good to Judy, and make haste to learn to write and—and—and—"

It only gradually dawns on the two little children that they have been left. Their grief is terrible.

When a matured man discovers that he has been deserted by providence, deprived of his God, and cast without help, comfort or sympathy upon a world which is new and strange to him, his despair, which may find expression in evil-living, the writing of his experiences, or the more satisfactory diversion of suicide is generally supposed to be impressive. A child, under exactly similar circumstances as far as its knowledge goes, cannot very well curse God and die. It howls till its nose is red, its eyes are sore, and its head aches. Punch and Judy, through no fault of their own, had lost all their world. They sat in the hall and cried; the black-haired boy looking from afar.

To soften this blow, the couple, although they are no relation, are to be known as Aunty Rosa and Uncle Harry. But quite quickly a hideous change begins. Aunty Rosa reveals herself as a vicious, frustrated, cruel and self-righteous Nanny-type of the very worst sort. She introduces them, but especially Punch, to lying, sin, 'showing-off', 'eating up', and introduces endless goods and bads, rules so many they can't be remembered, a nightmare scene over which broods the all-seeing, all-punishing figure of God.

Although, to give an example, she has taught him to read, she is furious when she discovers him doing it.

"I was reading," he explained, "reading a book. I *want* to read."
"You're only doing that to show off," said Aunty Rosa. "But we'll see. Play with Judy now and don't open a book for a week."

Playing now becomes a job and a job which must make a noise; he has to be heard to play. If he's found reading to Judy he is punished by being left alone. Aunty Rosa drinks wine, or what she describes as something for her stomach. This means she sleeps every day after lunch. Nevertheless she discovers one day that he has fixed the table so that he can rock it and make the toys tumble about to sound like 'playing'.

"If you're old enough to do that," she said—her temper was always worst after lunch—"you're old enough to be beaten!"
"But I'm—I'm not an animal!" said Punch aghast.

But beaten he is. And from now on his life becomes steadily more terrible. Judy is the favourite, with of course Aunty Rosa's son Harry; Punch becomes Black Sheep and is henceforward only called that. His day becomes an endless succession of prohibitions, traps, punishments. At first Uncle Harry mitigates this a little. He intercedes on his behalf, takes him for walks, and tells him stories of his past. But Uncle Harry

falls ill and eventually dies. Now Black Sheep is all alone. The regime
intensifies.

"But it wasn't a lie," Black Sheep would begin, charging into a laboured
explanation that landed him more hopelessly in the mire. "I said that I didn't
say my prayers *twice* over in the day, and *that* was on Tuesday. Once I did. I
know I did, but Harry said I didn't"; and so forth, till the tensions and the
questioning brought tears and he was dismissed from the table in disgrace.

Eventually he goes to school, but his 'reputation' has been broadcast
ahead.

"I suppose you warned all the boys of Black Sheep's character?" said Aunty
Rosa to Harry.
"Oh yes," said the censor of Black Sheep's morals. "They know all about
him."
"If I was with my father," said Black Sheep, stung to the quick, "I shouldn't
speak to those boys. He wouldn't let me. They live in shops. I saw them go
into shops—where their fathers live and sell things."
"You're too good for the school, are you?" said Aunty Rosa, with a bitter
smile. "You ought to be grateful, Black Sheep, that those boys speak to you at
all. It isn't every school that takes little liars."

Even the class weapon is no good. Black Sheep is now beaten both at home
and at school, and when he is not being beaten at school, he is being
bullied by the other boys egged on by Harry. And so it goes on—and on
and on. Because Black Sheep and Judy are abandoned by their parents
for five years. It is impossible in a short résumé, but Kipling conveys
brilliantly the passing of this appalling amount of time.

His pen sharpened by the memory of his own sufferings, he charts
the progression of Black Sheep's resistance into despair, into subterfuge,
into deeper despair, into furious resentment and rage when he threatens
and plans to kill Aunty Rosa and Uncle Harry and finally, his spirit
broken, into an attempt at the final solution. He tries to kill himself by
licking the paint from his Noah's Ark animals. This also fails.

Aunty Rosa, Harry and Judy go away for a holiday. Black Sheep is
left behind as a punishment, alone in the house with a servant who frequently goes out. He wanders about, relieved to be alone, but bored,
endlessly bored. He counts things, then measures the hall and the other
rooms using his outstretched palm as a ruler. He watches the sun in the
empty house.

Black Sheep would follow the rays of the sinking sun from the kitchens to the dining room and thence upward to his own bedroom until all was grey dark, and he ran down to the kitchen fire and read by its light. He was happy in that he was left alone and could read as much as he pleased. But, later, he grew afraid of the shadows of window-curtains and the flapping of doors and the creakings of shutters.

Aunty Rosa and the others return. Black Sheep now adds another sin to his already immense list—clumsiness. He keeps on knocking things over and breaking them. Finally, a sign how nearly broken he has become, he does lie about his school work (up till now he has always tried to tell the truth). His deception is discovered. Aunty Rosa's rage is terrible. "For three days Black Sheep was shut up in his bedroom—to prepare his heart. 'That means two beatings. One at school and one here. That one will hurt the most.'" After the Aunty Rosa thrashing, she stitches the placard—LIAR—onto his back. But when she tries to make him walk out with this on he fiercely refuses.

It is at this juncture that an emissary from Mama and Papa arrives. He discovers that Black Sheep is nearly blind. He divines other things. Various orders are given. Black Sheep is to do nothing. Mama will arrive in three weeks.

Aunty Rosa, confidently self-righteous, welcomes this return. She promises full exposure."'When your mother comes and hears what I have to tell her, she may appreciate you properly,' she said grimly, and mounted guard over Judy lest that small maiden should attempt to comfort her brother to the peril of her soul."

And at long last, so beautiful, so needed, Mama returns. Judy is open and sweet, but Black Sheep is cowering and awkward. When he goes to bed, his mother comes to him.

Black Sheep flung up his arm. It wasn't fair to come and hit him in the dark. Even Aunty Rosa never tried that. But no blow followed. "Are you showing off? I won't tell you anything more than Aunty Rosa has and she doesn't know everything," said Black Sheep as clearly as he could for the arms round his neck.

"Oh my son—my little, little son! It was my fault—my fault, darling, and yet, how could we help it? Forgive me, Punch." The voice died out in a broken whisper and the hot tears fell on Black Sheep's forehead.

"Has she been making you cry too?" he asked. "You should see Judy cry. But you're nice and Judy is a born liar—Aunty Rosa says so."

"Hush, Punch, hush! My boy, don't talk like that. Try and love me a little bit—a little bit. You don't know how I want it. Punch-baba, come back to

me! I am your mother—your own mother—and never mind the rest. I know
—yes, I know dear. It doesn't matter now. Punch, won't you care for me a
little?"

It is quite astonishing how much petting a big boy of ten can endure when
he is quite sure that there is no one to laugh at him. Black Sheep had never
been made much of before, and here was the beautiful woman treating him—
Black Sheep, the child of the Devil and Inheritor of Undying Flame—as
though he were a small god.

"I care for you a great deal, mother dear," he whispered at last, "and I'm
glad you've come back; but are you sure Aunty Rosa told you everything?"

"Everything. What does it matter. But—" the voice broke with a sob that
was also laughter—"Punch, my poor dear, half-blind darling, don't you think
it was a little foolish of you?"

"*No*. It saved a lickin'."

And here, or almost here, the story ends. In précis it sounds sentimental,
and of course it is; but such is Kipling's skill that it is also affecting. The
effect on Kipling of his own spell of foster-upbringing is problematical.
In my view it is probable that that vein of sadism which, to me, undeniably
appears in some of Kipling's work had its origins in the experiences
he describes in *Baa Baa Black Sheep*. And those experiences themselves
we shall find duplicated many times: the card LIAR on his back (which
Curzon also described), the type of 'sin' invented to justify a beating,
the immediate prohibition of any activity, even if laudable, once it was
seen to give pleasure—it is sometimes as though those unbalanced
women who were often so cruel to their charges had all been to the same
special school to learn how to impose pain.

But for our immediate purpose what is interesting is Kipling's attitude
to the mother. It is perhaps not all that odd that Black Sheep does not
find it surprising that his mother should never visit him in five years,
and only send someone to see how he is at the end of that long period.
Children accept what happens to them. But Kipling does not find it
extraordinary either. He never comments on it. Not only that, but the
mother springs back in Black Sheep's life as beautiful, as adored, as ideal
as she was when she went away. And here Kipling expresses, no doubt
because it is what he did himself, the psychological truth I stated earlier—
the need to preserve intact at all costs some image of someone loving.
True, he says "when young lips have drunk deep of the bitter waters
of Hate, Suspicion and Despair all the love in the world will not wholly
take away that knowledge." But we are left with the impression that in

fact, in an instant, all is as it was, with mother on her pedestal again. "There! Told you so," said Punch. "It's all different now, and we are just as much mother's as if she had never gone."

During the end of our period, that is to say from 1918 to 1939, it would seem that this intense, one might almost say fatuous, idealisation of the mother became less common. The pressures which I have outlined which were bringing mothers to take a greater interest in their children, combined with the slow, very slow, decline in the numbers of Nannies, did mean that mothers played more part in the upbringing of their children and thereby, inevitably, lost a good deal of glamour. Also for reasons having nothing to do with Nannies, male attitudes towards women, and women's attitudes towards themselves, were beginning to change during this time.

Nevertheless, time and again during my interviews, the idealisation of the mother occurred with all its old fervour. A Mr. W, aged forty-five, said, "I worshipped my mother. In fact in a sort of way I think it is because of my love for her that I've always felt there was something holy about women." Nanny Williams's Mrs. F used frequently to go away for five or six months at a time. When she came back her little son would not know who she was. "Who was that lovely beautiful lady who said goodnight Nanny?" "That was your mother." Though he never confided in his mother and only loved his Nanny he did, she said with some surprise, always regard his mother as a sort of vision of perfection.

You even get the same attitude today. Here is a singularly asinine comment, which Barbara Cartland made on a *Man Alive* programme by Desmond Wilcox called 'Who'll be Mother?'

Barbara Cartland: "Actually I believe it's a very good thing to have a Nanny. Ummm . . . if anyone . . . everyone could afford a Nanny, I'd like them to have a Nanny. Simply and solely because I think it's the mother to be the glamorous, glorious, wonderful person like they go to with all their troubles, not the strict disciplinarian. The Nanny does that, it's the Nanny who says: you shan't do this and you shan't do that. But the mother was a lovely person who comes in and tells stories and is beautiful and loving, and looks nice. It's much worse when you're all sort of . . . in a rage and cross and bathing them, getting hot and miserable yourself, do you know."

This idealisation of the mother itself had a number of consequences, one of the most interesting of which, though it will involve a fairly extensive sexual detour, I should like to examine now.

FIRST SEXUAL DETOUR:
ASPECTS OF VICTORIAN AND EDWARDIAN
SEXUALITY

One of the most interesting and popular developments in social history recently has been the discovery of the Victorian sexual underworld. Into its rich and hitherto scarcely mined seams deep shafts have been sunk. Kellow Chesney, in a book actually called *The Victorian Underworld*, has dug substantially in the main workings; Steven Marcus, in *The Other Victorians* struck out into pornography, flagellation and a fascinating account of the anonymous *My Secret Life* (which has itself been extensively published). And there have been others. Indeed, so stimulating have academics of all ages and degrees of distinction found this new area of research that while I was writing this book there was actually held a symposium at Cambridge on the general subject of Victorian sexual life, at which the attendance was unprecedented. Unfortunately, I learnt of it too late to attend.

It would only have confirmed, however, a picture that had already emerged. The Victorian upper, upper-middle and middle classes were always supposed to have led lives of stifling respectability, sexually either inhibited or self-disciplined to the point of chastity, and certainly completely faithful—and many of them did. But it now appears that beneath this there co-existed an underworld, luridly lit, acrid with the smells of sin, which is quite staggering both for its immense size and for its blatant, unashamed sexuality. Or rather this discovery would have been staggering at any time before today, when we expect people to behave like that (which is the fundamental reason, no doubt, why this research was directed where it was in the first place).

The premise of this underworld was very simple. Lower class girls were there to be enjoyed sexually by upper class men, usually (but not always) in return for money. Curiously enough it owed its existence in part to the same forces which gave rise to the Nanny: the incredible growth in population and the cruelly inequable distribution of wealth. The picture is not a pleasant one. William Acton wrote of the middle of the century; "Many thousand young women in the metropolis are unable, by drudgery that lasts from early morning till late at night to earn more than 3s to 5s nightly." Mayhew presents the same situation. Faced with biting poverty, indeed starvation, it is scarcely surprising these girls took to whoring in thousands. Figures are difficult to be certain about, but from around 1800 on there was a steady and continuous rise. By 1845 there were four thousand brothels in London alone. In 1851 sixteen whorehouse keepers were up in the dock at once, and that was just from St. James's. In 1869 some estimates put the number of whores in the city as high as eighty thousand. The life was not easy, nor was it particularly lucrative. The author of *My Secret Life* (probably born about 1825) wrote, "I got quite nice girls at from 5/- to 7/- a poke, and had several in their own rooms, but sometimes paying 2/6 extra for a room elsewhere." And as time wore on the ravages of disease and drink and the trade itself made life harder and harder. There are few things more tragic than an old, ugly, worn-out and impoverished prostitute, begging for a 'poke' for the price of a meal, or a drink, and eventually for nothing, for momentary comfort and companionship.

Yet the scene is not always tragic and degrading. Chesney paints a London seething with girls who wanted men. Girls in casinos and cafés or moving discreetly in the vast, murmurous, melodious gardens at night, many very young and very pretty, cutting a great swathe of sexuality across the centre of London, down through St. James's, Leicester Square and the Strand. And the same was true of other large towns. Nor were there only cheap whores and prostitutes. Many were very expensive, their dinners, their wines and their presents having to be chosen with great care. Harriet Wilson, for instance, though a little earlier than our period, at the height of her success had extremely smart apartments in Curzon Street. And it was accepted as perfectly normal, though of course never admitted, that a man should have a lower class courtesan, or more than one, before he was married. There is something exciting about this underworld London, underworld England, secret yet not secret, accepted yet ignored, where upper class Victorian men indulged fiercely the sexual pleasures which in the other half of their lives they pretended did not exist.

It is a sense of almost unrelieved excitement that one gets from the anonymous author of *My Secret Life*. This is an enormous work of over four thousand two hundred pages entirely devoted to a very detailed account of the relentless, endless and pleasurable pursuit and having of a great many girls. In the end, its author thought he had probably had over twelve hundred girls and "examined the cunts of a further three hundred" (this was one of the many things he enjoyed doing. Steven Marcus thinks he was secretly hoping to find a penis). Fifteen hundred is a respectable sample in survey terms; one can draw conclusions from it. This is particularly so as *My Secret Life* is not only almost certainly genuine, which is to say it is a work of autobiography and not of pornography, it is also extremely honest. One of the first things to notice about it, to reinforce the brief sketch of the underworld I have just given, is that nearly all his girls were lower class. There are a few upper class women, once he has a marchioness, but the vast majority are shop girls, waitresses, seamstresses, tarts, housemaids and so on. The second thing is that, though he is obsessively, compulsively promiscuous—there is a terrible description of his marriage and of how he tried to be faithful to his wife: it nearly killed him—one also gets a strong sense of pleasure from his book. Not just his own pleasure, which would scarcely be surprising; he clearly had considerable rutting energy, enjoyed sex and had an open experimental and uninhibited attitude to it which is remarkably contemporary. But he also expresses the pleasure of the girls he slept with. Quite often they would let him have them for nothing, just because they enjoyed it. They would discuss their orgasms with him. Sometimes he would set up a liaison with one or two of them which might last several months. But above all, he expected them to enjoy sex. It is this aspect of Victorian sex life, the pleasure side and its implications, which I should like to examine in a moment.

But first it should be noted that there is nothing inherently surprising about the Victorian underworld. For centuries the English upper classes, in a phrase which I believe is Cyril Connolly's, had used the lower classes as their brothel. There were obvious, practical reasons for this. They were willing and available. It was more discreet than affairs in one's own class (very important in an age which valued propriety). It was easier—class itself conferring attraction. If a child resulted, then it would just become one of the many lower class bastards, not interfering with inheritance or succession. And these cogent advantages were reinforced in Victorian times by two others. We know from Mayhew that venereal disease was extremely common among the lower classes. Once embarked, the fact of catching venereal disease, or even the fear that he might have caught it, could well confine a man to lower class sex. Also, in the nineteenth century a man was supposed to keep his wife, certainly as well and if possible much better than the manner to which she was accustomed (an echo here of the dynastic view of the family). Families were very large. Both these factors required money and therefore it was customary for men to marry late. Tarts were a natural consequence of this situation.

Nevertheless two things do need explaining. Given the population explosion, the English tradition of child upbringing and the unequal distribution of wealth, one could have predicted Nannies; given very large families, a great many Nannies. And given the factors I have outlined above one could certainly have predicted a good number of whores. But I don't think one could have predicted such a universal (and concealed) acceptance of the use of one class by the other. Nor do I think one could have predicted such enormous numbers. Eighty thousand whores in a city which, compared to modern London, was minute, is astonishing. And these numbers were duplicated in most of the major towns in England.

The second thing that needs explaining, which is in fact causally related to the first, is one aspect of the Victorian view of the sexual appetite. This can be found again and again, but it is very clearly expressed in a book, for whose discovery I am indebted to Steven Marcus, by William Acton called *The Functions and Disorders of the Reproductive Organs in Childhood, Youth, Adult Age and Advanced Life Considered in their Physiological, Social and Moral Relations*. In this he writes:

Having taken pains to obtain and compare abundant evidence on this subject I should say that the majority of women (happily for them) are not very much troubled with sexual feelings of any kind. What men are habitually, women are only exceptionally . . . there can be no doubt that sexual feeling in the female is in the majority of cases in abeyance . . . and even if roused (which in many instances it can never be) is very moderate compared with that of the male. Many men, and particularly young men, form their ideas of women's feelings from what they notice early in life among loose, or at least, low and vulgar women. . . . Any susceptible boy is easily led to believe, whether he is altogether overcome by the syren or not, that she, and therefore all women, must have at least as strong passions as himself. Such women however give a very false idea of the condition of human feeling in general. . . . As a general rule, a modest woman seldom desires any sexual gratification for herself. She submits to her husband, but only to please him; and but for the desire of maternity, would far rather be relieved from his attentions.

In a later passage he writes:

It is a delusion under which many a previously incontinent man suffers to suppose that in newly married life he will be required to treat his wife as he used to treat his mistresses. It is not so in the case of any modest English woman. He need not fear that his wife will require the excitement, or in any respect imitate the ways of a courtesan.

Now two things can be noted about these quotations. The second passage assumes something I have already mentioned, that large numbers of

Victorian middle class men will have had one or more lower class mistresses (courtesans were always lower class). But the second and much the most important point is the division of sexuality. In the first passage 'the majority of women' whose sexual feelings are in abeyance are evidently not 'low or vulgar women'. It is this group, which in fact plainly comprises all lower class women, which has passions as strong as men themselves. What in fact he is stating is the classic Victorian conception— lower class women have sexual appetites, upper class women don't. That is why in the second passge his wife won't require excitement, whereas his courtesan did.

This attitude could be proved from dozens of different sources. Indeed, it is a commonplace of Victorian study. Yet it is an attitude which is quite extraordinary. I know of no other culture (except perhaps early Athens) which has divided the sexual instinct up in precisely the same class-stratified way, both in its literature and in practice. It is not true, for instance, of the early Middle Ages in Europe. And it was an attitude which was quite new to England. In earlier centuries, if one ignores for the moment those intense but relatively small number of families strongly influenced by Puritanism, the English aristocracy and upper classes had allowed among themselves a fairly free and easy promiscuity. Certainly their women were not expected to be without appetite— one has only to think of Gertrude in *Hamlet*, or Restoration drama. There was a tolerant, uncritical acceptance of illegitimate children and provision was made for them. Joseph Banks, for instance, Fellow of the Royal Society and High Sherrif of Nottingham in 1735 had, when his father died, given three hundred pounds from the estate "in consideration of his believing John to be the natural son of his late father, and that his late father intended to have given him this provision, but omitted it by mistake." The very expression 'natural child' shows the normality of the event. It is a tender expression.

This enjoyment and acceptance of sexual indulgence outside marriage by both sexes in the aristocracy continued into the early nineteenth century. In his book *The Young Melbourne*, an early Prime Minister of Queen Victoria's who was himself one of six children only 'doubtfully related to their father', Lord David Cecil notes that the practice of upper class women having lovers was too common to arouse even comment.

> The historian grows quite giddy as he tries to disentangle the complications of heredity consequent on the free and easy habits of the English aristocracy. The Harley family, the children of the Countess of Oxford, were known as the 'Harleian Miscellany' on account of the variety of fathers alleged to be

responsible for their existence. The Duke of Devonshire had three children by the Duchess and two by Lady Elizabeth Foster; the Duchess one by Lord Grey. Most of them were brought up in Devonshire House. . . .

And this, one might think much more commonsensical conception of the equal bawdiness of men and women whatever their class, is reflected in the 'scientific' literature. The two quotations I gave from Acton's book are the only times he mentions women. The whole of the rest of the book, and it is not short, is about men and male sexuality. But in a similar work, *Aristotle's Master Piece*, an extremely popular and successful work of medico/sexual science in the seventeenth and eighteenth centuries, the emphasis is reversed. Far more space is given to women's sexual functions and appetites than to men.

Nor, it need hardly be said, does this Victorian idea—that upper class women had virtually no sexual instinct—survive with any great strength today. Yet, so far as I know, no adequate reason is ever given for the appearance, and equally swift disappearance, of so strange a theory. It is usually explained, vaguely and generally, by the increased influence of religion, Victorian morality, the process of civilising, the influence of Bentham and Locke and so on. To account for the wholesale decimation of the sex instinct of an entire class this is not enough.

Nor is it easy to say how long, in theory and practice, the idea persisted. Certainly, in this respect, Victorian times continue until 1914. One finds as many mentions in Edwardian literature to the chastity, the holy purity of upper class women, indeed to their active abhorrence of sex, as one does in the nineteenth century. There was the passage I quoted from Lady Hillingham at the head of this chapter—". . . close my eyes, open my legs and think of England". The source for this quotation is a little suspect. The sentiment expressed is without question typical and accurate. Since they were supposed to have no sexual instinct, Victorian and Edwardian girls were seldom told the facts of life. I can remember my grandmother, who was married in 1899, describing to me how on her wedding day her mother drew her aside and said, "There's just one thing I must tell you, Dorothy. Remember, whatever Gathorne does to you is *right*." As my grandfather, in my grandmother's phrase, could 'do nothing' for four days, her calm acceptance of this was probably helpful.

But although it undoubtedly declined during the 1920s and '30s, I think it probable that it continued with much greater force than is now realised. I recognised it in various guises during my interviews: "Of course his wife didn't like doing it as much as he did—women don't on the whole you know—he used to have shop girls in Eastbourne."

It is reflected widely in the literature, in the hopeless love affairs of Maurice Baring's books, or those pale, vapid, beautiful, untouchable heroines of Buchan, Rider Haggard, Conan Doyle, the women in Barrie's plays, in musical comedies, Chaplin's films, in fact in practically every popular novelist or playwright of the period one mentions. Nancy Mitford in *The Blessing* takes it as a matter of course that an aristocratic Englishman will have tarts. Sir Conrad Allingham enjoys making love, but it is "a pastime to which he devoted a good deal of energy with those whose profession it is, finding it embarrassing, never really able to let himself go with women whom he met in other circumstances". The women, that is, of his own class.

Evidence of the practical expression of the idea is also scanty. Once again, for this purpose, the Victorian age extends to 1914. In 1885 prostitution became illegal, and the number of whorehouses, common lodging houses and accommodation houses very slowly decreased. But there seems to have been little decline in the number of whores. All that happened was that, to escape detection, the single, independent adventurer became more common—the woman 'sailing on her own bottom'. These particular seams have not, so far as I know, been explored with any thoroughness for the '20s and '30s. My guess is that the demand for lower class girls, whether prostitutes or not, remained high, if declining, during this period. Certainly I can remember even after the Second World War how at night the whole of Hyde Park used to fill, shifting, scented, electric, with a great crowd of painted girls, professionals, amateurs, all totally flagrant, a strange and somehow apt reverse of the Nannies who thronged there in the day.

Because it will not have escaped attention that the rise and fall of the idea that upper class English women had no sexual feelings (which must in consequence have vastly increased any already existing tendency for upper class Englishmen to use lower class girls), this whole pattern fairly exactly coincides with the rise and decline of the Nanny. Plainly, this can partly be explained because, as I said, the numbers of prostitutes or willing lower class girls and the numbers of Nannies were to a degree caused by the same economic and population developments. This does not, however, explain the growth of the particular sexual theory I have outlined. In fact, I think the connection was much more intimate.

It may seem strange at first to consider the Nanny in relation to, even as responsible for, the sexual attitudes of the English upper classes. But in fact the reverse is true. An adult's sexual orientation is determined between the ages of one and five, and particularly between three and five.

During those years is established not just towards which sex (or sexes) the adult will direct his sexual energies, but much more minute particulars like the sort of partner chosen, the basic patterns of response, both physical and emotional, he or she will have with their partner, the degree of satisfaction the adult is capable of and so on. Subsequent events may modify these patterns and drives, or make them more or less difficult to achieve. They cannot alter them significantly. Plainly, then, Nannies and Nurses, who were frequently in total charge of practically all upper class and most middle class children during these precise years, can be expected to have played not just an important role, but a decisive one.

Two points have to be made here. It has been established by behavioural psychologists working from an enormous body of experimental and observed evidence, that little children *generalise* their responses from the particular events and people in their lives. If one dog bites them, they will be frightened of all dogs. Once they have found something they like in their mother's 'fridge, they will look in all 'fridges. Obviously, in practice the process is complex. If their father is kind and loving towards them, they will tend to like all men, or like all their father's friends, or like men who resemble their father. And generalisations made at so early an age impose tendencies which are permanent—though they will be modified. Thus a little child all of whose rewarding relationships have been with women, and who only had unrewarding and unpleasant ones with men, can be expected to prefer the company of women throughout its life. (For a full description of this process I would refer the reader to *Child Development and Personality* by Mussen, Conger and Kagan. See also Chapter 7.)

The second point is that most psychiatrists seem to agree that as far as boys are concerned there is a natural split between woman as mother and woman as sexual partner. The first is authoritative, nurturing, adored (and belongs to the father); the second he must in one sense be capable of dominating and he must be able to express his sexual feelings for. This is the basis of the Oedipus situation. A transition has to be made from one role to the other or, more accurately, the roles have to be fused; and how this is done, and how easily it is done, depends on the circumstances the child is in. Curiously enough, unlike many Freudian discoveries, this one seems applicable to cultures and societies far removed from our Western experience. One primitive tribe for example, recognises the transition, the fusion, by making each man copulate with his mother *once* in the ceremony which makes him an adult. In another, it is the custom for boys of fourteen or so to have adult mistresses much older than themselves until they reach the age of marriage. There are other instances.

If this transitional situation with the mother is true, and as I say most psychiatrists seem to agree that it is, then the Nanny must in one sense have made it more difficult. Because she removed the mother to an impossible position. If it is hard, or at least requires some effort of change, to transpose the role of an ordinary, close, active mother, how much harder must it be when the mother is distant, ethereal, idealised. It is scarcely surprising that many children couldn't make the effort. What they did, of course, was to transpose or, fuse the role of their Nanny. She had become the mother. And how natural this was. Because it was not only Nanny they saw all the time, who loved them and looked after them, but Nannies who looked after them in just those earthy, animal, often, for a child, overtly sexual areas the memory of which later would make the fusion so much easier. Nannies wiped bottoms and washed penises. Nannies fed. Nannies wiped up sick. Nannies gave baths and tucked up in bed. It was Nanny's arms that went round little boys, Nanny's breasts and lips they felt, Nanny they smelt. And Nannies were lower class.

The proposition is thus quite simple. The sexual transposition in many upper class Englishmen took place over their Nannies because their Nannies were closest to them. Their Nannies were also lower class. Because of the generalising process I described, therefore, many upper class Englishmen found it easier to regard lower class women rather than upper class women as the objects of their sexuality. The attitude which at first sight seemed so odd is in fact precisely what one would have expected.

Of course this is extremely speculative ground. To *prove* it I should have to find a great number of individual cases (I found a few), many going back in time, subject them to a fairly lengthy analysis, and *prove* that it was their association with their Nanny which made them prefer lower class girls and think upper class ones had feeble sexual appetites. And this of course is impossible. It can remain a speculation only, though I think a valid one. Yet it was a conclusion which was driven on me with more and more force as I read, and more particularly interviewed, for this book. Not only did people, almost without exception, say that they were always aware that their Nannies were of a lower class than themselves, and that from a very early age; but often I noticed that the air around the Nanny was, as it were, dense with sex.

Early on, for example, I was standing in a shop when an elderly and

distinguished acquaintance of mine came up and said, "I understand you
are writing a book about Nannies?" I said I was. He at once gripped me
by the arm and led me swiftly out into the street. I could feel that he was
trembling slightly. Once outside he stood very close to me (he is shorter
than I am) breathing heavily. "My entire life was altered by my Nanny,"
he said. "I have never told anyone about this before." He explained that
in those days (1901? 1905?) girls had drawers (knickers) which had a
fall-down flap at the back. One night, when he was about three, he awoke
suddenly to find his Nanny standing, back towards him, right against
his bed by the pillow. The flap was down. "There, right before my eyes,
were two absolutely enormous female buttocks—not an inch from my
nose!" He gripped my arm again and went back into the shop.

I was interested by his intensity and by the curious sensation it produced
in me—this whiff of infant sexuality from so long ago. At the same time I
was rather nonplussed. I wished I'd asked him exactly how it had altered
his life.

Curiously enough, two months later I was able to. I found myself in
the same shop with the same elderly gentleman. At once he came up to
me: "I believe you are writing a book about Nannies?" I said I was.
"Come outside. I have something to tell you that I believe will interest
you." Once more we went into the street and once more he stood very
close to me, trembling slightly. When he had finished—". . . two enormous female buttocks—not an inch from my nose!"—I asked diffidently
how it had altered his life. At this his eyes actually bulged with excitement. He put his face right into mine and said in a loud whisper. "Why
bottoms of course, *bottoms!*"

There was Brian Welsh who slept with his twenty-two-year-old
Nanny when he was five and six. She smelt of burning green wood and
to this day it is a smell that gives him an erection. But apart from particular
memories, there was often a generalised sense of physical warmth and
closeness. Until the eighteenth century it was customary to sleep two
or three to a bed—often a Nurse and two children. But the practice
of sleeping in the same bed with Nannies, though not usual, was by
no means uncommon. Quite often people described to me how they got
into Nanny's bed when frightened, or how they remembered when they
were five, say, and Nanny said they were too old to go on sleeping with her.
Alexander Weymouth remembered how when he was two or three, whenever he had wet his bed, he used to get into Nanny Mark's bed and put
his legs and bottom over her to dry his urine-wet body. She must, he
says, have been aware of this. He could remember how he tried to do the

same with her frigid sister (his own quite revealing adjective) and how she shrank away.

Gerald Brenan, in his brilliant autobiography *A Life of One's Own*, describes how at the age of four and a half, when they were in South Africa, he developed an intense, almost uncontrollable curiosity about women's private parts. One night a scorpion frightened him and Nana, as he called his Nanny, put him in her bed to comfort him. When she later came to bed herself, Brenan stayed with her. Immediately, he dived down to satisfy his curiosity. She stirred and pulled him up. But later, after waiting, he dived down again and this time Nana either asleep or out of her gentle, placid kindness, allowed him to explore her in her habitual silence. He remembers vividly to this day the feel and smell of what he found there and believes that this dive to discover something strange, this idea he had that it was something different from the ordinary converse with Nana—as indeed it was—affected much of his later life. It led him to think of sex in two different compartments. (It is interesting also that over quite a long period, which is not reached by this volume of his autobiography, he often preferred the company of shop girls, waitresses and so on, to girls of his own class.)

There is also the explicit initiation of young boys into sex by their Nannies—rare, though not unknown—but I should like to reserve this for a later chapter. Though it might be noted here that the author of *My Secret Life* was first stimulated by his nursemaid when he was five years old. "I recollect that she [his nursemaid] sometimes held my little prick when I piddled; was it needful to do so? I don't know. She attempted to pull my prepuce, when and how often I know not. But I am clear at seeing the prick tip show. . . ." Sometimes she seems to have become excited herself and been too rough with him. He can remember feeling pain, yelling out, her soothing him and "this occurring more than once".

Then I kept hearing rumours that German Nannies masturbated their charges. One man I asked said, "Quite true. And *ayahs* did it with their toes." Both statements seemed pure retrospective wish-fulfilment, until I read in Winnicott's *The Child, the Family and the Outside World* that in fact Nannies did masturbate little boys of two and three because they thought it soothed them, and that this too-young stimulation could be harmful later.

It was all this, besides other incidents not interesting enough to relate, the diffuse air of sexuality and class surrounding so many memories, and the *a priori* neatness of it, which more and more inclined me to the conclusion I have outlined above. (It occurred to me that the atmosphere in brothels is often like that of a nursery. There is a certain ceremony and routine. The same feeling of being ministered to.) I therefore began to ask every man I talked to about his Nanny whether or not he had had or would have liked to have had, lower class girls. This was not an entire success. Some people were irritated by it. But even the few I did find (three in all: two who said they preferred prostitutes, and one who pursued shop girls—"I like the smell of cheap scent"), even with these, though they had certainly been brought up by Nannies, there was no real way of establishing a causal connection. It would have involved a full Freudian analysis lasting several years. Before long I stopped asking people if they wanted lower class girls.

But whether you agree with my conclusion or not, I must, before we leave the subject, make some final observations and reservations about it.

The first is that, to a small extent, it was true that upper class women had less vigorous sexual responses than lower class women. I do not want to go into the inhibiting effects of a Nanny upbringing at the moment, but there can be no doubt that it was sometimes inhibiting, and particularly sexually inhibiting, on both men and women, and this did have quite a marked effect. Conversely, many lower class families were too big, too poor, too busy keeping alive to bother with the supervision, all the close, minor disciplines the Nanny had time for. Their lack of restrictions, their close physical proximity, would mean that sometimes they were more responsive, in a direct sexual way, than their middle and upper class fellows. *My Secret Life*, though the fantasy is often strong, does give this impression; and it is probably true, as he says, that working class sexual life began early: ". . . nearly the whole of the girls of the lowest classes began copulating with boys of about their own age when about fourteen years old." Acton in a book on prostitution corroborates this.

Furthermore, anthropologists have shown that in many cultures women's ideas of their own sexuality, and so to an extent their sexuality itself, is a response to what men want. If men wanted lower class women to have strong sexual appetites, they would have them; conversely, upper class women would try and suppress their feelings or pretend they didn't have them.

This last, among other developments, was a major cause of that saddest of all creatures, the Victorian spinster; that army of faded, withered maiden aunts which, like a heap of broken moths, filled the corners of every Victorian family house. Girls in Victorian and to an extent Edwardian times, as Mary Clive describes in *The Day of Reckoning*, were hedged in by their mothers with ludicrous strictness. They were not supposed to show men they were attracted by them, yet they were expected to get married. They were made to come back early from dances, made to refuse exciting invitations, chaperoned as if they were escaped nymphomaniacs. They were compelled to sit endlessly at home, frantic with ennui, tingling with health and energy, aching with what were virtually nameless desires, while they slowly grew grey and cold and old, dominated by their parents. A very old lady, the eldest of six unmarried sisters, once told Mary Clive that when she was a girl she had been invited to stay in Malta, but that she had not been allowed to go because her brother had said it would look as though she were trying to catch a husband. "But would it have mattered what people thought," she said, "if I had found somebody I liked?"

But the reverberation spread still further. If the women of your class can't feel sexually, if they are idols, they aren't really people. They can't think like you, talk like you, work like you, feel like you, they can't act as companions in any way at all. I have no doubt the sexual attitude towards women contributed considerably, at a remove, to the growth of that fusty Victorian/Edwardian (and into the 1920s and '30s) male world; that world of school and clubs and smoking rooms and men sitting on after dinner drinking port.

And it's odd how hangovers from this attitude persist today. For instance, there is far less agreement among psychiatrists about the formation and development of the female sexual response than there is about the male. Has it not been studied so closely? Why don't women have the difficulties we men have? Is it because women have always looked after children and so girls don't have the same problem of adjusting their image of men? And, if so, does it mean that now so many husbands are helping that we are in for some curious and dramatic changes? There are answers to these questions, though they are contradictory, and it would be interesting to discuss them, but, since what we are concerned about is a masculine attitude in a male-orientated world, they are not strictly relevant. One final observation about male sexual psychology might be made, however. The solutions to the problem of transposing and fusing the woman's role as sexual partner and as Nanny/Mother are presumably numerous. Men objectify sex, fantasise it—hence graffiti on lavatory walls. Or they degrade women—hence the Vicomte de Valmont in Laclos's *Les Liaisons Dangereuses*, or Montherlant's hero Costals in *Les jeunes filles* and *Pitié pour les femmes* (the French seem better at this sort of character). Or they objectify women, which does not necessarily mean degrade them as well, though it tends to. (Interesting in this respect is the way in which the members of Charles II's lascivious court in Hamilton's *Mémoires du Comte de Grammont*, certainly accurate in this respect, referred to the girls they slept with as The. Thus Miss Warmester became The Warmester, Miss Jennings The Jennings, Mrs Middleton The Middleton and so on.) It is plainly easier to make an object of someone if they are a different class (or colour) than you are, and there was therefore a purely psychological pressure on upper class men to choose lower class girls (and for lower class men to choose upper class girls). There are some striking examples of this in the nineteenth century. The author of *My Secret Life* actually seemed to regard lower class girls as almost biologically different. "She was a well-grown, good-looking woman about twenty-three years old, of the costermonger class. She looked like one who sold goods from a barrow, or a very small shop. She was commonly but comfortably clad, not warmly enough perhaps for well-to-do people, but enough so for her class who don't feel cold as we do." Or there were the 'Dollymoppers' of later Victorian years. A Dollymop was an attractive young lower class girl (apparently they were often nursemaids according to Marcus) who flirted with men and eventually went to bed with them. Dollymoppers were a great source of the 'virgins' who became so fashionable. But the word Dolly has strong suggestions of an object which is presumably why its use has persisted, in various forms, till today.

But the numerous solutions to the problem of transposition leads me to an important and obvious reservation, so obvious that it may not be necessary to make it. It would be quite absurd to suggest that just because someone had a Nanny it meant they automatically thought upper class women were sexless or wanted lower class mistresses. Practically none of the people I mentioned as examples of idealising the mother, for instance, as far as I know, had these reactions. Dr. Storr says that Churchill avoided sexual liaisons because he had been so profoundly horrified by the effects of syphilis on his father. Yet he is known to have had at least one upper class affair and may have had others. His relations with his wife were apparently excellent. Lord Weymouth's tastes are admirably catholic. No doubt the same is true of Compton Mackenzie. The point is that the childhood process of sexual development, though in essence simple, is in practice complex. Thus the generalising of a response needn't extend to a whole class but only women of that class with a certain hair colour or height or tone of voice; or the man will like women of his own class provided they look like his Nanny or smell like her or wear linen cuffs; or it may not be class he picks on but poverty and he will marry a poor upper class governess. The combinations and permutations are almost infinite. Furthermore, upper class men always felt they had to marry upper class women. We cannot know what fantasies may have fuelled their ardours, or how many slogged joylessly on doing, like Lady Hillingham, their bit for England. But no doubt a great many were agreeably surprised.

Because of course, and this the final point I wish to make, the fact is that the situation as viewed by men, and accepted by women, through Victorian and Edwardian times and on into the '20s and '30s just did not exist. With the reservation I made earlier, on the whole upper class women had precisely the same sexual appetite and responses as lower class women. The whole thing was a fiction.

I can remember my grandmother describing how her father, the Earl of Glasgow who was a naval captain in the late '60s and '70s of the last century, often used to be away. She remembered that frequently his disappearances seemed to coincide with visits from a young man, a cousin of theirs aged about eighteen. One morning when she was seven she went into her mother. She found her completely naked (her mother must then have been about thirty) sitting on the knee of their cousin who was also naked. Her mother turned round and they all stared at each other. "Go away, Dorothy," her mother said, "I'm busy." Lady Glasgow, despite the scantiness of her pre-marital advice to her daughter, was a woman of strong sexual appetite, a trait she transmitted to my grandmother. About her marriage, my grandmother, who was born in 1879, used to say, "Gathorne and I had great fun in bed."

But there is no need to prove that during our period upper class Englishwomen had perfectly ordinary sexual instincts. It is obvious enough. What we are studying, in fact, is a good example of that celebrated 'Victorian hypocrisy' which, far from being only Victorian, does seem to have been an ingredient in our national character for the last hundred and fifty years or so. That ability to hold in the mind totally contradictory and mutually exclusive ideas which, while tending to confusion in personal, was arguably a source of strength in public life. Men thought and felt one thing about women and sex, when at some level they were aware that precisely the opposite was true. Practically everyone knew about the gross underworld of tarts and prostitutes and loose women yet it was never mentioned and hardly ever appears in books. Gladstone was completely unable to understand any joke with a sexual reference. Not for the last time, and through no fault of their own, Nannies were a major cause of this situation.

CHAPTER FOUR

The Nanny as Mother; the Nanny–Mother Partnership

Other people's babies
That's my life!
Mother to dozens
And nobody's wife.

Other people's babies
Other people's prams
Such little terrors
Such little lambs!
Sixty-one today
And ought to be a granny
Sixty-one today
And nothing but a Nanny!
There, ducky, there,
Did the lady stare?
Don't cry! Oh my!
Other people's babies

A. P. Herbert

There is one last area of our subject where we can use Churchill's Nanny as a guide and an example. Then stranger and more sinister figures will take Mrs. Everest's place. This area, and it is one of the most important in this study, might loosely be called the Nanny as mother; related to it is the subject I will deal with in the last part of the chapter, the Nanny in partnership with the mother.

> Everybody's told me, dear, since I was seventeen,
> I ought to have been a mother—what a mother I'd have been!
> Mind you, minding babies isn't everybody's line
> But I wouldn't mind the minding, if I was minding mine.

Lady Diana Cooper said to me, "We were all of us perfectly accustomed to middle-aged men, when they got home, not going to see their old mothers and fathers but bounding upstairs to see their Nannies." One of these middle-aged men, now old-aged, was so affected when he began to describe the death of his Nanny to me that he burst into tears and we had to discontinue the interview. This area of the subject is so large—a continent —and so charged with feeling that it is difficult to know how to approach it. Having quoted some of A. P. Herbert's lines above, I think perhaps the best way is via Edward Sackville-West, the novelist of the Nanny.

Edward Sackville-West was born in 1901 and died in 1966. Among much other work, he was a distinguished critic, not only of books, but of music as well, writing for a number of years on that subject for the *New Statesman*. The Record Guide he produced with Desmond Shawe-Taylor was a bestseller. He also wrote a number of novels, among them *Piano Quintet*, *The Ruin*, *A Flame in Sunlight* and *Simpson*. Of these, by far the most successful (and best) was *Simpson*. It went into several editions when it first came out in 1931, and was reprinted again as late as 1951, when it again sold very well.

Simpson is entirely about a Nanny. It is in fact the fictional biography of one, of Ruth Simpson, following her from her early teens through to her death. It begins with her discovering that she has a vocation to look after children. This she does very early while looking after her youngest brother and sister.

> With the two children to look after she discovered a new kind of happiness which she knew would suffice her completely. But she did not give vent to her satisfaction, in that the family long remained ignorant of it. Her delight was in the delicacy of the child's body—the smoothness of its skin, the wonderful colouring of its face. Children seemed to her bodily perfect, and in contrast to them she found adults gross and shoddy and shockingly adult. But great as was her love, she did not romanticise; she did not wish Will and Dorothy always to remain children. With the quiet commonsense of a born realist, she knew that a supply of children need never be wanting to her and that, however painful might be the transition from one love to another, the pain would nevertheless pass. It was the body of the child which demanded her love and care, not its soul; that she left to take care of itself, knowing from her own experience that a mature mind is a more perfect instrument than an immature one and that to wish children to remain children is folly.

This vocation remains unaltered and unalterable. It is a destiny she must follow to its end—however terrible that may be. Other love emotions are neither ousted nor repressed, they are simply replaced. Thus, though what is known as 'a fine girl', she has no desire to marry, nor have children of her own. When Charles Tallyman, at the start, asks her to marry him, she replies:

"It's no use my thinking about it, Charlie. I don't want to marry you." She did not say "I don't love you." The phrase would have meant as little to her as "I do love you."

"What do you want to do then?" he asked, with surprising suddenness, and being so little of a fool.

"Be a nurse."

"What—in a hospital?"

"No. A child's nurse."

Charles Tallyman hesitated a moment and then said, in a reasonable tone, in which there was nothing arch or jaunty: "You could still have been that if you'd married me."

"But I don't want children of my own—as I've already told mother only she doesn't believe me."

"I don't think I do either."

"Then you'll have to lump it. I want to nurse other children, lots of them, all sorts and kinds, and chiefly babies."

"But they won't stay little," he argued, fascinated away from his intent by the strange ecstasy in her voice.

"Others'll come . . . I'll go to different families . . . I'll bring them all up. . . ."

"But—always, Ruth? You won't want to go on doing that for always. You'd rather have a home of your own, surely?"

"No. I don't care about it."

And so Simpson sets out on her odyssey. She rapidly develops the shapes, the sounds, the persona of a Nanny. She is firm and square, solid, her knees a lap, her breasts a bosom for crying on. She has a deep low chuckle with a curious click at the end. Her hair grows long and she does it up in long, complex coils on the top of her head, an operation which, like dressing and undressing, she can soon manage with immense speed, in the dark.

There is also her citadel, an inner recurring vision, a round room lined with windows which, as the book progresses, becomes less and less metaphorical and more and more concrete. Into this Temple, for that is what it is, she occasionally retreats or is drawn to find appearing behind each window in turn the figure of one of her children. They arrive here when 'completed' or in the process of completion. This happens when Simpson has done all she can for them.

Her odyssey lasts some thirty years (I think—no date is mentioned until 1912. But from some time in the '80s to 1920) and nearly four hundred pages. They are not in the least boring, but I do not intend to follow her closely through the five or six families which comprise her journey. What I should like to do is to make one or two general observations about the book relevant to our theme.

Sackville-West himself, to argue from his introduction to the 1951 edition, was quite definite as to his purpose in the book. Simpson he saw as a woman of action, but a woman of action controlled by a moral imperative—the need in her case to look after, love and 'complete' her children. In the abstract, these are qualities she shares with many great characters in history and literature, from Christ and St. Joan down to Danilo Dolci or the martyrs of modern Soviet Russia. The novel, in the series of family settings, shows how she copes and reacts to life in obedience to, almost in communion with, these deep springs within her character. It is a study of a particularly exalted type of character (if in a humble sphere) fulfilling its destiny. We watch how, whether she does not really like her charge, as with Martin the lonely albino, or loves him, as with Salathiel, whether the mothers are difficult or easy, how in every situation her course rings true, even if in the end, though she could not have suspected this, it leads to death.

On this level, and it is certainly one interpretation, it is essential that the novel should be highly realistic. And the scenes in the nurseries, Simpson sitting sewing by lamplight or dressing her children and sending them down to the drawing-room or briskly comforting, feeding, commonsensically at her exercise—all this is indeed accurate and real. Dozens of times Sackville-West catches perfectly the gesture or expression of a mood or situation. Consider this passage which, while incidentally evoking a nursery at desultory play, also exactly expresses the relationship of so many of the mothers in our period to their Nannied children.

> Sometimes in the winter evenings, without warning, Lady Tarent herself would suddenly come into the nursery and remain there, often for an hour at a time. Her entry always had a look of purpose, which faded, however, as soon as she got into the room, and disappeared entirely before she had been there many minutes. She was almost always dressed in dark blue, with infrequent diamonds which caught the light as if by surprise and seemed a reflection of her own perplexity. She would begin by trying to play with her children; but they soon noticed that she was an inexpert playmate and left her to play amongst themselves. Then she would relapse into a chair by the table and look at them from a distance with sadness and apprehensive love in her eyes. She had a habit of biting the inside of her cheek, which she pushed in with one finger; and the contemplation of her children was nearly always accompanied by this nervous fidget.

Meanwhile Simpson would sit by the fire and sew. Lady Tarent did not say much to interrupt the regular purr of the cotton being drawn through the stuff and the tick of the needle-point against the thimble. When she did speak, her tone seemed designed to disguise the haphazard nature of her question or remark.

"Do you think Helen's growing, Simpson?"

"Oh yes." (Simpson was in the habit of leaving out the "M'lady" on these occasions.)

Helen was sitting on the floor, cutting up, with a pair of blunt-ended scissors, some pieces of bright brown tissue paper which had once constituted one of the weekly dress patterns given away with each copy of *Home Chat*. She burbled to herself as she cut, with little crumpled face and bright, reddish hair. Her legs in blunt shoes like nutshells, stuck out in front of her. Nigel walked up behind her and tweaked her hair. She put her hands over her head as if to protect it from a shower of water, and let out a little scream of annoyance.

"Don't do that, Nigel, darling," exclaimed Lady Tarent. "Come over here now." She held him to her and began patting his hair, to arrange it, in the way all children loathe. He wriggled away. Lady Tarent sighed and let her hands fall into her lap. Then she rose to her feet.

"I suppose I must go and dress for dinner," she said regretfully. Then, apropos of nothing: "You're a great comfort to me, Simpson."

Or, another example, Sackville-West is, on one level, accurate about the power balance in a Nannied household. Plainly, for the Nanny to become the mother, the real mother must relinquish most of her authority, and in fact Simpson only rarely has any trouble in this respect. Early on, Nurse Barker, into whose position Simpson graduates from nursery-maid, says, "Mothers think, all think, they know more about health than nurses. That isn't true. If you know a child needs medicine, give it him; if the mother forbids you, give it him when she isn't looking. It's you who lives with the child, not she, and you're more likely to know what it needs and what it doesn't." It is only a step from this to Nanny having complete control—a step that Simpson soon takes. One of her rules is "not to give in to parents on purely professional matters". Professional matters in effect means everything of importance, but there is an ambiguity in Sackville-West's attitude here which I shall discuss in a later chapter.

At the same time, as one reads on, it becomes clear that there is another motive force behind the book, more fundamental than, and only very rarely contradictory to the artistic one I have outlined. Despite the 'little scream of annoyance' which Helen gives when Nigel tweaks her hair, practically none of the numerous children in *Simpson* are characters at all. They are most of them featureless; they are unbelievably good, quiet and docile. The quiet, indeed, from Simpson's point of view, often lonely nurseries never ring to the powder and shot, the crashes and explosions and power struggles inseparable from real children.

In fact, at its deepest level, the book isn't about real children, nor is it about Simpson's response to them, or how they react together at all. It is about something even more simple. It is about Simpson's love. It is a celebration of, a monument to, a long, elaborate and endlessly repetitive description of the love of a Nanny—and a monument to the strongest and most important love, one feels, that Sackville-West himself experienced. Repetitive because Simpson is a simple character. This does not make her unreal. No doubt children's Nannies often are simple—or appear so more than other people. But this simplicity combined with the early emergence of her adult character, means that her love does not change or develop, it merely becomes yet more clearly defined. Very soon the Temple reaches its final form (this quotation comes from page 63).

> The spinning, once flaming ball of her soul had at last almost cooled, solidified into a definite shape. The shape was that of a round room, with a low ceiling. Paned windows, stretching from floor to ceiling, occurred at equal intervals in the wall; each window gave onto a different landscape; each landscape was lighted in a different way—some by morning sunlight, others by grey twilight, one by moonlight. Many of them were dark, sightless gulfs. The light in the room itself came solely from the windows and was therefore an unnameable blend of many different qualities of light. Of the several landscapes each contained the living figure of a child, who moved freely about within sight of the room. Ariadne and Nigel and Helen Tarent were there, and Peter and Lucy and Rosalind and Christopher Price-Stables; each occurred at about three years old and remained there, unalterable as a photograph. The expression on each face was oddly similar: there was no joy in it, nor yet pain, but only the flower-like peace of faces that are asleep—or dead. The floor of the room was a maze of paths edged by low, dull flames. Up to each lighted window led the end of a path; but up to the dark windows was as yet no way. A mirrored Simpson, grotesque in a crackling, white apron, her square brown face busy and intent, walked ceaselessly up and down from one window to another collecting their contents to herself; the loop of her hair peaked out above her forehead, seemed to point at whatever she was looking at.

Sackville-West's infinite elaboration of this quasi-mystical love—often in renewed descriptions of the Temple—is rather surprisingly never tedious. Partly this is because it is surrounded by, rooted in, sound commonsense realism and humour. And partly because it is animated by passion. It is this passion and the form it sometimes takes, which made me speculate that the fundamental driving force behind the book was auto-biographical.

Two of the children Simpson deals with are different from all the others. These are her favourites and their role is crucial. Whereas the other children have had ordinary lumpish English names—Nigel, Martin, Peter, Christopher—these are called Salathiel and Childeric, and this heightening of romance is reinforced by an increasingly romantic and passionate use of language. The celebration of Simpson's love now begins to be echoed or joined by—and again I speculate—the creation of an ever more powerful combined figure: Sackville-West as he remembers he was as a child and as he would have liked to have been. Salathiel is strong, beautiful, confident, amusing, loving; it is he and his family who give refuge to Simpson when she is in trouble at the end. When the book finishes he is a young soldier, with hints of gay debauchery. Simpson loves him best of all her children. Yet she *gives* more of her love to Childeric, because he needs her most. Childeric is driven by extreme sensitivity to live in a private world of his own imagination. He is pale, almost translucent, fretful, delicate, and is often ill or having nose-bleeds. He does not love Simpson as much as Salathiel but depends upon her more. These two are entwined. In the Temple they share the same window. Childeric loves and hero-worships Salathiel.

Or rather, he does until he meets the German boy, Sepp.

A boy of his own age would have been no help to him: instinctively he desired, not a slave, but a tyrant—a leader. Sepp was sixteen, and in that face of coarse and violent beauty, that energetic, dark gold wire growing low on the forehead and far forwards on the temples, the lowering dark blue eyes and brutal mouth, thick neck and thunderous shoulders, Childeric completed the lives of many unfinished dreams.

For there went out from Sepp Karuschsit a purely physical radiation of astonishing force, compelling the attention of all other human beings who came near him.

For a moment, naked autobiography seems to burst through the texture of the novel. It is significant, also, that Childeric is, unwittingly, the cause of Simpson's death. After the war, she goes to seek him out, feeling he needs her, is 'uncompleted'. In her search, she gets caught up in a riot and is destroyed by a machine-gun wielded (though this is not entirely clear) by Sepp.

"Childeric!" she cried, as if this invocation were her last chance—as if it might accomplish, after all, in the passage of one word, the completion of her present task.

The pain had almost gone, leaving only the horrible core within her. But now that so much blood had flowed out of her body, she began to fail, though the crowd had cleared away from the place where she lay, alone, with her head near the kerbstone. She made one effort to rise; but it was no good. Sinking on to her back she saw the roof of her temple ruin in with a sudden roar and crackle, and she put up her hands to ward it off. But they were crushed savagely against her chest, and darkness—a huge, irregular saw—ground with a gathering shriek through her consciousness, destroying it for ever.

Certainly, in some superficial aspects, *Simpson* is undoubtedly auto-biographical. Edward Sackville-West's sister Lady Diana Hall said that Simpson herself was based on their own Nanny Hutton. There are numerous points of coincidence. Nanny Hutton came to the Sackville-Wests when Edward was born in 1901 and stayed ten years. She loved him and he adored her. She was eighty when she died in 1950, and was therefore born in 1870, so her life was more or less contemporaneous with Simpson's. When the family moved to Camberley, Nanny Hutton went too and made great friends with the Nanny of a friend of theirs. Simpson also goes to Camberley and it is there that she forms her only close friendship in the book, again with another Nanny. The Sackville-Wests weren't very rich and Nanny Hutton used to buy them things. Their mother was always urging her to save but she never would. This is another Simpson characteristic. Diana and Edward and Nanny Hutton all slept together in the night nursery, a small back room. She could remember Nanny Hutton's long coils of dark hair and her brown face, and how fascinated Edward Sackville-West used to be watching her undress, not just under cover of dark, but with her nightdress spreading out round her voluminous as a tent. He himself was extremely delicate when little and she was always having to nurse him through illnesses and once her devotion saved his life when he had pneumonia. In fact, his sister said, the little Sack-ville-West got a taste for being ill (one which he never entirely lost). He used to go everywhere in a bath chair. And he hated wool next to his skin. She could remember Fridays—when they had clean clothes—how he would sit trying to stretch his woollen combinations with a hair brush so that they wouldn't fit too closely.

How great the element of autobiography is in *Simpson* is not of course particularly important. It interests me because many of his observations about Nannies agree with mine and I am glad to find his were based on direct experience. The entire book is, if in a deep sense autobiographical, also a testimony to the great strength of the love a Nanny could inspire.

Though I am not concerned here with literary criticism, I might observe in passing that I think it is some insufficiently digested autobiographical element which explains the few, quite minor, flaws in *Simpson*. Occasionally the prose becomes over-wrought and even sentimental. The hefty character of Sepp is out of key and intrusive. And I found something unsatisfactory about the end. It is true that one can justify Simpson's destruction on the lines of the artistic interpretation of the book I gave earlier. It is the ultimate expression of the strength of her destiny. Yet it is more as though the motives behind this end, as well as artistic, were also personal. What these were is unknowable and unimportant—perhaps Sackville-West needed to exorcise his love for his Nanny, perhaps he was angry that she had left him when he was ten. No doubt they were muddled and even contradictory. It doesn't matter. Nevertheless, though both impulses, artistic and personal, impel the book to the same end— the death of Simpson—in a curious way they run counter to each other. One is planned, artistic, conscious, while the other is unplanned, irrelevant to art and probably unconscious. The result is that there is an acute sense of surging and unresolved emotions, of contradictory and contending forces, swirling round the climax of the book which results in muddle and confusion.

But these are very minor flaws. In fact it is the personal passion, when controlled, which gives *Simpson* its quality. Time and again it is lifted into flight by the remembered and continuing power of Sackville-West's own boyhood feelings. This is especially so when Salathiel and Simpson finally confront the love they have for one another. There is always something moving about the love of little children. But I think the love of little children for their Nannies is particularly so. It may have something to do with the humbleness of the Nanny. It is just because she is not the mother; as well as being disinterested she knows she must share her love. Partly it is because she knows the child will soon outgrow her. And partly it is because, so often, the Nanny has to go away.

"You'll find me the same when I come home to nurse your first baby, Salathiel—however old I may be by that time. Happiness keeps one the same, I suppose; it's those that get a lot of sorrow in their lives that get different. I've always been the same, ever since I went to nurse Lady Tarent's children at Vair—and that's many years ago."

All the shapes of her past come crowding into the room, taking advantage of the darkness to establish themselves secretly in the recesses of the air between herself and Salathiel; they filled the room with a lifetime of careful emotion, carrying like an army this burden of Simpson's farewell.

Suddenly, Salathiel unable any longer to bear the weight imposed upon his soul, started to his feet, struck a match and lit a candle upon the mantelpiece.

As if unutterably changed by her own words, Simpson was reborn to Salathiel's sudden eyes. He saw tears on her face; and his love for her overwhelmed him. Taking her violently by the hands, he pulled her to her feet, so that a gasping sob came from her throat.

"Oh you single heart!" He pressed his cheek hard against her.

For a moment she held him, then put him from her and turned away from the light. "Goodnight, dear boy. Bless you."

"Goodnight."

CHARACTER AND SKILLS OF THE NANNY

It might seem patronising to try to generalise about the character of the Nanny. Nannies were simply women and as various as that: there were witty Nannies, devious Nannies, murderess Nannies and lesbian Nannies (rare), drunk Nannies and scholar Nannies. What I am about to write, therefore, are only generalisations; I could supply a mass of exceptions. At the same time, all occupations that demand particular qualities or impose special conditions inevitably tend to make those that practise them resemble each other in certain respects or attract people with the qualities required by the conditions. This is perhaps particularly true of vocations—that is, occupations to which people feel called because of some special skill or need, occupations which frequently demand sacrifices they are willing to make to fulfil that need or use that skill. (And the reverse is true. When people in the same profession go mad they often go mad in the same way. I know a psychiatrist who specialises in bishops.)

Looking after children, though I am not certain if you could call it a vocation (I think Sackville-West exaggerates this a bit), if it is to be done well, unquestionably demands special skills and a special sort of character. I was frequently struck by similarities in the Nannies I interviewed. And more than similarity of character there was similarity of atmosphere. Mr. Wynne-Tyson, the person who produced a screen interview to prevent my interviewing him, said, when I mentioned I'd got on very well with Nanny Watson, that he got on well with all Nannies. He liked their ambience. The same is said to have been true of Churchill. He frequently used to go and sit with Nanny Soames. He enjoyed nurseries.

I have remarked already that in some respects Simpson was a simple character. Nannies often appeared so. An extreme example was Gerald Brenan's Nurse Annie, about whom he wrote:

> She was a large, stoutly-built woman who before my birth had been my mother's maid: at this time she must have been about twenty-eight. Nana, as I have always called her, was one of those people of whom there is nothing to be said except that they are good. Because of some impediment in her mind, she could not communicate: her large, pink and white face and pale blue eyes would beam with a steady benevolence, but nothing was put into words. She expressed herself therefore in her actions and no woman was ever more reliable and devoted.

By simple I do not mean stupid (though apparently stupid people often instinctively do the right thing. They just have another form of intelligence). Little children are usually simple in the sense that their demands are direct and generally single; they are not muddled by guilts or indecision. But this does not mean that they cannot also be complex—involving events in a certain order, or curious rituals and dressings up, pretending bricks are biscuits and Nanny a bird. Nor are they always easy to understand. They often want things they can't express. It is not surprising that the ability to think like a child, to consciously or intuitively enter and understand the world of a child, to be able to respond simply and directly to childish simplicity and directness is an enormous advantage. Nannies were often aware of this. Nanny Williams was minute—under five feet. She would have gone to a hospital in the course of her Welgarth training (this in the mid-'20s) but was too small to tuck in the beds. Yet she said her size was an advantage. It led her to identify with children. Several times she said, "You've got to be a child with a child. That's what Barrie said. Quite true." Several people who'd had very small Nannies agreed with this.

Often it requires considerable ingenuity to deal with children. One Nanny came to the house of a little girl whose mother had just died. Every night the little girl, Mary, would cry when she was put to bed and come running downstairs. Nanny invented a game: she used to say, "Who's teddy is that?" "He's mine." "Well look how he's yawning. I should put him to bed if he was my teddy." Mary agreed, so they used to take him upstairs, give him supper, brush him and put him to bed. Nanny would then say, "Do you know what he has just whispered go me, he says when you go downstairs he is going to get out and run down." "Oh but I's aren't going." So she was bathed and given her supper and said her prayers. Nanny kissed her and Mary hugged her and said, "God made you very playful, didn't he, Nanny?"

I could give dozens, hundreds, of examples of this sort of skill. My correspondence bulged with them. But, though they all have the charm of the nursery, in the mass they can become tedious. But certainly two things were true. Long years with children did end with many Nannies— in their simplicity, directness, honesty, concentration on the affairs of the nursery and so on—coming to a certain extent to resemble their medium. And they developed (and often seem to have been born with) a quite uncanny skill with children. I remember sitting in a railway carriage with a mother and a child of three who was screaming and yelling hideously and uncontrollably. A very old lady of ninety (a retired Nanny it later turned out) was helped in and within four minutes had completely calmed the little boy, by a mixture of distraction, gentleness, humour and patience.

Particularly, perhaps, patience. This was a quality Simpson possessed, and it is one essential to anyone having anything to do with children.

> The artless prattle of a child
> Drives everybody nearly wild,
> And who that for an hour beguiled
> A babe however clever
> For all the riches of the rich
> Would undertake a life in which
> They lived at that exacting pitch
> Ten hours a day for ever?
> Though even in the mother's joys
> A grander cycle dawns
> When we grow more like little boys
> And less like little prawns,
> Our Nanny, in a nobler strain,
> Would have us at our worst remain,
> A babe for ever pink and plain,
> Herself for ever Nanny.

It seems likely that at one point A. P. Herbert *was* a Nanny. Practically all the Nannies I talked to explained, usually with various anecdotes about how impatient mothers got, how essential it was to be patient with little children. "Patience and perseverance brought the snail to Jerusalem," said Nanny Murphy in the Francis Wyndham interview in *Queen* some years ago. Her photograph beside the interview, strong, kind, lined with experience, has much in common with many Nannies. They often have something of the calm, rock-like quality of great captains of the sea. Having weathered a million terrible storms in ten thousand teacups, they know their ability to face the tempest.

And it is this quality, as well as the knowledge of life gained vicariously through the often scandalous behaviour of their employers, which made them such good confidantes. It was not always a possible transition. Often they remained shockable. But many did not. I have already noted Nanny Marks's sensible attitude to gaol. One Nanny told me that one of her ex-charges—"Very popular, bless her"—used to come and ask her advice before every affair, and they seem to have been numerous. *The Blessing* opens with Grace being picked up by a good-looking Frenchman and instantly deciding to go out with him. She rushes upstairs and flings all her clothes out. Nanny comes in.

> "Good gracious. The room looks like a jumble sale."
> "Run me a bath, darling. I'm going out to dinner with that Frenchman."
> "Are you dear? And what's his name?"
> "Bother. I never asked him."
> "Oh well," said Nanny, "One French name is very much like another, I daresay."

Another woman told me that it was only by going to her old Nanny that she escaped from a potentially nasty blackmailing situation. Her Nanny comforted her, said that if he continued she must at once go to the police and then went and gave the man involved a tremendous telling off. He did not continue his blackmailing attempts. Nannies did not just view the world with the patience and tolerance learnt in the nursery; they could use the resource gained there too.

Nannies frequently shared Simpson's simple shape, as though like lilo's they inflated the better to comfort. Charles I, the last of the Hapsburgs, born in 1887, had one such, described by the Countess of Wittgenstein when she first arrived at the Palace in Favoriten Street to be lady-in-waiting to the Archduchess Maria Theresa.

> I beheld an enormous nurse puffing and panting on the steps in front of me, with a small boy of three by her side. This I realised at once must be the Archduke Charles, and I noticed the anxiety with which he watched her. "Now Nini", she flustered, "if you don't mind, we'll stop and rest a moment." And there he remained standing patient and thoughtful, until she was ready to proceed.

Charles apparently became more or less a saint. Even at the age of four the woman responsible for teaching him English, an Irish girl called Miss Bride Casey, found him giving away his shirts.

Another Nanny (mid-1930s), among many, who shared this as well as several other of the characteristics we have been discussing, was the Nanny of Peter Eyre the actor. The Eyres were a rich family living in America who moved, partly owing to the restlessness of Peter's father, a tempestuous man of violent temper, either from hotel to hotel or through a succession of huge country houses in Newport, Rhode Island, or Aiken, South Carolina. They had three houses in five years, as well as living in numerous hotels. There were seven children and they lived in a separate nursery world with the being-brought-down-to-see-parents routine and a great many servants.

She was called Jessie Robertson—Nanny Robertson—and her father was Scotch and her mother Cornish. But she was brought up in London and was a cockney. She spoke cockney. She came to us when she was forty, in 1935, five years before I was born, and left when I was about fifteen in 1955. So she stayed with us about twenty years.

She was very large, fat, stout. She moved all the time, she moved at a half-run, panting and talking non-stop. She couldn't stand still; she even ate standing up. She had a Scottish face, with strong features. A smiley face. But she was not pretty; she was plain. She had very wild hair, difficult to control, and she had a great many hairbrushes. She had a thing about them. She was always brushing her hair down and then whirling it out. She liked hair that stuck out—I think she thought it had something to do with health. Lively hair stood out. Our hair, therefore, was always brushed down and out. (Peter Eyre incidentally has particularly striking hair to this day.) Brushing her hair was practically the only attention she allowed herself to pay to her own needs. She thought people should dress colourfully. She always wore yellow; and striking yellow straw hats. These were huge, very large Diana Cooperish hats.

She is the only person I have ever known who was completely calm (except when it was about something to do with herself and doctors). She was never flustered or flurried. She was simple, straightforward and direct. She had a great sense of humour, a sense of ridicule (cockney). She was the only person who could deal with my father's violent temper. She could frighten him. She would dart at him with an upraised hairbrush and frighten him—and also make him feel ridiculous. When he was shouting and raving she would shut him up. Therefore, though we were all amused and laughed at her, we regarded her as an heroic person.

She was utterly dedicated; she had to be to last in such a tempestuous household. Also she must have been lonely. She was an Englishwoman alone in an American house. She didn't really have any friends, though she was sort of friends with some of the servants. For eight years she never had a day off. Then she had one and came back early. She was devoted to, and absorbed by, the children. She always preferred John, my elder brother and her first charge. But she never showed it. We never noticed it. She knew us all entirely, and ran us independently. I was musical. Though not at all rich she suddenly bought me a piano. In the same way, later on I became obsessed by animals. I used to read books about animals and get animal magazines. Suddenly she bought me a dog. She would initiate these purchases or suggest them to our parents. Her own life and concerns did not seem to interest her. She was always bringing us presents.

She was very observant. She had an instinctive knowledge about people. But at the same time, because her position in the house, with the children, was mid-way between servants and parents, she had an extremely clear objective view of those above and below her. She kept up a continual monologue of observation—you're looking a bit pale, hair needs a good brush, the fire's getting low. Because she did this with children she did it equally with grown-ups—you're looking a bit peaky. Or with camp men—she would answer in their own voice, imitating it. The result often seemed catty, and would amuse us. Yet in fact her observations were often very acute.

She used the word 'Anyway' a great deal. She would put it at the beginnings and endings of sentences. She would draw it out—*Any*-way. Sometimes she would use it on its own. Anyway. She was always talking—a soothing, continuous, comforting, observing commentary, gossiping monologue. A Nanny's day is a long monologue, or series of monologues and chats. Chat to maids, chat to parents, chat to children. This chat is always misrepresented in literature. It is made too jokey, its nature not realised. It is partly soothing and calming, like dentist's talk; and partly it is a sign that everything is under control, that it is being observed and ordered.

This observation was sometimes paranoic. She regarded chicken as particularly beneficial. She had a theory that when we had chicken, which I suppose we did quite frequently, the cook carefully opened it and scraped out most of the meat, sewing the skin up afterwards. She would say "Tut. Look at the chicken. No meat in it. She's taken all the meat. I can see the thread."

There was no thread.

She had a routine going to bed. She would go to the nursery door, lock it, bolt it, and put against it three or four chairs. Then she would go into her bedroom, lock it, and put one chair against it. Under her bed she had a bell, a torch, and pepper. She seriously believed that one night a burglar would soundlessly break into the nursery, soundlessly break into her room, and that she would then turn on the torch, blind him with pepper and ring the bell for help.

She was very demonstrative. She hugged us all a lot. She never got angry, she would ridicule us. Cockney—"Who does he think he is?"

I don't think she had many boyfriends. We asked about them. There seemed to have been very few. In fact only one. "I knew a young man who tried to be cheeky to me on a bridge. I gave him a good hiding." The feeling was that she had had a hairbrush handy.

She left when she was sixty. I was at school at the time. I was shocked that my parents could let her leave—but also shocked that she should want to leave. She lived in various places in the South of England and then eventually settled with her two sisters. She wrote to us all the time, sending presents. We used to go and see her from London. She treated the sisters like nursery-maids— they were allowed to see us for a few instants and then vanished into the kitchen. There was a huge tea which it was sometimes difficult to eat as we had always had lunch on the train. She would shout for one of the sisters to bring more tea or cake.

I gave her a dog. It became her charge, and her new baby. It died. I bought her another and I remember it shocked me rather how quickly it replaced the first. As I got out of the car, holding it, she gave a sort of yelp of excitement, seized the dog (the other had only died a few days before) and hurried into the house with it. It was an instinct, her Nannying instinct. I felt her life had been sacrificed to this instinct.

She always dreaded doctors. She was suspicious of them. "He's a humbug." Her skin went wrong—probably cancer. She simply covered it with calamine. She was seventy something. Then gallstones. Finally we heard she had cancer. It was terrible to see her. She had been a large active woman. Now tiny, bent, huddled in bed. At tea she just had one biscuit on a plate. I'd never seen her eat less than fifteen pieces of bread and butter and several cakes. When I went into her room I was so horrified and distressed I didn't know what to say. She said, "What an awful shirt you have on. It's a revolting colour." (It was purple.) Then turning to the others, "Can't we do something about his clothes?" As usual she'd diverted me. Soothed us over, along.

She died when I was abroad. I cried for days. Her life seemed somehow pathetic in retrospect, devoted to us.

THE SECURITY OF THE NANNY

There are several comments one could make about Nanny Robertson. It might be noted in passing that many Nannies were mildly neurotic— hardly surprising considering their unmarried state, their frequent loneliness, and all the other difficulties of their position. But though the unpleasant ones vented their frustrations on their charges, the kind ones managed to create some bypass—inventing emptied chickens, or putting pepper pots under the bed.

Daphne Fielding, for instance, Alexander Weymouth's mother, describes in her autobiography a series of absolutely appalling Nannies.

Finally, when she was seven, her mother engaged Nanny Saddington—a bright, quick, black-eyed woman, not five foot tall, with whom Daphne Fielding was at last happy. Nanny Saddington, despite or because of her kindness and gentleness, was a prey to quite strong aggressive tensions, but she contrived a harmless, if vivid, outlet for them. She attacked mice. She filled every corner of the nursery, the night nursery and the outlying environs with mousetraps, so that great care had to be taken when looking for biscuits or even toys. She would patrol her jungle with ceaseless vigilance. And she experimented with different mousetraps; not just the savage kind that went off with a bang and squashed the mouse, but various sorts of boxes and cages which caught and imprisoned them. Once caught they had then to be drowned in a bucket. A mouse, apparently, can survive swimming for hours before it will drown. Gentle Nanny Saddington would sit patiently watching its efforts until it was exhausted and then hold it under with a shovel.

But the aspect I wish briefly to discuss about Nanny Robertson is one which didn't actually come out when I interviewed Peter Eyre, but only emerged in conversation some weeks later. That is the fact that there was nothing weak or overindulgent or undisciplined about Nanny Robertson. The same is true of Simpson. Her nurseries ran like clockwork. And, though I have come across a number of bullied Nannies (my mother and her sister used to tie their nursemaid up with skipping ropes and tickle her till she screamed), on the whole it would be true to say that all Nannies, from the beginning to the end of our period, practised a firm, regular and disciplined routine. The day, often down to its minutest portions, was vigorously patterned with a series of rules, large and small, which were only very occasionally, if ever, waived. M. A. Gibbs has this imaginary mealtime conversation:

"May I get down, Nanny?"
"Not until you have finished your bread and butter, dear."
"But Nanny—"
"Eat up your bread and butter, dear."
The bread and butter is eaten.
"Not too fast, dear, and don't cram your mouth like that. It is bad manners."
"Can I leave the crust, Nanny?"
"No, dear. Waste not, want not."
"But I don't like crusts, Nanny."
"Never mind. Eat it up. You may be glad of it someday."
"It's all gone now, so may I get down, Nanny?"
"If you say please, dear."

"Please, Nanny."

"Wait till I take your bib off and then say Grace."

"For what wehavereceivedmaythelordmakeustrulythankfulamen. May I get down now, Nanny? Please."

"Yes dear, you may."

And this certainty about how to behave, when to do what and why, extended with the same simple directness into the world of morality. Many people wrote and talked to me about this. Lady Antonia Fraser, for instance, described how she had several Nannies and how, because she was the eldest, she was never liked enough. Then at last, when she was four, came Jean. Jean was eighteen, extremely pretty and attractive. Antonia Fraser fell in love with her (I felt a sense of mutual indentification —the call between two beautiful people which Genet speculates about). Though her mother Lady Longford was then anti-religious—a phase now passed—Jean was not. She was very religious. Antonia Fraser became a Christian because she was in love with Jean and has remained one till this day.

Or there was Miss de Bourbel, whose Nanny's faith and morality were of the simplest: she knew what was wrong—selfishness, lies, meanness; and she knew what was right—unselfishness, truth, charity. This faith was buttressed by Hell to which the wicked went and were burnt; and Heaven, a clear, clean, white place without sin or dirt, which secretly bored Miss de Bourbel. But Miss de Bourbel also, despite her mother's atheism, has been sustained all her life by the same strong and direct morality as her Nanny.

I want to leave until later a full study of Nanny regimes and disciplines, their severity or otherwise and their effects (quite such pernickety table manners and eating crusts for example, though at one time universal, seem to me absurd). But the fact remains that, provided they are not too strict, little children need firm and consistent rules of behaviour. The rules delimit their world, give it boundaries and shape; their consistency means that that world will last, that it and they are secure. If a thing is right one day and wrong the next it is as though their house was there one day and gone the next. And if they are left to decide what is right or wrong themselves, or if nothing is declared wrong, then it is as though they have no house at all. This is intolerable. So they go on behaving more and more outrageously until at last some limit is reached. In a later chapter we shall see that various studies have shown that beating and over-aggressive discipline lead to over-aggressive behaviour on the part of the child. But the same studies have also shown that over-aggressive children result from too permissive an upbringing as well. That is why the children of over-permissive parents are such hell to live with. You have only got to see the children of such parents to realise how much children need some form of rule and, often, how much less secure and happy they are than the children of strict parents.

Or you can read Spock. It perhaps hardly needs saying that, whatever you think of Spock, if you read him you cannot accuse him of encouraging permissiveness or loose discipline. On the contrary, he repeatedly stresses the need for consistent and firm rules provided they are reasonably applied.

> I never wanted people to bring up brattish children [he said in an interview a year or two ago]. My own two boys were very well behaved. I was never as permissive as I've been blamed for. I was striving to overcome the extreme rigidity of infant feeding in my book on child care. Then the whole of American pediatrics swung towards permissiveness, and threw the less secure parent off balance. A mother thought that if you could let a child decide how to eat, then you could let him decide how to sleep, how to play and so on. I was alarmed at the way my book was being misinterpreted. Parents were going from extreme rigidity to extreme flexibility overnight. In my pediatric practice in those days, I'd run into quite a few babies who'd learnt to tyrannise their mothers as a result.

The fact is that a text on something people feel very strongly about will be interpreted to suit them. Like the Bible (his book has sold twenty-three million copies) this has happened to Spock. My brother had a friend whose own upbringing had been extremely fierce, who thought he brought up his son entirely by Spock. Yet, because the little boy disliked having his teeth done, his father clamped his head between his knees and brushed his teeth so hard the gums bled—to 'teach him'. To teach him to be brave he strapped him on the back of his motorbike and took him on terrifying cross-country scrambles.

Time and again during my researches I was struck how the best Nannies had anticipated Freud, and therefore Spock. Not so much in areas where fashion and custom dictated what should be done—like pot training or infant feeding (though, as I pointed out, nineteenth-century feeding habits were often remarkably unrigid)—but in areas where experience and instinct played a major part. They often realised, for instance, that too much repression was harmful. Nanny Graveney (then aged seventy-five) said it fussed little children if they had to bury things in their head. Nanny Watson told me that the Nanny who had trained her, born in 1869, said that children should have their fling and should never be afraid of telling Nanny anything. Nanny Marks (who tended to indulge in emotional blackmail) knew that obedience follows love; children obey because they want the approval of those they love. They do not need to be, and should not be, frightened into obedience. It is perhaps less odd that Nanny tricks and Spock's were often the same. Both were practising pediatricians. Nanny Henderson (active in the '20s and '30s, when such flexibility was rare) explained to me the same method Spock advocates for preventing a baby tyrannising by refusing to go to sleep at night—let him cry progressively each time a little longer, three, four, five minutes, and so on. This sort of example could be duplicated throughout our period.

Fulfilling, therefore, so many of the precise conditions of a secure upbringing, it is hardly surprising that one of the *leitmotivs* of the Nanny as Mother is a sense of security.

> I can still feel myself physically enfolded in the warmth and safety of the great nursery on the third floor of the home in Lexham Gardens [wrote Leonard Woolf in *Sowing* (his childhood was in the mid-1880s)], the fire blazing behind the tall guard, the kettle singing away, and Nurse, with her straight black hair parted in the middle and her smooth, oval peasant face, reading the Baptist Times or the visions of the opium eater (de Quincey). Just as the spider-haunted garden remains in my mind as the primary pattern for all the waste lands and desolations into which I have wandered, in later life, so the nursery with its great fire, when the curtains were pulled and the gas lit and Nurse settled down to her reading, and occasionally far off could be heard the clop-clop of a horse in a hansom cab or four-wheeler, the nursery remains for me the Platonic idea laid up in heaven of security and peace and civilisation. But though in the course of my life I have passed through several desolations more desolate than the garden with its grimy ivy and its spider webs, I never again found any safety and civilisation to equal that of the gas-lit nursery

Mothers, of course, can give security, too. But there is a peculiar flavour to Nanny security which is rather different—and a flavour which is peculiarly English. It is somehow cosier. This is partly because it is restricted in space to the single, warm, enclosing space of the nursery. And this concentration is reinforced by the concentration of the Nanny—she has nothing else to do. It is cosy because it is simple and direct in the way that I have described. And its flavour is peculiarly English for two reasons. The world of the Nanny has begun to merge, so old now are her charges, with nostalgia for England's past; however inaccurate (and I think often it is inaccurate), the honeycomb, the Golden Shred upon the nursery table, glow with the warm and diffuse light which envelops late Victorian and Edwardian England and even, now, is casting tentative beams across the '20s and '30s.

And it is English because, of course, all the appurtenances of this security were so extremely English. Nabokov writes of his childhood in St. Petersburg and neighbouring large estates around 1900:

> The kind of family to which I belonged—a kind now extinct—had, among other virtues, a traditional leaning towards the comfortable products of Anglo-Saxon civilisation. Pear's soap tar-black when dry, topaz-like when held to the light between wet fingers, took care of one's morning bath. Pleasant was the decreasing weight of the English collapsible tub when it was made to protrude a rubber underlip and disgorge its frothy contents into the slop pail. "We could not improve the toothpaste so we improved the tube," said the English toothpaste. At breakfast, Golden Syrup imported from London would entwist with its glowing coils the revolving spoon from which enough of it had slithered onto a piece of Russian bread and butter. All sorts of snug, mellow things came in a steady procession from the English shop on Nevski Avenue; fruitcakes, smelling salts, playing cards, picture puzzles, striped blazers, talcum-white tennis balls.

Nabokov had a bewildering sequence of English Nannies: a dim Miss Rachel, remembered chiefly in terms of the Huntley and Palmer biscuits which they greedily and guiltily shared; "Miss Clayton, who, when I slumped in my chair, would poke me in the middle vertebrae and then smilingly throw back her own shoulders to show me what she wanted of me . . ." (a governess this, surely); Miss Norcott, languid, lovely and melancholy with aquamarine eyes. One night, at Abbazia, Miss Norcott was suddenly asked to leave. No explanation seems to have been given and for a day the tiny Nabokov was inconsolable despite "the hot chocolate the Petersons' old Nanny had prepared for me".

Despite these Nannies, or rather more probably because of their number, the main influence on his life was his mother. Yet one thing we do perhaps owe one or all of them. Nabokov learnt to read and write English before Russian.

> My first English friends were four simple souls in my grammar—Ben, Dan, Sam and Ned. There used to be a great deal of fuss about their identities and whereabouts—"Who is Ben?" "He is Dan" "Sam is in bed," and so on. Although it all remained rather stiff and patchy (the compiler was handicapped by having to employ—for the initial lessons at least—words of not more than three letters), my imagination somehow managed to obtain the necessary data.

Wan-faced, big-limbed, silent nit-wits, proud in the possession of certain tools ("Ben has an axe") they now drift with a slow-motioned slouch across the remotest back-drop of memory. . . .

Upon these simple but immensely solid foundations was one day to be erected that wonder of contemporary English literature—the Nabokovian prose style.

NANNY AS MOTHER (1):
TOTAL REPLACEMENT IN EARLY YEARS

Bearing in mind, then, those characteristics of simplicity, patience and firmness, the elements of security and a peculiarly English cosiness, and with the figures of Nanny Simpson, Nanny Everest and Nanny Robertson still fresh, let us look more closely at certain other aspects of the Nanny as (and with) mother.

The crucial point is of course the relationship with the mother: both the relations the Nanny had with the mother and more important the relationship the child had with the mother as a result of the Nanny situation. There seem to me to have been very approximately three positions. The first of these I have perhaps sufficiently dealt with; that in which the Nanny seizes power and the mother meekly acquiesces, sinking like Lady Tarent hopelessly and ineffectively into the background. "People all over the world want a real English Nanny," said Nanny Ellis to Francis Wyndham. "But would they realise that *they must not interfere*?"

The second, and on the whole the most common through the period, is that in which the mother is just not mentioned. That does not necessarily mean she has not played an important part, but it is a part that didn't begin until the child was five or six or seven. When talking about their early life it is inevitable that children who have had this sort of relationship should only refer to their Nanny. There can be an element of partnership in this situation, but it is a partnership which the mother, though her presence is no doubt felt during infancy, does not fully enter into until later on. And this is tacitly acknowledged by the kind of thing ascribed to her influence: love of poetry, interest in art or gardening and so on.

A great many examples could be given of this situation. Peter Eyre is one; Baroness Budberg is another—and she is also interesting because she is a further example of the quite extensive inroads the Nanny had made into the aristocracy of Imperial Russia around 1900.

Baroness Budberg's father was convinced, because it was the fashion then among the aristocracy, that it was essential for his children to learn English and indeed in certain respects lead an English way of life (before then the fashion had been for things French). He was a friend of Charles Dilke and through him met Maude Gonne, a heroine of the late nineteenth-century Irish Movement. The Baroness's father asked Maude Gonne where he could get an English Nanny and she suggested her niece.

Margaret Wilson, then aged about thirty-five, came when Baroness Budberg was born in 1892 and never left. She brought her up, with the aid of swarms of Russian nursery-maids and governesses, and then brought up all her children, finally dying in Esthonia in 1939. Baroness Budberg called her Ducki, her children called her Micki.

Although she was Irish, one of the striking things about Ducki's character, apparently, was its 'Englishness'. She was pretty, but it was a severe prettiness. There was always something rather spinsterish about her, something self-contained and prudish. Long after the Baroness had grown up and had several children, Ducki would be deeply shocked if she had more than one glass of wine. She had few, indeed no, friends and did not seem to need them, and during all the years she was with the Budbergs only went home once for a few weeks. She was strict and she was given to sulking. Like Nanny Marks she used to say, "Why do you make it so hard for me?"

But this blackmail method only works if you are loved. And it was plain that Baroness Budberg and all her children had all adored Ducki. Her strictness was always fair. She was very sweet, patient and kind. The great thing about her was she wasn't clever (she never really learnt Russian for example; all the Budbergs learnt Irish/English before their own language); this meant she was on a child's level. You could approach her. Baroness Budberg remembered with horror a 'clever' Russian nursery-maid. There was also something warm about her. She loved the Baroness feeding her own children to such an extent that she made her suckle her son for eleven months.

Amazingly for one so basically a spinster, Ducki had been married and had two children. Indeed she had originally accepted what must have been a rather frightening offer to go to Russia in order to send money home to them. One gathered, said the Baroness Budberg, from references to horrible and unfaithful men that her husband had behaved badly. She had no known love affairs or even attachments during the forty-seven years she was with them, though there was one situation which, but for Ducki's equable temperament, might have become fraught. As usual, the house was full of temporary governesses and tutors. That year there was a music teacher, a Russian governess, an English governess, a German governess and a tutor for the Baroness's brother. The Russian governess was a very big, powerful woman, who was extremely masterful. She became violently attracted to Ducki, an obsession which grew through the summer. She had increasingly furious, jealous rows with the other governesses. There were hysterics and storms of passionate tears. Moods of deep gloom. But luckily Ducki was calm and good-tempered about it and eventually, as they all did, the Russian governess left.

Ducki remained. She became an indissoluble and indispensable part of the family—and of Baroness Budberg's character (her mother also played an important part and the Baroness was interesting about it; but I would like to return to this later in the chapter). People used to say, especially in later years, that the only person she would obey or listen to was Ducki. There was no strain between them. For instance, Ducki had no settled wages. When she wanted money she asked for it and Baroness Budberg gave it. But she never seemed to spend money even when the Baroness's mother left her five hundred roubles (about five thousand pounds). Presumably she sent it to Ireland (one son died in the Boer War, but the daughter is still alive in County Mayo and writes to Baroness Budberg).

So indispensable did she become, so much a part of the furniture of the family (a recurring image in this history) that she even did things with them which she didn't really enjoy, like going abroad. The Baroness's father used to use her for smuggling banned books on these occasions—a practice which made her nervous. Once, as they came through the customs, the books fell with terrible thumpings from their places of concealment. The memory made Baroness Budberg roar with laughter. It was an absurd conjunction. Ducki could not only not read Russian, she hardly read at all. She would certainly never have read banned books.

Just before the revolution in 1917, realising that things were getting dangerous, the Baroness sent all her children with Ducki to their estates in Esthonia. Apart from trips to Europe, Ducki remained there for the rest of her life. As she got older, she gradually grew more crotchety, especially as the Budbergs were no longer rich. Long letters arrived complaining about expenses and new house-keepers. Once she got into trouble because a letter Baroness Budberg had written her, asking if she had enough butter, sugar and so on, was intercepted by the communist police. There was a well-known spy at the time called Paul Dukes. The police assumed the letter was written to him, sugar, butter and lard being code-names. Ducki soon dealt with them. She died in 1939,

Baroness Budberg and her daughter hanging on to the telephone in London crying.

I could give a great many other examples of this sort, all different except for the crucial common factor of the Nanny being the mother for the first five to ten years, and thereby gaining a fundamental emotional foothold which was never lost. But I should like to consider just one more because it introduces a role which we will look at more closely later, namely, the Nanny as Bard.

Alison Cunningham was born in the Fife village of Tarryburn in 1822. In 1851 she came to look after Robert Louis Stevenson, when he was eighteen months old, and set the foundations for a love which was to last all his life. She brought him up firmly but fairly, and represented all the warmth and security we have come to recognise. Stevenson was extremely delicate as a baby and little boy and Cunny, which was what he called her, nursed him through long illnesses. "She was more patient than I can suppose of an angel," he wrote. "Hours together she would help to console me in my paroxysms." And he wrote in a letter to her years later—"Do not suppose that I shall ever forget those long, bitter nights when I coughed and coughed and was so unhappy. My dear old nurse, God will make good to you all the good you have done, and mercifully forgive you all the evil."

His feelings about this aspect of her devotion are summed up in the dedicatory lines of *A Child's Garden of Verses* which were addressed to her.

> For the long nights you lay awake
> And watched for my unworthy sake:
> For your most comfortable hand
> That led me through the uneven land:
> For all the story books you read:
> For all the pains you comforted:
> For all you pitied, all you bore,
> In sad and happy days of yore:
> My second Mother, my first Wife,
> The angel of my infant life—
> From the sick child now well and old,
> Take Nurse, the little book you hold!
> And grant it, Heaven, that all who read
> May find as dear a Nurse at need,
> And every child who lists my rhyme,
> In the bright, fireside, nursery clime,
> May hear it in as kind a voice
> As made my childish days rejoice!

We are, as I have said, becoming familiar with the love and gratitude quite understandably felt for these 'second Mothers'. But from another point of view, perhaps the most interesting line in the verse is "For all the story books you read". Because there can be little doubt that Cunny was a powerful influence on Stevenson's literary development. She had, he said later, a natural and greedy pleasure in words, gloating over their sounds and shapes. She recited to him for hours: hymns, psalms, bible stories and especially appalling tales of the suffering and death of the Scottish Covenanters. Deeply and puritanically religious, she had a strong, superstitious, gloomy and imaginative Scottish mind. She was steeped in Bunyan. One of her set-piece descriptions was of 'the killing time', when the scarlet coated dragoons went hallooing through the heather, hunting down and hacking the Covenanters to death. Their walks together, little Stevenson beside his giant Scottish Nurse, usually ended in the cemetery. And as they walked, she would imprint on him her view of the Devil—which was a fierce and deeply personal one—or tell him frightful stories of the Resurrection Man, scaring him to death. That fascination with the macabre, the grotesque, the supernatural, which is woven throughout Stevenson's work, derives from these sessions with Cunny. One can see her influence in characters like Thrawn Janet, Dr. Jekyll and Mr. Hyde, blind Pugh and Long John Silver.

But there was a further side to Cunny—she was tempted by the demon of narrative. Stevenson could not read until he was seven, and she loved reading to him the penny serials written for Victorian servants. Together they would follow the fortunes of beautiful daughters, wicked baronets, honest fathers and pure lovers. If the moral was strong Cunny would read on avidly; but if the aim was too blatantly to entertain she would fight desperately against the terrible lure of story-telling. The reading would stop. It was a resolve they could only half keep. "Yet neither she nor I were wholly stoical," wrote Stevenson, "and when Sunday came round, we would study the windows of the stationer and try to fish out of the subsequent woodcuts and their legends the further adventures of our favourites." It seems reasonable to suggest that the superb narrative drive which Stevenson later developed, that love of story, had its origins in, or was at least stimulated by, these experiences. A narrative drive common to all his work and which, when combined with the Scottish covenanting side of his Nurse, produced the fine novels *Catriona, Master of Ballantrae* and *Kidnapped* (which has in fact a hunt through heather much like 'killing time').

Stevenson never forgot or lost touch with Alison Cunningham. In

1894 hearing she was ill, he wrote to her, signing himself "Your laddie, with all love, Robert Louis Stevenson". But in fact he fell ill himself and died a few weeks later. Cunny survived her 'Lew' nineteen years, dying in 1913 aged ninety-three.

NANNY AS MOTHER (2):
HER DEATH, HER LOYALTY, HER LOVE,
HER ROLE AS BUFFER

Once having entered the family as mother, Nannies took on, as far as the children went, many other prerogatives. The children were always 'their' children: "She was my third child", "One of my children came to see me today." This acknowledgement of an ersatz relationship, which can sound rather odd to our ears, was freely admitted by 'their' children and indeed the real mothers themselves. One correspondent, after detailing at some length the remotest ramifications of her family history, said about her Nanny (aged ninety-one): "So you see in my parent's descendants alone, she has five children, nine grandchildren and eight great-grand-children. As my eldest granddaughter is now fifteen, Nur (which was what they called their Nanny) may have a great-great-grandchild before she is a hundred!"

But there are a number of other more or less profound developments which either devolve from, or show further how fundamental was this central situation. One of these is the grief at the death of the Nanny. Even now, you can see from time to time in *The Times* or *Telegraph* the death recorded of "Miss Xxxx Xxxxx, beloved Nanny to the Xxxxx family." There have been obituaries to Nannies.

Often in my interviews people said how much they had loved their mothers "as well, of course". Yet it was noticeable that nearly always the mother's death was passed over almost without comment. It was the death of their Nanny which had affected them. There have been instances of this in some of the examples I have already given. Anne Talbot described how when her Nanny (whom she called, by her Christian name because she had first come as nursery-maid in 1899), Blanche Hannah was dying in 1928, all the children rushed round to the hospital, followed rather reluctantly by Anne's parents. When she died the children were deeply upset, especially Anne's brother who had been brought up by her from birth and called her Nanny. Anne Talbot was twenty-eight at this time. This grief was sometimes very sudden. I think the elderly man who broke down while describing the death of his Nanny to me was taken by surprise. He had not known, or had forgotten, how much he had loved her. And it is a grief whose expression and depth is common throughout our period. Only language alters, sometimes laying it on a bit thick as we go back in time. Here, for instance, is E. F. Benson, in his book *Mother*, describing the death of Beth who had been both his Nurse and his mother's.

> All her life she had given love, and all her life she had received it: there was never so blest and joyful a sojourning in the world which had never been a vale of woe to her . . . she had followed one instinct and that was devotion to her children; knew one law, and that was love.
>
> And then, rather suddenly, one night came the final failure of her forces, and the last face she saw and smiled at in the candle-light was mother's whom, seventy years before, she had first taken in her arms.
>
> There was my mother by her now, not in Beth's arms, but Beth was in hers; and just as Beth had leaned over her, listening to her first breaths, so now my mother listened to those quiet final respirations. There was no struggle at all, no wrestling with an enemy. Beth missed a breath and clung a little closer to my mother's arms, and then she turned her face towards the beloved of her heart, and died. . . . Out of the house which she had blessed with her love she was triumphantly borne, and she lies now, the little that was mortal of her, in the churchyard at Horsted-Keynes, Elizabeth Cooper, aged ninety-two, and of a spirit quite ageless.

As mother, the Nanny's identification with her family was total. It was 'our house', 'our carriage', 'we're going on holiday next week'. And her loyalty was total too. She defended her family and her charges against everyone and anyone—frequently in the face of reason. Someone observed that one of Archbishop Benson's children squinted. The Nanny said, "All babies squint." "He doesn't squint." And "He'll get over it." Often they were fearless in the face of considerable danger. During the Civil War in Spain the English Nanny of Paquitto Santo Domingo hung the English flag out of the window of their house and declared that it was British territory. She was successful and both Paquitto and his possessions were saved.

And not just danger. Nannies could be fearless in the face of death. *Fanny* by E. M. Almedingen is a delightful account of the Russian family of Poltoratzky in the late '40s and early '50s of the last century. They had an English Nanny called Gibson. She is old and deeply devoted to the whole family, a firm, kind, stable, loving woman. She is also, as she shows when put to the test, extremely brave.

Their house in Moscow is set on fire by an arsonist in the middle of the night one winter. They are all rushed out and stand on the hard-beaten snow in the streets.

At that moment my mother, a thick grey shawl over her head, seized Gibson's hand.

"Nanny, where's my baby, my Olga?"

"Pasha's got her, Madam."

But Pasha had not. For a second we stood rooted. Then my mother rushed towards the front door, but Gibson was quicker. We could see her flying up the stairs, whorls of thick smoke curling all about her. Then she vanished and my mother cried out:

"Let me go, Serge, let me go . . ."

But my father held her back.

Those were minutes, yet even to us children they seemed eternities. We dared not look across the hall. Then my father said quietly:

"She is coming back. She has got baby—"

We dared and raised our heads. Gibson had reached the first landing just in time. The railings on the top were blazing. She got down into the hall, shawl and cap off her head, her hair scorched. Almost blindly, she handed little Olga to my mother, saying hoarsely:

"She isn't hurt, M'm, she isn't hurt—but those rooms were ablaze—"

She shivered and would have fallen if my father and Kuzina had not caught her in time. And from that moment Gibson ceased to be a hireling. My father and Miss Jardine settled her in the first sledge. I heard Kuzina mutter to Masozuissa:

"That Nanny should get St. George's Cross for what she has done."

This loyalty was also evident in struggles with other servants. I want to keep a full examination of this until later when I go more deeply into the status and position of the Nanny and shall have to describe the ruthless and vicious power battles which raged behind the green baize doors (and frequently burst through them) in Victorian and Edwardian households. But there is an interesting variation in this theme in *Christmas with the Savages* by Mary Clive. This is an account of an Edwardian Christmas (loosely based on actual Christmases at Middleton in North Oxfordshire, with the Pakenham, Rhys and Villiers families) which Evelyn, the eight-year-old heroine spends with Lady Tamerlane and her grandchildren. There are three sets of grandchildren: the Glens, the Savages and the 'Howliboos'. Their Nannies are called Nana Glen ("Save your breath to cool your porridge"), Nana Savage and Nana Howliboo. The father of the Howliboos is the most important, and Nana Howliboo therefore thinks that she should be in charge of the vast nursery wing, seething with children, babies and nursery-maids. But Nana Glen has been coming there for longest and thinks that she should be. A power struggle breaks out, but it frequently takes the form of defending their own charges against the other Nanny or winning for them extra privileges. Nana Savage is for some reason totally apathetic and so Rosamond, one of the Savage children, takes on her role. She not only fights for the Savage interest, taking a share of green ivy and so on; but, which is interesting, fights for Nana Savage as well, having to deal with Nana Howliboo on her behalf. It is a delightful book, gay and rumbustious and shows how riotous and enjoyable the nursery world could be. There is a fine (and rare) portrait of a bullied Nanny who is treated by Evelyn, as she puts it, like mud. There are examples of the strange stories Nannies used to tell. Nana Savage said that her sister was stolen by gypsies and found in a quarry with only her chemise on.

One of the most striking things in *Simpson* is her love for Salathiel. But it is striking not just because of its power but because it supposes a peculiarly penetrating piece of observation by Sackville-West. I do not think it is something one could have guessed. That is the 'fixing' of the Nanny on to one of her children. Time and again I noticed that a Nanny nearly always had one child she remembered above all others. Many of the Nannies I talked to had looked after as many as fifty or sixty charges in their long years of service. But of all these, one always remained clearer and dearer than the rest. There was no particular rule about it. It wasn't the first necessarily, or the last, or the first they'd 'had from the month'. It was more as though at some stage in their emotional development they had reached a point where they needed to crystallise the up till then diffused maternal love which was their driving force. Perhaps a point when their desire to have a child of their own and the realisation that they never would reached their height together. It was then rather like imprinting in reverse. They suddenly locked on to the child they were looking after at that moment.

It seems likely that Anne Talbot's Nanny, Blanche Hannah, did this with Anne's brother. Nanny Watson, the screen Nanny Wynne-Tyson produced for me, had plainly fixed on to Elizabeth Briggs (or Swithinbank as she then was). Nanny Watson must then have been about forty to forty-five (this is early '20s) and had had numerous charges including, as she had with Elizabeth, children from birth. She said that leaving her children was always very painful, but that leaving Elizabeth was terrible. It had precipitated a nervous breakdown from which it took some time to recover. And it was with Elizabeth Briggs that Nanny Watson, now aged ninety and a fascinating figure to whom we will return, was ending her days. Or there was Nanny B who, some nine years into her career, went to the W's and looked after, particularly, their daughter Jane. She described how Jane had been her favourite child and how she could not bear leaving her. She remembered Jane coming to see her with a strict, even unkind, governess and how painful it was when the governess slapped Jane to prevent her bouncing on the sofa. They continued seeing each other regularly through the years and Nanny B promised that, when Jane had a baby, she would come and Nanny it. Finally, this moment arrived and Jane W wrote to her. Unfortunately, the call came while Nanny B was looking after a little boy aged two. It was a crucial moment in his life, and though she longed to go to her child Jane, she couldn't leave the boy. He needed her too much. Jane W was bitterly wounded and has since refused to see or speak to Nanny B, much upsetting her.

Now this small anecdote is interesting for three reasons. It illustrates the, to us, curious practice (though perfectly understandable if you are Nanny-orientated) of handing your own Nanny/mother on to be your children's Nanny/mother, even though you are the real mother. It shows how perceptive Sackville-West was in making Simpson follow Childeric even though she loved Salatheil best. Despite the reverse imprinting I have described, it was always the latest charge or the child that needed her most, that was most important to a Nanny. And finally it introduces us to another major role of the Nanny as mother. Because the crisis through which Nanny B's little boy was passing was the divorce of his parents.

Throughout our period, but particularly towards its end, the children of upper class families have been protected from many of the tensions and disruptions of family life by the calm buffers of their Nannies. Rows may convulse their parents' bedroom, the most flagrant infidelities take place there, furious silences be maintained for months, finally the marriage may burst asunder in acrimonious divorce. The children are unaware that anything is in the slightest degree wrong. Nothing penetrates the serene calm of the nursery. Nanny allows no hint of discord past her door. Lady L-M had three marriages, as well as several affairs, in six years—all stormy, the last ones inflamed by alcohol. Fortunately, she only had two children, Jonathan and Celia from the first marriage. And Nanny. The children sailed happily from house to house under the calm captaincy of Nanny, untroubled by, indeed ignorant of, their mother's riotous behaviour. They are now aged sixteen and fourteen (Nanny is still with them) and seem to have been quite unaffected by it.

Miss N wrote and told me how when she was Nanny to three boys the parents quarrelled, divorced, and then both refused to have any further responsibility for their children. Miss N had to bring them up single-handed, arrange their schools and see them through them. And apart from divorce, many people described to me how it was not until years later that they discovered their parents had had terrible rows, from which they were insulated by their Nanny. This whole phenomena—the Nanny saving the children from family discord—does seem to become more common as the period progressed, but this could just be that marital troubles have been a fashionable topic for a number of years and that it is easier to obtain evidence about them. Of course married couples had rows in Victorian times as well. P. W. H. Hutchinson (aged eighty-four when I spoke to him) said that he could remember at the age of five standing outside his parents' bedroom and hearing them shout at each other inside. After a short while, his Nanny discovered him there, picked him up briskly and marched back to the nursery. He asked her what they had been shouting about. "Your mother and father are going to take part in a play," said his Nanny. "They are rehearsing and learning their lines." Mr. Hutchinson said he accepted this at the time, but that he remembers wondering why this play was never mentioned and where and when it was to be performed. Or plays rather—because rehearsals, though only rarely overheard, continued for many years. He only discovered the truth when he had grown up.

This role of the Nanny as buffer was particularly valuable during a war. Nannies seemed to have had a particular aptitude for war. Partly it is because, concentrated entirely on the nursery, the lesser realities of battles, invasions, aerial and artillery bombardment and destruction, defeat or victory, life or death, failed to disturb them. And partly, no doubt, because they had had practice enough in the long and fierce campaigns waged against other servants and other Nannies. But it was as Nannies pure and simple that they did most good. One of the saddest sights in the Second World War were the evacuees. Droves of little children shivering in the stations of London and other major cities that were targets for bombs. They were scattered all over the country and, since they went without their parents, often suffered severely. This did not happen to upper class children. They simply moved out of the cities with their Nannies, and were as emotionally secure as though they had remained at home.

An interesting variant of this occurred in the case of Miss Virginia Johnstone. Her Nanny, Elsie Beeny, came when Virginia was three weeks old. She was (and is still at sixty-five) a lively energetic woman, the daughter of a picture-framer and gilder from Dover. When the Second World War broke out Virginia Johnstone was going to a day school run by Miss Faunce in London. The school moved to Wimborne St. Giles in Dorset, to the home of Lord Shaftesbury. From here Miss Faunce, desperate for staff, wrote to all the parents asking if any of them had a Nanny they would be willing to send with their child. Six came (or seven if you include a French Governess, who was extremely neurotic and unsuitable and soon left); among them Nanny Beeny, or Nanny Johnstone as she now came to be called.

At first the situation was prickly. Grand Nannies refused to speak to less grand Nannies (it was here that the Nanny who should have been called Nanny Laurence insisted on being called Nanny Hailsham, because her charge was half-sister to the Hoggs). But the difficult ones were weeded out. Soon a solid core of three remained: Nanny Johnstone, Nanny Maud, Nanny Tritton. Miss Johnstone endeavoured to describe them to me, but her memories were extremely imprecise. The Nannies, their appearance and characters, somehow merged comfortably together, all sharpness of outline lost in a blur of cardiganed cosiness. They became known collectively as 'the Nannies' and lived together, apart from the rest of the school. They had their own sitting-room where they played rummy on Saturday nights. They ate at a separate table, and wore Nanny clothes. They never came to evening prayers except on Sundays. Then they always came. They were always late. Virginia Johnstone remembered how at the end of term or on expeditions, everyone would be waiting in the buses. "Where are the Nannies?" They would be found finishing some small, flustering, tidying job. They became part of the prospectus. Many parents sent their children to Miss Faunce's because of the Nannies.

Their job was in essence Nannying. The girls—aged from seven to sixteen—were divided into families of twenty and slept four or five to a room, in one of which a Nanny slept. They helped dress, washed clothes, did plaits, got everyone ready for this or that. Organisation was haphazard. There were no lists or noticeboards. The will of the Nannies somehow became known. They were also in charge of health. There was no sick-room where a child could be isolated and if any of the children had measles or 'flu or chicken pox they were just put to bed in their own room. Not till the outbreak had reached epidemic proportions were the sick children isolated in one or more separate rooms. Epidemics were therefore extremely common. The role of the Nannies was more comforting than disciplining. If the dormitories got completely out of control, then the

Nannies would call in the staff to restore order. Though they got on well with the staff, they were separate from them—just as in fact they were back in their own households. The children felt that the Nannies were somehow more on their, the children's, 'side'. Miss Faunce was an astute woman, and she not only retained the services of the Nannies throughout the war, but succeeded in making the respective parents continue to pay their wages. Towards the end, however, Miss Johnstone told me, Miss Faunce "went a bit potty". She used to fly into towering rages at the smallest misdemeanours. The Nannies were very good at soothing away the effects of these scenes. It was a situation they were used to. Miss Faunce had assumed, in effect, the position of a difficult parent. During the holidays the Nannies returned with their charges to their own houses. It is hardly surprising that Miss Johnstone said she passed an extremely secure and enjoyable war.

NANNY AS MOTHER (3):
CHILDREN RESEMBLING NANNY; USELESSNESS
OF MOTHERS

There are two other effects, more superficial than the ones we have been looking at, which also flow from the Nanny as mother. The first of these is the way in which people often came to resemble their Nannies. I do not mean this in any fundamental sense. As far as that goes, I think there can be no doubt that in terms of security, confidence (or lack of it), sexual orientation and all the deeper character traits which I shall discuss fully in chapter 7 and which have already appeared and will continue to appear throughout this book, many, if not most, upper class children owed more to their Nannies than to their mothers. But the resemblances were often surface ones as well—tricks of speech, styles of dress and so on. Blanche Hannah, Anne Talbot's Nanny, had a very marked and direct way of speaking. For instance, when Anne Talbot was young she was very shy, very fat, and had a very red face. Blanche Hannah used to say of it— "Looks like a tom-tit on a round of beef." Yet this country directness— or the directness so described—is very marked in Anne Talbot herself. Or Peter Eyre's fine head of hair, plainly brushed down and out to this day, must be entirely due to Nanny Robertson. Mrs. D-G told me she could never understand why her mother, whose own mother had had impeccable taste, always decorated her houses in such a different, and really less attractive way. She described it as Woolworth's decoration. It was only when visiting her old Nanny one day (a Nanny she had shared with her mother) that she suddenly realised that her mother's taste in interior decorating was the same as her Nanny's.

Perhaps the oddest example of this effect is one which makes me wonder —though of course such a thing is impossible—whether there was not some truth after all in the old superstition that a baby imbibed something of the wet nurse's character along with her milk. When Gerald Brenan was born in 1894 he had, he writes, "a yellow, wrinkled face like a Chinese baby, long, straight, black hair and for many weeks I screamed day and night when I was not sleeping. The reason for this, I imagine, was that my mother was too ill to nurse me. Since baby foods had not been invented and nobody seems to have thought of a wet nurse, a she-ass which had recently been foaled was procured to give me her milk." Mother and son, he goes on, continued to do badly. It was decided to return from Malta, where he'd been born, to England. They get on a P & O steamer and his wet nurse and her foal are established in a cabin close to that of his mother and him.

My mother has often described to me the horrors of this voyage. We ran into a storm off the coast of Portugal, everyone was very sick and the cabin filled with cockroaches. Since I could not keep down my milk and lay in a coma, the doctor was sent for. He arrived reeling drunk and breathing out fumes of whisky. "Madam," he pronounced in a thick voice after a long, dazed stare at my cot, "Madam, you're washting your time in shending for me. Our lasht voyage out we had a baby that looked like this. Jusht put it through the porthole." However, thanks to my nurse's care, I got through the next few days and we landed at Plymouth. But here a new difficulty arose. The railway officials refused to convey a she-ass in one of their compartments unless a whole carriage was reserved. This at great expense was done and we reached Liverpool and finally Belfast without being separated.

How long this relationship continued he doesn't tell us, though he says that his grandmother was so delighted with the oddity of the journey that she proposed that the foal of his wet nurse should be brought up in the nursery with him. Yet like so many suckled by animals—Mowgli, Romulus and Remus—there is something magical about Gerald Brenan. His energy, his youth and his extraordinary quickness of mind are phenomenal. And it is true that he has always possessed that determination, that refusal to be moved from a course once decided on, which is traditionally associated with the donkey. It is this determination which enabled him to forge out a life of his own in Spain and write the quite outstanding books he has done. And the resemblance is there in quite small things.

When I visited him in his new house in 1971 he was busy planting his garden, though not with flowers. He was planting thistles.

Finally, since the Nanny was mother, mothers became incapable of looking after little children themselves. Whenever Nanny had a day off, or evening off, supposing there were not nursery-maids to take over, panic set in. One Nanny wrote and told me that she went away once and when she returned she found that the mother had sat up all night in a fever of anxiety, prodding her two-month-old son every ten minutes to see if he was still alive. But the almost invariable practice was to engage a relief Nanny. Not for an instant could mothers be left to cope with those incomprehensible creatures, their children. Miss Virginia Johnstone told me with pride, even awe, that when her Nanny had a day off her mother had looked after her. All her friends had had relief Nannies. And this situation goes back into Victorian times, even at one time involving the Queen herself.

Queen Victoria had a harsh childhood. "I was extremely crushed and kept under and hardly dared say a word," she said later. Her mother, the Duchess of Kent, was the chief architect of this crushing, though she was no doubt assisted by the Nurse, because when this woman died Queen Victoria plainly did not feel the tender emotion she might have done. "Received news of the death of my poor old nurse Mrs. Brock, which took place the day before yesterday. She was a pleasant person, and undoubtedly had, as everybody has, her faults, but she was extremely attached to, and fond of, me, having been with me from my birth until my fifth year, therefore it is impossible, and it would be very wrong, if I did not feel her death."

But, though strict with them later, Queen Victoria loved her own children when they were little and followed their progress closely. She saw more of them than many Nannied parents after her and used to take them on expeditions with her. One of these, to the Duke of Wellington at Walmer, involving the Prince of Wales and Princess Royal, is amusingly described by Lady Lyttelton. She was in distant charge of the Royal Nurseries; the functionaries were Mrs. Sly for the Prince of Wales and Mrs. Packer for the Princess Royal.

> They were met [wrote Lady Lyttelton] by immense crowds, and it was extremely fatiguing owing to the continual cheering, and all the excitement of wreaths and bonfires and triumphal arches, church bells and chorus all the way along, escort panting, horses foaming and carriages swaying with speed. The children will grow up under the strangest delusions as to what travelling means, and the usual condition of the people of England!

At one point Lady Lyttelton told Mrs. Sly to hold the Prince of Wales up higher so that the people could see him better. But immediately a fat lady seized the little boy, almost tore him from Mrs. Sly's arms and gave him a huge kiss. "Mrs. Sly has not yet cooled down, her rage was such at being taken by surprise."

However, disaster struck on the return from the expedition. Mrs. Sly had fallen ill, and by some appalling blunder the enormous retinue of nursery-maids, maids of honour, everybody's servants, the luggage and the children's things had all been put on to a separate train. When the Queen, Lady Lyttelton and Lady Finch took the two children on to the royal train at Windsor they found to their horror that they were in sole charge of them. Both under three, the children sensed at once they were in the hands of people who hadn't the faintest idea how to control them. They were seized with a wild madness. They rushed all over the carriage, crawled, scrambled, climbed, were caught, escaped, spilt things, broke things, poked things, shrieked and screamed and yelled. The Queen became irritated, then furious, finally exhausted, despairing and helpless. The children too became tired and cross and were then "squally and cried for hours". By the time they eventually arrived, the entire Royal party were complete wrecks.

THE NANNY–MOTHER PARTNERSHIP

There is one last aspect of the Nanny as mother which we must examine and it is possibly the most important of all. That is where Nanny and mother form a partnership and bring up the children together.

A combination of Freud's immense intellectual dominance and the particular family set-up which has evolved in Western Europe and America over the past few hundred years makes most people suppose that one mother (or mother-figure) and father with family, provided all is secure, stable and loving, is the ideal environment in which to bring up a child. This is by no means certain.

One of the most interesting suggestions in psychiatry today is that the central Freudian situation—the love of the son for the mother and his rivalry with his father; the love of the daughter for the father and rivalry with her mother—is in fact only a behavioural response to one particular, and peculiar, form of family arrangement. If you have a situation where there are several 'mothers' all performing the same duties, or if you have one dominant mother-figure for a large number of children, helped by assistants, that is if you have some form of what is called 'multiple mothering', or extended family, then you radically alter the family set-up. And it has been found that if you alter the type of family organisation which gave rise to the Freudian pattern, the Freudian pattern disappears. The suggestion is that the Oedipean reaction, so far from being integral to human nature as Freud believed, is only so when that nature is subjected to certain stresses.

The family, especially in the close form we have now, can be extremely stressful. With only the parents and one or two brothers and sisters, intense emotions are generated: desperate sibling rivalries, violent loves and hates for both parents, over-strong feelings of neglect or favouritism. The pressure and strain on the parents can be considerable too. If there are several figures giving love—mother, Nanny, nursery-maid, game-keeper, what have you—the intensity of these emotions is lessened, conflicts can be avoided. It seems likely that children are able to spread their emotional needs in a much more catholic way than we have become used to thinking. Certainly, some studies in multiple mothering on an Israeli kibbutz, which I shall go into later, suggest this.

Now this is all obviously very germane to a discussion of Nannies. At its best, the Nanny situation was a particular form of multiple mothering. The ideal of this form was very difficult to achieve. Nanny Ellis said, "It's a mistake for a Nanny to get too attached to a child. That causes jealousy on the part of the mother, which results in constant changes. It's the difficult mothers who have difficulty in keeping a Nanny." Jealousy and rivalry were of course the great stumbling blocks. Nanny N described to me a family in Holland where three Nannies had left because they could not have full control, but how eventually she managed a partnership with the mother and stayed.

Perhaps the ideal situation, at least as I see it, where the mother is the most important figure in the child's early life, but is closely assisted and helped by a Nanny, is only possible today—when Nannies have virtually disappeared. Today, at least some upper class mothers have an inkling of their responsibilities to their children, and are prepared to do something about it; and today they can, though still rarely, find Nannies who understand the importance of the mother's role and can relinquish authority.

Lady Antonia Fraser's household is a good example. It is mixed, flowing, rumbustious. She always has very young Nannies of sixteen or seventeen because, she says, they do not usurp her position. She is probably also harking back to her love for Jean. Lady Antonia looks after them during the early years (they never leave her till they are one) while the girls, called by their Christian names, do the chores. It is a large household and a shared one; there is a sense of something happening all the time, of shared affections and activities. If a child can't find love or sympathy with one of the girls or his mother, there is always someone else to go to. There can never be that sense that the whole world is desolate; somewhere, in the kitchen or with the new girl, there is hope. I often think it is no accident that one of the great explosions of English energy and hope took place in Elizabethan times, when large rambling and rumbustious households like this were usual.

The Nana in *Peter Pan* is another example. There is little more one can say about her, except of course that she is a dog. It is, apart from her species, a conventional portrait of a nursery-maid assisting the mother. I think, in fact, for a play written at such a highly facetious level, Barrie makes commendably little play with Nana. Only in one scrap of dialogue does he give way to temptation:

> *Mr. Darling* (depressed): I sometimes think, Mary, that it is a mistake to have a dog as a nurse.
> *Mrs. Darling*: George, Nana is a treasure.
> *Mr. Darling*: No doubt, but I have an uneasy feeling sometimes that she looks upon the children as puppies.
> *Mrs. Darling* (rather faintly): Oh no, dear one, I'm sure she knows they have souls.

But to return to the relationship of mother–Nanny–child, I may well be wrong in asserting the primacy in such a triangle of the mother. I am as influenced as anyone by the Freudian dominated *mores* of our time. Or perhaps, if not wrong, then unnecessarily idealistic. Children can survive, if crippled, backgrounds of appalling cruelty. We shall look at these. And they can get sufficient love and security in a vast variety of ways. It is this variety, these different routes, which are interesting; not the search for the single perfect one.

And, of course, it is precisely this, these different routes, but always with or via a Nanny, that we have in fact been examining in this chapter. Both Nabokov and Gerald Brenan had very close relationships with their mothers to which Brenan's Nana provided a warm additional security, and Nabokov's succession of women not much more perhaps, though no less, than the remembered and comforting gleam of golden syrup. Baroness Budberg said almost precisely what I have said; that it is possible for children to have numerous important love relations, and that she had one with her mother and another with her Nanny, Ducki.

Peter Eyre defined the areas of his relationship. His feeling towards his Nanny was strong but gentle. It was not a close passion. The fact that she was a servant may have had something to do with it. And she was, like a lot of Nannies, distant too. "There was an air," he said, "of cool it about her. Nanny Robertson would ask what I'd done, but she wasn't actually interested in the details of my acting. She just wanted to know I was all right. She would have liked to hear I was married, but wouldn't have particularly liked to see my wife—at least not more than once."

And in fact some of the very signs which earlier we saw reveal that the true balance of emotional dependence was heaviest on the Nanny, can also reveal the opposite. Frances Partridge said that her mother was often known by her initials—N.A.M.—and that when her Nanny, whom they called Nan, died, there was a mistake in the telegram so that it read "Nam died last night". For a day she was completely grief-stricken. Then she found out the truth and her relief was immense.

Frances Partridge wrote a long account of her Nanny, which is not only interesting for the reason above ("My mother and father are the people I dreamt about," she said. "I seldom dreamt about Nan") it is also a delightful and penetrating description which sums up many of the aspects of the Nanny we have looked at.

Lizzie Croucher was her extraordinary name, but she was always called 'Nan', even by my mother and father who would never have thought of her as their children's nanny, but always as a nurse. She came to look after my eldest brother when he was a baby in 1888 and remained in charge of our well-spaced-out family of six almost until her death. I was the youngest, so there was no one to supplant me in the honours and pleasure of sharing her bedroom. I used to lie in bed, snug and warm, and watch the fascinating ritual of her getting-up. There was never a flash of nudity, but every morning she magically got herself into a bodice and stays and long frilled drawers, and then put over them two flannel petticoats—one red and one royal blue. After that she brushed out her long, straight, pale mouse hair, plaited it tightly and fastened it in a small knot behind her head. (It was so fine and silky that she once made excellent substitute paintbrushes for us out of snippings from it when we had run out on a wet day in the nursery.) These red and blue petticoats gave one a warm feeling of reassurance, and so did her appearance. She was tiny, and therefore halfway between an adult and a child; with a pale face and a small round head like the top of a ninepin. Spiritually she was a natural object, a tree in the garden, something taken absolutely for granted and relied upon, someone who was always there in the nursery mending stockings, and who had a way of dealing with bawls, bangs, or knots in crochet that was probably purely instinctive, but worked. I can't remember any disagreeable or over-acute emotions attaching to her, not even jealousy; for although I'm sure she had her favourites—my eldest brother (her 'baby') and my sister Ray I think—her total devotion to all six of us completely rose above any tickings-off for bad behaviour or awareness of our failings. She was aware of them (I was 'spoilt blackberry jam') but accepted them as we accepted her. There was never the fear, as with parents, that one might disappoint her or let her down. She had no standards except pragmatical ones and her morality was a golden hazy myth centring around Gentle Jesus knocking on the door (in a picture in her bed-room). I can't imagine what her attitude to sex was, and doubt if she even knew the facts of life. Nor am I sure she was altogether kind to the succession of waxen-faced nursery-maids with a tendency to fainting, who carried up coals and hot water to the nursery floor of our house in Bedford Square.

Her origins were shrouded in legends connected with a very poor Dickensian life in the East End, a brother called Bill who drank, and parents who died young. So did her young man, Harry, and I was told she was a pale thin girl of nineteen when she came to us. We loved hearing about the Coxeters, the family she had been nursemaid to. After she arrived, our family was her entire life. On her days out she visited her brother Bill and dressed herself in a coat with a cape, while a pointed bonnet like a gnome's hat trimmed with jet and artificial flowers was tied under her chin with black velvet ribbon and pinned to her head with hairpins. A new bonnet for Nan was a great event, and we couldn't bear the slightest deviation from type. She wore elastic-sided boots.

With this enormously reassuring and benevolent little being inhabiting the nursery we ought to have had few childhood fears. But I certainly did, and I was much more likely to tell Nan about them than my kind and passionately loved Mother. (The only worry I told my mother about was that on my first day at school, wearing a crimson jersey and brown skirt, I had been teased as being 'a leg of mutton with blood running out at the top'. She laughed and I never forgave her. Nan would never have done that.) She somehow got me over my terror of going down the drain with the gurgling bath water (when I believed its mahogany lid would drop from its leaning position against the wall and shut me in, as into my coffin). And of having a black animal with big teeth called 'Aertex'. And of going downstairs to the drawing-room after tea in my white silk frock, because of the 'bogies' lurking on every landing. She cured me of these fears without making me feel ashamed of them. As for naughtiness, when she called for me to go to bed at the drawing-room door I often flew into a passion of tears, but Nan at last impressed on me that this was a fearful bore for everyone and coached me how to behave. When she called me I must 'get up at once and smile and say "Here I come, Nan" and come tripping along'. I learned my part and next evening my mother was amazed to hear me say: "Here I come Nan, here I come smiling and tripping along."

I wish I could remember all her runic sayings, like "If you want your hair to curl you must eat fried bread behind the door." (I did and it did.) And when later I slept with my next sister Eleanor she would call us with the mysterious formula: "Look at the *moon*; and the *stars*! And Eleanor's NOSE and Frances's WHISKERS" pouncing on us both with the last two, so as to rouse us thoroughly and send us into giggles. She led a rich religious life; it took very little to persuade her to sing us hymns in a high thin dragging soprano which seemed to me incredibly beautiful and moving (almost everything about her was this in some strange way) and she often talked about Jesus as though of a friend. "I dreamed of Jesus last night," she said once in the peculiar high voice dedicated to other worldly things. "He came to me carrying a beautiful blue vase, and he said 'Nan', he said, 'please clean this for Heaven.' "

As we all grew up she changed her role, and gradually became a sort of court jester or attendant sprite, often making comic or ironical comments on our life. She could always tell when Eleanor and I had been quarrelling on the way back from school, and when we asked how she knew she said: "It's the way your eyebrows draw together." Our friends became 'her girls' and 'her boys' and only once do I remember any of them losing their status, because she wanted to be called '*Miss* Anna'. Nan said: "She's not one of my girls any more." Her mantelpiece was crowded with china ornaments, presents from us and 'her girls' and 'her boys'. Except that 'rheumatiz' began to plague her I think she was extremely happy and this may have been the source of the comfort she gave us. As she grew older she seemed to grow smaller, and as we got beyond her control she began to dominate the other servants in the same quiet way she had dominated us, and trying in vain to keep up the standards which inevitably collapsed with two world wars and my father's death. His gentlemanly, if liberal and agnostic outlook, deep respect for mahogany and linen and hatred of spots and stains, was replaced by my Irish mother's more bohemian way of life and leaning to women's suffrage and socialism.

Nan was probably unaware of these changes, and still queened it over the rest of the staff. But she loved fun, and hen-like cackles or shrill screams used to emerge from the servants' hall, especially when she was teased by our handsome young chauffeur whose hair was as curly as Bubbles's.

There were marriages and children. Nan became 'gran-nan' and left off her apron for a dignified black dress with tiny buttons down the small protuberant bosom. When some of the family marriages took place in registry offices without clergy, bridesmaids or bouquets, it was Nan who had to be prevented from discovering this hideous irreligiousness. My own deviation was far the worst. What was to be done when I left home to set up 'in open sin' with no wedding ring or 'Mrs.'? Nan was an almost insuperable obstacle. She couldn't possibly swallow such a horror, so she was told I was having a quiet wedding and I was embarrassed and dismayed to be woken on my 'wedding morning' with tears and six teaspoons. Poor Nan got more and more rheumatic and finally developed *tic-douloreux*. It was the saddest sight to see her tiny white face contract as she rocked her head in her hands in spasms of terrible pain. At last, no help for it, she went to an old folks' home. Her 'children' all visited her there, where she sat among a lot of ancient figures ranged round the wall in chairs. She had quickly and quietly taken a dominant and queenly place among them, and showed us off proudly to them and them to us. It was deeply embarrassing and painful, and not long after I got a telegram to say she had died.

CONCLUSION

To conclude, then, the subject of this chapter, that is to say the good Nanny in place of or in conjunction with the mother, must plainly occupy an important place in any book on the subject. Indeed, if a great many of my correspondents had their way, she would have been the whole book. She has tended to be so in past studies. Unfortunately in future chapters our view of the Nanny will have to alter—sometimes only slightly, sometimes violently.

It is noticeable, for example, that all but one of the Nannies described (not counting the Nabokovian succession) stayed on in their families for a great many years, often for the whole of their lives. They were all kind. No attempt was made to analyse the various disciplines which were an essential part of the security they engendered. Is it feasible to try to see how many Nannies fit roughly into this category? Perhaps they were only a small minority. And besides all this, people were often extremely ambiguous in their attitudes to their Nannies. The desperate need for love and security when small, led them to imagine they had had it when they had not. Or there were confusions and resentments about the role of their mother which they tried to hide. There is an element of this ambiguity in *Simpson* which must be looked at. And there is a school of thought (though I do not belong to it myself) which would say that it often doesn't help a child to have too much sheltering when young. This school would suggest that numbers of people, particularly boys, emerging from the enveloping arms, climbing off the ample laps of their Nannies into the brutal realities of English prep schools, suffered shocks from which they never really recovered.

Nevertheless, despite these blows, including the fairly innocuous one which must result from the exploration in the next chapter of one of the wilder shores of Nannydom, the figure of the Nanny as represented by Nanny Robertson, Simpson or Nan Croucher must not suffer.

Women give birth indiscriminately. Nannies sometimes chose the career because they were fitted to it. There is not the slightest doubt that such women were often far better mothers than the mothers themselves would have been. They interrupted and so put an end to that terrible chain of passed-on instability and unhappiness. Children from broken homes break homes; those who were beaten, beat; and one of the most depressing of modern sights is the neurotic or selfish mother bringing up her children so that they will bring up their children to be neurotic or selfish, and one sees not so much the sins as the mistakes and miseries of the parents descending far beyond the seventh generation, to infinity. And good Nannies, these Nanny Robertsons and Nan Crouchers, existed throughout our period—it is a question again of the Nanny Block. The qualities of a Nanny Everest could be found, indeed, at any time up to today. It was women such as these who prompted by far the greater bulk of the 259 letters sent me. I had the impression sometimes that the minute publicity the book received (a paragraph or two in *The Times* and the *Daily Mail*; a brief appearance on Southern Television) had nevertheless thrust it like a lightning conductor into an atmosphere electric with remembered love and gratitude. For the first time it could be discharged; and was so in page after page, often in very moving words. It was women such as these, able to devote themselves to their children to a degree perhaps never possible before or since, whose love produced not just a Churchill but thousands upon thousands of secure and happy human beings. It must be remembered throughout this book that as a way of bringing up children the Nanny system, at its best, was very good indeed.

CHAPTER FIVE

Second Sexual Detour:
the Nanny as Wife, Spinster,
Mistress, Lover

William Bridges (aged four): "When I grow up Nanny I'm going to marry you. I'm going to marry you and you'll have lots and lots of babies."
Nanny: "Yes, dear, that's right."

Nannies did not just act with, or in place of the mother; sometimes of course they became wives and mothers in their own right.

Lady V-W. told me of a family she knew during the 1920s whose mother was always singularly reticent about her background. Even the father, who had married her when she was twenty-seven, knew little about it. She seemed conversant with the ways of grand houses. She was a Campbell; an Irish branch of the Campbells, she said. One day when they were all strolling in the park (the eldest child now seventeen, the youngest ten) a man of about twenty-five had rushed up to their mother, opened his arms and cried "Nanny!"

Even odder was the situation, or probable situation, that existed in a family in Westmorland before the 1914 war. Here, a correspondent told me, the mother was extremely vain. She had one child, and apparently the birth was very difficult. The mother also became obsessed with a terror of losing her looks. A Nanny was engaged, a fine buxom Westmorland girl of particularly striking Celtic appearance; dark, with high cheek-bones, where the wife was fair with a rather languid, long, mournful though lovely face. Thereafter, a curious pattern emerged. The Nanny was supposed to have periods of insanity and these always coincided with the birth of a new child. The mother would apparently become pregnant, be seen in the town once or twice in maternity clothes; then the Nanny would go off her head for a month or so, disappear, and when she had regained her sanity and returned—there would be a new baby. The first child, a girl, was long and fair like the mother; all the other children were dark (the father also had fair hair). "But," wrote my correspondent, "the Nanny always kept her place. And though, as you can imagine in a remote country district, the rumours simply flew around, no one was ever quite sure whether what seemed to be happening *was* happening."

But the usual course of events was more normal, though even here it is probably true that it was harder for a Nanny to get married than for other servants. The plain fact is that their employers didn't want them to get married. They wanted them to look after children. Nanny Williams, the Nanny who said "You've got to be a child with a child," married after fourteen years as a Nanny. She described part of her Nanny life (this is the mid-1920s) in terms reminiscent of the Thurber cartoon: "It's Perkins, sir. We're having a bit of a time below stairs." She said that the nursery-maids were the emissaries between the nursery and the kitchen, indeed the whole outside world. A nursery-maid knew all the scandal. She also knew exactly when Madame was going out and when she'd be back. So that—though of course on no account were Nannies supposed to be courting or have boyfriends or lovers or anything like that—if they did then the nursery-maid could tell them the safe time. She remembered once Madame was away and five of them were entertaining their boy-friends to tea in the nursery. All at once—there was the Lagonda flowing up the drive. She's never seen china and men move so fast. Another time, cook told Madame that Nanny had a boyfriend. Madame didn't believe it for a moment; nevertheless she pretended to go out one evening, and then concealed herself. Nanny Williams led her boyfriend up the back stairs, and horrors—there was Madame stepping out of the nursery!

As well as the natural isolation of the nursery, the long hours and the short time off, all of which must have made it difficult for Nannies to meet men, I came across a fairly large number of other instances where the mistress either subtly or blatantly impeded her Nanny's effort to get married. One bribed her Nanny to stay with an extra hundred pounds a year. Mrs. Hurrell, who it was still evident had been extremely pretty, was Nanny to Major-General Bruce-Scott when he was with the Gurkhas in India (this is again the '20s). She said she was the only young girl in the area and had a whole regiment to herself. It was all right when Mrs. Bruce-Scott was away. The Major-General wasn't so strict and she had a whale of a time. But Mrs. Bruce-Scott drew the line. Nanny was not allowed to mix with the soldiers on any account. "But I married one all the same!"

Nanny McCallum agreed that it was hard courting if you were a

Nanny, and it must have been particularly hard for her since she met her husband in Scotland while her family, the family she worked for, lived in the South of England. But she said it was impossible when you were a nursery-maid. Once you had become a Nanny at least you could regulate your own time a bit.

But, as well as natural or imposed obstacles, there was sometimes a more profound reason why Nannies did not get married. The love for their charges became very deep. They received offers of marriage but felt unable to abandon their children. This theme is slender but persistent; its melancholy note of renounced happiness runs through our period. Curzon, despite his fearful experiences at the hands of Miss Paraman, was forced to leave his children with a Nanny after his wife died. Fortunately he chose well. His daughter, Baroness Ravensdale, wrote a book called *In Many Rhythms*, where she says:

> The real prop and backbone of my life was our Nanny Sibley. To her I owe— if I possess them at all—the flowering in one of God's gifts of love and kindness to others. I reckon her sacrifice for us is an example that is unbelievable in a selfish age, and I only heard of it on her death bed, from our second nurse, Rhoda Hyslop, who since than had been a devoted Nanny to my sister Cynthia Moseley's children. My mother, in failing health as we were leaving India in 1905, asked Nanny Sibley to bring us three children back to England before marrying her fiancé in India. My mother died in 1906. Nanny Sibley never returned to her fiancé though he came to England to plead with her. She gave up her life to the three of us, and she died of cancer when I was twenty-one years old.

Noël Oakeshott, who gave me a great many interesting facts I shall have occasion to use later, told me that her Nanny had turned down an offer of marriage because she couldn't leave the current baby. Anne Talbot said that Blanche Hannah was extremely attractive. She was a Kentish girl, large, firm and finely built with particularly splendid breasts. Her brothers were all either guardsmen or policemen. Yet she loved Anne's brother so much that she turned down a great many proposals and in the end never married. I could give numerous other examples, and it is undoubtedly true that Nannies did become devoted to their children and did sacrifice their lives to them—if not getting married is judged a sacrifice.

At the same time, I can't help wondering how common this was. On the whole Nannies, like practically all women of their time and most now, can be expected to have got married if they had had the opportunity. If they didn't, it was because no one asked them or they simply didn't want to. It is true that they loved their children and didn't like to leave them—yet, as we shall see, many, if not most, did leave their children, not for any motive as fundamentally compelling as love and marriage but simply to better themselves or continue their careers. They suffered. Some had nervous breakdowns. But they left.

There are other sides to this. I often gained the impression (through reading, but particularly in interviews) that Nannies, in their attitude to sex, were on the whole inhibited, disapproving or frightened; particularly as regards themselves (about others they could be very tolerant). This is something about which one can only be extremely tentative; it is not for instance remotely possible to be statistically convincing. Yet, though I often met warm and gay Nannies, I never met one you could quite call sensuous.

Figures like Miss de Bourbel's Nanny were far more usual than their reverse. Although a warm woman—they shared a bed together and Miss de Bourbel's earliest memories are suffused with the close cuddles and enveloping safety of her Nanny's body—she had a horror of sex and dirt. She loved cleanliness and associated it with godliness and chastity, whereas sex was dirty, somehow evil. She was a virgin and relieved to be one. She used to describe how once, inadvertently, she had seen a fully grown, developed, completely naked male. It had been an appalling experience. She told Miss de Bourbel that the facts of life were to be found in the Bible.

Similarly, when one goes into the boyfriends of Nannies, they often become rather insubstantial. Like Nanny Robertson's young man, they turn out to have been driven off with a hairbrush. Simon Wilson told me that his Nanny always talked about a boyfriend who, he discovered when he grew up, she had in fact met only once. Nanny Marks had boyfriends, and had once actually been engaged she said. When he was at his public school Alexander Weymouth tried to find out exactly what she had done with her lover. She answered, more bluntly than he'd expected, "I never did anything dirty, if that's what you mean." But far more often, Nannies had no past in this respect. They 'couldn't be bothered with that sort of thing', it 'didn't interest' them, they 'hadn't the time for it', and so on. It was rare even to find figures like Baroness Budberg's Ducki, who, apart from her brush with the powerful lesbian figure of the Russian Governess, was supposed to have nursed a lifelong but secret passion for Baroness Budberg's father.

Nanny March, who taught the Goldings' Nanny, always admitted that she wished she hadn't given up Nannying to marry. Her Irish husband drank and ill-treated her. She found she missed her earlier charges and wasn't as fond of her own three children as she'd been of them. When her children had grown up she went back to Nannying. Nanny March was one of those instinctive Nannies, herself a little childlike, whom children instinctively loved and trusted, and I think she provides a clue to an aspect of the Nanny character relevant to the subject of their marriage.

One of the fundamental things about a Nanny's position was that in the final analysis she was not responsible. The children were not hers, they were their mother's. It is true, too, that one of the most fundamental things about childhood is that you do not have any responsibility. Growing up is learning to become responsible for yourself and in the end, usually, for other people. Now many Nannies enjoyed their lack of responsibility, though this only came out obliquely. It is an enjoyment that will show more clearly in the interviews and examples I shall use later to illustrate the Nanny's position in the household. But, after all, it does not require much imagination, or need demonstrating, to see that it must have been a great relief not to have to decide, at a superficial level, where the money was coming from, or the food, or to which school a child was to be sent. At a deeper level, it must often have been a relief to feel that the child you were looking after was not yours. You did not bring him into the world. You need not worry so intimately about his future. You could always leave and get another child. A weight was lifted. I think that a reverse side, as it were, of that childlikeness we have noted, was sometimes a deep fear of responsibility. I think some women became Nannies not out of the sense of vocation which Sackville-West gives Simpson, but because they instinctively knew that they could never marry and have children because of their fear and dislike of sex and their reluctance to assume the burdens of family life.

Certainly it is impossible to generalise about this, but it is an aspect that should be borne in mind. It does not mean that they were worse Nannies. Nor does it lessen the tragic side to a Nanny's life. That people suffer because of defects or inadequacies in their characters does not make their sufferings less painful. And there is tragedy in the condition of a Nanny. The tragedy of loneliness when old, your 'children' grown up and gone and seldom, if ever, coming to see you. The sadness which all women feel who would have liked to have given birth and haven't, and would have liked to have been loved by a man and haven't, that sense which Auden catches, of humanity flowing forward and the Nanny somehow, in the end, always having been on the fringe.

Now the leaves are falling fast,
Nurses flowers will not last;
Nurses to their graves are gone.
But the prams go rolling on.

THE NANNY SEDUCED

Despite the fact that many (perhaps most) Nannies did not marry, there are other Nannies throughout our period who were no strangers to the pleasures and perils of love and lust.

In 1862 Emmeline Lott went out to become what was in effect the Nanny (her charge was only five) to the son of the Grand Pasha Ibrahim, Viceroy of Egypt. She wrote two books about her experiences, and in the first has a vivid description of bedtime. "The last meal of the day was presented to the Viceregal children, each child being attended by its own head nurse, who literally spoon-fed them." They were then undressed and bathed, and re-dressed elaborately for going to sleep. And now every-one—children, nurses, Nannies, slaves, male and female attendants, all to the number of perhaps forty persons—everyone launched for the night into what Emmeline Lott describes as "one full-swelling bed". This consisted of a single colossal mattress, or giant cushion, very thick and soft, which completely filled one reception hall. Over this bed was dropped a gauzy canopy, an enormous bell-shaped mosquito net whose folds partly obscured the light, already dim, which came from a silver brazier burning in a corner of the hall. And it was in this great sea of a bed, Emmeline Lott delicately hints, whose concealing billows heaved and seethed with the writhings and agitations of the youthful attendants, the half-naked slaves, the Nannies, nurses and charges, that during the long, hot Egyptian nights there took place what a latter-day Nanny would have described as 'goings on'.

But it was not all pleasure for Nannies going East in the nineteenth century. There were dangers as well, particularly on the journey out. In her second book, *Nights in the Harem*, Emmeline Lott warns of a certain Madame Tedesco in the Via de la Scala in Florence.

The business of this second disgrace to her sex was to advertise in foreign papers . . . when her unhappy victims were entrapped, under the pretence of being supplied with situations, with cool deliberation this person showed herself in her real light as a mere jellal, or slave-dealer, and absolutely sold the more prepossessing of these fair exotics to foreign nobles of wealth. When the poor fading flowers had ceased to adorn the conservatories of the Florentine Villas they were packed off, as mysteriously as smuggled wares to Egypt, to decorate the saloons of Signora Tedesco where Pashas, Ministers, members of the diplomatic corps, merchants, and roués of all countries nightly congregated.

Finally, after this long and arduous apprenticeship,

> Many of the choicer plants from this foul soil were transplanted into the palaces of Egyptian Princes; there they vegetated, sumptuously tended, perhaps, but in such *durance* vile, that no intelligent friends or relatives ever reached them. Many were, many are still, walled-up in these retreats and will pass away to the tomb under conditions which no mortal dare seek to unveil.

Such exotic temptations were rare in a Nanny's life. More usually, as as can be imagined, it was the father of the house who provided them. Often this was done quite honourably. The 2nd Earl of Arran, for instance, married his children's nursery-maid in the early nineteenth century, and had, by her and his first two wives, twenty-three children. (He also had, incidentally, roughly the same number of illegitimate children and such numerous progeny confused him. There is a story about him in Dublin that while walking outside his house on St. Stephen's Green he met a little girl out with her Nurse. "You're a very nice little girl; whose little girl are you?" he said. "I'm Lord Arran's little girl," she said. Neither knew the other.) One of the psychiatrists with whom I discussed certain parts of this book told me he had a patient whose father married the Nanny after his wife left, and had three children by her. His patient was one of the first wife's children and was fairly disturbed, among other things, by the change. She is a lesbian and wants a baby from a sperm bank.

But sometimes the approaches were less honourable, if understandable. A particular difficulty was the grandfather, suddenly jolted into late flowering lust. One correspondent, in an informative piece I shall quote from later (she had a prostitute Nanny), describes such a case:

> Finally, there was Mademoiselle, willowy, pretty, vulnerable, who burst into homesick tears when, having travelled from France, she asked to be shown her bedroom, and was shown instead a narrow bed in the nursery where we were all standing.
>
> Because she was French she was allowed to eat in the dining-room, and she got on very well with my father—"You are so *amusant*, Major," she would exclaim, making my father more and more *amusant*. But she got on even better

with my grandfather whom we stayed with for holidays. He was over eighty, huge, ponderous, unimaginative, and, for the previous fifteen years, following the death of his wife, without joy or emotion. He must have picked up from somewhere that women like to be given fur coats, so he gave Mademoiselle a very expensive one. And then, a few months later, wanting to show his admiration again, and being imaginatively rigid, gave her another. (Probably they were musquash and pony, which were fashionable at the time.) The family behaved as if they feared he would go completely wild, and decided Mademoiselle must be sacked. I can imagine the pain and depression this must have caused him, the late flame so officiously extinguished.

Something of the same sort seems to have happened to the old Marquis of Bath. But these elderly gentlemen could be coped with. The fathers themselves could do more damage. This is not the place to discuss Mr. Kent, but his practice of sleeping with his children's Nurses led directly to two murders. And numerous Nannies told me of their experiences in this sphere. They ranged from the comparatively mild, like Nanny Dickson who described to me how she was being interviewed once in Mrs. Boucher's famous agency in Basil Street. She was being interviewed by a Frenchwoman who kept on saying, "You are too young, you are too young." As Nanny Dickson was twenty-seven at the time, she was flattered but surprised. The Frenchwoman said finally, "I will be 'onest with you. If you come, my 'usband will never be out of the nursery." But one Nanny told me that after repeatedly rejecting the advances of the husband, he became very drunk one night and tried to batter down the door of the night nursery, terrifying the children and having to be forcibly removed by the butler and a groom.

The saddest cases are those where the emotions of the Nanny are un-expectedly awakened. In 1937 Mr. J. L., a good-looking young man aged thirty-six, began to fall out with his wife. Foreseeing divorce and wishing to keep the children, he decided to get the Nanny on his side. She was a spinsterly figure of about forty-seven, taut but well under control. Mr. J. L. took her to the opera and the theatre a number of times, and then out to dinner. He began to do this regularly. The Nanny was first pleased, then excited and finally, although she managed to conceal it, fell violently in love with him. She thought he was serious. He observed the excitement—which he thought something of a joke and, already having a reputation as an eccentric, used to describe it to his friends—but was unaware of her love. He took her to more operas and once to a garden party at Buckingham Palace. The rift between his wife and himself became open. They parted; Mr. J. L. keeping the children and refusing to let her have them. It was now the Nanny showed the depth and extent of her love by risking her life in his service. She was guarding the children fiercely but one day the wife and her lover came and snatched them. Unhesitatingly the Nanny flung herself in front of the speeding car and only just escaped being killed. After this, with the wife and children gone, and all need to pretend presumably over she became unable to contain her emotions. For the first time Mr. J. L. became aware of them—and of her attentions and expectation. He was embarrassed, irritated and in any case no longer needed her; he was coming to a more amiable arrangement with his wife. He decided that the best thing to do was to sack the Nanny, which he did. The unfortunate woman became completely distraught. She bombarded him with letters, first passionate, finally abusive; she accosted him in the street; wrote furious and desperate letters to all his friends and finally collapsed into hospital with a prolonged nervous breakdown.

But Nannies were not always just the innocent victims of masculine selfishness or lust. They were quite capable of seeking adventures on their own, sometimes finding their satisfaction in the very nursery itself. But before I go into this, there are two strange Nannies I would like to mention, rare as to type, but interesting in that they show how wide a variety of human nature we are studying and how dangerous it is to generalise.

Occasionally, criminals were for a short time Nannies. They will once or twice slip wickedly in and out of this book or for a brief moment lurch, usually drunk, across its pages. One such was Nanny Joan, Nanny to the McSorley children before the Second World War. She was large and jolly, with a big, loose mouth and a line in coarse, vulgar phrases. Veronica McSorley said they knew the phrases—'Shut up', 'belt up', 'button your lip'—were coarse because their mother would shudder and then take Nanny Joan outside and reprimand her. Nanny Joan terrified and dominated Mrs. McSorley, who was a frail woman and often unwell. She could not bring herself to sack her, disliked her, yet was fascinated by her. One summer she escaped with her husband to Juan-les-Pins, leaving Nanny in sole charge. Never exactly inhibited, Nanny Joan now blossomed. Veronica remembers how, evening after evening, she would tell the children about an illegitimate baby she had had and then, led on by association and becoming stimulated, would describe in great detail numerous other sexual exploits which, though they didn't understand, excited them. She also systematically ransacked the house. Veronica remembers how she would come into a room and find Nanny Joan going through the drawers, setting valuable and disposable objects to one side. She would look up, smile her 'red-lipped huge smile' and calmly conduct the little girl out of the room. On top of this, she ran up enormous bills. Wisely, just before the McSorleys returned from Juan-les-Pins, she packed her bags and left. Later they found out that she was an ex-convict from Holloway, sentenced for theft and 'improper practices'. They also learnt that she was supposed to have been a lesbian.

I only came across one other instance of even suggested homosexuality among Nannies. No doubt it existed, but it seems to have been more overt among governesses whose emotions tended to turbulence and were more apt to get out of hand. But Bridget Tisdall wrote me a brilliant account, strong with the stinks and stings of childhood, which happened to end on this particular note.

> One last Nanny I must mention. She was a breakaway from tradition: young, commanding, her name was Lilian: a Nanny with a Christian name! She ruled her mistress with an iron rod: they were inseparable. Her eyes were light grey, slightly protuberant. Her mouth was pouting and sensual. Her soft, mouse-brown hair fell wildly over her forehead. She reminded me of a leopardess, ready to spring. She had a charming laugh, and beautiful, even, white teeth. Her skirts were short for the period, and she would wear white muslin blouses with floppy bows at the neck. She was brusque with her charges, pulling them roughly out of high chairs, smacking them and making them stand in corners. The screams in Lilian's nursery were hideous. I remember the table covered with spilt food, the floor with spilt pots, and Lilian reigning among the chaos like a disdainful queen, elbows hunched on the table staring enigmatically into space.
>
> Her mistress died young on a journey to Switzerland. It was rumoured in Lilian's arms. Here, I felt, was a mystery which made a mockery of the nursery world; a breath of passion divorced from senna pods and hot milk. Lilian kept herself to herself, never mixing with the orthodox Nannies. I wonder now if what I sensed was true, or if she eventually married.

THE NANNY SEDUCING

I was talking generally about this whole subject of Nannies and marriage and sex one day to someone when she said she was sure she knew a man who'd been at Eton before the war with a boy who'd married his Nanny. I asked her to find out. She wrote to her friend and after some time a letter came from him saying, yes the subject did ring a faint bell—"I

Mrs Everest, Nanny to Winston Churchill

A fine study of a
Nurse with
children, circa 1860

Park scene, 1890

Nannies live to a great age. When I did my research, Fanny Clamp was the oldest Nanny in the world. She was still extremely sharp and retained a sure touch with children (her room was always ready for them, full of little presents). Born on 10 June 1864, she was the daughter of a butler. At 17 she became nursemaid to Lord Clinton, who had a house in Curzon Street and estates in Devonshire and Scotland. When she was 20 she rose to be Nanny to Dr Paget in Harley Street (grandfather of Christopher Mayhew). She could still – at 106 when I saw her – remember cows in St James's Park, and seeing Queen Victoria in the Park (fourteen times). By the time she was 30 she was 'sick of the rich' and went to work as matron in a home in Berkshire. She lived at the end of her life with one of her former charges, Mrs Chudley.

Children in their nursery, 1884

Illustrated London News,
11 September 1920

Edward Sackville-West, aged 11 months

Heatwave in Hyde Park, 1917. It is noticeable how no one has removed any clothing at all.
1938. Nannies at a society wedding outside St Paul's, Knightsbridge, waiting to see the bride.

Nanny Marks, Nanny
to Alexander,
Caroline, Christopher
and Valentine Thynne
in the 1930s and 1940s.
ABOVE outside
Longleat.

LEFT with Lady
Caroline Somerset and
her two children.

The pram parade in Kensington Gardens, February 1933

The Parade Ground at the Norland Nursery Training College,
Hungerford. This photograph was taken in 1971, but exactly the same
manoeuvres take place today – and every day.

Lord Curzon (with watch chain)

seem to remember dimly it was someone who *ran off* with his Nanny."
I have tried in vain to locate this figure. But I think the fact they had to
'run off' says something: it indicates difficulty, perhaps parental disapproval, rows and scenes; also feelings too strong to be controlled;
and it suggests an element in them both of dash and daring admirable
in anyone, but particularly in the Nanny, who must have been nearing
forty, a late age to uproot oneself from the nursery and set out on the difficulties of a new and married life.

Yet in many ways, if true, this young man was only acting out a fantasy
which was almost universal. Nearly all little boys wanted to marry their
Nannies, and one of the most touching things was how often the Nannies
would tell me about it with pride: "Oh yes, he wanted to marry me, all
right. 'When I'm grown up I'll marry you,' he used to say." But only
rarely are infantile fantasies acted out explicitly. The inhibitions and
taboos are too strong. Nevertheless you sometimes get a sort of false
simulacrum of it; something which resembles the playing out of a fantasy
while it is, in reality, something far simpler. No doubt, for example, if
I had been able to pursue the Etonian who had married his Nanny,
I would have discovered he had simply run off with an eighteen-year-old
nursery-maid engaged to look after his cousins. This brings us to an aspect
of our subject which I think is best approached, as was the Nanny as
mother, via a novel.

Balthazar, the hero of *The Beastly Beatitudes of Balthazar B* by J. P.
Donleavy, is a Nannied boy. But, because of the idle wandering wealthy
life of his parents, Nannies continue to play a dominant role in his life
long after the normal age. He is at prep school, aged eight or so, his
knowledge of life dependent on Beefy. (This passage is interesting,
incidentally, as an example of that attitude towards the sexual appetite
in upper and lower class women we discussed in chapter 3. Donleavy was
born in 1926.)

Beefy said

that nipples could get big and hard but he was not positively sure of this yet.
And girls were of two types. One to whom you did the vile and odious thing
and whom you would not love. She would be a servant, a waitress or a maid or
be in a back alley of the town. But girls you loved were cousins at the race
meetings or partners at dancing school or at aunt's and uncle's house in their
pretty dresses. You married them and always they had their own bed and
dressing-room and you would not go in there unless it was desperately necessary.
Beefy never said what he knew about Nannies for each one he had departed
after a few days.

During this period, Balthazar receives a letter from his old Nanny.

> My dearest Balthazar,
>   I have the sorriest thing, for me at least, to have to write to you. My father who has not been well for some time has been taking a slow turn for the worse. My mother who has arthritis cannot look after him alone. And so I have written to your mother that here I must stay. I did so much want to look after you during the Christmas holidays in Paris. A new Nannie, your mother tells me, has been engaged and I'm sure she will be very nice. She will collect you from school and bring you back to Paris on the train.
>
> With all my dearest love always,
Nannie.

And so Miss Bella Hortense enters his life. She is long, cool, beautiful, young, gay, gentle, sweet. Her job is to take him to Paris in the holidays— this sensitive, elegant, extremely rich little boy—and there to be his companion. He calls her Nanny. Once, when he is nine, there is a thunder-storm and he creeps into her bed and she comforts him. He grows fast, early becomes a young man. He plays chess with her. They have great fun together in the holidays, grow very close and gay. He notices the swell of her large white breasts against her poplin shirt tucked lightly into long, grey skirts swirling elegantly around long slim legs, and her arched eye-brows. He notices she is very noticeable to men, he hears sometimes what they say. When he is twelve she says it is time for him to call her Bella. When he is twelve he is so tall that he reaches above the lobe of her ear and, walking in the soft summer air one Paris night she says suddenly, abruptly, she must go, he is ruining her life.

"Bella, I didn't know I was ruining your life."
"It was unfair of me to say."
"You told me it was nice these holidays like this. And you could give all the gentlemen about Kensington a merry dance. And you had your nice little change of situations."
"Oh God, what a mess. Don't you see I love you. And you are far too old to be loved like that."
A strange shiver comes upon the back of the head and goes down the spine and lingers between the legs.

When they got back to the huge Paris house where they are alone together, stalking each other awkwardly, she soon leaves and goes to bed. He comes to her room, bends and peeps through the keyhole. She hears him. He can see nothing. She calls him in. She is lying in bed, and they talk and talk. She is gentle and they talk. He wants to marry her—she explains it is impossible. But he has made a declaration and been turned down. He gets up and goes, hurt. She calls him back, very gently, and makes him sit on the bed and turns out the light.

> And her hand felt and took his hand and she pulled him gently down. Her fingers up through the short hairs on the back of my head, and cool as they touch in behind my ear. Tumbling down into her arms she whispers O God come to me. Her kisses over my mouth. On the cheeks and eyes. Her tongue along the side of my neck and deep into my ringing ear. All the bells of Paris. And stormy choirs sing when it is not yet morn or Sunday but her silky long slender arms, smooth wrists, and soft slim hands. She breathed her breath catching in her lungs. And I can hardly breathe at all. Her hard teeth as she bites into my mouth. Her hand at my throat to undo my tie. Pulling herself up out of the sheets. Hair strips of shadow hanging around her head. I watched in the garden once her fingernails as she sat and scratched her thigh and they made long white marks on her sunny skin. Distant fingers unbuttoning my shirt one by one. And close by lips kissing me upon the breasts. Bella tell me what to do. Nothing, nothing. Just take off your clothes. And so strange to wonder. Of all these years of dreams. To reach one day in the laundry room to secretly touch her drying underclothes more close to her than I ever hoped to be. And now lie side by side all along her body, and feel it pressed to mine, like two bodies all of your own. One here and one you reach around. Bella is what we're doing love. Yes, yes. Hurry tell me how. You'll see, you'll see. And I see . . . can I touch and put my hand running over you, you're so smooth. Yes you can, you can and come on top of me. Bella, Bella it's coming out of me. It won't stop. All over you. O darling you mustn't mind, sweetest and dearest, let it come out over me, you must not mind. Bella tell me what did I do. It's all right now. It should have been inside you. Yes but it's all right, you mustn't mind.

And so they talk again. How she's longed to seize him and cuddle him. And how it's impossible. And he—so rich—says his money will get them out of any trouble. And she tells him about his uncle Edouard, making the most delicate of passes; and then goes on to be jealous of the girls he'll one day have. And he remembers how men looked at her and said things to her about her. The night is hushed and faint. They lie hearing the noises of Paris, the slow sounds that pass across a city. The cry of a street philosopher calling out. He wonders what it meant, when the men said what they'd like to do to her. He asks her.

> And Bella is this what they do. When I put my hand here and feel your breast the way it swells up from the rest of you. And I don't yet know what you've got

down there in your secret hair. Yes dearest it's what they would do. They would kiss me only I'm kissing you. They would grab me tightly, only I'm grabbing you. And they would do what I'm telling you. Come Balthazar on top of me. On top. Like that. And never would I want you to be them. You're sweet and sweet. And my own loveliest little man of mine. Get in between my legs. There. God it's so hard. I'll guide you in. Don't worry, don't worry. O God there you are, there you are. O God Balthazar. You have it up in me. And all the thoughts you never knew you'd know. Of some strange miracle happening to it there. In that part of her. Was it her. Like her face and teeth and hair. These speaking lips so close. Just step out of my brain and into hers. And hello where the holy grail. Like rolling down in grass in all the wet sweet smell of hay and stop and stare up into a sky of chestnut blossoms. White white planets everywhere. Bella. Have I done it right. Yes. Yes. O Bella O Bella please it's coming out of me, it's coming out of me, hold me please. Yes yes my dearest let it come. Bella don't let me die, please. And bleed away all my blood. O Balthazar I won't let you die or bleed away all your blood and God I'm dying too. In all the nooks and crannies and shadows of the sheets. Torn back from bodies one wild one pale. Her hand bumping and counting on my spine. And put my fingers on the hard bone behind her tiny ear. Your face Bella has your eyes closed. And you smile all around your mouth. Everything now so still. Save another long cry from the street philosopher. In search of the holy grail. And you went back up on your shoulders and groaned and groaned. Bella it wasn't unhappy was it. No not unhappy, you silly boy. I worried you were in pain, you went all so stiff and shook. Sweet that's the way it is when it happens, with happiness, happiness. Why then do you have tears in your eyes. I don't know why. Tell me why. Bella. You must. Tell me why you're crying and you are. And her elbows pointed out into the dark as she held up her hands.

And so they talk again—again she says how impossible it is, and he says he'll save them, and she tells him to go. He won't. Go. Won't. Please. No. And eventually they lie together and sleep. The dawn comes and she tells him to get up and go and brush his teeth and she'll bring his breakfast.

A last day. In circumstances of embarrassment his mother returns. They are caught. Miss Hortense must leave immediately. She tells his mother she loves him, she would like to marry him. But she leaves, she leaves, she leaves.

Goodbye Miss Hortense, goodbye.
And when
The channel
comes
And you slip out
on the

grey and greeny
white
whisper to it
And say
God love you
Tonight.

We may seem to have moved some considerable distance from the Nanny. Indeed Miss Hortense was a Nanny in name only; and quite soon not even that. But the distance is not as great as one might think. Little boys, baby boys, must often have dreamt just such dreams, though in the confused language of the subconscious, of which Donleavy describes the adult (fictional) reality. How many Nannies have stirred with Miss Hortense's feelings—however much disguised—appalled to sense how close to sexual is the maternal lust?

And not dreams only. Simon Wilson said that when he was seven, his brother's nursery-maid used regularly to take him into the linen cupboard and fondle and excite both his penis and herself. We have already come across something of this sort with the author of *My Secret Life*. Another correspondent described how his Nanny, who came when she was nineteen and left to get married when she was twenty-seven, used to take him into bed with her when he was eight and caress him and press him against her—he could remember her groans—in a way which later he realised was frankly sexual. Had he been more precocious no doubt much the same thing would have happened to him as to Balthazar.

One of the most interesting cases of this sort is that of Byron. Interesting not only because in a rough way it is an exact parallel to Balthazar B's, but because Byron's brilliant American biographer, Marchand, who seems to have been the first to unearth the facts, builds a fundamental analysis upon the poet's youthful experiences.

Three people influenced Byron's very early life: his mother and his two Nurses, the sisters Agnes and May Gray. His mother was a loud, irritable, rowing character with whom his relationship was tempestuous, open, powerful and also intermittent. Much of the time he was left with his Nurses. The elder sister Agnes Gray was a pious, Bible-reading Presbyterian. She introduced Byron to the Bible and to Psalms, creating a love which was to last all his life. "I am a great reader and admirer of those books [of the Bible]," he wrote to John Murray, "and had read them through and through before I was eight years old."

However Agnes Gray left to get married and her young sister May took over and remained with Byron until he was eleven. She, too, was apparently a pious Presbyterian and may possibly have read him the Bible. But her real proclivities lay elsewhere. For long periods she had sole care of the boy, particularly when he went to Nottingham for tutoring or to have his foot seen to. And it was in Nottingham—though no doubt their indulgences had continued surreptitiously at home—that her true character was in the end discovered. In August 1799, Byron's attorney Hanson was pursuing various enquiries on his behalf in that city when he discovered something that caused him to write an impassioned letter to Byron's mother and secure May Gray's instant dismissal.

> I assure you Madam . . . [he wrote] her conduct towards your son while at Nottingham was shocking, and I was persuaded you needed but a hint of it to dismiss her. Mrs. Parkyns, when I saw her, said something to me about her, but when I found from dispassionate persons at Nottingham it was the general topic of conversation, it would have ill become to have remained silent. My honourable little companion tho' disposed to retain his feelings, could not refrain, from the harsh usage he had received at her hands, from complaining to me, and such is his dread of the woman that I really believe he would forgo the satisfaction of seeing you if he thought he was to meet her again. He told me that she was perpetually beating him, and that his bones sometimes ached from it; that she brought all sorts of company of the lowest description into his apartments; that she stayed out late at nights, and he was frequently left to put himself to bed; that she would take the Chaise-boys into the Chaise with her, and stopped at every little Ale-house to drink with them. But, Madam, this is not all; she has even—traduced yourself.

No doubt such behaviour, if true, is quite enough to justify the dismissal of a girl in charge of an eleven-year-old boy. But what Hanson had in fact discovered horrified him so much that he did not reveal it until Byron's death. This he did in a conversation with Hobhouse in 1824, which the latter recorded.

> With respect to the early development of these propensities [he is writing of sexual propensities] in Byron I am acquainted with a singular fact scarcely fit for narration but much less romantic and satisfactory than the amour with Mary Duff [a childhood romantic passion, totally platonic]. When nine years old at his mother's house a free Scotch girl used to come to bed and play tricks with his person—Hanson found out and asked Lord B—who owned the fact—the girl was sent off. . . .

Precisely what these 'tricks' were, it is impossible to say. Byron, writing about his youth in his *Detached Thoughts*, said: "My passions developed very early—so early, that few would believe me if I were to state the period, and the facts which accompanied it." This, and other things he later hinted, suggest intimacies akin to, even the same as, those Donleavy describes. Certainly it is physically possible. But one should beware of imposing on the past the expectations of a permissive age. More interesting are the effects on Byron himself.

Professor Marchand says that the fact this experience was with someone who had taught him the Bible may have been an additional shock. It may in part have laid the foundation for his lifelong hatred of cant and hypocrisy. But he goes on, "It is strange how little account has been taken of Byron's plain statement that his passions were developed very early and that this 'caused the anticipated melancholy of my thoughts—having anticipated life' " (this phrase, incidentally, being another which suggests that his intimacies with May Gray were fairly advanced).

Marchand says that in fact the effects went deep, particularly since the experience with his Nurse occurred in parallel with a second development —the growth of a concept of pure love. Shortly after May Gray was sacked, there was a repetition of his ideal affair with Mary Duff—which also heralded his 'first dash into poetry'. This was inspired, wrote Byron, by

the ebullition of a passion for my first cousin Margaret Parker . . . one of the most beautiful of evanescent beings. I have long forgotten the verses, but it would be difficult for me to forget her. Her dark eyes! Her long eyelashes! . . . I was then about twelve—she rather older, perhaps a year . . . I do not recollect scarcely anything equal to the *transparent* beauty of my cousin, or to the sweetness of her temper, during the short period of our intimacy. She looked as though she had been made out of a rainbow—all beauty and peace.

My passion had its usual effects upon me: I could not sleep, could not eat; I could not rest; and although I had reason to know that she loved me, it was the torture of my life to think of the time which must elapse before we could meet again—being usually about *twelve hours* of separation!

The fact that the May Gray experience—coarsely, even grossly, physical— took place at the same time as this romantic vision, caused, Marchand argues, a dramatic split to take place in Byron's relations with women. The ideal loves, as well as inspiring him to poetry,

became the constant symbol to him of the ideally beautiful impossessed love, the sort of image that usually develops in adolescence but that in Byron was a dominating vision between the years of eight and twelve. It had numerous counterparts or embodiments male and female during the rest of his life. The other, the primitive sexual awakening, caused disillusionment, the melancholy which springs from physical disgust and the failure of a real experience to measure up to the ideal. The first carried him into love with young girls and boys; the second into the cynical search for 'fine animals' like the baker's wife in Venice.

This analysis is extremely interesting, and it was as far as I know, completely original in Byron research when Marchand wrote it. It is also, of course, speculative. As with Churchill, one can never be certain about such things. But I must confess it does seem to me rather a lot to lay at the head—or body—of May Gray.

For one thing, to return to the beginning of Marchand's argument, there is no direct evidence that May Gray read him the Bible or had— as her sister definitely did—a particularly profound religious effect on him. What with Ale-houses and Chaise-boys I cannot believe she threw much enthusiasm into her Bible-reading—supposing she still had the energy for it. And if her role as Bible-reader was carried out, if it were at all, with little or no conviction, then her lapses into sensuality need have led to no awareness of hypocrisy. And even if it did, I see no reason why Byron should have been led thereby to dislike hypocrisy.

Because in fact there is no evidence that he disliked his experiences with May Gray. Marchand talks of the melancholy which springs from physical disgust, but Byron had many reasons for melancholy. It seems to me more likely that his seduction was a source of pleasure. His outpourings as reported by Hanson sound like someone caught out in something he enjoyed, guilty because his interlocutor clearly disapproved, and piling everything he can think of on to his partner to avoid blame. After all, the practices, whatever they were, had been going on for two years— from the age of nine to eleven. Byron had never complained before. It is supposed that he didn't complain to his mother, either about the beatings or, presumably, the sex, because he didn't dare. But in fact Byron's relationship with his mother wasn't like that. He was always fiercely independent and bold with her. He never feared to attack her. He would not have been afraid to complain. When May Gray left Nottingham Byron gave her a gold watch and never referred with any particular opprobrium towards her thereafter. I think common sense would suggest that it was the excitement and satisfaction he had experienced with her which led him later to pursue 'fine animals'.

Furthermore, I don't think that the distinction Marchand makes between these fine animals and the ideal loves is nearly so clear cut;

not later, and not even in these early years. His description of Margaret Parker is excitedly physical—"Her dark eyes! Her long eye-lashes!" A little after this he fell in love with Mary Chaworth, an eighteen-year-old beauty who was a distant cousin and already engaged to someone else. She was a lovely and romantic girl and Byron's love for her was apparently of the same sort as his love for Margaret Parker, but writing about it later he noted:

> When I was fifteen years of age it happened that in a cavern in Derbyshire I had to cross in a boat (in which two people only could lie down) a stream which flows under a rock, with the rock so close upon the water, as to admit the boat only to be pushed on by a ferry-man (a sort of Charon), who wades at the stern stooping all the time. The companion of my transit was M.H.C. with whom I had been long in love, and never told it, though *she* had discovered it without. I recollect my sensations, but cannot describe them—and it is as well.

Confusion between sacred and profane love, as we saw in an earlier chapter, is very common, if not universal, in men. It is a reflection of the dual and contradictory feelings towards the mother: woman as protector and nurturer, woman as sexual partner. Byron certainly had this split and May Gray might conceivably have increased it a bit. (Though we do not have here, as in the earlier chapter, the situations of lower class nurse and idealised mother. Byron's relationship with his mother will not allow it.) But my own feeling is that the most one can say is that May Gray brought into early play, and thereby intensified, propensities which were in any case likely to be strong and strongly pursued.

They would be strongly pursued because Byron's crippled foot, as well as driving him to excel, would naturally impel him to excel at something which would both be manly and which would prove his physical attraction.

The form they took ran in the family. Byron's father, Captain John Byron, chased women—successfully—all his life. Here he is writing from Valenciennes in 1790, a year before he died. It is the middle of the French Revolution, but Captain Byron, as usual, is thinking only of sleeping with chambermaids and actresses.

> As for me, here I am, and in love with whom? A new actress who is come from Paris, she is beautiful. . . . As for Madame Schoner—she fairly told me when drunk, that she liked me, and I really do not know what to do. . . . For my Amours, these are all finished and everybody says Je suis trez amoureux but tres inconstant . . . and I believe, I have had about one third of Valenciennes, particularly a girl at L'Aigle Rouge, an Inn here. I happened to [be] there one

day, when it rained so hard . . . she is very handsome and very tall, and I am not yet tired.

Byron inherited his sexual energies from his father. The free Scotch girl was merely the first to harness them.

LATER SEXUAL ATTITUDES

I do not think it would be safe to draw any general conclusion from this chapter—though perhaps in the area we have been studying that is a conclusion itself. Although I retain the impression that on the whole Nannies appear either to have been frightened or uninterested in sex, I cannot be certain of it. Nor can there be any question of the Nanny Block. Indeed one must suppose that Nannies shared in the gradual liberation of behaviour which took place after the First World War. There is certainly some evidence for this. Jaime Parladé and his younger brother had an Irish Nanny who came to Spain in the mid-'30s when she was eighteen. She was very large and very beautiful and Jaime Parladé remembers the wonder of her beauty and how her life fascinated them, as well it might. She had a succession of lovers and every day used to take the two boys, then aged four and one and a half, into Malaga cinema and leave them, by a special arrangement with the usherette, in two front seats from three to six while she went off and slept with the current Frenchman or Spaniard. To this day Jaime Parladé has a startling knowledge of certain specialised areas of late '30s cinema.

After the Second World War the evidence becomes quite plentiful. For example, Miss de Bourbel says that her Nanny, still alive, aged ninety, has now come to accept things which before she wouldn't have believed possible in Hell. Before Caroline and Nicolas Hill were married her parents made a great fuss about them sleeping together. One weekend they went to stay with her old Nanny. While unpacking their suitcases Nanny discovered their Dutch cap. That afternoon she said to them, "It's a lovely day. Why don't you go for a picnic? I'll pack you one." They did and when they eventually arrived at their destination and unpacked the picnic they found (and later used) the Dutch cap at the bottom of the basket. I was told a number of other similar stories. One can argue retrospectively that if Nannies changed then, they did before.

The situation today, though outside our period, is gloomy. The moral forces of the Nanny, as so much else about her, are in disarray. The *au pair* girl bears little or no resemblance to her. A couple began to call their *au pair* 'Nanny' after she had been looking after their children for six months. But shortly after this elevation she came and told them she was pregnant. And G.C. engaged a Nanny through an apparently impeccable source. She was nineteen and trained. His wife had to go away for a week and the first night she had gone, the Nanny came and climbed into his bed. I asked him what he had done. "Naturally," he said, "I sacked her on the spot."

CHAPTER SIX

The World of the Nanny

But forty years of croup
Forty years of fights,
Long, long days, dear
And short, short nights—
Sixty-one today
And ought to be a granny
Pensions for the widows, eh?
But what about the Nanny?
There, ducky there
Nannies don't care!
Don't cry! Oh, my!
Other people's babies.

A. P. Herbert

I should like now to examine, quite briefly, the political, economic, educational and social sides of our subject, with some of whose emotional and psychological aspects we are becoming familiar: the training of the Nanny, her wages, uniforms and conditions of employment, her numbers, her position in the household (the Nanny as warrior), the Nanny community (the Nanny as gossip, the Nanny Mafia), some final and fantastic convolutions of Nanny snobbery, and last, the old Nanny, in retirement, fading, dead. I shall also look at the various changes and developments which took place during our period in the attitudes to child upbringing and try to evaluate how extensively they affected the attitudes and behaviour of Nannies.

On the whole, Nannies trained other Nannies. This was probably always so (certainly the progression nursery-maid to Nurse was common in the eighteenth century); but after 1850 it quite swiftly becomes formalised (along with the uniform). By the 1880s the classic pattern is established: nursery-maid, nursemaid or under-nurse, possibly a spell as second Nanny, and then finally taking over from the old Nanny and becoming a Nanny in her own right. Or moving to a new household—passing out as it were—as a fully-fledged Nanny. After 1900, but more particularly 1920, nursery training colleges start to make themselves felt. There is a certain amount of evidence that towards the end of our period various exigences encouraged the use of more eccentric, untrained material.

The classic course began very young. Nanny Williams ran away from home and knocked on the door of the first house she came to—Mrs. F's—when she was thirteen and a half. Nanny Hurrel was fourteen. Noël Oakeshott's Nanny was twelve. And these young girls, especially if they hadn't had brothers and sisters to look after, were extremely ignorant. Mary Anne Gibbs' Nanny used to tell of a nursemaid who said that her charge screamed incessantly from morning till night.

"But what do you *do*?" said Nanny.

"Oh," said the nursemaid, "I just sits and bears it."

The point of the training was to learn the routines of the nursery and all the tricks and rules which governed infant upbringing—which themselves constituted an elaborate routine. This element of rigid routine, which persisted in child upbringing until very recently, need not surprise us. For one thing, it seems easier to bring up children under a routine. You don't have to think what to do, or when or why. It is laid down. And routine appears to make discipline easier. For another, a routine makes it much simpler to teach someone else. And because you are receiving something hallowed by time you feel fully confident in it (an essential ingredient for anyone dealing with children); when you pass it on, enriched now with your own experience, you bring to bear all the weight of this time, now greater still, and the force of your own involvement. No wonder the Nanny systems and routines often persist to this day, oblivious of recent discoveries in child upbringing, either imposed by the few surviving Nannies, or else inflicted on their children by those who were brought up by Nannies but who cannot now afford them.

The training could often be very strict, almost military. Nanny McCallum joined the Tates of Tate and Lyle when she was fourteen in 1924. Her mother was a lady's maid "so it was natural I should go into service". She was taken on six months' approval, and once this was over, given a wage of fourteen pounds a year and her uniforms. These consisted of six cotton dresses for morning wear, stiff white collars and cuffs and a wide belt, and frilled mob caps. In the afternoon, she changed into a grey silk alpaca dress. She wore ordinary stockings and, an indignity, the housemaid's flat shoes.

Her R.S.M. was a martinet—Nanny Stansford, born in 1860. She was thin, sarcastic, with a grey bun tightly wrapped. She was extremely strict, both with Master John and Nanny, then nursery-maid, McCallum.

"You'll get a training from me," she said, "you'll remember for the rest of your life." Every night, McCallum had to be in bed by nine o'clock, nine-thirty on her day off, but when she came in she had to report to Nanny Stansford that she was back. She had to take Nanny a cup of tea before she went to bed, washing up the teapot in the 'still room' afterwards. One night McCallum left three tea-leaves in the still room sink. Nanny waited till she had taken off her uniform and was asleep and then came storming in, made her get fully dressed and clean it all up. "The girls of today would never stand for it."

Her day began at six o'clock. She got up and, from the housemaid's box, cleaned out the fire, blacked the grates, polished the brass and then swept and cleared the nursery. Once a week the green fitted carpet had to be washed by hand. At seven o'clock she took Nanny Stansford her first cup of tea. Then came breakfast. There was a lift, said Nanny McCallum, but old Nanny wouldn't have that used.

I had to go down and get the breakfasts. Master John had his first. Then us. I've seen Nanny take half an hour to get him to eat his porridge. If he didn't— into the still room with it and he'd have it for tea. She'd never give in. If he didn't eat it, he'd get nothing. After breakfast, potting.

Potting! What a performance! This was the high spot of our day, the most important event in it. Or events rather, because it happened incessantly. All through the morning, afternoon and evening, regular as clockwork, out came the pots. They were put on the pot before the end of the first month. Out of nappies by ten months. It was the beginning, the very fundament of their training. Nowadays they don't start till two!

After potting, there were clothes to wash and mend. Then out for a walk. And we did walk—from eleven-thirty till lunch. Here, once again Master John fed separately—no doubt on porridge. Then the nursery-maids, then Nanny. This meant six separate journeys (for two courses) to the kitchen. Cook created. Why can't she use the lift? After lunch, potting again (didn't matter if the heavens fell, potting was done). Then rest.

And so on, every moment of the day regimented to the second till nursery-maid McCallum collapsed exhausted into bed at nine o'clock. Her training lasted eight years, when, gazetted a Nanny, she joined the family of Colonel Freeman.

Of course this pattern allowed for considerable variation. The Nanny in charge could be kind and considerate. Nanny Williams just helped in the house for three years and was then sent to the Welgarth Nursery Training College. Nanny Buckles's father was a postman with ten children, and they all helped bring each other up, which was really how she learnt. She was training to be a nurse when she got rheumatic fever and had to take a year off. Someone suggested she look after children and she was a Nanny from then on. Nanny Watson was born in 1882 and learnt dressmaking so that she could become a sewing-maid in a big house. When she arrived, the daughter of the house was about to return to Jamaica with her two children, aged ten months and two years. The nurse failed to turn up. "On the Saturday I was asked if I'd go instead. On the Sunday I said yes. We left on the Monday. I had no training. The mother taught me all I know. We did it together." Nanny Watson had an eventful trip. During the crossing, they ran into a tremendous hurricane. Huge seas battered the tiny boat, three lifeboats were torn off and lost and an iron bench wrenched itself from its bolts and hurtled to and fro across the deck above her cabin. But as she had never travelled before she imagined it was always like this and remained quite calm.

But despite these variations, and excepting the nursery training colleges, the usual pattern was as I've described: a period of apprenticeship under another Nanny, a gradual promotion, the attainment of full Nannydom.

This uniformity was also expressed literally, in a uniform. Before 1850 Nurses and nursery-maids seem more usually to have worn the same type of clothes as other servants: the Nurse of the Kents in 1860 wore clothes of an ordinary servant girl, nursery-maids were dressed like housemaids; the head nurse would wear the more expensive and distinguished dress of the housekeeper. But after 1850, when the growth and specialisation of the Nanny really got going, a uniform begins to evolve sensibly. If you deal with babies and infants all the time you need protective clothing. As, incidentally, do hospital nurses. This is probably why a Nanny's uniform seems sometimes to resemble a hospital nurse's, though since both crystallised after the Crimea, when the nurse was very popular, there may have been indirect influence. During the 1870s and '80s the basic pattern became set: some form of cap, bonnet or boater, possibly a piqué or cotton dress for mornings, long skirts of grey alpaca in winter, white in summer, wide belts, sometimes cuffs and collars, boots.

Within this pattern there was naturally enormous variations. Nannies followed fashion like everyone else, if slowly. In Edwardian times, they often wore short black cloth jackets with leg-of-mutton sleeves over their dresses; these long dresses, covering the boots, had no train like their mistresses. In the '20s, skirts became short, boots disappeared, as did boaters, though you still find bonnets. There were variations in different households. Sometimes the hats or caps were immensely elaborate frilly affairs which had to be anchored into the hair with long twisted pins. The first Head of Women Police at New Scotland Yard, the late Mrs. F. Stanley—a formidable woman whose powerful character was formed in ferocious battles with her Edwardian Nanny—liked to recall in her declining years how she would seize one of these tethered hats and wrench it off, together with enormous bunches of hair. She remembered the sensation vividly, the involuntary scream of the Nanny, her pleasure at how much it must have hurt. Then there were the nursery training colleges, the brown/fawn/white striped dresses, with stiff cuffs and wide belt, of the Welgarth; the brown and fawn capes of the Norland. Often Nannies who hadn't been to a college but had been trained by a Nanny who had, wore some variant of these.

The Nannies themselves often introduced interesting, or fantastic, variations. We have seen the swooping Diana Cooperish hats of Nanny Robertson. Instead of hats, complex use of hair was very common. Ursula Siddel's Nana Pewter, the daughter of a roistering sea-captain, had auburn hair which reached half-way down her thighs and which she whirled up round a face like Dante's. She died at a hundred and one. A frequent and appropriate shape for hair was that resembling a teapot. A Nanny Robbins used to paint her bonnet from time to time with black lacquer which had a peculiar and memorable smell. And it should be mentioned here that that same relaxation we have noted in other spheres towards the end of our period is applicable also to the Nanny's uniform. It gradually became less unusual to see a Nanny without one. The Nannies at the prep school wore cardigans, sensible skirts, aprons. A certain amount of riff-raff infiltrated the Nanny ranks and kept the clothes they were accustomed to. But despite this, and despite the variations I have indicated, and others I haven't, it remains true that a uniform was far more common than not (its absence in a Nanny is always commented on); and that throughout the period, just as you could always have recognised a soldier despite much wider differences in dress, so you could always have told that a Nanny was a Nanny.

CHANGING ATTITUDES TO CHILD UPBRINGING; INFLUENCE OF NURSERY TRAINING COLLEGES; NUMBERS OF NANNIES

The attitudes that we found so influential in the centuries before 1850—namely that children were little adults, but little adults with evil faults which had to be eradicated as quickly as possible—persisted strongly into Victorian and Edwardian times. Edwardian children's clothes were still miniature grown-up ones. Girls had a multitude of underclothes like their mothers, vests, combinations, a cotton bodice to which knickers buttoned, petticoats. Over this they had long dresses, little jackets with mutton-chop sleeves, a muff, fur bonnet, white socks and long, many-buttoned boots and a long coat. Their hats were large, made of straw and lined. Boys were dressed in sailor-suits or like little fathers in knickerbockers and short jackets. Not till the '20s were children's clothes made for children. Here is a remark, typical of the time, chosen from an article in the 1880s on children's books: "One great fault of children's books as a class is that they are about children who are made to appear martyrs, geniuses, *personages*. Little boys and little girls ought not to regard themselves, as these stories teach them to do, as possible personages. . . ." Mrs. Fairchild in Mrs. Sherwood's *The Fairchild Family* says, "All children are by nature evil." And that caning, slapping, beating and all forms of violent punishment were a common way of dealing with young children throughout these years is so well known as to require no illustration.

Nevertheless, throughout the nineteenth century and into the twentieth a number of profound historical movements and enormously influential people were at work, which gradually altered these very old and deeply-rooted ideas. Oddly enough, in the life of one of the earliest reformers, a Nanny-figure plays a crucial role.

Anthony Ashley Cooper, the 7th Earl of Shaftesbury, was born in 1801 and died in 1885. He had an intolerable upbringing. His father was hard and cold to his children and his mother, the daughter of the 4th Duke of Marlborough, ignored them completely. She was only interested in fashion. "I and my sisters," wrote Shaftesbury, "all three of them older than myself, were brought up with great severity, moral and physical, in respect both of mind and body, the opinions of our parents being that, to render a child obedient, it should be in constant fear of its father and mother." And not just them—a child should be frightened of everyone. His parents were not just brutal themselves, as far as they could they were overseers of brutality in others. Shaftesbury also wrote about them, "The history of our father and mother would be incredible to most men, and perhaps it would do no good if such facts were recorded."

Fortunately their tyranny was not total. Maria Millis, an old servant of the family, became devoted to the gentle, serious little child and was in effect his Nurse. She loved him, protected him, and used to read the Bible to him. She probably saved him psychologically; he himself felt—and there seems no reason to doubt it—that these twin influences, cruelty and kindness, influenced his entire life. The memory of childhood suffering quickened his sympathy in relation to the sufferings of the little children who slaved in the mines and factories of nineteenth-century England; the love of his Nurse showed him that their alleviation was possible and imperative. Not unless you have been taught to love can you love other people. So flowed those Factory Acts and other reforms associated with Shaftesbury's name.

They were of course revolutionary. Not only, almost for the first time, had Parliament and the country been made to behave altruistically towards little children, as though they were real people—but these were *lower class children*. The novelty of the attitude is the more striking. Shaftesbury was an extremely important figure in bringing about this change of attitude, which slowly gathered momentum through the nineteenth and early twentieth century. He was helped by Charles Dickens, whom my friend Julian Jebb has described as 'inventing childhood'. Certainly his children, for the first time in literature, are proper 'personages'; and though on the whole he uses children to excite our terror and pity, as instruments to emotion, the fact that he could do so is significant.

And this slow change in attitude was expressed in practical ways. Nurseries became nicer. In 1888 Mrs. Panton wrote a book called *From Kitchen to Garret—Hints For Young Householders* many of whose pages could be used today in an article addressed to (rich) young marrieds. Your nursery should be light and roomy, with a window opening top and bottom. Make it cheerful and pretty, wallpapers pale blue or pink. And how about having a dado running round the lower half of the walls in a contrasting shade of washable paint? Inset your cupboards to avoid banging heads. Don't be afraid of furniture that might seem strange to the nursery. A huge sofa is a god-send to a tired Nanny—and the children can use it as a ship!

Sometime after the mid-century the pram—that vehicle of the Nanny— was invented. This is one of those technological developments—comparable to the internal combustion engine in the outside world—which revolutionised a way of life. The Nanny became mobile. This led, in time, to those great gatherings of Nannies in parks and squares which were already common in the 1870s (Maurice Baring describes visits with his adored nursemaid in the late '70s) and which grew more and more popular, reaching their height in the 1920s and '30s. These concourses strengthened, if indeed they did not create, that sense of a Nanny community, of a privileged world within a privileged world.

But prams, though convenient for adults, were also for the comfort and enjoyment of the child. In the late 1870s, for the first time, a baby could lie down. Then, in 1883, the Nurse and the baby are suddenly brought closer together. The Army and Navy Stores bring out a pram where, again for the first time, they face one another. It is called 'The Sociable Vis-à-Vis', costs five guineas, is made of wicker and has four wheels.

Another figure who is very important to this aspect of our study is the child educationalist Friedrich Froebel. He opened his first kindergarten at Blankenburg in the Thuringian Forest in 1837 and ran it according to rather vague philosophic and religious principles which, though in a hazy way, can be seen to owe something both to Locke and Rousseau. The most important of these was the belief that little children already possessed innately ideas and skills which it was the function of education to develop. There was no need to train or impose; nor could there be any question of repressing the childishness of children. On the contrary, it was to be encouraged. The second important principle was vaguer: all living matter was a unity, a pantheistic oneness which had something to do with the Union of Father, Son and Holy Ghost. A child could only develop, therefore, if he was in tune with nature.

But, as so often in the history of ideas, arguable theory led to sensible practice. Union with nature meant that children only had to attend classes in the morning; in the afternoons they went for walks and studied stamens, grew watercress and so on. The innate ideas in children were brought out by giving them the tools and tasks which would elicit them: paper, chalks, paint, clay, beads to thread, ring laying, pea work, balls and blocks to play with. As a matter of fact, to see his system in practice, somewhat modified and stripped of its philosophic concepts which are nineteenth-century and German, one has only to look at the infant teaching systems practised in nearly all nursery and primary schools in England and America today.

Froebel's ideas could lead to absurdity. As early as 1876 *Mother Songs*, the product of the Baroness von Marenholtz-Bulow in Dresden, had reached England and been translated. Professor Graham Wallis, in a famous criticism of the system, drew attention to these. Even though the verse he quotes may actually never have been used in a Froebel Kindergarten, it is indicative of the attitude Froebel could evoke.

> We are but little toddlekins,
> And can't do much, we know,
> But still we think we must be nice,
> For people love us so.

Nevertheless, on the whole, his ideas, in the context of nineteenth-century ideas about child upbringing, could do nothing but good. They reached England in 1874, which was when the Kindergarten Association started, and in 1876 Miss Emily Lord (later to become Mrs. Emily J. Ward), a member of the Froebel Society, started a small school, which also trained young teachers, run on his lines. As time passed she noticed that the girls she taught, while frequently not particularly talented teachers, were often naturally 'good' with little children. "Good, conscientious, industrious, bright, domesticated girls, and I frequently asked myself the question—'Is there no work in the world where these women can realise their best selves?'" Suddenly in 1892 Mrs. Ward saw what these best selves were—they were Nannies. Thus started the Norland Nursing School at Notting Hill Gate to train girls to be nurses for young children.

At the start (the note can still be detected today) there was a strong emphasis on class. Mrs. Ward had a firm grip on reality and she saw that if the apostles of her methods were to get a hearing, and wield sufficient power, they must be raised socially. "Girls," she would say to each intake as it left, "Nurses—take your silver-backed hairbrushes to impress the servants." The early Norland Books (which recorded the whole life story of each Nurse) gave as one of the reasons for the School existing the fact that it could "offer a new career to gentlewomen by birth and education, and to girls of good education and refinement". Elsewhere the Books emphasised, "Nurses do not take their meals with the servants, but the presence of a nursery-maid at the nursery meals should not be objected to."

The early training was clearly both Froebel-inspired, and also designed to allow the young Norland Nurse to fend for herself in the world of the nursery. It included the following: needlework, cutting out, cooking, laundry, Natural History, brushwork and blackboard drawing, singing and story-telling. The following moral qualities were also instilled: punctuality, neatness, personal neatness, tact, temper. From the first a Norland Nurse was forbidden to hit a child. "The Norland Institute does not recognise the necessity of whipping or slapping and therefore no Norland Nurse is allowed to use corporal punishment in any form." This enlightened view—which, despite the gradual change in attitudes we are charting, was amazing for the 1890s—has remained a key feature of the Norland training. By 1930 the curriculum had grown to include these subjects: principles of education, practice of education, all aspects of child psychology, hygiene, nursery management, nature study, children's drawings and children's games. The same moral qualities were instilled but they now included something vague and bracing called General Tone.

Now there is a certain amount of evidence which suggests that old-fashioned attitudes towards children persisted in many Norland Nurses despite this training. I shall come to this later. There were fashions in infant feeding and pot training in the '20s and '30s which militated against the freedom the Norland programme suggests. Nevertheless, assuming for the moment this training produced its best results, it was very much in advance of its time. It set standards of kindliness, of stimulating and enlightened 'teaching' of young infants which, had they been generally followed, would have done much to mitigate some of the miseries we shall soon be examining. It was a channel, also, through which the new and exciting discoveries in child psychology might have been expected at last to reach those who could most benefit from them. And not the Norland Nursery Training College alone. The Princess Christian Nursery Training College opened in Manchester in 1901; some time later another college opened at Windsor. In 1911 the Welgarth Nursery Training College opened in London. There were one or two others of lesser size and importance. All the colleges differed in one way or another. But for our purposes at the moment it is enough to take the Norland training as representative.

It is clearly of vital importance that we see this development in its true perspective. While working on this book I talked to an American Research Fellow engaged (with a giant team) on a study of English domestic servants in the twentieth century. Although my subject was not in her field, she had gained the impression, she said, that from 1920 on the college-trained Nurse fairly swiftly dominated the field. The numbers of nursery- or Nanny-trained Nannies dwindled, and by 1939 they were already quite rare. Consequently, she said, any history of the Nanny divides neatly at the First World War, with the Nanny proper before, the college Nurse after. This is certainly a stimulating idea and it has additional interest because it would mean that patterns of infant upbringing changed quite decisively between these two periods and would explain certain apparent changes in upper and upper middle class social behaviour. To see if it is an accurate picture we must make a detour, but an absolutely necessary one, into the numbers of Nannies.

In the census return for 1861 the number of children's Nurses is given as 92,606, against a total of 1,065,836 domestic servants. In 1871 there are 103,908 nurses, and 1,303,194 domestic servants. Children's Nurses comprise, that is to say, approximately a tenth of the total domestic labour force. And this is confirmed by the fact, which we noted at the time, that in the analysis of advertisements in *The Times* from 1822–1882, children's Nurses are an average of one-tenth of all domestic servants asking for or offered places. After 1871, census returns no longer divide domestic servants into such detailed categories; the totals continue to rise, however. In 1881 there are 1,803,810 domestic servants, in 1891, 1,900,328. At their peak in the mid-1890s it is probably true to say the English upper classes were employing around two million servants. This would give us a figure of 200,000 Nurses and Nannies.

There is evidence, however, that this may be a considerable underestimate. The early census returns were by no means a hundred per cent accurate, and it is notorious that the hardest categories in the population to pin down are the moving ones. The nature of the Nanny's job made her itinerant: in any one year approximately one-fifth of all Nannies were either about to move, moving, or had just moved (This figure is based on, as near as I can calculate it, the *average* length over our whole period a Nanny stayed with a family.) Furthermore, the figure of Nurses given to the census would almost certainly not include the nursery-maids, since these were not yet proper Nurses. These, too, were often moved about the house as necessity dictated. They were probably listed as housemaids, yet there could be, as we have seen, as many as three of these to a nursery and in terms of the effects we are studying they were often as influential as the Nanny herself. Furthermore, all the literature, the social comment, including my interviews, suggests a very much larger figure. As I quoted earlier, at the end of the nineteenth century you were considered "barely middle class if you did not have a nursemaid for the children". Anne Talbot, born in 1899, said that her family were considered extremely poor; yet they had a cook, a Nanny, a nursery-maid, a housemaid and when another child was born another nursery-maid was employed. My own guess is that probably in 1901 an income of about four hundred pounds a year—equivalent today of about four thousand pounds in purchasing power though worth considerably more in terms of employing servants—was more than sufficient to procure you a Nanny to look after your children. At a conservative estimate then, and I do not think this is too great a figure, we are dealing with something like half a million Nannies; at the least, perhaps two hundred and fifty thousand.

From 1901 to the outbreak of the Second World War the number of domestic servants according to the census returns remained approximately static. Here are the figures: 1901—1,332,965; 1911—1,314,024; 1921 —1,209,704; 1931—1,333,224 (an increase no doubt due to the Depression). The population on the other hand rose steadily from 32·5 million to approximately 44·8 million. Very roughly we can say that, relatively, the number of domestic servants decreased by approximately a quarter during this period; though we are still dealing with approximately the same absolute figures.

It is interesting that these absolute figures of Nannies remain more or less constant (within say twenty thousand) throughout our period— that is between two hundred and fifty thousand and half a million. These figures are, of course, for the number of Nannies existing at any one moment. To get a *total* figure of Nannies from 1850 to 1939—a time-span of eighty-nine years—we will be erring very much on the side of strict fairness if we allow three generations of Nannies. That is to say we are studying a figure, at the lowest of three-quarters of a million, and at the highest of one and a half million Nannies. The second in my view is the most likely. In fact, as I explained earlier, the number of Nurses began to grow larger from 1800 onwards. If one were to take these into account the total number of Nannies and Nurses is probably as high as between two and two and a quarter million.

What happened to the Nanny during her relative decline (as regards the total population) from 1901 to 1939? At the top of the scale very little. Grand houses and rich parents continued to live much as before. But as we go down, common sense and the evidence of letters and interviews suggests a loosening of the structure. Certainly, Nanny would be one of the last servants to be relinquished. Along with cooking, children were by far the most demanding of domestic tasks. The Nanny custom was by now firmly established. Mothers panicked at the idea of looking after their children and were in any case probably less fitted for it than at any other time in history. What happened was that Nanny had to help out in the home. She continued to be *called* Nanny because that gave both her and her employers status. So when the First World War came we find Anne Talbot's Blanche Hannah doing the cooking (actually this war seems to have had little real effect on domestic servants, certainly not the older ones. There was no conscription of women, and only of men in 1917). Mrs. F, presumably fallen on less affluent days and become still weaker, relied on Nanny Williams for more and more. Nanny Williams described one mealtime (they are all eating together!) when the parlourmaid was in a rage. Each time she came in, she thumped the dishes down with such force that they were all splashed with gravy, rhubarb, etc. All Mrs. F could do was say faintly, "Deal with Miss X please, Nanny."

And of course in these circumstances the choice of Nanny material tended to become more catholic. The correspondent whose grandfather kept on giving musquash and pony fur coats to her Nanny demonstrates this development very well. In fact I would like to quote some further pages from her letter, because, while showing that the Nanny lost little of her power and influence, she also demonstrates that loosening of the Nanny structure I mentioned earlier. The picture one should hold in mind for the 1920s and '30s is a combination one: a continuing and still very numerous top stratum of the conventional, wealthily-employed Nannies we are familiar with; the rise of new tasks for Blanche Hannahs and Nanny Williamses; and the appearance of the sort of figures and situations we find below.

I had eleven Nannies in eleven years and added each to my prayers, so that, when I was twelve, I prayed: "God bless Nanny Jarman and Nanny Bertha Stroud, and Penny and Jimmy and Sister Rumgeld, and Sister McLaren, and Lossy and Fieldie and Carry and Bertie and Millie." Yet, with two exceptions, I never again met or heard from any of them when they left. . . .

In continuing to pray for these lost Nannies, some of whom I had hated, I must have been praying for, and trying to preserve, my own past. . . .

During the Depression a queue of would-be Nannies stretched right round our block and up to our doorstep in response to an advertisement that offered five shillings a week more than the standard rate for untrained Nannies (25/–) and promised no housework and no teaching. The queue was directly outside our nursery windows; we peeped at the women with a real sense of humility: how *could* so many women want to look after *us*? We knew it was a dull, boring job. We also knew what they did not, that they would have to sleep in the day nursery, without even a dressing-table of their own. In the drawing-room, hour after hour, my mother interviewed these desperate, lonely women, frequently asking capricious questions to vary the monotony. "Do you play the violin? Can you turn somersaults?". . . .

Nanny Bertha Stroud was an early Nanny and thus had more effect on us than later ones. She was a coarse, stupid and rather unkind woman who looked like a dutch doll. One of her punishments was to open her round, dark eyes very wide, and keep them fixed on me, unblinking, until I screamed. She discovered my sister had claustrophobia, so used to pull the bedclothes over her head and hold them there. She was also fond of cleaning out our noses with long cones of cotton wool. Her sister, also a Nanny, and Nanny to our first cousins, enjoyed this too, and I remember when we were staying with these cousins for a horrifying month, both Nannies cleaning out all our noses, and daring us to move by showing us an old cottonwool cone half covered with blood—the result of a child having moved. We also, during that dreadful time, had to eat, nearly every day, potato soup that looked like sick, and made us sick. A strange thumping under my pillow used to wake me at night, and I would lift the pillow with terror to see what was beneath. I gradually realised it was my own heart. This Nanny frightened me continually for two years. . . .

When she (Miss Jimpson—'Jimmy'—a nice Nanny who came after Bertha Stroud) left to get married in China, a horrible experiment arrived—Sister Rumgeld, an elderly, ugly Scandinavian with a deep voice. I couldn't face the fact that Jimmy was really gone, and felt that if I called out to her often enough she would suddenly be there again. So the whole evening I kept calling, from the dark night nursery to the light day nursery, where Jimmy used to sit, sewing our clothes: "Jimmy—Jimmy, are you there?" and every time the answer came: "No, it is not Jimmy, it is Sister Rumgeld." She said it with a guttural satisfaction, as though her name was an improvement.

Sister Rumgeld was so awful—she never smiled, she had no interest in us whatever, she behaved like a sergeant major—that I complained about her to my mother (the only time) and got her sacked. "She's *awful*," I said, and my mother had to agree.

Mrs. Lossiter-Smythe looked rather like Vita Sackville-West (probably the reason my mother engaged her). She was quite nice to us, but the only thing I now remember about her was her description of how she disciplined her son, Charles. She used to put his head down the lavatory and pull the plug on him. I got the impression boys were very difficult and had to be treated severely, and Mrs. Lossiter-Smythe knew the secret.

I needed to give love, and, having no one better than Mrs. Lossiter-Smythe, made her a huge and useless apron from embroidery canvas, with her nickname —Lossie—worked in woollen roses across a big centre pocket. I felt more love for the woollen roses than for her, really.

The woman who had been a prostitute stayed only a short time. Her accent was so 'refined' as to be grotesque. She wore a fawn suit and white satin blouse and seemed to us half-witted. She stole things. Just before she left for good I heard her saying, over and over again, to my parents, "Ay was just having a wee lay-down."

The cook, Mary, was soft, plump, dreamy and bone-idle. It must have seemed an amazing turn of fortune for her to be waited on in the nursery, and to have almost no work at all. Once I was sent all the way home from school for having a large hole in the back of my stocking. "It's not my fault—it's Mary's. I don't know how to darn—*she's* supposed to do it!"—cut no ice in a place where it was very rare for girls to have Nannies.

I wonder now what our Nannies did during the day when we eventually went to school. Perhaps they had a wee lay-down in the nursery, undisturbed. The fact that they had to live in the nursery was the reason we went to bed so early—

at eleven I still had to go to bed at half-past six, and, of course, there were years of reading under the bedclothes with a torch because of the boredom of lying awake.

Betty Field was youngish, pert, and entirely orientated on a place called the Wishbone Club, where she went quite often. Once she asked me what kind of man I would like to marry when I grew up. I said instantly, "A Poet." "Oh *no*," said Fieldie, "Poets sit about drinking *tea!*" At school I drew a picture I entitled: *An Etonian with his best girl*. The rather upper-class house-mistress, with difficulty, and going red, said she thought the caption 'rather vulgar'. I cried with mortification: I had thought I was immune from Miss Field's influence, and realised I was not. I saw instantly that the caption was vulgar. Then, Miss Field went to a fancy-dress dance at the Wishbone Club, and made her outfit herself. It consisted of a very few green leaves, because she had decided to be Eve. She had a flat chest, broad hips, and very short legs. I remember her turning round and round in front of our glass in the night nursery, asking me how she looked. I thought she looked vulgar, but didn't say so.

In 1939, with the number of domestic servants still at about one and a quarter million, the number of Nannies, at the least, was some hundred and forty thousand; for reasons already given the figure was probably somewhere between two hundred and fifty thousand and three hundred and fifty thousand. The War finished them off—or finished them as a force of social significance. Now, if my correspondence is anything to go by, young Nannies fought—in the W.R.A.C.S., W.A.A.F.S., as Wrens, in war jobs up and down the country. Even older Nannies did their bit. One old Nanny ran a market garden and a farm of fifty acres. Another took three companion Nannies and helped staff a British Restaurant. After the war, even by 1951, the number of domestic servants had barely risen to half what it had been before while the total population continued to soar. For the first time, by war and legislation, the wealth of the upper classes had been effectively cut into. As I said earlier, it is the Second and not the First World War, not only in this important sphere but in class attitudes, in our position in the world, in our social and sexual values and so on, that future historians will judge to have been the great watershed in British history.

Meanwhile, what of college-trained Nurses? Between 1892 and 1939, 3,832 girls entered the Norland Nursery Training College. From this must be deducted the number of those who failed to reach the required standard or dropped out during the course—approximately two hundred. A more serious deduction must be made for marriage. The marriage rate amongst Norland Nurses has always been extremely high, possibly, since a fee has to be paid for the training, because a 'better class of girl' is attracted to it. Before the war it was estimated that one-third of the students would marry; nowadays the estimate is three-quarters. A deduction of a quarter over the period will therefore be generous, which leaves 2,724 Norlanders. Between 1901 and 1939, 1,068 Nurses passed through the Princess Christian College in Manchester. Calculations similar to those above leave us with a figure of 809. For the other, smaller colleges the numbers are as follows: Princess Christian College, Windsor—496; Welgarth Nursery Training College—509. To this I shall add 500 nurses to compensate for any errors and cover any small establishments which may have escaped my notice. The total number of Nurses for the entire period is 4,994—say 5,000. But this is a *total* figure; at the beginning, college-trained Nurses could be numbered in tens and then hundreds. We are dealing, therefore, with a little group of 5,000 college-trained Nurses in an army, a host, of nursery or otherwise trained Nannies numbering anything from three-quarters of a million to two and a quarter million. The effect of the college-trained Nurse was negligible.

There is a more fundamental reason for suggesting that the Nanny attitude to children changed less swiftly than has sometimes been supposed. One of the most important influences in this sphere was of course Freud. Once the paramount importance of early childhood experiences is recognised; once it is seen that what the adult develops into *is a result* of those experiences, then clearly the way is open to a radical reappraisal of how one should treat children. But Freud himself was only part of a far more momentous revolution in human thought which took place throughout the nineteenth century. It seems inevitable, now, that in its early days scientific enquiry would lead steadily deeper down and further back in its search for explanation. It must always exhaust what is on the surface; hypotheses which stand up to facts that are close to them must be tested against facts less close (involved here, as well, is that unending human desire, particularly strong in the nineteenth century, for a total, universal picture). But this search further back and wider both induces and predisposes another nineteenth century development; the idea of growth from a beginning, of change and development which takes place in logical accordance with that beginning. This is in essence what we might call the modern historical view of life and it is not surprising therefore to find that it really began in the study of history itself at the German University of Gottingen in 1760. Here, in their determination to remove history from the realm of theology and philosophy, German historians developed two weapons: a critical and scientific approach to the evidence;

the opening up of National Archives (comparable, in a sense, to the authentic memories of early childhood). These weapons became their most effective, as Professor Butterfield shows in his brilliant book on the subject, in the hands of Ranke and Acton. But we see very similar processes at work in many spheres of nineteenth-century thought. Darwin is an obvious example in biology; Freud is another in the field of human psychology; Marx is a third.

But changes of this magnitude in the direction of human thought take time to absorb. Only gradually do they permeate and work their way down into the mental texture of a society. One must question how quickly the humble Nanny was affected. During the 1920s nursery magazines—as well as chat, knitting patterns and stories—began to contain very sound advice about bringing up children. Some Nannies caught an echo of Freud in that they were vaguely aware of the serious and long lasting effects that incidents and atmosphere in early childhood could have. Nanny W described to me how she'd known one Nanny who had caught her little boy, aged three, playing with the poker in the fire. She had immediately heated the poker to red heat and made him grasp it, not at the red-hot end but near enough to be extremely hot. That's why, Nanny W said, the little boy had always stammered.

But I was much more struck by how little attitudes seemed to have fundamentally changed. Then, as today, Nannies often praised the new freedoms, the greater closeness between children and parents, while running their nurseries in exactly the same way as before and doing their best to keep children and parents apart.

As we have seen, of all attitudes those towards the upbringing of children change slowest. It is possible to say and read one thing and to do the opposite. My own feeling is that not until after the Second World War did the change become effective. Then, the upper and upper-middle class mothers, deprived of Nannies but not of children, with not the faintest idea how to bring them up, created the demand for information which was met by books, classier magazines, the wireless and, later, television. Lower class mothers as well, deprived of the advice they had once obtained from relatives now that the close family group began to disintegrate, set up a similar demand similarly met. The clinics which had grown up in the war to dispense rose-hip syrup and orange juice now began to dispense advice. And so on. Here, again, it is the Second World War that is the watershed.

I have gone into this aspect of our subject at considerable length for two reasons. First, the total number of Nannies, as I said at the beginning, is obviously relevant to the social significance of this study (though actually as I shall hope to show, less important than might be thought). But secondly, other books on this subject have assumed a steady and uninterrupted swelling of benevolence. Now I don't want to deny that attitudes did become very much more humanitarian, more enlightened, corporal violence diminished—this is no place to evoke the Nanny Block. But it is necessary to administer a corrective to that rather sloppy picture of the Nanny from 1850 on, just getting nicer and nicer and nicer. She didn't. The atmosphere in 1960, say, differed very much more from that in 1930, than that of 1930 did from 1900, or 1900 from 1850.

THE NANNY IN TIME OF WAR

The picture then, within wide variations, remains the Nanny-trained Nanny serving an apprenticeship and becoming herself a Nanny. The length of the apprenticeship, the specialisation of its subject, the isolation of its world produced a concentration on the nursery and its events which was often extremely marked. From this concentration there flow a number of interesting consequences.

One of these is the curious aptitude Nannies seem to have had for war. Often their bravery was the result solely of their nursery-centric view. Mrs. Priscilla Napier described to me a house just outside Plymouth in 1940. A day-light air-raid had just begun. The two-year-old said, "What's that noise, Nanny, what's that noise?" Nanny: "Bombs, dear. Elbows off the table."

Ducki, the Nanny of Baroness Budberg, showed a similar indifference to the realities of warfare. When the First World War broke out, the Baroness's husband was at the Berlin Embassy. No one had expected a war, least of all the Embassy. In fact the First Secretary had just gone on holiday. The Ambassador sent an urgent telegram telling him to return. The First Secretary wired back: "Why?" Baroness Budberg herself had sent Ducki and her son aged one to a house twenty miles outside Berlin. She telegraphed for them to return at once; she would meet them at the station at such and such a time. The country was in a ferment. Troops were being mobilised, trains cancelled, houses requisitioned. She was appalled at what might befall Ducki and her son, especially as the Nanny only spoke English. The station was particularly chaotic, seething with soldiers and frenzied crowds, desperate either to arrive or to escape. Suddenly, amidst the furore—there was Nanny! She sailed, said the Baroness, like some large serene cloud somehow above the turmoil, the little boy holding her hand. She appeared not to notice what was going on. Her only comment was a faintly irritated one at being sent for at such short notice.

But Nannies were often called on to show courage and resource of a still more positive nature. There is an excellent description of one Mary Fellows, born in 1868, whom Fitzroy Maclean discovered at Tiflis in deepest Georgia, U.S.S.R. He describes in *Eastern Approaches* how she had survived the First World War, the Bolshevik Revolution and now, in 1937 lived on in Tiflis. He asked her if she had any trouble with the local Soviet authorities. "None to speak of. They keep trying to make me give up my English nationality but I tell them not to be so silly."

Jessie Wheeler was Nanny to David Pryce-Jones's mother and afterwards to him. She had gone out to France as a nursery-maid and remained there, never learning French, for the rest of her life. She was a woman who held strong and clear-cut moral views and, as she showed when the Second World War broke out, of indomitable courage. David was then four, and they were living just north of Paris. Also in the house was his six-year-old cousin Propper de Callijon and her Nanny Staynor. His mother had gone still farther north to be near his father who was in the army. Suddenly—France fell. His mother and father escaped at Dunkirk, but David and his cousin were trapped. Not losing a moment, the two Nannies fled south with their charges to Cannes in Vichy France. It was felt to be only a matter of time before this too was taken over by Hitler. Everyone was frightened of the German troops, who were everywhere. Jessie Wheeler's contempt for them remained absolute. David can remember how she used to sit on the green-painted benches which were set at intervals along the front. One day, a German soldier came and sat next to her. Jessie stood up and said, "Do you think I am going to sit on the same bench as a Boche? Go away." The soldier went.

In 1941 it was decided they must go to Spain. You need a cool head to smuggle a little boy, at dead of night, through enemy territory. David can just remember a rowing boat over a lake in darkness. They eventually arrived at a small port on the Spanish Mediterranean coast. It was infested with fleas. Jessie (well into her sixties) would sit calmly watching while her stockings became covered black with fleas, and then swiftly peel them of and plunge them into boiling water. The game was to see how long her patience and control would hold out.

But even Spain was not considered safe enough. Nanny Wheeler and David Pryce-Jones fled farther and farther south until they reached Morocco. Here they stayed a year until finally in 1942 the Consul-

General arranged for them to be flown home via Portugal. They flew on the same service in which, shortly before, Leslie Howard had been shot down and killed. When they landed at Bristol they were front-page news. She would, David said, in other circumstances have made a first-rate guerilla leader. Her love and calm preserved his soul; but it was her bravery and cunning that saved his life in those long and often dangerous years.

It is not surprising that there is a well-known cartoon showing a naval commander in the middle of planning an attack and saying to his colleagues, "I wonder what Nanny would have done now?" And the mothers were often quite aware of these latent powers and were prepared to use them. During the last war Lady A prepared a simple but dramatic contingency plan in the event of a German invasion. Her daughter was to be sent with her brother and her Nanny, together with five other families and their Nannies, to a remote Hebridean island. The Nannies were to be completely self-sufficient. Lady A collected an armoury of guns and fish hooks and drew lists of what the Nannies were to catch and shoot and how they were to cook it. In some ways it is sad the plan never had to be put into operation.

But perhaps the strangest account of a Nanny at war occurs in literature, in a short story called *Mary Postgate* written by Kipling in 1915. It reveals the quite extraordinary lengths to which the anti-German war hysteria at this time allowed people to go. And it shows very clearly that vein of sadism in Kipling which some critics deny; a vein of sadism which it is possible to argue was a direct result of the experiences he described in *Baa Baa Black Sheep*.

Mary Postgate is the forty-four-year-old companion to elderly, crippled Mrs. Fowler. After she has been there a while, Miss Fowler's nephew Wynne comes to live with them. Wynne is already eleven, so Mary Postgate can in no sense be called his Nanny. Yet as the story progresses Kipling quite deliberately makes her behave as though she had in fact been his Nanny. The beginnings of her love for him are subtly pushed further and further back into the past. This is a necessary move because, for the logic of the story, to justify its horrifying end, her love for Wynne must appear to have deep roots. And so, almost from the moment Wynne enters the story, Mary Postgate takes on the role of ex-Nanny. She buys him clothes, packs him off to school, grieves or rejoices over reports. He has the gruff and teasing affection, the old nicknames—'Gatepost', 'Postey'—which conceal and reveal a deeper love. It is her photograph he takes to training camp, not Miss Fowler's. And Mary Postgate loves him. When his plane flies overhead she lifts her lean arms towards it.

When, at the end, she burns his childish nursery possessions she lights a match which will "burn her heart to ashes".

Apart from this love—and the fact that she has seen a great many uncles and cousins die, and has a large nose and large feet—there is nothing more to Mary Postgate's character. She has never done anything and never will. "Would you have been anything except a companion?" Miss Fowler asks her. No, replies Mary, she imagines not. Kipling represents her life as wasted. Even her love for Wynne, which she has always kept hidden, is no longer of much use once he has grown up and gone to train as a pilot.

It is after Wynne's departure that the story begins to move with almost indecent haste towards its grisly climax. It is as though Kipling can barely control his excitement at what he is about to make Mary Postgate enjoy. Wynne is killed on a training flight. Mary feels a surge of fury against the Germans, which on Miss Fowler's advice she suppresses. They decide that the best thing to do is to burn all his possessions in the incinerator ('the destructor') at the bottom of the garden. Mary Postgate sets off into the wet misty afternoon to get some paraffin from the village. She is returning from there when a German plane flying in low and with its engine cut so that no one will hear, lets fly with its guns and brutally shoots up a little girl, Edna Garrett, killing her more or less in front of Mary Postgate's eyes.

She returns to the destructor, brooding, and trying not to brood, on the bestiality of the Germans. While lighting it—it is now raining—she hears someone groaning behind "the dense Portugal laurels". Investigating, she finds a wounded airman at the bottom of a tree. Not one of ours, because "their heads were dark, and glossy. The man's was as pale as a baby's and so closely cropped that she could see the disgusting pinky skin beneath. . . . He seemed helpless except for his horribly rolling head."

Mary Postgate knows exactly what to do. Her beloved Wynne had left them a huge revolver firing flat-nosed dum-dum bullets which he explained were forbidden by the rules of war to be used against civilised enemies. "They're good enough for us," Miss Fowler had replied. "Show Mary how it works."

She fetches the gun and returns to the destructor. Not, however, to kill the German, though she threatens him with it and tells him to stop asking for the doctor. No, she is used to death. Kipling gives a catalogue of all the people she has seen or known die, ending with Edna Garrett and Wynne. "The thing beneath the oak would die too." She would

guard It till then. Poking the fire in the destructor, warming herself
at its flames, she settles to wait for Its death. And gradually it comes to
her that she is performing a function. No man could have done what she
was doing—he would have fetched help, taken It into the house. A woman
should have a family and husband, but one who hadn't could still be
useful. And not only useful, as she listens with expert ear for the sound
of Its death, she realises fulfilled, satisfied, too; fulfilled in a direct physical
way, in a slow, long-drawn out orgasm of pleasure at suffering and death.

> She thumped like a pavior through the settling ashes at the secret thrill of it.
> The rain was damping the fire, but she could feel—it was too dark to see—that
> her work was done. There was a dull red glow at the bottom of the destructor,
> not enough to char the wooden lid if she slipped it half over against the driving
> wet. Thus arranged she leaned on the poker and waited while an increasing
> rapture laid hold on her. She ceased to think. She gave herself up to feel. Her
> long pleasure was broken by a sound that she had waited for in agony many
> times in her life. She leaned forward and listened, smiling. There could be no
> mistake.
>   She closed her eyes and drank it in. Once it ceased abruptly.
>   "Go on," she murmured, half aloud. "That isn't the end."
>   Then the end came very distinctly in a lull between two rain-gusts. Mary
> Postgate drew her breath short between her teeth, and shivered from head to
> foot. "*That*'s all right," she said contentedly, and went up to the house where
> she scandalised the whole routine by taking a luxurious hot bath before tea, and
> came down looking, as Miss Fowler said when she saw her lying all relaxed on
> the other sofa, "quite handsome"!

WARS WITH OTHER SERVANTS

From the intense concentration of the Nanny on her job there flowed also
a lively sense of her own importance. It was an importance, however,
which occasionally had to be won, and then held, in protracted, fierce
and sometimes even bloody battles.

Late Victorian and Edwardian households were often very large.
Anything from six to ten indoor servants was usual; while as many as
twenty or thirty not uncommon. I can remember my grandmother—
certainly well off but not considered very rich before the First World
War—telling me how she didn't even put on her own stockings. She
just held her leg out and said, "Stockings!" Households and balances
of power obviously differed widely, but on the whole they divided into
four: the kitchen, under the head cook; the general household, bedroom,

linen, etc., under the housekeeper; the pantry, dining-room and all areas (like the master of the household's clothes) covered by male servants, under the head butler; and the nursery under the Nanny. In theory, each of these areas was separate and autonomous; in practice they merged, co-operating or clashing. It is difficult now, and perhaps wasn't even possible then, to give a very accurate general picture. Cooks, for example, saw themselves as supreme in the kitchen, and wouldn't have admitted the possibility of a comparison as to status with the Nanny. Most Nannies, on the other hand, saw themselves as certainly superior to the cook, almost certainly to the housekeeper, and only the butler, partly because he was a man but mainly because he had the ear of the master, was sometimes recognised as more important.

The great strength of the Nanny's position, of course, was that she looked after the children. This not only gave her the mistress of the house, but also, when her children grew up and if she was kept on, the authority of a mother herself. I was told many stories of how old Nannies exploited this situation, often quite amiably if with considerable strength. The wife of Dr. Alington, headmaster of Eton from 1917 to 1933, was a dominant woman, but she was not nearly as powerful as the Nanny, Nanny Shirlaw. Quietly, Nanny Shirlaw ruled the house. The particular pivot of her power was the nursery tea. Anyone visiting Dr. Alington—and in his long years at Eton a great many famous men and women came to see him— had to have tea in the nursery, presided over and delicately controlled by Nanny Shirlaw. The teas were delicious: dozens of different cakes and buns, tissue-thin sandwiches, honeycomb and home-made jams. Nanny Shirlaw was afraid of no one. My informant still thrilled to recall an encounter with Clive Lewis, then nineteen and, as Captain of the Boats, an immensely important figure in the Eton hierarchy. "If there's any more butter thrown at the ceiling, Master Lewis, you'll finish your tea in the bathroom." But she would have done the same, and did, to an over-frivolous member of the Cabinet, or an earl who spoke out of turn.

But dominance was not always achieved easily. In the tussles that developed the mistress, endowed, whatever the strength or weakness of her character, with the divine right of class, was always the arbiter. Even feeble Mrs. F fulfilled this role. Nanny Williams told me of a typical encounter. Three meals running brains had arrived in the nursery. Furious, Nanny Williams stormed down to the kitchen. "Does Nanny have to have brains when the child does?"

Cook said, "Just because you're the Nanny you think you can have what you like. I cook what I like."

"We would have had it out," Nanny Williams said, but fortunately at that moment Mrs. F appeared.

"What is wrong, Nanny?"

"We've had brains three meals running."

"What happened to the fish, Cook?"

"The butler fancied a piece, Madame."

Despite what she regarded as a technical victory, Nanny Williams continued to have a lot of trouble with Cook. This was quite usual. Cooks resented having to prepare completely different meals for the nursery, probably at different times and going to a different place. Their irritation explains why so many Nannied children remember nursery meals with boredom and distaste. The other great rival of the Nanny was the governess. Her arrival marked the beginning of the end of nursery rule. It was these two that Nannies chiefly fought.

Now, so long after, only a few legendary tales remain of whole campaigns, as the Horse is all that people remember of the Trojan struggles in the twelfth and thirteenth centuries B.C. Also, of course, as large households declined, at a rate we needn't bother to evaluate, the necessity for such fighting declined too. Fortunately almost at the end of our period (during the '30s), a complete war is preserved entire in the Journals of the present Lord Weymouth.

Nanny Marks was kind, even over-indulgent according to the Marquis of Bath, with the four Thynne children—Caroline, Alexander, Christopher and Valentine; but, though minute, she was also fussy and belligerent and had to fight ceaselessly to maintain her position. Intermittently, her foes attacked on most of the fronts a Nanny had to defend. There was, for instance, the war between Nannies. The then Lord and Lady Weymouth lived nearby Longleat at Sturford Mead (this is from 1934 on), but every Christmas they would return to the big house together with their Wilson and Stanley cousins. Because as the Nanny to Alexander, the heir to the house, Nanny Marks regarded herself as head Nanny, Nanny Harrod (of the Stanleys) and Nanny Bolton (Wilsons) used to gang up against her. Angry exchanges were frequent (an interesting parallel here to *Christmas with the Savages*). However, the alliance was always very precarious. One of the little Stanley boys and one of the little Wilsons hated each other and always fought. This immediately brought Nanny Bolton and Nanny Harrod into conflict, a circumstance which Nanny Marks grew adept at using to her advantage and sometimes even brought about.

She also had a difficult time with cooks. One in particular sent up such revolting food that Nanny Marks was eventually forced to complain —both to Cook and to Lady Weymouth. Next meal Cook sent up a raw skinned rabbit. This event in fact heralded the cook's loss of sanity. In the scene which followed the dispatch of the raw skinned rabbit, she locked herself in the kitchen and went berserk, hurling pots and pans around the kitchen and breaking it up. She had to be collected by attendants from the local lunatic asylum.

But Nanny Marks's major war, lasting a number of years, was with the governess, Miss Vigers. From the start, Miss Vigers seems to have decided there would be conflict and laid her plans accordingly. The very day she arrived she began to tell stories of how in her previous past at Lady Somerlyton's the Nanny had tried to interfere with the education of the children. "But," said Miss Vigers, "Lady Somerlyton kept the Nanny firmly in her place." Aware herself of the enormous social gulf which did and should separate a Nanny from a governess, she tried to impress it both upon the children and on Nanny Marks. She openly abused her with being a 'mere servant' and of 'trying to put on airs'. Nanny Marks began to loathe Miss Vigers. But at this stage, says Alexander Weymouth, she couldn't seem to formulate her dislike, couldn't quite put her finger on what was wrong; she became slightly incoherent when Miss Vigers was mentioned.

Matters developed swiftly. Thinking, with a knowledge of the realities of power no doubt gained from her study of history, that she would greatly strengthen her position if she could get her hands on the Exchequer, Miss Vigers offered to organise the paying of the other servants in order to lighten the load on her mistress. Nanny Marks was furious. She stormed down and refused point blank to be paid by anyone else but Lady Weymouth—a concession immediately granted her.

There followed the battle of the knickers. Miss Vigers, consolidating her hold on Caroline, had all Caroline's clothes transferred from the nursery to the schoolroom. She found that a pair of pink knickers was missing and assumed at once that Nanny Marks had concealed them out of obstinacy. Returning, apparently calm but no doubt inwardly seething, to the nursery she demanded the knickers. Alexander Weymouth, from Nanny Marks's subsequent accounts, has reconstructed the following conversation.

Nan: I haven't got Caroline's pink knickers.
Miss Vigers: You must have got them: they're down on her clothes list, but they're not among the clothes you handed over to me.

Nan:	I tell you, I simply haven't got them, Miss Vigers. They're not here, and what could I possibly have done with them?
Miss Vigers:	It's no good asking me what you've done with them. You've eaten them I expect.
Nan:	I've done no such thing. Come in and look for yourself.

Nanny now shut herself in the night nursery, leaving Miss Vigers to rout fruitlessly through toy cupboards, under cushions, behind rocking-horses. Finding nothing, she tried to get into the night nursery only to discover that the door was being held fast. A tug of war developed, Miss Vigers shouting, "Open the door! Open the door!" She was stronger than Nanny, so the door began to open; but now Nanny suddenly let go, the door flew open, and Miss Vigers overbalanced backwards. Before her enemy could recover her dignity, Nanny left the field having won, she always claimed in after years, not just a moral victory but a physical one, as Miss Vigers was still lying flat on her back. She also said it was proof of Miss Vigers's madness that she should accuse anyone of eating pink knickers.

Quarrels and arguments of this sort were continual. As month followed month, they began to wear Nanny down. She became obsessed with the idea, quite justifiably, that Miss Vigers was trying to drive her from Sturford. Miss Vigers once said to her, "Yes, so far I've only got Caroline. But Alexander will be starting lessons with me soon. I'll take them away from you one by one. Even that little baby [Valentine] will belong to me one day." Time is on the side of the governess. Nanny Marks fretted and brooded and eventually had some form of nervous breakdown. She woke one morning and found, she said, she 'simply hadn't the energy to move'. Dr. Graham Cambell prescribed a long holiday and a temporary Nanny, Mrs. Broom, took over.

Realising her moment had come, Miss Vigers struck. She saw that her best plan of ousting Nanny was to establish Mrs. Broom as a preferable alternative. She formed, therefore, a close alliance with her, and they further strengthened their cause by procuring the sympathy of a Miss Simms. Miss Vigers now began to hint openly to Lord and Lady Weymouth that they would be wise to take this opportunity of getting rid of Nanny Marks. Her chances were further improved because the whole family was about to go to France when, provided Nanny Marks stayed away, Mrs. Broom could become even more deeply entrenched.

However, Miss Vigers failed. Mrs. Broom was disliked by the children so Miss Vigers's plan was weakest at its most fundamental point. And

Nanny Marks knew precisely what was going on. She returned well before the French holiday—and in fighting trim. On the holiday she re-established her control and position with the children and, especially since Valentine was still a very small baby, became once more indispensable.

On their return, Alexander moved down from the nursery to a room near Miss Vigers and Caroline. The family was now split into schoolroom children and nursery children. In the holidays, Miss Vigers went away and the schoolroom children returned to the nursery, to be spoilt by Nanny and commiserated with for having to be with Miss Vigers. But in fact both antagonists now realised that each was firmly fixed in her respective position. They had arrived at a balance of power. Hostilities continued, but were confined to pin-prick scheming and bitchy remarks—continued indeed for years. While at his prep school, Alexander used to write to his mother and ask if Nanny Marks and Miss Vigers were still having their rows.

It could have gone on till the end, when time would have brought the children one by one under Miss Vigers's control, as she had long ago prophesied. Then suddenly the true source of a Nanny's power delivered Miss Vigers into Nanny Marks's hands and enabled her to annihilate her and her kind for ever.

The instrument of her triumph was Christopher. He continued to love Nanny Marks and resisted all Miss Vigers's attempts to wean him. She therefore loathed him, castigated him as a nursery boy and used to terrify him—shouting at him and beating him with a ruler. Her presence paralysed him and he became totally unable to concentrate, particularly on reading. For a while he obtained relief by noticing that if he looked at her lips he could see her unconsciously mouthing the words that she was expecting him to say. However, she discovered this and thereafter hit his hands with a ruler if he so much as raised an eye from the page. The next ruse he employed was to hide all the reading books before the lesson but this too was found out and led to further beatings.

At the end of 1941 Miss Vigers was abruptly sacked. The reason was that Christopher had become too terrified of her, and since her dislike of him derived directly from his continuing attachment to Nanny Marks, Nanny's assumption of a great victory was quite justified. She flaunted it through the household and, taking advantage of her success to secure the future, urged Lady Weymouth that it would be better to send Christopher to the Lord Weymouth school as a day-boy, rather than risk another governess. Lady Weymouth agreed, and no other governess was ever engaged. From then on Nanny Marks's position was unassailable.

THE NANNY COMMUNITY

Although many Nannies lived rather isolated, lonely lives, it is also true that this intense concentration on, and the specialisation of, their subject, the similarity of their lives, the fact that children like and need to meet other children, these and other factors gradually produced a rather loose Nanny community. Magazines and journals slowly appeared to cater for them: a monthly, *Nursing Notes*, in 1899; *Baby—The Mother's Magazine* in 1907, a guide to bringing up children which was more often read by Nannies; in 1915 came *Creche News*, now the *Nursery Journal*, and in 1925 *Nursery World* which is still going strong.

These publications were read by quite large numbers of Nannies. But within this wider community smaller, more intense, more local groups sprang up. Nannies met each other at parties and gossiped about their employers and themselves (older Nannies sitting together, separate from the younger Nannies); getting to know each other, they recommended Nannies to their employer's friends. Nanny Buckles gave me a particularly strong sense of a Nanny community. The gossip they had! She wouldn't let on—but, well, they were only human. "So I wrote to a Nanny I knew. . . ." She knew Nanny Soames and confirmed what I had heard, that she was very well set up in Paris. Very well set up *indeed*. In fact she'd heard that Nanny Soames didn't really like coming back to England at all now.

Plainly, the Nanny community was strongest in London (though many families had country houses as well). And the centre of the Nanny community in London was the park.

Hyde Park! How an old Nanny, as Englishmen did once to Agincourt, thrills still to the mention of that name. For many, the richest moments of their lives passed there. Nannies were going to it before the First World War, but it was during the 1920s and '30s that it seems to have reached the zenith of its popularity (a development no doubt facilitated by technical improvements in the pram). The morning might be spent in numerous Square Gardens, but in the afternoon Nanny and children set out for the park. Many walked literally miles to reach it, ignoring nearer, greener, less fashionable recreation grounds. And when they reached it—what a sight! A vast concourse of Nannies, thronging, drifting, sitting, rocking, more numerous than the buffalo upon the plain, more talkative than starlings at a moot. Here the gossip seethed and flowed, though transmitted often through the Nanny medium of nods and chuckles, pursed lips, raised eyebrows, shaken heads, fiercely criticising their employers, boasting about them, complaining, reminiscing, talking about past scandals, past positions, and all the while watching and discussing their charges, reprimanding misdemeanours, inflating small dramas, removing minute specks of dirt (Nanny Buckles used to take a complete change of clothes to the park for her children because the drawing-room ritual followed immediately upon it).

For these same children, the park was not necessarily so stimulating. Here is another extract from the memoirs of her childhood by Bridget Tisdall, whose fine lesbian Nanny I quoted earlier.

> My sister and I had a double pram for a short period. Then I had a pram of my own, and after that, a mail-cart, which was simply a more impressive form of a push-chair, with a hinged floor which could be converted into a pram. It, like the prams of that day, was a very solid affair with large spoked wheels and a black leather hood with a white lining and frilly pillow. I would be wheeled daily into Hyde Park up Sloane Street . . . past Gooch, now Harvey Nichols, across Knightsbridge, past the French Embassy and the stags on Albert Gate. Here sat the Balloon Woman with her bunch of balloons and red and yellow windmills on sticks which the Nannies bought for their charges. We would then cross Rotten Row, pass the little sylvan, fenced-in inclosure with its rabbits, moorhens, lake and waterfall, and turn right into The Daisy Walk where upper-crust Nannies with crested prams sat knitting, complaining, and generally comparing each other's situations. It was rather dull in The Daisy Walk. We toddled about, picked daisies, and were called to attention with monotonous regularity by Nannie. If a little boy pinched a little girl their respective Nannies were at each other's throats. Such were the meagre facts of life encountered in The Daisy Walk. An air of convalescence hung over it on those sudden, hot Spring days so peculiar to London. The children were always getting over, or in the middle of, streaming colds, heavily wrapped up in spensers, coats, scarves, gaiters, these last done up with a button-hook which, if the button didn't fly off, often hooked up a piece of leg with the button. Spensers, which Nannies adored, were much hated jackets made of thin stockinette worn under winter coats. They wrinkled and tickled. "Nannie, I'm boiling" was the continual lament.
>
> As a baby I wore a pelisse of cream serge bordered with beaver. My appearance was greatly admired, as I then had naturally curly hair. "Strangers stopped the pram," my mother informed me. Straight hair was abhorred. It was ugly. That was enough.
>
> If you were naughty you had to sit beside Nanny and rock the pram. Odd it may seem, but children obeyed. Nasty little boys had a thin time in The Daisy Walk and were often taken home yelling and kicking, while the little girls looked on disapprovingly.

Sometimes I was wheeled up the hill to the Serpentine where I was allowed to throw bread to the ducks. I longed to feed the sparrows, but it was considered messy. There was an old man on this side of the park who was always covered in sparrows. His coat pockets were full of fine, white breadcrumbs, and when he offered them to the birds, a pinch at a time between his grimy finger and thumb, I felt quite hungry.

The park had plenty of red squirrels in those days. But even then, I felt there wasn't enough to do. All one's movements were so heavily supervised; the only wild animals of any size were the rabbits, and they too were fenced in.

The Daisy Walk at the east end of the Serpentine was certainly the most fashionable spot to go. But you could see Nannies all over the park. Another favourite spot was up behind the Albert Memorial. Here, quite recently, the young Nanny who looks after David Pryce-Jones's children had a conversation which can lead us into the final aspect of the Nanny community which I want very briefly to study.

The Pryce-Jones Nanny had wheeled herself behind the Memorial and sat down on an empty bench. After a while an older Nanny appeared, pushing a pram on which was painted a small gold coronet. She sat down too, and they eyed one another. At length the older Nanny turned to the younger one, coughed, and said "Excuse me, Nanny, is your mummy a titled mummy?"

"Actually, no," said the Pryce-Jones Nanny.

"You will excuse my mentioning it, Nanny, but this bench is reserved for titled mummies' nannies, Nanny."

NANNY SNOBBERY

But then it isn't everyone can say
They used to bath the Honourable Hay
Lord James Montagu, Sir Richard Twistle-Thynnes,
Captain Cartlett and the Ramrod Twins.

Other people's babies
All my life
Three dozen mothers
And not one wife.

Of course it isn't everyone can say
They used to bath the Honourable Hay,
Lord Charles Cobley—had a present from the King—
And now, they tell me, he's a Bright Young Thing.

The aspect I mean, of course, is Nanny snobbery. I have perhaps already given sufficiently numerous examples and sufficiently cogent reasons, to explain the existence of this snobbery. But the growth even of the rather vague and loosely defined Nanny community we are discussing had three effects upon it. First, of course, their snobbery was intensified. They became competitive. Second, they became extremely adept at recognising and commenting on snobbery in others. Peter Eyre had a very good governess called Isobel Taylor who had also taught Jacqueline Bouvier (now Onassis) and all her brothers and sisters. "Typical Newport snob," said Nanny Robertson. She *was* a snob, said Peter Eyre, though more an intellectual than a class or wealth one. She was thought to be a communist. In fact Nanny Robertson was a far more direct Newport snob. She refused to let them play with a wealthy nearby family because she believed the father had something to do with garbage.

The third effect was more curious. It took many years for an outsider to master the complex, subtle distinctions, the nuances of accent, attitude, behaviour and misbehaviour, which went into, indeed go into, that living, changing thing—English upper class snobbism. And Nannies were outsiders. Suddenly they found themselves thrown into a world in which the very air was electric with snobbery. As a result, they had to invent snobbish distinctions—rather as prep school boys, and for the same reason, create crazes, fashionable words, special clothes. Their invention runs through the thickets of my correspondence and my interviews like some extraordinary creeper thrusting out great tendrils and huge eccentric flowers in search of a sun it cannot see. Mrs. Goriely's Nurse Binfield (*c.* 1927) said jelly must be eaten with a fork, you can tell a gentleman because he has buttons on his coat and they *undo*, nice (that is upper class) children never whisper, have white knicker-linings, and Chilprufe next to the skin. Vulgar children (always vulgar; it was common to say common) said Hip, hip, Hooray; 'we' said Hurrah. Nanny Ellis, Nanny to the King Spark children, said Cadbury's chocolates were all right, but Fry's were common. In a pram, it was polite to have the hands resting primly on the pram cover. She also said it was common to play in a large front garden where you could be seen. Later, in the First World War, the Dutch Queen Wilhelmina took a house near the King Sparks and used to sit in her porch looking onto the front garden. The King Spark children told her she was being common to sit in a front garden. "I sit," said the Queen, "where the sun is." Compton Mackenzie's Nanny always called dripping honey, as she considered dripping vulgar. And so on.

These, and the numerous other aspects of Nanny snobbery I have dealt with earlier, were spread unevenly and in various degrees throughout the Nanny community. They did not, however, diminish as time passed. On the contrary, as Nannies became more rare, so their position became stronger and more elevated, and their sense of snobbery more refined than ever before. Today, the Nanny in a grand household is at the height of her power. Nanny Soames, for example, reigns in Paris. Her tea parties are the equivalent of a reception at the Duchess de Guermantes. While to be asked to one of her dinners is something all the Nannies in Paris strive for, but few achieve. Once a week, I understand (but my informant may have exaggerated), the entire Embassy is given over to her—kitchens, dining-rooms, staff—and she entertains. I have a picture of the Ambassador and his wife slinking out to some local bistro. The style a Nanny in Paris is accustomed to now is further indicated by this description of one employed—if 'employed' is quite the term—by one of the smartest Parisian families.

> (We) gave Nanny a lovely cottage last August—I furnished it with pieces from the house in North Berwick, we bought 'Louis fittings' for the electric lights from Peter Jones!—garden equipment, etc. . . . The last Christmas dinner took place on December 27, 1969 at Montefontaine. It was just a 'diner cottillon' each Nanny (usually eight) either emanating from the house of Rothschild (Nanny Sergeant) or from a 'nouveau riche' international Parisian family. They had to have lobster, turkey, foie gras, plum pudding and mince pies, champagne flowing—crackers and English decorations, lots of holly and mistletoe. . . .

Most of the Paris Nannies have cottages in Wiltshire they will eventually retire to. The distinguished French family de Valdenair, who have an English Nanny, also have race horses. In the late '40s their horse Pearl Diver won the Grand National. The Nannies in Paris were delighted, since they all won considerable sums of money. Seeing them pass in the streets shortly after this someone said, "There go the landed Nannies."

This is all outside our period, but like scientists studying prehistoric biology we can often trace back, and date, from species existing today, developments which were already beginning in the past. And oddly enough the most complete, and most amusing, account of this whole area of our subject (though in an advanced stage)—the small community, its power, its snobbism, the part played in it by the park—has been written by an American describing the British Nanny in New York. This comes from a story, 'The Nanny Mafia', in *The Kandy-Kolored Tangerine-Flake Streamline Baby* by Tom Wolfe. As you read, hear Manhattan:

All right, Charlotte, you gorgeous White Anglo-Saxon Protestant socialite, all you are doing is giving a birthday party for your little boy with the E.S.A. (Eastern Socially Attractive) little-boy bangs in his eyes and all his little friends. So why are you sitting there by the telephone and your malachite-top coffee table gnashing on one thumbnail? Why are you staring out the Thermo-Plate glass towards the other towers on East 72nd Street with such vacant torture in your eyes?

"Damn. I knew I'd forget something," says Charlotte. "I forgot the champagne. . . ."

"OK, Charlotte. Champagne for your little boy's birthday party?"

"You're damned right," she says. "For all the Nannies. I'm not kidding! If we ever tried to give a party for Bobby and his little friends without champagne for the Nannies, we might as well, you know, forget about it.

"Bobby's Nanny is mad enough as it is. All she can do is drop what are supposed to be very gentle hints about the V . . .'s party for little Sarah. Do you know what Van gave each kid as a *party favor*? An electric truck. I'm talking about a *real electric truck*. Of course, they're nothing much really. They're *smaller* than a Jaguar. By a little bit. The kid can get inside of it and drive it! They cost five hundred dollars, five *hundred* dollars. Can you imagine that? We had to carry the damn thing home. You should have seen us trying to get it into the cab. Of course, Van is absolutely petrified of the Nannies." For her party Charlotte has some sort of bird with a tape recorder in it. But she knows their Mrs. G. . . , whom they call the Black Widow, isn't going to be happy with it.

"She wanted to have the party in Robert's father's house on 70th Street in the first place. I'm serious! She doesn't like this apartment! It em*bar*rasses her! Do you know what it is? Do you know who runs the East Side of New York? The Nanny Mafia. There's a Nanny Mafia!"

The Nanny Mafia. They congregate, we learn, in Central Park, in the playground just over the stone wall next to Fifth Avenue, at the foot of East 77th Street. They are status symbols—the English ones the most status-y status symbols of all. Unabashed snobs. (The Irish ones act British.) And they're on the phone the whole time. About everything. About how common so-and-so's apartment is, where everything looks cheap except the wedding presents.

You know, you're invited to dinner, says Charlotte, and this poor couple, as soon as you walk in, you can see they've gone to a lot of trouble, flowers and indirect lighting, yellow glows, city lights, and they've hired a butler. The girl always has on some kind of Ravish-Me hostess outfit and looks like Little Heidi of Switzerland conscripted into a seraglio. So pathetic. And the furniture is always sort of Department Store Louis, if you know the kind Charlotte means. Then you sit down to dinner at this *awful* table and then suddenly here is the fabulous silver and china, Winslow table settings, apparently the real thing, *fabulous!* The comparison is just too crushing. It's always obvious. Where it came from. Their parents and their parents' friends shelled out and gave it to them when they got married. Haven't you ever been in that kind of apartment? It's too—Charlotte doesn't know—it's not even pathetic. Well, Charlotte didn't mean to go on about that. But that's exactly how the Nannies think!

Everyone with a Nanny does what the Nanny says—children's clothes, children's parties, décor, everything. And the network! They spend half their time trading information. "Such information! Never mind politics, industry and culture. The Nannies deal in intelligence that is close to the soul. Who was seen insinuating his trembly knee between whose silky shanks in the crush at whose party."

She wasn't going to have a Nanny. But then one day she took Bobby down to Central Park and was just completely frozen out. There's nothing lower than a mother who brings her own baby to the Park. And not just that. She had the wrong kind of baby carriage. It was white. It was too shiny. The wheels were too heavy-looking. It was made in America. They (the Nannies) looked at the thing the way people look at Cadillacs or something.

"The only acceptable one is the Brabingham," says Charlotte. "It's a very old make. They have to be shipped in from England. It costs a fortune. They're dark blue with all sorts of fine handwork, you know, and, oh, I don't know, all these little touches here and there. I don't know what we did with ours or I'd show it to you."

Lord, the Nannies are absolutely dictatorial about what you have to buy. Charlotte remembers the first day, when she went into the playground by herself there was this poor little girl, about six, who came in with her nurse. The nurse was a colored girl. Neither of them knew a thing, poor dears. The little girl saw these other little girls her age, and, oh, she wanted to play with them. Her little eyes lit up like birthday candles in her little buttery face and her little legs started churning, and there she was, the original *tabula rasa* of joy, and friendship. Did they let *her* have it! Rather! The first girl she came up to, Carey K. . . .'s little girl, a real budding little bitch named Jennifer, if you wanted Charlotte's frank opinion, just stared at her, no smile at all, and said, "My shoes are Indian Walk T-strap." Then another little girl came up and said the same thing, "My shoes are Indian Walk T-strap." Then Jennifer says it again, "My shoes are Indian Walk T-strap," and then they both start whining this at the poor little thing, "My-shoes-are-Indian-Walk-T-strap!" And the little girl—all she had done was come into the playground, to try to make friends, with the wrong shoes on—she's about to cry, and she says, "Mine are, too," and little Jennifer starts saying in that awful sarcastic sing-song kids pick up as one of their early instruments of torture: "Oh-no-they're-not-your shoes are *garbage!*" So the other little girl starts saying it and they start chanting again, and the little girl is bawling, and the colored girl can't figure out what's going on—and the other Nannies, Jennifer's Nanny, all of them, they're just *beautiful* as Charlotte remembers it.

"They just sat there through the whole performance with their masks on, until their little terrors had absolutely annihilated this poor kid, and *then* they were so concerned.

"'Now Jennifer you mustn't tease, you know. Mustn't tease.' The whole time, of course, she was just delighted over how well Jennifer had learned her lessons."

The Nannies dictate that kids have to have Indian Walk shoes. They have to get their hair cut at this and that hotel. And clothes! Charlotte gives upon clothes.

There is no such thing as knockabout clothes in the Nanny's entire rubric of life. There is all this business about herring bones, Shetland weaves, light flannel, heavy flannel, raw silk even, Danish sweaters. The only thing that saves even the wealthiest family from total bankruptcy is that the kids start going to school and watching television, after which they demand dungarees and their tastes in general deteriorate medievally. Until then, however, the Nannies have all picked Cerutti on Madison Avenue, and so all the kids go trooping off to Cerutti for clothes.

"Of course," says Charlotte, "there's this place in England the Nannies really prize. They get practically emotional over it. There's a photograph of the Duke of Windsor as a baby, on the wall, and it's signed, something like 'Best of luck to my dear friends, Sincerely, Edward, Duke of Windsor.' Do you see why they love the place? The message, naturally, was written by his Nanny. So here is the Nanny Mafia speaking through the throne of England!"

A Nanny will do anything to get you to go to England just so you can get to this damned store.

"Robert, you know, is always handling these bond transfers, for the Swedes, and he goes off to Stockholm, for the Belgians, and he is off to Brussels—everywhere, for some reason, except England. If the Black Widow doesn't let up, I swear, he is going to crawl in there on his hands and knees one day and ask to be sent to London. I'm only kidding about that. Actually, Robert is rather level-headed about Mrs. G. It's me who—well, these are formidable people. They have power. I'm sure some of these people, like the party caterers, for example, wine them and dine them. They ought to, if they don't. . . ." The telephone rings. Charlotte picks it up. "Hello Robert. . . . Well, all right . . . I suppose so . . . that's fine . . . I guess that's fine . . . All right . . . Goodbye."

She untwists and faces me again, looking kind of blank. "That was Robert. He's been talking to his father about the party. . . ."

CONDITIONS OF SERVICE, RETIREMENT

As a career, being a Nanny had a certain amount to recommend it. If my information is representative, the wages were not large but they were adequate, probably rather higher than the normal run of domestic servants.

Lady Cecilia Ridley was a young mother in the 1840s whose letters have been preserved. She had a difficult and cantankerous Nurse called Wells who grumbled and complained about everything. She complained particularly about the position of the nurseries. "We cannot alter the position of the nurseries," said Lady Ridley, "unless we pull the house down." Wells was paid 20 guineas a year. I think this was high. I have figures of £11 and £13 a year for the 1860s and 1870s respectively. For 1905 I have a sum of £15 a year. In 1916 one Nanny was paid £20 a year; another had £18 and £6 beer money. In 1924 Nanny McCallum got £14 a year, but then she was only fourteen years old. For the mid-'20s I have figures of £65, £52 and £70 a year. A good cross-section is provided by Priscilla Napier. Her mother's Nanny in the early 1870s was paid £10 a year; her own Edwardian Nanny £30; her children's Nanny in the '20s £60; and her grandchildren's Nanny now gets £600 a year.

Of course, some employers were very mean. Nanny Watson, because she had come untrained and been taught by the mother, received virtually no wages at all. This continued for some years. The mistress had a view of salaries, said Nanny Watson, as being immutable. Nanny Watson eventually asked for a rise. The mistress said it was quite impossible. She simply couldn't afford it. The idea was quite out of the question. Eventually she said she might manage a rise of a pound a year. But on the whole the Nannies I spoke to had been satisfied with their money. It was, after all, pocket money. They had no other expenses whatever. Often their clothes and travelling were given them free. A minor but indicative role is the Nanny as Bank. Richard Usborne and his family frequently borrowed from their Nanny, and he once heard a mother saying she wouldn't pay her thirty-year-old son's subscription to White's Club until he'd paid back the fifty pounds he owed Nanny.

Accurate generalisations about whether it was more or less pleasant to be a Nanny are obviously impossible, but there are various other factors which should be borne in mind. In larger Victorian and Edwardian households where servants were plentiful the work cannot have been too exacting. There are numerous examples of five people—for instance a Nanny, two under-nurses, a nursery-maid and a serving maid—looking after three children. Such profusion declined, but as recently as 1939 J. V. can remember her mother, Lady V, doing the ironing for their Nanny. Often Nannies wrote to me nostalgically recalling the comfort, even luxury of their Nannying days. Nanny Hurrell never went down the back stairs, it was always the front stairs. A chauffeur took her and the child everywhere. "We never went on a train or anything common like that." Nanny Edwards bemoaned the difficulties of bills and things and said she missed the feeling of being looked after. Nanny McCallum remembered Nanny tea parties, a footman to each Nanny. No doubt they and the others exaggerated, but a sense of ease remains.

And many Nannies did things, met people, went to places they would never have seen in any other circumstances. They travelled the world, occasionally settling in its remotest corners. Wives today not only look after the children, they have to cook, clean house or flat, continue to attract their husbands, and sometimes even work as well. Their travelling is limited by money and the absurdly short holidays most men get from their jobs. And much of this activity, just as or more demanding I can't help feeling than the work of all but the most hard-pressed Nanny, is made still more difficult because it takes place in conditions, often, of loneliness and isolation, unbuttressed by the bustle of a large household community.

There is a simple but affecting phenomena in Nature whereby a plant which has not been pollinated retains its flowers long after its fellows have gone to seed. Far into the autumn it stands, straight and bright, patiently awaiting its destiny. It may not fall till winter. The same is sometimes true of women. But the ordinary spinster (this was especially true in the past) can be subject to tensions which interfere with this process. Nannies, on the other hand, had many mundane stresses lifted from them. And more fundamental ones as well. Through their children they satisfied what were often strong maternal instincts. The figure, therefore, of the alert, vigorous Nanny, retaining authority and position well into her seventies and even eighties, is quite a common one. I got a strong impression that Nannies lived a very long time.

The evidence I have for this, as for the whole subject of retirement, is not really numerous enough to be statistically convincing. It is true, too, that people with very old Nannies often wrote to me to boast about them. Also, in search of information about late Victorian and Edwardian times, I deliberately sought out the oldest Nannies I could find. Nevertheless the Nannies described in the bulk of my correspondence, and most of those I saw by chance, seemed surprisingly strong and surprisingly old. I'm sure I've never seen so many vigorous old doctors, say, or solicitors or farmers.

Many, perhaps even the majority, of old Nannies probably retired as other servants did, that is back into one branch or other of their families, into homes of one sort or another, or, if they were fortunate, into some form of independent, if poor, existence on money saved during a long lifetime. Nevertheless my researches suggest that on the whole they did better than other servants, and commonsense would support this. Up till 1939 it was by no means uncommon for old servants to be given pensions, either of money or homes. In the person of a Nanny the motive would be much stronger. I frequently came across instances where, like Churchill to Nanny Everest, one or more ex-charges were paying their old Nanny an allowance. Much less common, but not restricted to the landed Nannies of Paris, was the gift or lifetime's loan of a house or cottage. Nanny Marks, her battles long since won, lived till she died last year in just such a cottage at the gates of Longleat. Elsie Beeny, the prep school Nanny, has recently bought and furnished a house in Hythe with the help of all her past and present children. At sixty-five, she is still working. The house is to retire to. Much more usual, too usual to make examples useful, was the old Nanny living on in the house. It might be noted, however, that this figure was by no means always the comfortable, wise, alert old woman as depicted by Evelyn Waugh, for example, in a conventional portrait of a Nanny in *Brideshead Revisited* or the Nannies in *Scoop*. I recall, among several, a crotchety, senile, difficult old lady who had been looked after for years in a great gloomy North Kensington house—goal of an embarrassing and fruitless visit. Another in Suffolk, where money, which once made easy the support of a redundant servant, had gone, and an unfortunate couple struggled to maintain an old mother and an old Nanny.

Sometimes Nannies, on retirement, supported their employers. The grandfather of Jaime Parladé in Southern Spain lost a lot of money on inspired schemes far in advance of their time. Around 1900, for instance, he imported cows into Malaga to provide milk, but the Malaganians, used to goat's milk, became frightened and obstinate about the cow's milk and refused to drink it. He also had the idea of making electricity from the waterfalls on his estate. But the expense of bringing the current the vast distance to Malaga finally broke him and he died not long after. Fortunately, he had engaged an Irish Nanny called Anne Dunn for his children, and on her retirement this woman lived with Jaime's grandmother in Malaga and supported her by sewing and teaching English. Anne Dunn is buried in the Parladé family vault, in the top and most coveted position.

There was one final thing I noticed about the retirement of Nannies, a factor which showed up in nearly a quarter of my interviews—and that was, even when they had 'retired', how vigorously the Nanny instinct continued to operate. They found it impossible to stop (I detected at times pleasure in the exercise of power). Nanny Watson stopped nannying when she was sixty-seven, but found she couldn't settle. She eventually joined a Quarrier's Home for orphans and stayed till she was seventy-seven. Nanny Hurrell found the same, and took to fostering children. Nanny McCallum looks after the old ladies of Eastbourne at night: "The things I could tell you of what goes on behind Eastbourne's doors!" Nanny Williams runs a nursery school. And so on.

Perhaps the oddest example I encountered was of another Suffolk couple. The husband's old Nanny—seventy-eight—came to live with them, but as their grandchildren were seldom there she had no function. Gradually, she took over the dogs. She moved them up to the nursery. She fed them, took them for walks, gave them rests, bathed them and put them to bed, when the couple would come and kiss them good night. In fact she developed an entire nursery routine from morning till night, excluding, as far as I know, only potting—and that, if puppies had come along, she'd no doubt have managed to squeeze in too.

CHAPTER SEVEN

Some Effects of
Early Upbringing

In ancient shadows and twilights
When childhood had strayed,
The world's great sorrows were born
And it's heroes were made.
In the lost boyhood of Judas
Christ was betrayed.

George Russell

Plainly, any profound understanding of the effects the Nanny could have requires some knowledge about the results of early upbringing on later adult development. So far in this book, I have been able to include the requisite information where appropriate in the text. Some of it no doubt was well known. It is now necessary to make a fairly brisk detour in order to explain more fully one particular aspect of child psychology; it is a detour, however, which is not only intrinsically interesting, but will throw considerable light on some of the things we have already discussed, as well as those to come.

Most people, while they pay it lip service, are very reluctant to face up to the importance of infant and child upbringing in character formation. Nor is this surprising. The effects of a disturbed childhood often don't manifest themselves for many years; till adolescence or the late twenties. They may even be repressed till middle age. And the ways in which they manifest themselves are very different from the events that occurred. The connection is seldom susceptible to the vague, apprehensive, unskilled introspection most of us bring to it. Those events themselves and our early reactions to them are often frightening. It is unpleasant to think that our identities were substantially laid down before we could play any part; the responsibility for doing the same to our children is awesome.

No wonder we shrink from facing up to the significance of our early years, and this reluctance often made my research for this book very difficult. After some months of work, for instance, I received a very promising and amusing letter from Jon Wynne-Tyson, the successful and enterprising owner of the one-man publishing firm Centaur Press Limited. His mother, he wrote, was a highly intelligent and emotional woman, a successful novelist and promising actress, who, as she would certainly admit, should probably never have been a mother. From 1924, when he was born, till 1930 he was looked after by his Nanny—'Nin'. His mother was a Christian Scientist and was determined he should not become emotionally dependent on her or his father. He was to have only one father/mother—God. (Nin too became a Christian Scientist and when he was ill instead of medicine they used to 'work him over' to get rid of 'error'.) Since he was not to depend on his parents he seldom saw them; he became therefore very dependent on Nin, despite the fact that she was an extremely unpleasant woman. She was fifty in 1924, Victorian in outlook, fat, resentful, strict, very strong-willed and seething with the bitterness of a frustrated spinster. She used to shake him violently, holding him up in front of her red face and screaming at him. He could still remember the pleasure he'd got from biting her bottom once when she was leaning over the nursery fire. Most of his early memories were of conflict and revenge: of refusing to get on the tram because he wanted another ride on the ferry; or of getting under the bed and clinging to the leg nearest the wall to escape the clutches of stout, enraged Nin, reaching out and breathing heavily.

Now I wanted to get at those early memories. They would counteract the, I suspected somewhat over-sugary, pictures I was being given at that time. I made an appointment and hurried down to Sussex. Imagine my amazement on finding that Mr. Wynne-Tyson had only allowed ten-minutes for our interview. Interviews always took at least an hour and a half and usually longer. Not only that, but he had also arranged what I recognised was a screen interview. ('Screen' is a Freudian term for a dream, memory, association or whatever, put up to hide the dream, memory or association the patient is reluctant to face.) There was a wonderful old Nanny of ninety nearby and he'd arranged for me to have tea with her. But even during our brief ten minutes I realised Nin had submerged again. Could he tell me a little about their rows? He couldn't really remember much. Not about refusing to get on the trams because of wanting to ride on the ferry? No. What about hiding under the bed while furious heavy-breathing Nin scrabbled for him? Mr. Wynne-Tyson looked vaguely out of the window and shook his head. His mind was blank.

Yet, as I say, this reluctance must be overcome if we are to evaluate the significance of the Nanny with any accuracy. It is not just that every study of criminals, the mentally unwell, the socially maladjusted reveals almost invariably that these situations have their origin in early life experiences. It is that very careful studies have now established that things much more intimate, minute and close to us are formed there too: the type of personality we will have, whether aggressive, shy, independent, devious and so on; the sort of wife or husband we will choose and whether we will choose; our ambitions, fears, needs, jobs; in fact all our characteristics, down to quite small details, though they will be modified later, are particularly the result of the intimate experiences of childhood. Heredity, of course, also plays a significant part. Heredity will dictate whether a person is short or tall, fat or thin, a man or a woman; it will probably have a strong influence on whether he is stupid or intelligent. Apart from such fundamental influences, one can say in general that it will incline a character in certain directions. But the evidence today continues to be that these directions will be altered, brought out or repressed to a quite overwhelming degree by the environment.

The most obvious way to approach this subject is through what one might loosely call psychoanalytic theory. That is to say, the body of theory which, while owing a great deal to Freud, has now gathered to it a large amount of new or modified material, deriving from the results and study of analysis, which is generally accepted by most psychiatrists, psychoanalysts, etc. It is information of this sort which we have already encountered from time to time. What I would like to look at now is what may be a less familiar approach and one which has special relevance to the next two chapters—that of behavioural psychology.

When I said 'studies have established', it might be wondered what studies and how much reliance can be placed on them. How can one 'establish' anything, prove anything, about something so complex as the human character? The answer is one can't, but one can so nearly prove things that to deny them becomes unreasonable.

For instance, if a psychologist wants to prove that parental rejection (or in our case Nanny rejection) leads to a proneness to delinquency or anti-social behaviour, he can hardly set up an experiment. He cannot ask a large group of parents to reject their children for several years to help his study. What he can do, however, is study a group of children known to have been rejected and compare them to a similar group of children who have not been rejected; similar, that is in age, intelligence, sex, social and economic background, etc. If there is always a significant amount more delinquency and anti-social behaviour in the rejected than in the non-rejected, then to say the least his hypothesis is supported.

But of course this was not a true experiment. The psychologist couldn't control all the factors. In this study, for instance, which has in fact been done many times, it has been found that rejected children often come from homes where there is a great deal of friction between parents. In these cases, therefore, it is possible that anti-social behaviour is a response to inter-parental tension as well as rejection.

Not only have many studies of this sort been made, but they have been very thorough, have used large samples and have been conducted over long periods of time. Margaret Ribble studied six hundred children for several years. In the Fels longitudinal tests thirty-six men and thirty-five women were studied continuously from birth, through nursery school, later schools and then, with continuing interviews and observations, into adulthood. In a moment I shall outline some of the ways in which what happens in early upbringing can effect people—but it should be remembered that it is studies like Fels and Ribble which have provided the evidence from which we can deduce those effects.

Mussen, Conger and Kagan, in their book *Child Development and Personality*, to which I am indebted for much of the material in this chapter, point out the central role which learning theory plays in behavioural psychology. It is not therefore a diversion to look at this theory for a minute.

To learn something is to establish an association between a stimulus and a response. Stimuli can be very varied—a bell, a breast, a traffic light, a thought. And the response can be very varied—running from class at the bell, drinking from the breast, starting the car at the lights. When the association has been set up—drinking from the breast, leaving class at the bell—we say the child has learnt to drink or learnt that the bell means he can go home. And the same is true of thoughts. If the child had an accident and was sick, then if he thought of the accident later he could be or feel sick again.

Learning happens more quickly and more effectively if a person has a strong motive, say the desire to get home quickly from school. And it happens more quickly if the response is rewarding, that is if he can go at once when the bell goes, and if home is pleasant. Now motives are what make a person act. A few of these are innate—food, warmth, water, air. The rest are learnt. This may sound odd. Surely, one thinks, aggressiveness, the need for mother love, the need for status and so on are also instinctive, automatic. Learning theory would say not. They are certainly very powerful motives, but they are only potentials, they can lie dormant—not until they have been activated, rewarded, learnt, can they exist. Not until a baby has been fondled and kissed and fed by his mother does he 'learn' to love her. In a famous experiment monkeys were removed from their mothers the moment they were born. They were never fondled or cuddled. Their feeding was quite impersonal. When they were adults the desire and ability for physical contact was completely absent. They could give birth; but they would not hold or nurse their babies, which soon died. In practice of course all the major motives—the need for love, security, sex, status, control over environment, etc.—are activated. But because they are in essence learnt, they are enormously modified by the way in which they are taught. A child who is not fondled a great deal by his Nanny, with whom physical contact is kept to a minimum, is likely never to show much interest in it later. A baby treated roughly, to whom contact is often painful, may come in later years to dread it. Whereas a child who is given a lot of cuddling, to whom physical contact has always proved rewarding, will probably enjoy it in later years.

Generalisation is a useful term in learning theory. We found it helpful in chapter 3, for example, where I examined the Victorian and Edwardian idea that lower class women had stronger sexual feelings than upper class women. As I explained then, if a child is hungry in the night and has learnt to steal from his mother's fridge at home, he will do the same in other houses he visits. If he dislikes his father, he may come later to dislike his father's friends, or men who resemble his father in some way, or even all men. (The actual form the lesson later takes is of course infinitely varied.) Denial is another useful term. It means that if something very unpleasant happens children pretend that it hasn't. Children openly ill-treated by their Nanny will insist she was kind and loving. If their families reject them, they will say they are adopted and that their 'real' families love them.

Once started, and it starts at birth, the personality, the character, develop in a series of learned responses of an almost inconceivable comprehensiveness, swiftness, complexity, depth and detail.

A child's desire [write Mussen, Conger and Kagan] for his mother's [or in this book his Nanny's] love may originally have developed because of her role in meeting his primary needs through such acts as providing warm bottles, rocking and cuddling, changing nappies, removing safety-pins and adding blankets on cold nights. Once developed, however, this motive (i.e. desire for maternal love) may serve as part of the basis for learning (i.e. activating) further complex motives. For example if the mother gives love only if the child is being orderly and conscientious the child may develop a need for conscientiousness that will be manifested even if the mother is not there. He may even learn to do many complex acts, such as always putting his toys away carefully, keeping his clothes clean, washing his hands frequently, and always doing what he is told, in order to satisfy the motives that are based, have grown from, his need for maternal affection.

Sometimes the degree of detail, its strength, is astonishing. Winnicott describes an infant who had a woollen covering which he loved. Before he was one he had become interested in the various coloured threads and liked pulling them out according to their colours. This response, this interest in the texture and colour of wool, never left him. In fact, when he grew up he became a colour expert in a textile factory.

So all-embracing and complex are the patterns set down in the first years that I can only indicate a few of them, and of these only outlines. The most important is this: following the principle of stimulus generalisation, it is on the reaction and responses the child gets from its Nanny that it will base its reaction to people generally. If she is rewarding then he will look for rewards—affection, trust, love—from people all his life. But if she is not, there is a danger the child will not, as an adult, seek rewards from people. He or she will be emotionally cold and indifferent.

Discipline is a tricky subject. A child is being asked to give up something it wants and if it does so it should be rewarded. In exchange, the mother or Nanny should praise and give love. If she *only* punishes, she becomes an object of fear or anxiety. She also often defeats her own ends. Long-term studies have shown, for example, that over-aggressive physical punishment increases bad and aggressive behaviour. The child is being told not to do something by someone who is actually doing it. He is likely to learn as much by the Nanny's successful aggression as he is by the fear and pain of punishment.

A child's concept of himself between the ages of two and four is based on what the most important people in his life think of him, that is his mother or Nanny. At the same time language is very important. Words *are* what they represent or convey. And so a child's idea of himself is determined by the labels his Nanny attaches to him. If she continually calls him 'dirty', 'smelly', 'naughty', he will begin to regard himself as those things and feel guilty and unworthy. Later, when he learns that people avoid dirty things he may behave as though he expected people to avoid and reject him. On the other hand, if he is told he is clever and good, he will begin to think he is, and in a challenging situation respond in an appropriate way. Self-confidence can be created or it can be crushed.

The conscience is formed in the first few years. If the Nanny rewards and punishes a child in conformity with consistent principles, then children learn how to view their actions even if the Nanny is absent. They see it through her eyes and thus develop a conscience. If her rules are not enforced or are inconsistent, then no conscience or only a weak one develops.

The role of the sexes are imprinted in early childhood. Little boys are expected to be tougher, more aggressive, less 'cry-baby'; little girls to be sweeter, more obedient, gentler. Tests have revealed that this sex-role imprinting is reflected in adulthood. Adults believe completely in the innate quality of differences in fact trained into them as children.

Imitation and identification are important. A child will imitate its Nanny for several reasons. If she is loving and rewarding, then pleasure is associated with what she does and she is imitated for that alone. Between three and four a child sees that Nanny has powers and privileges he doesn't —she can stay up late, she needn't eat up, she can spank. He thinks he can get these powers by becoming his Nanny and therefore imitates her. And he imitates to gain approval. As time passes imitative behaviour becomes automatic. It becomes an entrenched part of a child's personality and later heroes or heroines, and wives and husbands, will be found on analysis to be deriving a large part of their energy from those early figures who watched over us when young.

And so on and so on. Much of the influence of early childhood is practical, automatic, almost, when pointed out, obvious. This does not mean that the influence is simple. It is immensely complex, so complex that you can never say in detail how a person, even a baby, will react to his environment. What you can say is what aspects of the environment are important and how in general people may be expected to react. Thus you can say that the very early behaviour of mothers or Nannies towards their children is important as regards those children's ability to form later human relationships; and you can say that if that behaviour is violent and unrewarding, or if they are frequently absent or even leave, then that ability will be severely impaired. Also, of course, this early training will be modified or reinforced by what comes later. Incapable emotionally of love, distrustful of people, physically distant, the adult will see that 'love' and 'marriage' are socially desirable and embark on both. He, or she, will often cause great suffering. Some quality long ago admired in the Nanny will be reincarnated, with alterations, in a major-general. But all studies of this subject show that the shape of the personality, the direction our lives will take, the forces that will motivate us, are all laid down in the first six or seven years and cannot be fundamentally changed. When one adds to this the whole sexual and emotional development which has already appeared and will continue to appear as relevant parts of psychoanalytic theory surface in this book, it will be evident that the Nanny's power to do good or evil, to warp or straighten, to build or destroy, was virtually unlimited.

CHAPTER EIGHT

Separation from the Mother

"Say you're sorry again."
"I'm sorry, Mummy."
"You mustn't bang doors like that, darling."
Darling he thinks—that empty word.
From *Morning* by Julian Fane

Bearing in mind the last two chapters, particularly the portion in Chapter 6 dealing with the very slowly changing attitudes towards children and child upbringing, we are now in a better position to study further the most important ingredient of the Nanny situation—separation from the parents.

The most important of these can be put quite simply: Nannies left. They arrived, they stayed a few crucial years, and then they departed. How long they stayed, how often they departed, it is a little difficult to generalise about. Noël Oakeshott (pre-1914 childhood) told me that a Nanny would usually leave when her child was five, because she didn't want her next employer to think she had lost her touch with young babies. Other informants confirmed this. Mrs. Sitwell, on the other hand, one of Nanny Watson's charges, told me that Nannies left when the youngest boy went to prep school. They were always given a clock. The picture is complicated because there is some evidence that before the First World War households and families were larger and people richer. Nannies may have stayed longer. After the war, especially with the more raffish material we have noted, Nanny turnover quickened. My own impression is that around five was probably the usual age (this is the reason I estimated that in any one year one-fifth of all Nannies were on the move). Of course there were wide variations in this. Some Nannies, a minority, would stay thirty, forty or fifty years in the same family. I have several examples of over sixty years. Many others, perhaps a majority, left before five: they were sacked, or got fed up, or were offered a better position.

By the age of two the love of a little child for its Nanny is the most violent and important emotion in its life. Nor is it a simple emotion. It is profoundly physical, by which I mean sexual. The child will have felt jealousy, possessiveness, longing, passion, peace, adoration, desire . . .

Mussen, Conger and Kagan say that by two a child's feelings "acquire the strength and variety of adult love". If this loved figure (loved even if unworthy of it) departs, the child's despair is terrible. The symptoms can resemble those of babies deprived of food. The effects are permanent.

It is not surprising, therefore, to find that the annals of Nanny literature are filled with desperate descriptions of these incomprehensible and brutal partings. I could give dozens of examples; three will suffice.

F. Anstey (the pseudonym of Thomas Anstey Guthrie), who was born in 1856, is interesting for two reasons. His father was a genial, kindly man and his prep school was not, as Victorian prep schools went, all that horrific. The origins of *Vice Versa* probably lie, therefore, in the nursery, and here we do indeed find a despot—Fanny Channer, "a dark, sallow, hard-featured woman of about thirty". But in this context the significant thing about Fanny Channer was that she had been preceded by another nurse.

> I can just remember a nurse I had, and of whom I was very fond, when I must have been about that age [three], how she had to leave, and how one night she reappeared in my nursery and kissed me and we both cried. . . . I have an impression she was young and pretty and had to leave because she was discovered flirting in Kensington Gardens with a soldier. . . .

Even if not unkind, as here, the Nanny that followed the departure of that early and most basic love was often doubly hated. She was probably unconsciously held to be responsible for the event that brought her arrival.

In *Goodbye For the Present*, Eleanor Acland (born in 1878) describes the sacking of her beloved Miss Reed—Reedie. 'Milly' is the authoress. She is told that Reedie is going away on holiday and goes to her room interestedly to watch her pack. She begins to notice that Reedie is packing a great many, indeed all her dresses. She is seized with misgiving.

> "Reedie, when you coming back to Milly?"—though the actual words I do not remember, nor the actual words of Reedie's answer. But the sensation of the word 'never' in that answer remains, and the awfulness of seeing her suddenly burst into tears, there on the floor beside her trunk—the first grown-up tears Milly had ever witnessed.

In a panic Milly clutches at Reedie's hands, tries to pull them away from her eyes, they will not come. . . . She doesn't want to go, she has to go. Because she has 'spoilt' Milly. In her stead there comes "to reign over our Nursery Kingdom—Maria Barley".

Milly is only just over two when Reedie goes, yet writing in 1935 the grief of fifty-five years before catches her with all its original force. She loathes Barley.

But the age at which the Nanny went made little difference to the suffering of the child. We saw how even in their late teens Churchill and Peter Eyre were upset when their Nannies left. Dormer Creston, writing about her Edwardian childhood in *Enter a Child*, was seven when her Mary was taken from her. Her book, occasionally but understandably empurpled by self-pity, gives a classic picture of a little girl whose only warmth, love and stability came from her Nanny. Her mother was weak, distant, ineffectively and vaguely 'kind', whose sole desire was to escape and immerse herself in *The Times*, eating hot buns. Her father was more positive.

> His great principle as a parent was, not friendship, but discipline. He had in fact a craving for discipline that was so strong as often to obscure his other, most excellent qualities [we never learn what these are], and he could not resist bending all his energies on this child-fly that happened to be myself. I give him credit for believing that he always behaved exactly as a father should behave . . . but, meantime, across nursery and schoolroom, lay the shadow of Sparta.

But she gives examples of his behaviour which make it plain that he was activated by motives in which aggression, resentment and sadism played as much a part as his idea of parental duty. One time, aged four, she has just been interviewed by him about some childish misdemeanour. She becomes so terrified that, on leaving, she knocks a silk-covered cushion off the sofa and is unable to replace it. Each time she puts it back it slips off again. Her father watches angrily silent until at the fifteenth attempt she manages to lodge it. She turns and walks from the room. Suddenly he bellows at the top of his voice, "Walk straight! Straighten your back! Straighten your back!"

He is not only incapable of contact, but actively and invariably resists her attempts to establish it. She describes how, when she was three, she spent weeks making a birthday present for him, cutting out illustrations of bowls from a gardening catalogue and painting them. On the day, highly excited, she hurries down to the dining-room. Her father ignores her entrance, so she goes across and arranges the discs before him.

> One of my father's slogans was: *Speak out, don't mumble*, so now, endeavouring in no way to tarnish the occasion, I said with great clearness: "Many happy returns of the day, Father. I've brought you a present."

Without putting down his paper, he turned his head and glanced down at the untidy little deposit at his elbow: then without speaking, turned his head back to his paper and went on reading.

In her lonely, loveless, boring and often frightening babyhood, the one stable and comforting figure is her Nanny, her 'Mary'. Though a somewhat weak figure, she is constant, a 'lifelong companion' from whom she is never separated. Until, when she is seven, Mary is abruptly removed from her. First, she is sent to the country for a week without Mary (their first separation). When she asks for Mary on her return everyone is guiltily evasive. No one will tell her. Even her mother, dragging herself out of *The Times* and away from her buns, forces herself, with no doubt unconscious irony, to offer unexpectedly a game of Happy Families. At length she finds out from one of the servants: "Why, *don't you know*, Miss Dolly? She's never coming back! She's gone for good, she has!"

"For a second I seemed to see Ellen's face transfixed before me. Something was swelling inside me . . . some hideous realisation of grief coming to birth . . . straining against my ribs . . . suffocating me." In a panic, she rushes up through the house.

> Up again past what had been the nursery, up to the room at the top of the house where for the last year Mary had slept. I turned the handle and stumbled in. The little, shut-up room, clammily cold, received me into its darkness. Groping my way across I found the bed, and throwing myself on it face downwards felt the soggy honeycomb texture of the coverlet pressing against my cheek. I knew it at once as Mary's old bed-coverlet that she had always used as long as I could remember. Now it seemed the one part of her that was left to me. Dragging up a wodge of the stuff into my arms I buried my face in it and my anguish broke forth.

She catches exactly the animal sense of loss and the frenzied quality of her little girl grief which no doubt roused the sadist in her father. Some months later, terrified now of being left alone at the top of the house, she receives from him a harsh and heartless 'talking to'. Her sense of abandonment and unhappiness reach a climax and she thinks she should kill herself. She hears a voice saying, "Kill yourself! Kill yourself! Kill yourself!" She is eight years old.

A system which sets up a solid, all-important bulwark and then suddenly, arbitrarily and at a vital time, removes it, must be much vitiated as a method of bringing up children. Even in the modern marriage, which shows evidence of being itself less and less reliable, the mother doesn't just suddenly vanish. And there can be no doubt about it—the Nanny going was the *rule* not the exception. In book after book, letter after letter, interview after interview, from the beginning to the end of our period, I found descriptions of this event and the pain it caused.

Just how fundamental is the departure of the Nanny was brought home to me when I visited the Norland Nursery Training College in Berkshire. The aspect I particularly wished to examine was what sort of psychological background the girls were given—a subject which was supposed to be fully covered. It is dealt with during the morning lectures and unfortunately I was seriously hampered by M4 construction work round Reading which, at that time, in the interests of speeding the traffic of the future seemed unable to allow any movement at all in that of the present. The practical training, however, is remarkably thorough and comprehensive. It lasts twenty-one months (with holidays) with a further probationary year as an actual Nanny. It costs a thousand pounds (sometimes grant-paid). Although it is stressed that the young Norland Nurse is not a servant to help with the housework ('silver-backed hairbrushes') she is expected to control all aspects of her nursery; and the nursery is of course a miniature house. Accordingly she learns cooking, laundry, needlework and all forms of housework. Three months are spent in a hospital. And finally the great bulk of the time—nine months—is spent learning how to deal with children of all ages up to seven. But it is the very practicality of this last and more important part of the course which throws doubts on the thoroughness of the psychological training. Because the last part was in fact particularly practical. It is not a question of lectures or wall charts or changing nappies on dolls. The twenty prams which surge across the gravel each afternoon at Denford Park are full, there's a smell of milk in the air at the nursery wing, the scent of clean bottoms, you hear proper screams—the medium at the college is real live guinea-pig babies.

The babies come from the professional classes, from parents on holiday or looking for houses or getting divorced; also quite a number come from foreign diplomats. They stay two or three weeks, frequently for a month or two, sometimes for several months and recently two have stayed for four years. The system is that each baby is given to a girl student for a month (or if it is staying five or six weeks given for the whole of that time). The student does everything for the baby—sleeps with it, feeds it, baths it, looks after it twenty-four hours a day. Then, at the end of the month, she has a new baby. A baby there for four months will change hands four times. And, since the children left at the college are of every age and since the same system is followed, the young student gains an extremely thorough, practical, tested knowledge of how to deal with children from almost when they are born up to around seven. In this respect it is an admirable system.

But it has been established in recent years beyond all doubt (particularly by the Platt Report) that little children up to the age of five or six suffer enormously if they are suddenly removed from their mothers and put into institutions, however kind. Two or three days are painful; two or three weeks or months can do irreparable and permanent damage. It has also been found that if such visits to an institution are unavoidable then children are much happier if they are looked after by one person throughout their time—not six mother-substitutes in six months but one. Even quite unsophisticated institutions—council orphanages and the like—now do this as a matter of course, with immensely beneficial results.

Why was it not done at the Norland Training College? I was told I needn't worry. Children settled in very quickly under 'skilled hands'. Within a matter of days they were absolutely quiet and as good as gold (this apathy is in fact a far worse sign than crying or anger would be). But the main reason was that the pain of these little partings would prepare the girls for the many later and much more painful separations inevitable in a nurse's life.

This of course is rubbish. Emotion cannot be trained out of one. The reason for switching every month is the practical necessity for each nurse to have experience of children of every age. But this conversation did make me wonder just how sound the Norland lectures on child upbringing were. It would be quite impossible today to give a course on this subject and not stress the importance of the mother and the importance of having the same stable mother (and father) figure throughout childhood and indeed as long as possible, at least into adolescence. But it then occurred to me that this was the one area where, in a training college for nurses, you would expect to find schizophrenia. Because the entire purpose of the training was first to replace the mother and second to leave the child around the age of five and go and replace another mother. No doubt the lectures did stress the importance of stability and continuity and the role of the mother; the facts were at once forgotten. So much so that an institution which, above all others, should have sternly refused to take babies away from their mothers, in fact actually advertised for them.

There were factors exacerbating the departure of the Nanny. In some ways I think a marriage or a love affair which breaks up is more painful than one that is ended by death. Death is final, but separation is a prey to torments—where is she (or he) now, with whom, might she not return, why did she go, what did I do wrong, what was so terrible about me? The Nanny's going was rendered more inexplicable, more painful, because she was still there. Letters arrived from her, opening the wounds. She paid visits. In one case the Nanny went to work in the local bank and her little girl was confronted by this loved figure, now cold and distant behind a barrier, each time she accompanied her father when he cashed a cheque.

Nor was it only Nannies who left. Alexander Weymouth, before the arrival of Miss Vigers, had a young and pretty governess called Miss Russell of whom he was very fond. Oddly enough, Nanny Marks liked her too, and Alexander can remember them all playing games together. At the time of Edward VII's abdication crisis they used to play the Mrs. Simpson game. Miss Russell and Caroline acted as King Edward and Mrs. Simpson, Nanny and Alexander were 'Mr. Baldwin and supporter'. They had to run around preventing 'King Edward' and 'Mrs. Simpson' holding hands. Once they succeeded in getting together, the roles were reversed. Then suddenly Miss Russell left (Nanny Marks said it was because Alexander's grandfather had become attracted to her). Alexander was miserable. As opposed to the security of large households where the little upper class children could depend on the servants for love and affection, was this insecurity—much loved figures would often disappear abruptly, without explanation and without trace. Lady Antonia Fraser said that she has always associated love with leaving. No doubt we have here another reason why the literate members of the English upper classes respond so avidly to Proust.

Children suffered; but Nannies suffered too. They attached themselves deeply to their charges, sometimes without knowing it. Noël Oakeshott and her brother Penderal Moon bullied their Nanny Ford unmercifully. "If she attempted a reprimand, we rushed into the night nursery and jumped up and down on her tin trunk shouting 'I'm off to Pimlico'. Once I climbed onto a chair to reach the nursery medicine cupboard, and consumed some cold cream before her very eyes!" Yet when Nanny Ford left she had a breakdown lasting nine months; and breakdowns for this reason were common. I have already mentioned Nanny Watson and Nanny Richardson. Out of a total of eighteen in-depth interviews, one quarter of the Nannies had had a nervous collapse of some sort or another on leaving a child they particularly loved.

It was for this reason much less than to use them as examples of ideal behaviour (though they came in handy for that too) that Nannies so often talked about their old charges to the new ones. They couldn't get them out of their minds and only found relief in telling endless stories about them, showing photographs and little gifts, writing to them. From Nanny Everest on, this is so common as to make examples superfluous. Towards the end of her life, an old Nanny's memory would be thronged with her children, fixed immutably at three or four by their false death, and rendered more vivid by it—rather as the children in Simpson's Temple were vivid and unchanged. Nanny Strode sent me a poem she had written and which had been printed, a tribute to the universality as far as Nannies went of the emotion it expressed, in *Nursery World*.

> What memories come
> When things are still,
> I'll cherish them,
> I always will.
> My little ones, they are no more,
> Yet, still I see them by the door.
> A tiny hand to hold again,
> A cuddle now to dispel pain.
> Where are they now?
> All gone away.
> But in my memory they will stay.

The pain and damage caused by a loved Nanny's departure could be very great. It is appalling how little notice was taken of it. Nannies themselves, as we have seen, were sometimes vaguely aware of it. Lady Walberton's Nanny, in *Queen* magazine some years ago, said of a child misbehaving near where she was being interviewed by Francis Wyndham, "If that child had had only one Nanny all its life it wouldn't be such a pickle. It's the constant changes that are bad for them." But she, like Nanny Oxborough, was an exception. Simpson, for instance, because of Sackville-West's totally unrealistic conception of "completing" a child, didn't mind leaving in the least.

> But Ruth [Simpson] was much too excited to feel much sorrow of departure. . . . Will and Dorothy, much as she loved them, were becoming things of the past. . . . This was no heartlessness; she did not feel less love for the children she had just left behind her; but her regret at leaving them was transient—swallowed up by the excitement of her new charges.

Most Nannies, since the pain touched them so closely, preferred to ignore it or suppress it. Their own grief they bore as stoically as they could, unless it became unbearable (a cumulative process sometimes) when they broke. As to that of the children they had left, they took refuge in comforting phrases: "They'll get over it soon," "Two or three weeks", "He's a bit unsettled", "A child soon forgets", and this is understandable. But what of the parents?

The responsibility of parents, particularly the mother, for the evils resulting from the Nanny system is extremely difficult, perhaps impossible, to evaluate. What, after all, could they do? As often as not, if they didn't give the Nanny notice she would leave of her own accord. "You had to improve your lot," Nanny McCallum said. The Nanny method of bringing up children soon became the accepted one. Everyone did it. And, while it is not true that children got over the loss of a Nanny quickly or easily, it is probably true that few mothers noticed the symptoms—withdrawal, loss of appetite, regression to an earlier stage of behaviour, indiscipline and so on. Such things do not show up in an hour in the afternoon and a ten-minute visit in the morning—supposing the mother knew the child well enough to recognise them, which was unlikely. The new Nanny or governess or schoolmaster where the boy or girl had been sent were either familiar with such behaviour from past experience and knew it would pass or else supposed it was normal for the new child. The Freudian-orientated or inspired attitudes and discoveries which would change this situation penetrated, as we have seen, with extreme slowness.

Nevertheless, it is hard here, and even more later, not to feel anger at the gross selfishness and superficiality of many upper class mothers during this period. While their children often suffered, they had nothing to do, and did nothing, but enjoy themselves—or try to. Even within the Nanny system, it was their *business* to know something more about their children. And of course, in a guilty, ineffective and evasive way they often did. In two of the cases I quoted earlier—from the autobiographical studies by Eleanor Acland and Dormer Creston—the departure of the Nanny was deliberately concealed from the child. This was quite common. Furthermore many of these same mothers had undergone exactly the same experience that they were now forcing on their children. They knew what it was like to lose a loved Nanny. There is a certain amount of evidence that towards the end of our period some mothers did realise that all was not well—both here, in the area of the Nanny leaving, and in the danger of allowing possibly cruel women completely unsupervised control in the nursery. Their realisation seldom led them to do much about it.

As with the landed Nannies, we find an advanced example of this embryonic but evasive guilt in the present day (as regards Nannies generally and leaving, I should point out; not as regards cruelty. The Nanny in question was plainly a good one.) It occurs in the television programme I have already quoted from. Jeremy James is talking to the Buchanan-Michaelsons, who have two little children.

Jeremy James:	What do you look for in a Nanny?
Jane Buchanan-Michaelson:	Umm . . . someone who loves the children. And she does . . . very very good.
Jeremy James:	What does she have to do, what do you expect her to do?
Jane B.-M.:	Umm . . . completely look after them. And she takes them for walks. About all really, you know.
Robert Buchanan-Michaelson:	I think there's more to it than that.
Jane B.-M.:	She really loves them. She's very kind to them.
Robert B.-M.:	And they're very happy with her.
Jane B.-M.:	She's brought the baby up completely, I mean . . . you know she was ten years . . . ten days old, wasn't she.
Robert B.-M.:	I think my wife would have found it umm . . . perfectly feasible for her to do it, but as I said it would . . .
Jane B.-M.:	I think with one child . . . I could have brought one, but not two.
Robert B.-M.:	I think my wife's rather giving the impression that she's not capable of looking after the children, I know perfectly well that she is. There is a sort of social life involved in her life and mine, that means quite a lot of care and umm . . . attention to it. You can't give dinner parties which are bad and you can't give dinner parties or entertain people from abroad er . . . unless you see that they have a very pleasant time.
Jeremy James:	Mr. Buchanan-Michaelson is rich and busy. He's a property developer. Mrs. Buchanan-Michaelson is a busy property developer's wife with all that that involves. They're a typical, though not particularly common four-car Chelsea family. One each, one for the staff and one for spare.
	CAR DRAWS UP
	Mrs. Buchanan-Michaelson could you describe the sort of average day? What do you do?
Jane B.-M.:	Well, not very much really. I get up fairly late. Umm . . . James comes back from school at about lunch time and I see him, usually I have lunch with him, and the baby. I go out. I go to the hair-dresser, sometimes I go out to lunch, shopping, back again and we go to the theatre in the evening, have people for dinner, go out to dinner.

Jeremy James: How often do you have people at home?

Jane B.-M.:   Er . . . about twice a week. Dinner parties.

Jeremy James: How often do you go out?

Jane B.-M.:   About twice a week.

Jeremy James: How often do you take the children out with you?

Jane B.-M.:   Well, they're a bit young at the moment. Not all that often. They go out to tea parties. But I really don't take them with me shopping or anything, because they're a bit young.

Jeremy James: What happens if your Nanny, for instance, wants to have a day off, or does have a day off?

Jane B.-M.:   She has one on Thursday and er . . . I look after them until about three o'clock and then there's a relief Nanny comes in and helps me with tea and putting them to bed.

Jeremy James: So in fact you don't have too much to do?

Jane B.-M.:   Umm . . . not all that much, no.

Jeremy James: Do you think you have enough?

Jane B.-M.:   Mmm . . . I think so. I see them quite a bit in the daytime. And er . . . they adore me.

Jeremy James: Some people might say that in fact if you're going to have children one's first priority ought to be to be with them and to bring them up for their own good really.

Jane B.-M.:   Well, some people's opinions. It's not mine. I don't think it really matters to them as long as they're loved. And they're loved by three people, the Nanny, my husband and myself.

Jeremy James: Some people might also say that if you're not going to bring up your children and you're not going to put them first, then perhaps you ought not to have them.

Jane B.-M.:   Oh no. I mean I was brought up this way and I expected my children . . . after all they're very happy children, aren't they? I think it's the way you're brought up.

Jeremy James: Do you think it'll have any effect at all on the children when the Nanny leaves?

Jane B.-M.:   Yes, I think when they go to school and she leaves, yes. I remember when my Nanny left I was very upset, but umm . . . they get over it in a couple of weeks, really they make new friends at school and er . . . they get over it. I think they're a bit fickle, children, when they're young.

Finally, what are those effects which children 'get over in a couple of weeks'? There are, I think, three. The first is of very minor importance but of a certain interest. Adults seldom remember what their mothers looked like when young. Continuous contact with the face as it has aged means memory has blurred and merged with successive memory and a mother, at least until the child leaves home, has always looked as she does now. This did not happen with Nannies. I was struck again and again how strong and how precisely their features were remembered over the years. I realised that the same thing happened to the children I have already described with the Nanny—departure fixed her face vividly, even violently, in their minds.

More serious was the sense of insecurity engendered. A loved Nanny is not just the most important figure in a little child's world, she *is* that world. If the world suddenly erupts and disappears, the child is very severely shaken. It will be *permanently* more insecure and anxious than it would have been otherwise; and the earlier and more frequent the disappearances the more profound the insecurity.

But the most damaging result of a Nanny leaving is the effect it has on the child's (and therefore future adult's) ability to form and maintain any further close human relationships. A child's desire to pursue, and the ease and pleasure he gets from pursuing, and forming, human relationships depend on the rewards he received from the very first relationship—in this case with his Nanny. The realisation of the satisfaction to be obtained starts to take place very early; many psychiatrists would say in the first few months. If that early relationship was warm and close, and continues so, then for the rest of his life, despite subsequent disappointments, the child and adult will continue to seek and find satisfaction from other human beings. But if this early relationship is suddenly severed, if, in effect, he is punished (for so it seems) for loving, and not rewarded, he will naturally be very wary about how he sets about it in the future. It will be much more difficult for him to commit himself. The gradations of response are obviously infinite—depending on the age the rupture took place, how close the relationship was and so on. Some people, whose Nannies left late and who had formed relationships with other people, survived, only in a fairly minor way inhibited and shy in future human contact. But where love relationships are early and frequently broken the effect can be very serious. Some children reach a state where they no longer seem to mind. But this absence of reaction in a child—often no doubt greeted with pleasure by mothers and Nannies—is either (I quote again from *Child Development and Personality*)

because he has never experienced a continuous loving relationship or, more frequently, the relationship he has had has been disrupted so severely that he has not only reached but remained in a phase of detachment. As a result he remains detached and so incapable of experiencing either separation, anxiety or grief. Lesser degrees of this condition are, of course, more common than the extreme degrees, and sometimes give the impression of unusually vigorous independence. Analysis, however, shows that the springs of love are frozen and that their independence is hollow.

The springs of love are frozen—for a moment the dull language of the text book strikes vividly. But it goes further than this. Following the principle of stimulus generalisation which we discussed in chapter 7, it is on the reactions and responses it gets from its Nanny in the early years that a child bases its reactions to people in general. And these reactions in turn form the basis of the adult's later attitudes of "social . . . trust and affection or of mistrust and hostility towards others."

Now, as with one of the primary sexual effects of the Nanny (the effect I described of upper class men assigning sexual appetites only to women of the lower classes), I think it is almost certainly true that a whole range of rejection symptoms of the sort outlined above existed in the English upper classes and that they were frequently due to the departure of their Nannies. But to be truly convincing the hypothesis would have to be backed by numerous case histories stretching back through our period. One of the psychiatrists I talked to about Nannies said that in twenty-five years' London practice he could think off-hand of seven patients whose neurotic and inter-personal difficulties he had been able to relate directly to the departure of numerous Nannies. He had no doubt that he would find others if he went over his old notes. Out of all the people I interviewed I found that the four shyest and most difficult to talk to (all unmarried) had in fact lost their Nannies and then lost the replacements at an early age. But proper confirmation must wait interviewing and analysing on a scale I had neither time nor skill for.

Nevertheless, excessive misanthropy and neurotic shyness was sufficiently common to be accepted, indeed almost admired. It entered Victorian and Edwardian literature in the form of heroes who, after some trifling rebuff from the woman they 'loved', renounced women and in fact all human relationships for ever. In the novels of the 1920s these men went to work in the colonies. If someone mentioned love or marriage they turned white and left the verandah or sat drinking whisky far into the night. These sad, crippled men (and their feminine counterparts) were matched in life. One correspondent had a cousin who was turned down at the age of twenty-eight, so woundingly that he decided never to marry. Yet when my correspondent met the woman many years later and became friendly with her, she found that the woman never even knew the cousin had proposed to her.

As to the general picture of the English upper classes during our period, it is a cliché, certainly among foreigners, that they were inhibited, cold, withdrawn, shy, hostile to all but their own countrymen or, more exactly, their own class or family, and so on. Like all generalisations, it is almost as easy to prove its opposite. But, though I don't intend to do it, I think it would be possible to show that English people (and particularly upper class English people) during this time were often more rigid and distant than they need have been, that human contact was difficult and frightening to them, and that this was a development which had taken place, or had at least become more marked, during the nineteenth and twentieth centuries. Of course it would be ludicrous to lay this entirely at the door of the Nanny. There were other complex and interacting causes—religious developments and various social customs principally—some of which we touched on in the historical survey of Chapter 2. Many men and women were excessively misanthropic long before Nannies ever existed and will be for centuries now that they have gone. But the fact that vast numbers of the upper and upper-middle classes were reared under a system which, at crucial moments, removed the figure from whom they were learning the value of human relationships almost certainly played an important part in bringing this situation about.

ALIENATION FROM THE MOTHER

The next result of that separation from the parents, whose final and more harmful consequences we are now examining, is not so clear cut. Broadly, it could be described as alienation from the mother: but this is difficult territory. People find it very difficult to admit, or even discover, their true feelings about their parents, especially if, as often happened in our period because of Nannies, they were expected to love them when they were really indifferent to them or even loathed them. There are other reasons for the difficulty. The feelings themselves were often confused—interactions of resentment and gratitude, dislike and idealisation, desire to respond and inability to do so. And the Nannies themselves were frequently extremely cunning and hypocritical in the methods they chose to bind their charges to them and to destroy the influence and love of the mother. But, roughly speaking, three areas can be defined.

The first of these was the situation of the unkind Nanny. Very occasionally, a mother rescued her child from the vengeance of its Nanny. Firbank has described such a deliverence.

> The hand was raised
> The child was there!
> Bending over the back of the chair.
> A step on the staircase, a voice there came,
> Calling the nurse a terrible name.
>
> She paused!
> There was not time for more,
> The stick went crashing thundering to the floor.
> Her eyes spoke volumes, doom and woe.

But much more usually the opposite was the case. A classic example is Compton Mackenzie.

Born in 1883, Compton Mackenzie claims a clear, continuous and total memory from before the age of two, and certainly on the evidence of his partly autobiographical novel *Sinister Street* and *Octave I* of *My Life and Times* his memory of his childhood is remarkable. For the first few years, it was a life of travelling, because his father was an actor with his own company.

> Every week, except for five weeks in the summer at Lowestoft, a different place and sometimes different places in the same week. Sunday after Sunday in the train. From that faraway year of 1884 comes back the metallic sound of the footwarmers being pushed into the compartment, and after that my being put to sleep, and as I lie looking up at the roof I see the oil swinging to and fro in the lamp that sheds a rather feeble light.

Until he was four, life was idyllic. He had two Nurses whom he adored. First Bush and then "that pretty and lovable little Welsh girl called Mimmie". Unfortunately, Mimmie caught diphtheria and—an event he describes as a catastrophe—a woman called Annie Curry was engaged to take her place.

> I suppose in fact that Nanny was not much more than fifty-five at this date, but to me she seemed the oldest and ugliest woman in the world. My mother was always convinced that anything she herself very much wanted to do was the wrong thing to do and so from the first she allowed Nanny's early Victorian notions about what children should and should not do far too much latitude . . . she was always fearful of being accused of spoiling me and therefore surrendered.

Annie Curry is clearly the model for Michael Fane's Nanny in *Sinister Street*, a figure an example of whose unkindness we have already seen. But it was an unkindness which was so persistent, which lasted for so long and which was exercised upon an object so small, that it amounts to cruelty. Michael Fane's Nanny, like Compton Mackenzie's, used every weapon to humiliate, frighten and make all aspects of his life unpleasant.

She was rude and sarcastic.

Michael disliked being looked at by anybody or anything, and this bar [in his cot] had a persistent inquisitiveness which already worried him.

"Why does he look at me?" Michael would presently ask, and "Nobody wants to look at such an ugly little boy" Nurse would presently reply. . . .

"What was that noise?" asked Michael.

"Your own noise," said Nurse sharply.

"It wasn't. It was lions."

"And if it was lions, what next?" said Nurse. "Lions will always come when little boys are naughty. Lions don't like naughty boys."

"Michael doesn't like lions."

He took refuge in the impersonal speech of earlier days, and with a grave obstinacy of demeanour resisted the unreasonableness of his nurse.

"What was that noise, Nanny? Do tell me."

"Why a train, of course. There's a molly coddle. Tut-tut!"

"A train like we rode in down from the country?"

"Yes, a train like we rode in from down in the country!" Nurse mimicked in outrageous falsetto.

She filled him with fears. The coal-yard of the nearby railway frightens him.

"Could I be left there?" he asked.

"Left where?"

"There." He pointed to the coal-yard.

"Don't point!" said Nurse.

"What is that place?"

"The place where coal comes from."

"Could I be left there?" he persisted.

"Not unless one of the coalmen came over the wall and carried you off and left you there, which he will do unless you're a good boy."

Michael caught his breath.

"Can coalmen climb?" he asked, choking at the thought.

"Climb like kittens," said Nurse.

She used food as a weapon, and also medicine. In *Octave I*, little Compton Mackenzie and his father meet a man in the street.

"That was Mr. Condy. You've heard of Condy's Fluid?"

Heard of it? It was one of Nanny's favourite forms of medical torture. To gargle with that horribly positive taste of nothing needed all the honey and borax we could get out of a teaspoon to counteract the taste of Condy's Fluid. To meet Mr. Condy himself was as impressive an experience as it would have been to meet Dr. Gregory of the powder.

As well as slapping him and punishing him, the whole tenor of her behaviour was harsh and unpleasant.

Michael and Stella [the sister in *Sinister Street*] were now lifted out of the cots and dumped on to the cold oil cloth and marched into the adjacent bathroom, where their faces and hands were sponged with a new sponge that was not only rough in itself, but also had something which scratched buried in one of the pores. During this operation, Nurse blew violent breaths through her tightly closed lips. . . . Michael was lifted up and thumped down into another high chair and pushed close up to the table so that his knees were chafed by the sharp edge and his thighs pinched by a loose strand of cane. Nurse, blowing as usual through closed lips, cut up his meat, and dinner was accomplished in an atmosphere of greens and fat and warm milk-and-water and threats of Gregory powder if every bit was not eaten.

Overtly, both in *Sinister Street* and his autobiography, Compton Mackenzie is at pains to stress how much he adored his mother, yet it is plain from both books that his real feelings about her were very mixed. Certainly, as I showed earlier, one part of him did adore her—indeed idolised her. At the same time he bore her a deep resentment, both for allowing him to be treated in such a way, and for leaving him so frequently and so long.

He cannot trust himself to show this resentment often or very clearly, but it surfaces from time to time. When Michael's mother comes back from her many holidays she always asks him if he's been perfectly happy. Though he has been miserable, Michael always says yes, because that is what she wants him to say. His mother is always quite satisfied. In *Octave I*, he describes how once his Nanny told a lie about an accident.

My mother certainly did not believe her and it has always been a puzzle to me why she was ready to leave her three children in the charge of a woman over sixty who could tell such a lie. I suppose the reason was that Nanny was a competent and economical housekeeper and that her devotion to gin was at this time unsuspected.

But he shows himself most fully by his constant and furious outbursts in the autobiography against psychiatry and psychiatrists, as though he

were aware of more complex movements below the surface he so enter-
tainly skims—and was frightened of them. One particularly revealing
passage occurs apropos one of the many very moving early scenes in
Sinister Street. It is Mrs. Fane's last night with Michael before embarking
on another of her long absences.

That evening, just when Michael was going to bed, there came a knock at the
door, and a tall fair man was shown into the drawing room.

"How d'ye do, Mrs. Fane? I've come to ask you if you'll go to the theatre
tonight. Saxby is coming on later."

"Oh, thank you very much, Mr. Prescott, but I really think I must stay in.
You see," she said smilingly, "it's Michael's last night of me for a long time."
Michael stood gazing at Mr. Prescott, hating him with all his might and sighing
relief at his mother's refusal to go out.

"Oh Michael won't mind; will you Michael?"

Nanny came in saying "Bed-time! Tut-tut-tut! Bed-time!" and Michael's
heart sank.

"There you are," said Mr. Prescott. "Here's Nanny to say it's bed-time.
Now do come, Mrs. Fane."

"Oh, I really think I ought to stay."

"Now, what nonsense. Saxby will be furiously disappointed. You must.
Come along, Michael, be a brave chap and tell your mother she's got to go out;
and here's something to square our account."

He pressed a little gold coin into Michael's unwilling hand.

"Would you mind very much if I went?" his mother asked.

"No," said Michael tonelessly. The room was running round him in sicken-
ing waves of disappointment.

"Of course he won't," decided Mr. Prescott boisterously.

While he was being undressed, Nurse asked him what he was holding.
Michael showed the half-sovereign.

"Spoiling children," muttered Nanny. "That's for your money-box."

Michael did not care what it was for. He was listening for his mother's step.
She came in, while he lay round-eyed in his cot, and leaned over to kiss him.
He held her to him passionately; then he buried his face in his bedclothes, and
while she rustled away from him, sobbed soundlessly for a long while.

In *Octave I* we learn that this scene was based on a real incident when, the
night before they went away once, his father persuaded his mother to go
out with him. Compton Mackenzie at once defends his mother by suggesting—on no evidence—that it must have been to see someone beneficial
to his father's career. One might suppose they would have explained this
to him. But what is significant about the passage is that in describing the
incident Compton Mackenzie has stirred the ghost of his long buried

resentment. At once, fearful of the threat they hold, he launches with only apparent irrelevance into another attack on 'psycho-analysts' (showing, it might be added, a somewhat hazy knowledge of this subject).

I know that many people when frustrated allow the frustration to cuddle itself within themselves for some psycho-analyst to wheedle it out of them, thus giving him the satisfaction of supposing he has released them from any inhibitions. I have not been lucky enough to obtain direct evidence from the patient himself of any such achievement by psycho-analysis. I am not presumptuous enough to deny the possibility of a cure by psycho-analysis, but the experience of my own introspection, when I do very rarely indulge in it, has convinced me that my own memory of my thoughts and behaviour when very young are much more reliable than any theories I have read. When psycho-analysis became the fashion in the early twenties I read everything Freud and Jung and Adler and others had written. When I moved my library from the Channel Islands to the Outer Hebrides I left behind on the Island of Jethou about two dozen volumes of psycho-analysis; they had ceased to provide me with any food for thought.

So I am not prepared to be told by some devotee of psycho-analysis that the Oedipus complex entered into the failure of my mother to resist my father's wish for her to do what somebody presumably of importance to his career wanted him to do. What I learnt that evening was something completely objective about human behaviour, which was of great benefit to my happiness in the future however painful the lesson was at the time.

The lesson he learnt was this: "You can never again in life afford to depend on the love of somebody. . . ."

There are valid excuses to be made for mothers who let their children be ill-treated by Nannies and I shall make them. They had no relevance to the children. Even weak mothers appeared to be the authority figures in the house, they said they loved their children—yet they did nothing. Compton Mackenzie can stand for a great many children whose feelings towards their mothers were complicated and confused by the mixture of love, distrust, and repressed resentment.

The situation of the cruel Nanny is relatively clear cut. More usually the feelings were vaguer and harder to define. They could range through anything from a simple unease and confusion, a mild alienation deriving from the mother's lack of function, right up to an overt anger that the mother should expect a love and obedience she had done nothing to deserve.

In *Simpson*, for instance, there is a distinctly ambivalent attitude towards the mothers. These are invariably inferior to Simpson in both love and care, yet they are neither cruel nor unconcerned. Sackville-West repeatedly stresses that Simpson is *not* the mother. There is a dramatic scene where she is asked point-blank to take on this role.

> Simpson sprang to her feet. "No I can't. I must refuse that. I'm not the boy's mother and *never could have been*, so I can't behave as if I were—"
>
> "But no-one wants you to *replace* Mrs. Cresset."
>
> "That's what you say. But it's splitting hairs. No Ma'am, I'm sorry; but I'm only a nurse, and a nurse I must remain." Simpson stood in the midst of excitement and perplexity. Her soul dictated every word to her in the clearest accents. . . .

Yet what the mother's role is Sackville-West does not seem to know—not surprisingly, since with this charge as with all her charges, it was being totally filled by Simpson. He seems to suggest at one point that the difference is that the mother, just by *being* the mother, had some mystic, almost magic position in a child's life. It was recognised and accepted automatically by the child. She held this position by right. She had to do nothing to earn it or justify it or keep it. The Nurse's love, on the other hand, was given without this magic fillip (which was why Churchill praised it), a child could feel he had somehow created it.

Now there is truth in this, of course, though there is nothing mysterious or automatic about mother-love. For one thing society expects them to love their children, so they set out to do so; society expects their children will love them, so they expect it too. But more important, mother-love is already wakened by her pregnancy and the birth. It grows very quickly as she cuddles her child and feeds it and looks after it; and so it would be with the child. But under the Nanny system this essential nurturing and loving is quickly taken from the mother, and it is this nurturing which awakens the child's love, which earns it, which makes it a proper relationship, and not some mystical essence automatically emanating from the biological mother. Therefore many children, quite rightly, loved their Nannies more than their mothers. They recognised this instinctively, but were at a loss to explain it—since even their Nannies told them they should 'love' their mothers. Sometimes they reacted with guilt (I suspect that Sackville-West's attitude to mothers in *Simpson* is a reflection of his own guilt that his love for his Nanny was so much greater and more important than his love for his invalid mother).

A somewhat more positive example occurs in *Morning* by Julian Fane. This is an account of two years (seven till nine) in the life of a young boy and a Nanny. But in contrast to *Simpson*, where the children were vague and unreal (*Simpson*, as I said, is in fact a description of an ideal love, a prolonged metaphor) the hero of *Morning*, Vere, is intensely real—it is the reality of his trials, his wounds, his terrors, his loves whose accuracy gives the book its quality. His life is played out within the love of his Nanny and the nursery-maid Flora. They are its focus, the sources of his emotional interplay, his strength. When ill, it is them he needs, not his mother. "He is often frightened. His coughing and sickness frighten him. Only Nanny's hand, or Flora's—only their ready hands for which he reaches at all hours of the day or night, still his fear." The portrait of his Nanny—stable, quite strict, loving and sensitive—could well have taken its place in an earlier chapter with Nanny Robertson, Everest and Simpson.

But it is Vere's relationship with his parents that we are concerned with here. Both he and they are confused about the role they are supposed to play. He wants to respond to them, but can't—because they can't respond to him. Partly because they seem dead, without emotional muscles. And partly because they cannot respond accurately. They have no intimate knowledge of him. Yet at the same time they expect the manifestations of affection and the obedience, particularly obedience, which a child can only give freely to someone he genuinely loves. When obedience is exacted without, as it were, having been earned by love, then the result is resentment. Fairly late in the novel, Vere's resentment against his father, a constrained and distant figure, bursts out when his father maltreats a horse Vere has come to love. But it is also implicit in his attitude to his mother. She is shown as totally inadequate, usually lying in bed surrounded by newspapers. She frequently misunderstands him and offers irrelevant advice. And she too expects an obedience she has done nothing to deserve. There is an incident after Vere has built a house in the garden. The building of this house has been extremely important to him, but when he shows it to Mal, his governess, it collapses on top of them, hurting his head. Vere is bitterly ashamed, but too proud to show it. He goes to have his head 'seen to' by Nanny and then, still in an agony of humiliation, dashes out on to the lawn, banging the side-door open violently in front of him.

"Vere!"

It is his mother. She is standing with his father outside the schoolroom french windows.

"You're not to open the door like that Vere, you'll break the glass," she says. "Go back and shut it properly."

He does as he is told and starts across the lawn.

"Vere! Say you're sorry to your mother," his father calls.

"I'm sorry," Vere shouts without pausing.

"Vere! Come here!" The boy stops. "Come here." But he does not move. He would rather die. "Say you're sorry again."

"I'm sorry, Mummy."

"You mustn't bang doors like that, darling."

Darling he thinks—that empty word.

In *Memoir in the Middle of the Journey* Julian Fane has more recently given autobiographical accounts both of his Nanny and his mother. The Nanny, Nanny Harvey, is substantially the same as in the novel. It is a powerful and a moving portrait. But his mother is shown far more sympathetically. She appears to have been a substantial figure with whom he had a relationship. And if this is an accurate picture, and it certainly reads as one, then the skill with which Julian Fane has constructed a typical Nanny-reduced mother in *Morning* is the more to be admired. There can be no doubt that she, and the feelings she aroused, were usual throughout our period.

But the most common reason for the alienation of little children from their mothers was that they were deliberately set against them by their Nannies. Nor is this surprising. Nannies loved their charges, and this love sometimes seems to have been intensified by the knowledge that its duration was limited. "*She's* got him for the rest of his life." They often could not control their jealousy, just as, and equally naturally, mothers were often tormented by jealousy of their Nannies.

The expression of this jealousy could be quite mild. When the Thynne children sat snivelling at the top of the stairs, dreading grown-up Sunday lunch and the disciplines of "Hold your fork straight!" after Nanny's lax administration, Nanny Marks would say, "Don't worry, you'll be back in the nursery soon." Miss de Bourbel described how, in the gossip about their respective employers which flowed endlessly in the Daisy Walk, her Nanny had developed, for reasons of discretion in front of her three-year-old charge, a whole series of 'silences', pursed lips, nods, frowns and raised eyebrows. Miss de Bourbel soon learnt to interpret—or exaggerate—these and attributes her estrangement from her mother to the barrier they erected between them. Frequently I heard in my interviews a note of contempt which cannot have been lost on the children. Nanny Williams: "The parents didn't know *how* to look after children. They shouldn't have had them. They couldn't relax, couldn't let themselves go."

But frequently the jealousy was more passionate or its expression more violent. The Nanny of George VI used to give his arm a savage twist before shoving him into the drawing-room. Even after forty years, Nanny

Hurrell could not conceal the bitterness she had felt in her relationship with the mother of her Kenneth. She described how the mother used to pack her and Kenneth off alone for months at a time, to the Isle of Wight or the country or, when they were in India, to Kashmir to escape from the heat. Not unnaturally, Kenneth loved her and almost forgot his mother, or remembered her only as a figure of vengeance, since Nanny Hurrell wasn't allowed to punish Kenneth but was expected to hand him over to the mother for slapping. "They lost their children. They didn't want them. It was their fault—but they didn't like it. She didn't like Kenneth not loving her, but she had put up with it." She described a scene she clearly remembered with horror and rage. Kenneth, aged five, was being 'trained' to eat in the dining-room, but since his Nanny was there and since he resented his mother trying to bully him into obedience, he played up: spilt food, emptied finger bowls, insisted on sitting next to Nanny until eventually everyone lost their tempers—Kenneth howled, the mother turned on Nanny Hurrell and furiously blamed her for not teaching him good manners, and Nanny sat and seethed at the mother's ineptitude.

Jealous mothers would sack Nannies, order them about, countermand their instructions, criticise them behind their backs or to their faces in front of the children—and by fighting against a love whose growth they had in fact done everything to encourage, they alienated themselves. Among many examples, I had one letter, anonymous, which quivered with the pain of still torn feelings. It described how the Nanny, a country girl, had looked after two little rich children, whose parents spent most of the time in West Africa, occasionally sending instructions for extra staff to be employed or sacked. When the Second World War came the Nanny took the children to her parents' tiny cottage, looking after them, sending them to school and so on. They saw their parents only once during the entire war, but they also received a constant stream of letters trying to win them back from the Nanny and warning them against the 'common environment'. "The little girl found these letters cruelly hurtful." As the letter progressed it became rather confused, almost incoherent. There were references to the 'giant struggle' and 'fearful animosities', as though there had been some fight at the end of the war between the Nanny and the parents as to who should have the children. It ended: "They [the parents] still fight over my children, although I do my best to protect them."

At best, mothers and Nannies set up conflicts of loyalties which bewildered and unsettled their children. Another letter described how a Nanny became so dominant she forbade the mother to take the children on holiday. Instead, she took them herself. The mother wrote a letter sacking her when they got back. "My fragile pretty mother would not speak to Nanny. Misery in my innermost being. A month later she was gone."

Any conclusion as to the effects this widespread situation might have had must be extremely tentative and I shall reserve the attempt for later in the chapter. But three points should be made now. First, as with leaving, this alienation of the mother occurred throughout our period—we are faced with the Nanny Block again. But again, as with leaving, I have the impression it became more common during the '20s and '30s. The disintegration of the green baize door, the slow diminution in the number of domestic servants, the vaguely apprehended feeling that parents should perhaps have something to do with bringing up their children, all these acted to force the Nanny and mother together. But instead of beneficent and fruitful partnerships developing, the result more often seems to have been to intensify the squalid and damaging tussles for the hearts of the little children.

The second is that we can note a fairly obvious effect. Nannied children were supposed by convention to love their parents. Often they hardly knew or actively disliked them. As a result, many Nannied children pretended to like and respect their parents and so we find yet another sinuous vein of hypocrisy, of false feeling, that can be traced back, through no fault of her own, to the Nanny.

Through no fault of her own because, and this is the third point, given the Nanny set-up it was inevitable. Closeted for years with their babies and children, the possessors often of strong maternal feelings, with no other outlets for their emotions, it was certain Nannies should love their charges and be loved in return. They were bound to resist attempts to lessen that love. It was equally certain that mothers, who also loved their children, should be jealous of a love they instinctively felt should be theirs. Indeed, this tension was so integral a part of the Nanny/child/mother relationship that I was interested to find it, in embryo as it were, at the Norland Nursery Training College.

When I said earlier that the entire purpose of the Norland training was for the nurse to learn how to replace the mother, I did not of course mean this literally. In their training the very reverse is taught. They are told that the position is one of partnership. But, as we have seen, a true partnership between Nanny and mother is difficult to achieve. Apart from any emotional bias, unified control is much easier, and single control depends on single affection. Furthermore, the very thoroughness of the training, the time taken, the many things taught, mean that the young Nurse must long to use her skills, skills which do, effectively, leave nothing for anyone else to do. And when I went round the college I actually saw their schizophrenia in action again as regards the role of mother *vis-à-vis* the Nurse, as I had earlier with their attitude towards the Nurse's departure. I asked a senior member of the staff who was showing me round if she didn't think it was better if mothers brought up their own children. She agreed readily. Then she said, but of course some mothers were no good— they were neurotic or too highly strung, or lazy or selfish or didn't understand children or only liked children of a certain age. When any of these things happened a Nurse was better. She expatiated on the advantages of having a skilled Nurse in this sort of situation. But gradually, as she talked, I was fascinated to see how she was insensibly led from particular circumstances which do, no doubt, sometimes justify a Nurse, to more and more general ones, to whole clumps of reasons why in quite normal circumstances skilled hands were best, until in the end she had worked her way round to face the opposite direction and said with finality, "You know, let's admit it, practically all children really prefer a Nurse. They like it better when they are brought up by someone who has been properly trained to do it."*

*I should perhaps say here that my visits to nursery training colleges were not made to judge how adequate or inadequate the teaching was in 1972. I wanted to see if I could find out the sort of Nurse they would have turned out before 1939. My impression is that although they were probably quite advanced in their attitudes to discipline and very thorough in their practical training, in certain more fundamental aspects they were not particularly enlightened.

Nevertheless, a number of the impressions I gained certainly implied some criticism of the system – particularly as practised by the Norland Nursery Training College. I was, for instance, fairly caustic about their custom, still followed, of advertising for babies.

The College read the proofs of my book and made the following comment: 'We would point out most strongly that we advertise to be of service to parents who have parted with their children either through illness or fatigue and the Norland thinks that it gives a service to both parents and children in many cases where the local authority cannot help.'

I should also say that in practical terms some things have altered since I did my research (though I suspect the psychological attitudes I outline in the text are less easily changed). As a result of further studies into the damaging effects of fragmented substitute mothering on children separated for varying amounts of time from their real mothers, the Home Office decreed, during the 1970s, a rapid run-down of institutional care for such children. Today (1985) foster mothers are provided wherever possible, who will give the single full-time care that a mother would.

As a result of this the Welgarth, which depended on local authorities to provide them with children, had to close down.

NANNY DISCIPLINES

Democracy, oligarchy, aristocracy are all forms of government impossible in the nursery. Separated from the parents, the only constitution (apart from anarchy, which is no constitution) was, as we have seen, a despotism —benevolent or otherwise. Sometimes it took the form of what might be called a bullied despotism. I can remember my own Nanny, Nanny Paton, a gentle creature who used to suffer from terrible migraines. When these occurred I would get my bricks out and drop them one by one back into the box, watching Nanny Paton being sick. We saw Evelyn in *Christmas with the Savages* treating her Nanny 'like mud'. But in the vast majority of cases, the Nanny rule was strict. It is the actual, practical nature of this strictness—whose theoretical evolution and slow demise we have already studied—I want to look at briefly now.

The strictness of child upbringing had deep roots in British history. Nannies inherited this tradition and continued it. But during the nineteenth century the strictness of child upbringing was coloured by that peculiar mixture of smugness, hypocrisy, religion, rigidity and almost violent conformity which we call Victorian morality. This development, of enormous interest, had causes too complex and profound for us to get involved in here. It was partly an extension of the Puritan tradition—but the Puritan tradition compounded by a number of different and powerful forces. The rigidity and violence of the conformity for instance, were, particularly as the century progressed, unconscious attempts at defence. Defence first against social and economic forces which were undermining the class structure; and second against intellectual movements which were destroying the religious, philosophic and social ideas upon which, along with much else, that class structure depended.

But as far as the Nanny herself went, the effect of this development, of this Victorian morality, was simple and long-lasting. It led to that whole pattern of behaviour designed to prevent their children becoming 'spoilt'.

The Norland Nursery Training College has responded by putting all their short- and long-term stay children into the charge of two student nurses. These remain with the child throughout but share the care. This goes part of the way to remedy the objections I made earlier. It does not go the whole way. The Robertson Centre in London has established beyond doubt that, in this far from ideal situation, *one* mother substitute is by far the best solution.

I like to think [wrote Lady Christabel Aberconway in her autobiography *A Wiser Woman?*], indeed I do believe, that the first friend I made, and made entirely by myself, was Oscar Wilde. Surely I do remember that bulky form bending over my pram, and a glove being removed and myself clasping a soft white finger and grabbing a sparkling ring? And I can still hear my Nanny saying to another Nanny, and later to my mother, "That *dreadful* Mr. Wilde stopped me *again* today and talked to Baby—and she *smiled* at him!"

Many years later when I asked my mother if my first Nanny really had said this my mother was amazed that I had remembered, for I was only just two years old when my parents moved from their house in Tite Street. My mother said she remembered the incident most clearly and added that she had reproved Nanny, saying, "I'm sure Mr. Wilde won't do Baby any *harm*; and, in life, it is important to smile. Nanny, you don't smile enough."

This instinctive disapproval of the Nanny of anything pleasure-giving and anyone pleasure-having (and though this was before Wilde's downfall, how right, from her point of view, Christabel Aberconway's Nanny was) this disapproval turned in as well as out. Jessica Mitford describes in *Hons and Rebels* how her very large sister, Unity, was simply given the name 'Hideous' by their Nanny, who always called her that. Anne Talbot said that her Nanny never praised them, and always dreaded the praise of parents. The highest praise she ever received was once, when just going out to a party, her Nanny said, "You'll do." And in fact many Nannies believed that it was bad for children to be excessively praised or encouraged—they would get 'swollen heads', start to 'show off', in a word be 'spoilt'.

This essentially Puritan attitude underpinned and added to that structure of strictness we looked at in Chapter 2. Within the absolutely necessary routine of many nurseries a whole host of restrictions, prohibitions, absurdly detailed timetables evolved, whose sole purpose seems to have been to nip the bud of pleasure whenever and wherever it appeared. Noël Oakeshott (pre-1910) described a life devoid of jam and cake, and so infrequently allowed a drink that she remembers suffering from thirst. Her father before her had always been overdressed, and as well as thirst had usually felt too hot. He discovered that by putting ink on his ears he could keep them cool. He did this every day at school washing it off before returning home. One day he forgot one ear, with disastrous consequences. Examples could be endless: gloves worn to prevent thumb-sucking; silence at meals; silence in the night nursery; no playing on Sundays; walking in peculiar queues and at special times; the banning or mutilating of books because the pictures gave pleasure; endless washing and brushing;

insistence at all times on the phrases of politeness, on please, thank you, no thank you, and so on. Sometimes the practices were so elaborate and eccentric that one suspects the same invention of manners as we found invention of what was common and what not, and for the same reason. Baroness Budberg's Nanny made them sit with a napkin across their chest secured only by being held under each arm. This taught the correct posture at table. Frequently, one hand had to be held palm down on the table while the other was used for eating. One Nanny taught her children to do up their shoelaces only with forefinger and thumb. Another insisted that on setting out for a walk, the left foot should be advanced first.

Now all this, which most people today would probably regard as over-detailed, over-strict upbringing, does not necessarily imply unkindness. Children have to (and want to) be taught how to behave; and this sort of teaching was regarded as right and indeed, at the beginning of our period, at any rate, spiritually essential. Nevertheless, such a restrictive regime—and in innumerable different forms it was widespread—did allow irritable or neurotic Nannies, or cruel ones, to express their resentments under the guise of doing their duty.

Hair-washing [writes Bridget Tisdall] took whole afternoons; there were no hair-driers in 1910. My wet hair was rubbed with a towel and then combed. As it had then formed into knots it was extremely painful. "Tangles, Nanny!" I used to scream with my eyes watering and screwed up. Nanny was merciless with the comb. After this ordeal I would sit in front of the fire-guard with my hair hanging over my face until it dried. Curl rags at night made one's scalp sore, and wherever one laid one's head on the pillow there was a lump.

That mixture of automatic repression and putting down, faintly insane rules and superstitions, yet all just tempered by minute indications of rough kindness, is well caught in a fine if farcical piece of writing from Alan Bennett's *Forty Years On*. Note how each statement is enshrined in a cliché—the thought has become sanctified by repetition.

(*Nanny Gibbons is played by Matron, and is a much more intimidating presence than Nursie. At first only a voice behind the screen, she casts a monstrous shadow on the wall as she unbuckles her black bombazine armour and talks to the little boy in the bed.*)

Boy: What time is it, Nanny?
Nanny: Time you were asleep, young man.
Boy: What time is it?
Nanny: Time you had a watch. Time you learned to say please. Time you knew better. Go to sleep.

Boy: What are you doing, Nanny?

Nanny: I'm doing what I'm doing. Go to sleep.

Boy: Nanny!

Nanny: What?

Boy: I've got a pain in my leg.

Nanny: Do you wonder you've got pains in your legs when you don't do your
business. Well next time you'll set there till you do. Forgotten to
fold your vest, young man. I can't turn my back for two minutes.
And clean on this afternoon.

Boy: I feel sick.

Nanny: Do you wonder you feel sick sitting on them hot pipes. How many
more times must I tell you, you sit on them pipes you'll catch piles.

Boy: What are piles?

Nanny: You mind your own business. Piles is piles, and you'll know soon
enough when you catch them because your insides'll drop out and
you'll die and then where will you be? Lie down, sitting up at this
time of night.

Boy: What time is it?

Nanny: Time for Bedfordshire. Time you had your bottom smacked.

Boy: Can I have an apple?

Nanny: No you can't. Apples at this time of night. Apples don't grow on
trees you know. *(She has a drink from a bottle.)*

Boy: What's that?

Nanny: That's Nanny's medicine.

Boy: What for?

Nanny: It's for Nanny's leg. Nanny's got a bone in her leg.

Boy: Can I have some for my leg?

Nanny: No, you can't. Going out without your wellies on, do you wonder
you get pains in your legs. You go out without your wellies on,
you'll go blind. That's why St. Paul went blind. Went out on the
Damascus Road without his wellies on. See, did I say no? Lie down
this minute. If I have another snuff out of you there'll be ructions.
Give me a kiss. Kisses make babies grow. Night, night, sleep tight.
God bless and go to sleep or the policeman'll come and cut your
little tail off.

Nanny Gibbins, incidentally, was partly based on Jonathan Miller's
Nanny, a woman given to vast, vaguely terrifying statements, in the
manner of a Thurber character. Jonathan Miller once asked her what death
was. "It's the peace that's passed all understanding," she said. "*All*
understanding?" said Jonathan, horrified by something so enormously
incomprehensible. "*All* understanding," said his Nanny. It frightened
him for years.

I have already described the attitudes to beating and indicated the rate and extent of its decline, but, in the area we are now, it is when one comes to punishment that the line between fair if strict discipline and unjustified harshness becomes ever harder to draw. Listen to the satisfaction in Nanny McCallum's voice:

> Nursery life was very strict. If they had jam for tea they didn't have cake. The parents were tough too. C.F. [the father] was a good example. The children were often given 'stick'. Right from the beginning, when they were very small, I've taken a child into the bathroom, father has come up, then slippered that boy till he couldn't sit for two days. A real good proper thrashing. You could hear him yell. And a very good thing. We never punished them. The father did. That gave them a lively respect for their father. As a result they were very good children. Very quiet. Very self-contained.

Sheila T (1920s) described to me how her Nanny used to quiver with excitement when it came to a beating—which it did several times a week— and used to go herself and cut the canes she used from a grove of long swishy bamboos which grew by the lake.

I received another fine account bearing on this subject from Lady Anne Hill. I shall quote it in full because to split it would spoil it. But in fact it covers far wider ground (pre-1910) than the rather limited area of beating very small children—and indeed this points to a difficulty throughout this book. Long before the present chapter we had seen examples of all three of its principal subjects—the Nanny leaving, alienation from the mother, and the strict routines and disciplines of the nursery. The divisions I have made for the sake of clarity and momentum, though I think they are illuminating and valid, are in a sense artificial. Nannies were multifarious —a Nanny described early on will often have thrown light on a subject discussed much later, just as a Nanny dealt with now will reinforce, or correct a view already put forward. A study of this sort is an infinitely complicated picture in which each successive part alters the weight, the value, of those that have gone before and no final view can emerge before the very end.

> My first Nanny [wrote Lady Anne Hill] was horrid. I am told that I was wrongly fed by her in infancy, and that in consequence I was ill for some years. Everybody who knew me then recalls how appallingly I used to scream. One of my brothers remembers her laying me over her knees when I was still in long clothes (I imagine aged eight months or younger), and beating me hard on the bottom with a hairbrush. This she continued to do frequently when I was bigger.

I lived in the country, where I seldom saw any children except my brothers, who were four, nine, ten and eleven years older than me; but every summer holidays a number of cousins, mostly Scotch, would come and stay, sometimes as many as eight at a time. Their visits were intoxicating to me. I remember on one occasion, when I was about four, tearing round and round the corridors with them, and getting 'over-excited', screaming with laughter until I was sick and did what we called 'the nose trick', which made me laugh more than ever. "Nanny'll beat me," I said to my eight-year-old brother. "Stuff a towel up your drawers and you won't feel it," he said. This he helped me to do, both of us nearly swooning with giggles. But when the time came she found it, pulled it out, and beat me harder than ever.

Being 'over-excited' (laughing too much and being 'silly') was a great pleasure that was much frowned upon. If ever I was particularly enjoying myself, my every movement would be followed by my Nanny's eyes as she knitted, with a chilling, sour, disapproving look on her face. "It'll end in a cry," she would say in her lugubrious, ominous, sing-song voice; and it usually did.

This Nanny kept the nursery extremely cold; curtains and blinds, if drawn, billowed in the east winds. I had chilblains, often broken and bandaged on my fingers all winter; I also had a sensation then, sometimes, from cold, that I have never had since, as if an elastic band were stretched tightly round my forehead.

I had a thing the matter with me at that time (bacillis coli in my bladder I think it was called) that made me often be sick for several days on end, when I would get thin, with my ribs showing, 'like a famine child' the grown-ups said. It also had the effect of making me never hungry. It was naturally considered important that I should eat when I could: in consequence I often had the experience (described in many memoirs of that epoch) of disliked uneaten food being presented to me, cold, at a later meal. I took two hours to eat my breakfast, an hour for the revolting lumpy porridge, quarter of an hour for the egg that I minded less, and three quarters for the sour soft dull apple. I think as well as being ill I must have been pretty obstinate to dare go slow to quite the extent I did.

I remember nothing nice at all about this first Nanny; nonetheless, when she took to saying that I was such a naughty little girl that she was going to leave I screamed as hard as ever I had, hugging her round the legs and begging her not to. However go she did. Her actual departure I don't recollect; but I do recall, clearly, later, being alone in the nursery awaiting the arrival of the new Nanny. The feeling that this was the most extraordinary unbelievable occasion, the fear and the shyness must have been just what a motherless child feels when her father tells her she is to meet a 'new Mummy'.

When the new Nanny did come she smiled at me and said in the kindest way, "I think we are going to be friends." My heart melted and I loved her from that moment; my happy nursery days date from then, and they were very happy. There was an immense security in the day-and-night nursery life. When I was in bed, there was always the light under the door, and often the murmur of voices from the other side of it. I don't remember her ever being 'out', or going away for a holiday, and meals were brought to us in the day nursery by the nursery-maid, so Nanny was never further away than the distance of the bathroom-lavatory, not more than a dozen yards; screams or even shouts, if made, would have been heard. In this respect it was nicer to be brought up by a Nanny (if she was nice) than by even the best of mothers. For a mother, the time when she least wants to be with her children is when they most need her, bed time, which is usually about the time her husband comes home from work, when (in many families) it is drink time, and friends may come for drinks or dinner; or she may be going out for the evening. It is also the time of day when she is most tired. Strange baby-sitters come, possibly ones who don't know much about children, and who may not particularly like them; they may hardly speak English. They also usually come and go, different ones with different ways on different evenings.

The conclusion I draw is that the happiest possible childhood may perhaps be one where both parents love their children, and are lucky enough and rich enough to find, keep and pay for a really nice Nanny, so that the child is lapped in treble security. Perhaps fifteen or twenty families in England are now enjoying this happy situation. Forty or fifty years ago there would have been many more. But I think a far higher proportion of children were seriously unhappy then than now, the poor ones because of the consequences of the wretched poverty of that time, the richer ones because their parents so often did not perceive things that were wrong—that a Nanny was unkind, or that a kind one who had been with the child since infancy had for some reason left, leaving it as bewildered and bereaved as if orphaned, but without its being accorded the sympathy and status of an orphan.

How much harm my bad Nanny did me it is difficult to say. I was certainly much more 'disturbed' than my children or grandchildren were. I had horrific bad dreams nearly every night. and my fear of them and of the dark was so great that I was only really carefree in the mornings; by after lunch I would be beginning to dread the end of the day. It is not worth enumerating my various other neurotic fears and worries. My father died of TB in a sanatorium in Scotland when I was just four, and my mother was with him and away from me for many months before this, and so it is impossible to tell whether my troubles were mostly due to his death and her absence and subsequent unhappiness, or to the unkindness of my Nanny.

THE NANNY AND FOOD

A portion of this account introduces another area on which this whole spectrum—of strictness, puritanism, doing the child 'good' by preventing it becoming spoilt, and yet sometimes using all this as a cloak for harsher feelings—shines with particular intensity, and that is food.

A baby's food, the milk it receives from bottle or breast, is the first and by far the most important manifestation of love it receives. It remains immensely important psychologically throughout childhood. It is recognised instinctively as a vehicle for love. People who love their children—if I may quote what I wrote earlier on this subject—want them to eat heartily. It pleases them; it is a way of sharing their love. Similarly those who do not particularly care for their children and are guilty about it, feel that by filling them with food they can somehow compensate for their lack of love. And even without love, food is after all what keeps us alive and makes us grow. It is scarcely surprising, then, that on both counts— emotional and practical—there should have grown up a practice of very strict feeding. If a child didn't want to eat anything, he should be forced to. It is only unfortunate that not only was such strictness quite unnecessary, but it usually brought about exactly the opposite reaction to that intended.

The medium itself was often not pleasant. Towards the end of the eighteenth century and beginning of the nineteenth century it was believed that raw fruit and vegetables were bad for children. Their diet on the whole was plain and stodgy: bread, mutton, rice pudding, porridge, milk. This solid fare was inherited by the Nanny, but the care with which it was prepared was often, as we have seen, much diminished by the irritation of the cook at having to prepare it at all.

Sometimes, it should be said, Nannies recognised this and were patient and tried to help. Peter Eyre described how Nanny Robertson never, or seldom, used a knife to cut up food. She used a spoon and used to dollop it out. Years later he asked her why and she said she thought children didn't like clean neat slices of food. It was less intimidating and made them more comfortable if it were given them in heaps. Bridget Tisdall's Nanny, rather surprisingly, was understanding.

> I had a hot-plate. It was decorated with blue and white fishes on a white ground and rested on top of a metal base which was filled with hot water. The base, a circular tank with a flat bottom, was rather similar to the container of an oil-lamp, with a hole and a screw cap on one side into which hot water was poured. I remember scraping away the shepherd's pie with my spoon in order to find the fishes. I was a dreamy child and my lunch was a leisurely affair. Paradoxically, Nannie was patient at meal-times. She would wait for quite a time with a spoonful of food poised in mid-air while I gazed out of the window. She would also, like all well-trained Nannies, peel and de-seed grapes then

pop them into my mouth, and cut bread and butter fingers which she dipped into the yolk of softly boiled eggs. Nothing has ever again tasted so heavenly.

But far the greater number of Nannies were punctiliously strict. So common were stories of being made to eat up, of having breakfast porridge for lunch and then for supper again, of sitting for hours staring at a piece of bacon rind or gristle, that I am at a loss which to choose. Three almost at random will suffice. King Peter II of Yugoslavia (born in 1923) had English Nannies.

> I remember Nurse Bell, my first Nanny, and one of the many English people who were to be concerned in varying degrees with my education and development. Nurse Bell's care of me was very unimaginative. Somehow I got tired of lemon juice, rice pudding and what she called 'pap'. But she certainly succeeded in fattening me up. I was like a little balloon. She taught me to say my prayers in English . . . her place was taken by Miss Crowther, known as 'Crowdy' in the family . . . like Nurse Bell, Miss Crowther also paid great attention to my diet.

The court physician, a Doctor Ambrozic, puts him on a strange diet consisting entirely of grapes, with particular emphasis on the pips and skins.

> I had no alternative but to accept Dr. Ambrozic's dietary, but with the cunning of childhood, I found what I thought to be a 'way out'. I sucked the grapes dry, but tucked the skins and pips into the side of my mouth. Miss Crowther used to spot the bulge in my cheek and give it a good press. I had to swallow the lot.

Strictness was overlaid by Puritanism—one slice of cake only, not jam *and* cake, bread and butter before jam or cake. Puritanism and strictness often hid meanness. Compton Mackenzie again offers a typical example.

> It may have been at tea on that blighted afternoon that I (five now) thought of a way to exasperate Nanny by telling her that I preferred my bread without butter. I was tired of the way she always transformed butter to scrape, of the way in which, if a dab of butter was happily caught in one of the holes of the slice of the real bread we had in those days, she would excavate it with a knife and turn it into another bit of scrape. I was tired of the way she would mutter that too much butter was not good for me and, as it seemed to me, obviously enjoyed depriving me of it. If I told her that I preferred my bread without butter she would be deprived of the pleasure of depriving me. So whether it was on this particular afternoon or not I cannot be sure, but it was about this time that I declined butter on my bread, and to this very day I never eat bread

and butter unless urgent politeness to an anxious hostess compels me to accept a single slice.

But strictness does not necessarily imply unkindness. When I interviewed Nanny P I had tea first with Mr. and Mrs. Googe (Nanny P's Mary) and Mrs. Beddington, Mrs. Googe's sister who had also been looked after by Nanny P. It was a large, very rich, very comfortable English country house; Mr. Googe was in rather long white tennis shorts, the tea was delicious. We discussed Nannies for a while—their uniform, their wages, when they left—and then talked about other things. Suddenly Mrs. Beddington said, apropos of nothing, that the one good thing the old-fashioned Nanny had done was to make children eat up. Nowadays they didn't learn to eat properly or enough. Her grandson only ate Frankfurters. It was just as well he was American. This prompted Mr. Googe to say that he could remember nothing at all about his entire childhood except that his Nanny had made him eat bacon. He had hated it. Somehow he had always managed to distract her or get her out of the room and then hidden it behind the large chest-of-drawers. One spring-cleaning they'd moved the chest-of-drawers and found hundreds of rotten and rotting slices of bacon. (He did not seem to think it odd, though his sister-in-law pointed it out, that he'd become a pig breeder.)

But it was Mrs. Beddington's remark—some vehemence in the way she'd said it—which stuck in my mind. Its significance became apparent when I was talking to Nanny P, half an hour later, about the time she'd looked after the two sisters. It was when she was approaching the crisis in her life which I have already described. Mary, she said, was a very good little girl but a terrible feeder. She just *would* not eat. The battles they had! Nanny P tried every trick she knew. But Mary still refused to eat. The battles grew worse—furious and exhausting for them both. Mary, like Augustus in Dr. Heinrich Hoffman's *Struwwelpeter*, now began to grow thin, so they decided to take her to a specialist in London to whom Nanny P explained the situation. He was a very distinguished specialist and, Nanny P said to me, the interesting thing was that she was able to pin-point the very moment when he'd discovered what was wrong. She was explaining how the trouble was not that Mary wasn't hungry but that she wouldn't eat up at table. They knew this because when they went to feed the bantams she would surreptitiously eat all the bread they took. It was then, said Nanny P, that the specialist made his diagnosis (no doubt he had made it long before). There was nothing wrong with Mary, he said. It was her attitude. She was suffering from what he might describe as 'negativism'. The way to deal with it was not to bother about it. Pretend you don't mind, he said. Above all she mustn't do what she had been doing, trying to get food down Mary by force.

The training, habits and convictions of a lifetime are not lightly discarded. It seems likely that Nanny P found these instructions very difficult to carry out. At any rate, Mary only got over her 'negativism' very gradually and she was four or five, which was when Nanny left, before she was eating satisfactorily. Just how tenacious was Nanny's belief in feeding strictness is shown by the fact that a few months after her arrival at her next post she discovered to her horror that the new child was developing exactly the same trouble. She too *would not eat*. "I used to lie awake at night," said Nanny P, "worrying over it. I couldn't understand it. I couldn't sleep for worrying about it."

There was nothing remotely unkind about Nanny P. There was no mistaking the protectiveness and goodness of her—she radiated warmth like a fire. She was also extremely bright and intelligent. But she had been taught that children must, if necessary, be compelled to eat up all their food and so that was the regime she imposed. With her, as with so many Nannies, the fault was one of doctrine, and though that doesn't mean that Nannies didn't do damage, it does mean the damage was mitigated by the kindliness which shone through.

How widespread and long-lasting was this feeding strictness and what were its effects? For the first two-thirds of our period—say from about 1850 to 1920—it would seem to have been almost universal, though there were exceptions and endless variations as to the degree of strictness. As the period ends children's meals certainly seem to become more pleasant and parents and, to a degree, Nannies, become more knowledgeable about diet. There is also evidence, though not a great deal, that that indulgence we have noticed creeping in elsewhere was also felt here. But this was counter-balanced (some psychiatrists—I shall discuss this later—would say more than counterbalanced) by increasingly rigid routines of infant feeding and caring. During the '20s and '30s babies were treated like clockwork toys—fed every four hours, put on the pot every two hours, changed, bathed, dressed, even kissed and spoken to only at stated times. Their wails of hunger or distress were ignored. A particularly strict series of routines was the Truby King method.

As to the effects all this had, it is extremely difficult to generalise. Perhaps at the outset I should say that forcible feeding, insistence on 'eating up' and all the rest of it is entirely unnecessary. Worse—it is what today would be called counter-productive. Certainly, children have to be taught what to like and what not; as Geoffrey Gorer has pointed out, there is no instinct in the matter. In Britain and the U.S.A. we think it is 'natural' to like sweet things; but Belgian mothers find that the pudding is the hardest thing to get their children to eat. In North Africa you can see children chewing raw red peppers that would make an adult European or American weep. But the point is children enjoy eating. It is a rewarding activity.

Provided different foods are introduced with tact and not pressed, provided it is appreciated that in fact they have years ahead of them in which they can learn to like things, they will take to enough new things without trouble. And they quickly learn what foods they need. In an experiment some years ago children between the ages of three and five were allowed to eat exactly what they liked from a large selection of foods for a fortnight. At the end of that time, though there had often been 'runs' on certain types of food, all the children had chosen a balanced diet. Furthermore, adults fuss needlessly when children don't eat. They can go for several days with nothing or very little to eat and come to no harm at all. Attempts to force children to eat, to impose new foods, to create routines where none are needed simply result in the rebellions, battles and refusals I have described.

There were other more varied results. Lady Anne Hill is now an excellent cook, and eats with incredible rapidity (in a sense I suppose one can say that Nanny has won). Bernard Shaw's father had been strictly but insufficiently fed when a child and had, Shaw wrote, "such a horror of childish hunger that he insisted on unlimited bread and butter being always within our reach". It is noticeable that English adults brought up by Nannies often have strange phobias and dislikes about food—they won't eat crusts or rice-pudding; like Compton Mackenzie, they don't like butter on their bread; I have a cousin who can't eat raspberries, spinach, pears, yoghourt (reminds him of junket), over-soft boiled eggs, any fruit with pips in it and much else. They frequently feel compelled to finish anything they are given to eat—however disgusting—(this need to 'eat up' persisting into later life sometimes attaches to bottles of drink). Again, another reaction, English upper class people of the nursery generation sometimes seem to expect and even *want* disgusting food. Having been fed on it for so long when little, they came to think that food *ought* to be disgusting; since they were often forcibly fed, they feel you *have* to force yourself to eat—and plainly the more disgusting the food the more forcing required.

But in fact I don't think it is really possible to make any valid generalisations on the subject. Reactions and conditions were too variable. Certainly it would seem likely that the close relationship in a little child's mind between love and feeding, combined with the very unloving administration of it in many nurseries, may have contributed to that inhibiting of the ability to form loving relationships we have already noted. It is impossible to prove. The most one can say is that the mistaken strictness of Nannies when it came to feeding certainly created compulsions, aversions and inhibitions as regards food for the rest of their charges' lives, and that it often made mealtimes, which should have been pleasant and enjoyable, among the most stressful, upsetting and revolting episodes of the entire nursery day.

CONSEQUENCES OF ALIENATION AND STRICTNESS

> *The British Nanny must be a general*
> *The British Empire lies within her grasp.*
> *Tradition, discipline and rule*
> *Must be the school.*
> *Without them disorder, anarchy . . .*
> *In short you have a ghastly mess.*
>
> Father in the film of *Mary Poppins* describing what he needs in an ideal Nanny and why.
> © 1963 Wonderland Music Company, Inc.

The strictness of the Nanny imprinted her on the minds of her little charges as a figure of fear and authority so powerfully that they retained it for the rest of their lives. At this moment (I am writing at the end of 1970) the Shah's Nanny in Tehran, now immensely old, is a figure of considerable power. Her ear is sought, her salon attended, and she has been decorated with high orders. She is practically the only person the Shah is frightened of. I noticed this often during my interviews. Mrs. Beddington, the elder of Nanny P's charges, was quite a formidable county woman. She was large, assured, voluble and confidently upper class. Yet as the time approached for me to go and see Nanny P she, and indeed all of them round the tea table, began to show a noticeable reluctance to take me up. Eventually Mrs. Beddington said well, if I was quite sure I wouldn't have another cake or cup of tea—I was completely sure, was I?—she supposed she'd better take me. By the time we'd reached Nanny's flat this big, dominating woman had become a little girl again. She paused, hovering, at the door and then whispered, "You just stay here a moment. I'll go in first and see if it's all right." Ponderously, on tip-toe, she crept into the room whispering, "Nanny? Nanny?" I heard them murmuring, then she came back and beckoned me in. I half expected to see someone physically at least as commanding as Mrs. Beddington, but there in front of me was a tiny, bent old woman (eighty-nine in four months) with sparse grey hair, quick, kindly eyes and two sticks to help her walk. "I'll leave you two to it," said Mrs. Beddington scurrying thankfully back to adulthood. This continuing power of the Nanny was demonstrated again and again by the number of my informants who wished to remain anonymous.

Indeed, so strong and universal is this strand in English upper and upper-middle class life that in 1954 it was still possible to base an entire play upon it. The farce *All for Mary* by Harold Brooke and Kay Bannerman—which was extremely and deservedly successful (it subsequently became a film)—has virtually speaking only one joke in it: the power that Nanny Cartwright still has over her old charge Humphrey Millar—'Humpy'—and the power she assumes over Clive Norton, the ex-husband of Mary to whom Humpy is now married. I should like to quote a certain amount from it because, as well as being amusing, it gives a good feeling of the nostalgia and atmosphere surrounding a late '20s Nanny.

Humpy is frankly idiotic, re-succumbing to Nanny's world like a zombied dachshund; Clive, a bit of a cad (that is he drinks whisky and smokes), puts up a token resistance. The play begins with these two getting chickenpox (they have never met before) and being rushed into isolation at the top of their hotel. A nurse is sent for to look after them. She arrives and turns out to be Nanny Cartwright, who was expecting to find two little boys. Here she is at the end of Act I, establishing control.

> *Nanny:*   I think there must be some mistake. Mr. Victor said I was to look
>   after two boys. I didn't know he meant grown-up boys.
>
> (*Humpy has been gazing intently at Nanny*)
>
> *Humpy:*   Nanny!
>
> (*He crosses to Nanny*)
>
>   Don't you remember me, Nanny? I'm Humpy.
> *Nanny:*   Humpy? Let me think—*not* my Humpy Millar?
> *Humpy:*   Yes, Nanny.
> *Nanny:*   Well! How you've grown, dear.
> *Humpy:*   Have I, Nanny?
> *Clive:*   Of course you have, you idiot!

(*Nanny crosses below to bed L and puts the toy boat on the L of the truck. The attaché-case on the R. She removes her gloves and, opening the case, puts them in then closes the lid but does not fasten it.*)

Nanny: And what are you doing out of bed, Master Humpy?

(*Clive moves to R drops the teddy bear on the floor by the door, picks up his bottle of whisky, glass and cigarettes and then comes to base at foot of bed R and sits.*)

Humpy: I'm going to look for my wife, Nanny.

(*Nanny moves towards him*)

Nanny: What next? And you with chickenpox!

(*Nanny leads Humpy to bed C. He slips off his slippers.*)

Into bed with you, you naughty boy.

(*Humpy gets into bed*)

Humpy: But Nanny, I'm in such dreadful trouble.

(*Nanny tucks him in. Clive pours himself a drink and replaces the cork in the bottle; the glass in his right hand, the bottle in his left hand, the cigarettes in his lap.*)

Nanny: Now, don't fret, dear. Things are never as bad as they seem, are they?
Humpy: No, Nanny.
Nanny: Have you been scratching, dear?
Humpy: No, Nanny.

(*Nanny raises an admonishing finger*)

Yes, Nanny.
Nanny: That's right, dear. It's always best to tell the truth.
Clive: That's right, be a good little boy and maybe Nanny will give you a lollipop to suck.

(*Nanny turns round and moves down to Clive*)

Nanny: Now then, I can see you're quite above yourself and I don't have to look far to see the reason why.

(*Clive is drinking*)

No more of this, dear.

(*She takes the bottle*)

And no more of these.

(*Nanny takes the cigarettes, crosses to her attaché-case and opening it, puts them in, shuts the lid and fastens case. Clive rises and moves to R of Box C, putting his glass down on the box at foot of bed R.*)

Clive: I won't stand for this.
Nanny: Won't? That's a little word we never use up here.

(*Moves towards Clive*)

That's a funny word. Now, into bed with you.
Clive: Who do you think you're talking to?
Nanny: To a young man who's forgotten his party manners.

(*Nanny is close to Clive*)

Still, it's never too late to mend and we've plenty of time to teach you.

(*Nanny turns him round and pushes him towards the bed R.*)

So into bed for a start.

(*Clive turns protesting*)

Clive: This is ridiculous. Don't be silly. No! No!!

(*Nanny pushes Clive on to the bed and swings his legs up*)

Nanny: That's all right, dear. You don't know me yet.

(*Clive, protesting, is got into bed. Nanny holds him down with her right hand while with her left she pulls the clothes over him. Clive subsides as the blankets smother his protestations.*)

Nanny: But you soon will.

(*Clive's cries are inaudible*)

You soon will!

The curtain falls

This joke is miraculously maintained through three Acts, sometimes with great ingenuity, sometimes, as here again, with a simple but effective use of the Nanny ambience.

Clive is now desperate for whisky, which Nanny has hidden.

Nanny: (*To Humpy*) Would you like a glass of barley-water, dear?
Humpy: No thank you, Nanny.
Nanny: (*To Clive*) Would *you* like a glass of barley-water, Mr. Norton?
Clive: No!
Nanny: I think there's a little word missing. No, what?
Clive: No, dammit!
Nanny: That wasn't the little word I meant.

This is all relatively clear cut. When we come to more profound effects, it is much more difficult. What is one to make, for instance, of Compton Mackenzie? Here is someone who had a very strict, even cruel Nanny, would appear to have been partially alienated from his mother, and is in several ways a classic figure in this study. He has lived a very long time. He has been extremely successful. He certainly feels he has had a full and satisfactory life, and is in fact determined to be, and to be seen to be, happy. Any deep effects it is impossible to gauge, because Compton Mackenzie cannot bear to think deeply about himself and his refusal to introspect does not let us in. "I am temperamentally incapable of dwelling upon unhappiness." It is probably this shrinking to see into himself that accounts for the superficiality which prevents him, in my view, reaching the front rank as a writer. On the other hand, it may well be that his childhood experiences made him a writer in the first place. The enormous energy he has shown could well have been fuelled by the resentments engendered by Nanny Curry. He could read at two, and describes how he escaped from his Nurse's torments into a world of books and fantasy. Certainly, he himself suspects something of this sort. "I should agree with that critic I mentioned about the advantage to a creative writer of an unhappy childhood and I believe that the contemporary passion for turning childhood into an Eden before the Fall will have an adverse effect on the creative literature of the future. . . ."

Compton Mackenzie, despite outbursts of rage against his Nanny, psycho-analysts, and concealed resentment of his mother, prefers to think of his Nanny experience as valuable.

> My old nurse's attitude was indeed a valuable insight into human unreason-ableness and was much better preparation for my future than would have been the fondness of those devoted Nannies to whom quite a few people look back with the same kind of sentimental regret as they look to the happiest days of their life at school. . . . Moreover the rigorous denial of indulgence and the transformation of the simplest desires of a child into 'treats' undoubtedly trained me not to expect that life when grown-up would be entirely easy.

He would also probably say that she taught him good manners, self-discipline and those standards of right and wrong without which civilisa-tion collapses. And a great many people would agree with him. Continu-ally, in my interviews, people lamented the strictness of the old Nanny upbringing, and said how wonderful it had been. And, at the start of any discussion as to the necessity for strictness, one should perhaps say that, to a degree, they are perfectly right.

We have seen earlier that children, in order to feel secure, require a certain order and discipline in their lives. But they also have a lot to learn. Manners, for instance, those politenesses that facilitate and make more pleasant the flow of social life, are not innate. The children of Nannies were polite and life was enhanced thereby. And the same is true of many little nursery disciplines; they are useful and socially desirable— punctuality, fair play, conscientiousness, neatness and tidiness. Elié de Rothschild told Count Friedrich Ledebur that when he was in a German concentration camp he could tell at a glance those Frenchmen who had been brought up by an English Nanny. They sat calm, their bed space neat, their clothes folded. While a Frenchman not brought up by an English Nanny would be struggling and fighting, trying to get a better position or an extra blanket.

But, more profound than this, Nannies instilled a very strong moral code. This imposed two imperatives. First, that authority must be respected and obeyed. Second, that it was wrong to indulge the self, to which the corollary is that the best actions are those directed towards the good of others. These are the root results of a strict Nanny and of not spoiling. This morality made, in some respects, for a great certainty in private life. It also of course, probably to a greater extent than we realise, underpinned (and underpins) whole areas of English behaviour: the incorruptibility of the Civil Service, the respect for the rule of law, the acceptance of and obedience to the State. It underpinned the British Empire, and in this context I should like to quote some lines from a review Laurens van der Post wrote in the *Sunday Times* two years ago.

I believe, like a multitude of others, that a full and honest reappraisal of the meaning of the vanished British Empire is one of the most urgent historical tasks of our time.

I am perhaps one of the few people who can say this without being suspected of Imperial bias. I myself come from a people who fought against the British for more than a hundred years, was conquered by them and was brought up to hate all that the Empire represented. Yet somehow I managed to grow up not only to feel no hatred of the British Empire, but utterly convinced that, in its time and context, the good in it outweighed any harm.

The secret of my almost alchemical change lay in the extraordinary quality of the men who served the Empire, the way in which they used the exercise of immense power without being corrupted by it. Of course, it is easy enough to produce glaring exceptions, as in all generalisations. But what amazes me today is the nostalgia with which I recall the closing phases of the Empire, as I myself experienced them. And this nostalgia arises precisely because corruption by power was being eliminated so thoroughly that at the end of the Second World War, it came near to being the first Platonic system of Government that the world has ever known.

Countless forgotten British men helped to bring this about. For a century or more it had increasingly become the wish for many of the best among the youth of Britain, in the universities and Services, to spend their lives serving peoples of alien cultures in far countries, such as tribal Africa and the ancient civilised world of India.

Now, these are vast subjects—the British Empire, respect for the rule of law, obedience to and acceptance of the State—they have long and complex histories and many roots. Here, as elsewhere, it would be absurd to try to exaggerate the part the Nanny played. Also attitudes and developments of this size are part of the self-perpetuating process of history; they create and affect each other. The attitude and behaviour of the Nanny were as much, or more, a result of the society which ruled an Empire, as that society was a result of her. Nonetheless it should be noted that the morality, the sense of obedience instilled by the majority of Nannies were precisely those necessary for the creation and continuance of many basic aspects of English society in the late nineteenth and early twentieth centuries, and that the Nanny was the dominant figure in the lives of most of the men and women who ran that society. To that extent she deserves her share of praise—if praise is what you feel disposed to give.

Because of course there were other sides to that society. Consider Nurse Binfield, Nanny to Mary Goriely, thundering from her pulpit in 1927, "There are three sorts of sin: little sins, bigger ones, AND TAKING OFF YOUR SHOES WITHOUT UNDOING THE LACES!" Or is it really necessary to sit at table with the palm of one hand resting face down beside one's plate? It doesn't matter which foot you put forward when setting out for a walk. Why shouldn't little children have jam *and* cake *and* bread *and* butter?

The fact, and it doesn't need belabouring, is that many, probably most, Nannies went beyond, often insanely far beyond, the discipline necessary for learning the various social lessons indicated above. You can teach a little boy good table manners without, as happened to one of my correspondents, strapping his elbows to his side. Children can learn the value of authority in far gentler circumstances than too many Nannies often provided.

But this over-strictness had a number of quite definite results. Whole swathes of Englishmen and women were not just polite; they were far too polite. They were terrified of not being polite. They were polite when they should have been rude. The only thing I could get out of Mr. Wynne-Tyson in my ten-minute interview with him was that he was horrified by sticky fingers. His children could terrify him by advancing with outstretched hands chanting, "Sticky fingers! Sticky fingers!" And it was true. When he asked me if I'd like to wash my hands, so compelling was his gaze, so forceful his desire, that I did what I hadn't done in that unnecessary nursery way for thirty years, I went meekly and washed my hands. Or take neatness and tidiness. Elié de Rothschild did not say whether the Nanny-brought-up Frenchmen, sitting demurely in their immaculate bed spaces, were more likely to survive than the other ones—a question somewhat to the point in a concentration camp. The last thing a very drunk Nanny-generation Englishman does before passing out is to stagger round his room, frequently falling over, trying to fold up his clothes, put shoe trees in his shoes and finally, now probably being sick but despite this, cleaning his teeth. James Lees-Milne in an amusing autobiography describes how his father was so obsessed with time and punctuality that, whenever they travelled, the whole journey was timed to the minute and the mile. As they proceeded his father frantically consulted complex maps and charts, now slowing almost to a stop if they were early, now fuming and honking, racing ahead because they were thirty seconds late at such and such a crossroads. We shall see that Curzon is a particularly good example of this sort of behaviour.

But in fact examples could be endless, from life, from my interviews, from autobiographies and biographies. Far too many Englishmen and women of our period were hedged in, driven by, obsessed with hundreds of totally unnecessary disciplines drummed into them by their Nannies.

And it goes deeper than this. If you make a great many rules for a child and then always reward him for conforming and punish him for breaking them, if you never allow him to behave spontaneously, never, say, at the age of two let him crawl by himself and climb dangerously and untidy the house, if you never let him do things on his own and find out that there is a value in questioning authority, a value and rewards in experiment and exploring and poking about, then he will grow up, in the vast majority of cases, to behave like this in adult life. He will behave well. He will conform. He will want and need rules, conventions, recognised authority. He will want clubs and rules about dress and length of hair and formal unchanging patterns of social behaviour. Not only that—if his Nanny upbringing has been excessively strict he will require them still more. It is possible to crush and damage the will of a little child to such a degree that he needs the iron brace of outside discipline and convention to support him. Furthermore, we have seen how the Nanny leaving was a major source of insecurity. It was not helped by the Nanny's habit of withholding praise. Children *need* praise. It is good for them. They need to be encouraged and told they look attractive and are clever and brave. The more they are told these things the more they will become them, because at an early age a child sees himself through his parents' or his Nanny's eyes. If they say he is naughty or dirty or showing off he feels unworthy and unconfident. You don't spoil children by praising them.

But another more potent creator of insecurity, though less significant than leaving, was that alienation of the mother we looked at earlier. To a child, the Nanny and the mother were the twin sources of authority and security, in various combinations (but as we have seen with the weight predominantly in the Nanny's favour) they were the joint platform on which his life rested. They were his world. But if the two parts of the platform were at variance with each other, if the world heaved and split, it was hardly surprising if the child developed a sense of fundamental insecurity. And the stronger the tension, the more antagonistic the mother and the Nanny were, the greater the degree of insecurity. As I pointed out in an earlier chapter a number of recent child studies designed to find out the reasons for severely disturbed and insecure children have strongly indicated that interparental (i.e. inter-authority) tension is as powerful a factor as marked rejection. And of course the insecurity induced (often unwittingly) by all these various facets of the Nanny upbringing made the need for protection and safety provided by their rigid disciplines, the desire to conform, the terror at breaking the rules, all the stronger.

At its most dominant, when many of these factors operate together, the Nanny discipline became the very bone and skeleton of her charge's character. And you see this in the vehemence with which that structure is defended or its absence attacked. Partly the vehemence seems sometimes to have elements of revenge. "Because I had it, so will he." But mainly it is that, because these old Nanny children feel that they would collapse, become engulfed by nameless lusts and aggressions and fears without the complex structure of rewards and inhibitions built into them, they also feel society will collapse without a similar set of rules. They cannot realise that a perfectly adequate degree of good manners, self-discipline, sufficiently high moral standards and the rest are obtainable without the absurd routines and prohibitions they themselves endured.

There were undeniably strong elements of inhibition, conventionality and conformity, too rigid social taboos which made many people's lives during our period much less free, spontaneous and happy than they could have been. And, just as she received praise for the benefits, so the Nanny must bear her share of blame for the evils resulting from this situation.

THIRD SEXUAL DETOUR: THE CHAMBER POT

There is one last area, involving us in a final sexual detour, in which the strictness of the Nanny operated and where the results were arguably even more serious. The landscape is Daliesque, dominated, as by a grim, towering and distorted castle, by an enormous chamber pot.

"Over my grave," Nanny Ellis used to say, "they should put an up-turned potty." Up-turned, presumably, to show it was empty. A full one would have been more appropriate. The best potty is a full potty. It will come as no surprise now to learn that nowhere were the Nanny disciplines more rigorous than in the sphere of toilet training. Nor, it should be noted, is this surprising. Before nappies, disposable or otherwise, strong disinfectants and the rest, cleaning babies was a considerable problem. St. Bernadino of Siena (1388–1444) drew attention in one of his sermons to how enormously a woman "travaileth in washing and cleaning by day and by night". Swaddling clothes were a nightmare to clean and endless washing was part of the medieval routine. Writers recommended annointing little limbs with oil of roses to sweeten them. Even in the '20s and '30s nappies had to be boiled sterile. The quicker a baby could be pot-trained the less work for Nurse and nursery-maid. A clean child is one who pleases Nurse, and a child who pleases Nurse is good. So arrived the equation of cleanliness and goodness which was later raised by those who had suffered the regime into something almost mystic—Cleanliness is next to Godliness.

The Nanny inherited what had almost certainly always been a tradition of fairly strict toilet training and by a process we have seen duplicated made it stricter still. Throughout our period she threw herself into the task with an energy which was never less than firm and which sometimes bordered on the savage.

> This Nanny [wrote Lady Anne Hill] made as much of an issue over my bowel movements as over what and how much I ate.
>
> I was put on the 'article' (a common late Victorian and Edwardian euphemism for chamber pot) and told to do Number Two (also called Big as opposed to Little) as soon as I had finished my long long breakfasts. If I said I didn't want to, I was told I must 'try' and would be left sitting for up to half an hour or more. This was most uncomfortable and gave me agonising pins and needles. What a relief, what triumph, when I could shout, "Done it, Nanny!" What a worry

when I couldn't as this meant I would have to have Syrup of Figs in the evening. Syrup of Figs had "Children love it" written on the bottle, but I found it literally nauseating, and I was constantly being sick over it before bedtime, on several occasions twice over in the same evening. . . . An extra worry was my belief in what Nanny said that not 'doing it' was alarmingly bad for me. However my brother and cousins' giggly attitude towards these matters prevented my becoming really hypochondriacal. To get out of earshot of the grown-ups and say "Big, little, knickers, belly underneath" would set us off, tumbling and rolling about in the wildest convulsions of laughter.

Children still laugh at these things even when brought up by the most liberal and permissive of parents; but they cannot know the spice that danger added to our giggles, the ever-looming possibility that Nanny might suddenly appear from nowhere and start grimly scolding and slap-slap-slapping us all, turning our wild laughter to equally wild sobs and screams.

Pot training began very early, in the first month or so. Thereafter it was continued, in a sense, right up to the moment the child left Nanny's care. Every day he or she was questioned—often having to show some proof—about whether they had 'gone'. If they hadn't, some alimentary explosive was given them to blow the little faeces out. Training took several forms. At first—innumerable placings on the pot, dozens a day. Once the baby or child had learnt, the most common method of persuading a child to go was to leave him or her there, like Anne Hill, till something 'happened'. Eleanor Acland describes in her autobiography how "It was nursery law that we might not quit the water closet till we were fetched." Once one of them was forgotten from tea until bedtime and sat there for five hours.

But Nannies could be more fearsome and positive. They had weapons: fingers, suppositories, the pot itself. Here is Bridget Tisdall again:

I had two Nannies. The first was called Hilda Fig. She left when I was six months old. I have no recollections of her, except her name, which still seems to me to have a benevolent ring. The second Nanny was Nanny Moore. She had known a more exalted position with Lady May Cambridge, but appeared to settle down with us, who could only boast of a Daddy in the Household Brigade.

In some respects Nanny Moore was a fiend. I was never allowed to sit by myself in the lavatory and have a good dream. She always came in with me, and standing beside me holding sheets of Bromo paper, exhorted me to try. I tried until my rectum ached. Whatever turds I had must have been made of stone. Nothing ever came out. My rectum ached, my tummy ached, with 'trying'. There she stood, a tyrant in her white starched apron, filling the lavatory with terror and misery. After what seemed to me hours of trying I would shuffle off the lavatory seat. Nanny would peer into the bowl: Nothing! I knew I was in for a dose of Gregory Powder or Syrup of Figs. I was the victim of a sort of bowel fever. I went to bed haunted with the guilt of not going and the thought of a dose the following day. Sometimes she would try to make me 'go' on the pot. If nothing happened she inserted a suppository up my rectum. I remember the horrible sensation of the ice-cold suppository and extreme humiliation to this day: the feeling of having something done to one, an invasion of privacy, was quite horrible.

But in Bridget Tisdall's pot life confusion was introduced by a conflict of aim between Nanny who urged evacuation, and the nursery-maid who had to deal with the results.

> There was chamber pot etiquette in the nursery. Number One was applauded, but Number Two was a severe breach. I imagine Rose, our nursery-maid who waited on Nanny and brought up the meals, was not too keen on emptying pots: piss plus turd produced revolutionary rumbling and upset nursery hierarchy. It was an accident with agreeably sinful overtones.

But Nannies could go much further than this. One of the psychiatrists I discussed this subject with had a patient whose Nanny used to tie him to his pot with straps. Simon T was allowed two 'tries', separated by half an hour each, and then given a thorough smacking and Gregory powder. Perhaps the most unpleasant instance I found was of a Nanny who used to insert her finger, causing considerable pain, deep into her little boy's rectum, allege she could 'feel it there', and upbraid him for 'holding back on her'.

In England, until very recently (and still among a great many people I suspect), it was thought 'natural' to bring children up strictly in this sphere. It is not. Dozens of cultures are the reverse of ours. The Siriono of South America, for instance, never punish a child even if it urinates or defecates on its parents. The mother makes no effort to train the child till it can walk, and even then it is done with endless help and encouragement and no punishment.

Similarly we tend to dismiss its effects. Yet severe toilet training had (and has) a number of perfectly well attested results. The most obvious of these was demonstrated to me by a surprise appearance of its reverse. "I think you're right," said the quite elderly man I was talking to, "we probably were made too anxious about the whole business. But, even now you know, the relief when you have achieved, finally, a really satisfactory evacuation is very great. I think the enormous pleasure one experiences at a good motion counterbalances the despair at an inadequate one, or the horror at none at all.''

Such very strict training meant that throughout our period an absolute horror of constipation was very common. This was the more unfortunate as it is possible, though impossible to prove, that constipation—as an unconscious and retrospective act of rebellion, a withholding of what was being prised from them—was itself more common. When one of Nanny Williams's charges hadn't 'been' for a week she was rushed to hospital, where an enema produced a copious flow. "She hadn't had a turn out for a week. She was just lazy—that's all.'' Nanny Williams advocated starting pot training at three weeks.

Enemas, purgatives, middle-aged men and women frenziedly scrutinising the lavatory bowl—even doctors, on no medical grounds whatsoever, no doubt because they too had been brought up in the same way, added to the furore. The solution of one late Victorian doctor, Dr. William Arbuthnot Lane, still practising in the early '20s, was little less than heroic. By massive surgery he simply removed the whole colon, thus making constipation impossible. Yet, according to Dr. D. W. Winnicott, the fact is that dangerous constipation is very rare. Children (and adults) can go for two or three weeks without defecating and suffer no harm at all.

A great many studies have shown that the deeper complications resulting from over-strict toilet training—marked use of shame, rigid schedules, frequent putting on the pot and leaving there, etc.—can have two much more difficult effects.

The first is anxiety. It is actually physiologically impossible to pot train a child before the age of about six months or more. The sphincters which allow it to control bowel and bladder movements are not sufficiently developed till then. (Nannies will frequently boast much earlier triumphs; but of course nearly incessant potting—like covering most of the numbers on roulette—produces a high enough quota of wins for one to ignore the losses.) Yet the baby is continually urged to do it doesn't quite know what, which it physically can't do anyway. Later bed-wetting and other anxiety symptoms have frequently been traced back to this. But insistence on conformity in this very sensitive area spreads out. It reinforced that tendency to rigid behaviour, to the formation of compulsive habits of cleanliness, neatness, economy and so on that we have already commented on. It also reinforced the timidity engendered by over-strict disciplines, the feeling it is not safe to make a response unless certain it is correct.

There is another psychologically damaging aspect of over-strict toilet training. Tiny children don't distinguish between the organs of elimination and what is eliminated; indeed the whole genital and excretory area—penis, vagina, anus—and the functions and sensations associated with it are inextricably intermingled. Anxiety over one leads to anxiety over the other. "Some of the emotion that is engendered at this period (aged two)", write Mussen, Conger and Kagen, "over bowel and bladder functions spreads out and encompasses sexuality, since the organs of sexual functioning and excretion are the same"—or so close as to be the same. Once again frequent studies have shown that anxiety and difficulty and guilt over sexuality in later life often begin here.

To put this in its context it might perhaps be a good idea to look briefly at certain, now quite well known, aspects of Victorian and Edwardian sexual life (aspects which continued strongly, however, into the 1920s and '30s). Once more let William Acton and his admirable commentator Steven Marcus be our guides.

In the book I have already quoted from, Acton begins by describing in a page and a half the 'Normal Functions in Childhood'.

> In a state of health no sexual impression should ever affect a child's mind or body. All its vital energy should be employed in building up the growing frame, in storing up external impressions and educating the brain to receive them. . . . The sexes, it is true, in most English homes, are allowed unrestricted companionship. Experience shows, however, that this intimacy is in the main unattended with evil results. . . . At any rate, in healthy subjects, and especially in children brought up in the pure air, and amid the simple amusements of the country, perfect freedom from, and indeed total ignorance of any sexual affection is, as it should always be, the rule. . . . Thus it happens that with most healthy and well-brought-up children no sexual notion or feeling has ever entered their heads, even in the way of speculation.

But Acton now reveals the true cause of his concern, the enemy against whom his energies are really bent. Because the page and a half describing 'normal' sexual functions is instantly followed by twenty pages describing abnormal functions. Here Acton shows that childhood sexual play and masturbation were widespread and well known. They were disapproved of. They were evil. But they existed. And so we find a typically contradictory Victorian attitude (but one which, as I say, had a very long life): children are both non-sexual and pure, yet at the same time are dangerously over-sexed and continually being aroused and tempted by evil stimulations.

Everything contributes to rouse the childish sexual appetite (or boyish sexual appetite rather; girls, of course, for reasons we have discussed, had no sexual feelings whatever): bed-wetting, washing the penis, reading, "irritation of the rectum arising from worms. . . ."

The penis can even excite itself. Of the foreskin Acton writes worriedly: "It affords an additional surface for the excitement of the reflex action, and aggravates an instinct rather than supplies a want. In the unmarried it additionally excites the sexual desires, which it is our object to suppress."

The dangers in childhood were considerable. In youth they became dreadful, and chief among them was masturbation. Here is Acton's description of a boy who habitually masturbates:

> The frame is stunted and weak, the muscles undeveloped, the eye is sunken and heavy, the complexion is sallow, pasty or covered with spots of acne, the hands are damp and cold, and the skin moist. The boy shuns the society of others, creeps about alone, joins with repugnance in the amusements of his school fellows. He cannot look anyone in the face, and becomes careless in dress and uncleanly in person. His intellect has become sluggish and enfeebled and if his evil habits are persisted in, he may end in becoming a drivelling idiot or a peevish valetudinarian. Such boys are to be seen in all stages of degeneration, but what we have described is but the results towards which *they all* are tending . . . self-indulgence, long pursued, tends ultimately, if carried far enough, to early death or self-destruction.

Here we have, in fine ringing prose, the classic Victorian and Edwardian statement on masturbation. In various forms, it was repeated endlessly. It was the accepted belief. It was both the cause and symptom of the pathetic alienation of whole generations of upper and upper-middle class men from their own sexuality; the creator of pointless marriages and impoverished, often very unhappy, lives. Because, as Marcus shows, as an attitude it branched out. All sexual activity became dangerous. It must never be over-indulged in. When he comes to deal with marriage, Acton adds to the catalogue that attends sexual excess heart failure and loss of memory. In fact, marriage could be especially dangerous. Having kept an iron control before it, the newly married man goes virtually mad, intercourse "is indulged in night after night", and the result for the man is "simple ruin".

> A medical man called on me [demonstrates Acton], saying he found himself suffering from spermatorrhea [this was a disease the Victorians had actually invented which was supposed to result from excessive loss of semen]. There was general debility, ineptitude to work, disinclination for sexual intercourse, in fact, he thought he was losing his senses. The sight of one eye was affected. The only way in which he lost semen was, as he thought, by a slight occasional oozing from the penis. I asked him at once if he had ever committed excesses. As a boy, he acknowledged having abused himself, but he married seven years

ago, being then a hearty healthy man, but it was only lately he had been complaining. In answer to my further enquiry, he stated that since his marriage he had had connection two or three times a week, and often more than once a night! This one fact, I was obliged to tell him, sufficiently accounted for all his troubles.

What could be done about it all, all this masturbation and sexuality? There were devices. In fact as late as 1921, Havelock Ellis and Albert Moll were still able to recommend in the second edition of their *Handbuch der Sexualwissenschaften*, a special *Onaniebandagen* or *Korsette*. These were tiny metal suits of armour which fitted snugly round the genitals and were secured on to a locked belt to make masturbation impossible, or at least much less pleasurable.

But the main weapon must be self-control leading to continence. This will be a hard and difficult task. It will depend on the exercise of will. And so we are led straight back to the child, whose infant training is the most powerful source of all these ideas. Because will "is a matter of habit. Every victory strengthens the victor . . . the whole force of his character, braced and multiplied by the exercises of a lifetime, drives him with unwavering energy along his chosen path of purity." Since will is a matter of habit, the earlier the habit is inculcated the better. But where should these early habits be imposed? Now, without realising it, Acton returns to the area from which, no doubt deep in his unconscious, he had set out. He equates the habit of sexual control and continence with the habit of early bowel control in children. Stern discipline in one, he says, will lead to stern discipline in the other. The two functions have become confused in the mind of the man just as they are in the minds of little children.

And in fact the equation of sex and bowel movement/control is a common (if often unconscious) one in Victorian and Edwardian discussions of the subject. It is frequently noticeable in the pornography of the time. For instance in *Rosa Fielding or a Victim of Lust* (1867), when Albert first sees Rosa: "The gentleman was in that state of lust that two or three judicious rubs from the hand of his fair cousin would have released his evacuations." Similarly, it is often suggested that strict pot training affects attitudes to money and certainly the financial tinge to Edwardian and Victorian sexual language is also striking. To have an orgasm is 'to spend', over-indulgence spells 'ruin', chastity is spoken of in terms of saving, as an investment for the future.

There were of course other reasons for the growth of sexual repression during the nineteenth century. Marcus argues, for instance, that Victorian improving ambitions required very determined efforts, self-control, the acceptance of rewards deferred and so on, and that these attitudes were automatically transferred, in some way he does not indicate, to sex. There were the usual religious strands at work. But psychiatry would suggest, and the evidence confirms, that bowel training is one very important element in the development of adult sexuality and Nannies were crucial to this. Perhaps the later (1925) Nanny word 'potty'—"I felt quite potty", "he was a bit potty if you ask me"—had an element of truth in it, containing a covert and unconscious reference to what may sometimes have caused the 'pottiness'.

But Nannies could act in a more obvious way against sexuality than this. I wrote earlier of the atmosphere of fear and disapproval about sex, the lack of sensuality, which often seems to surround the Nanny. Anne Talbot had friends whose Nanny used to say with a sense of relief about kissing, "Well there's more girls doesn't do it than do." A frequent threat, no doubt hiding an unconscious but strong desire, was to 'cut your tail off'— a little boy's tail being his penis. Little girls were warned how terrible men could be, how dangerous, how disgusting. There were whole dictionaries of euphemisms, and then, when a euphemism had taken on too clearly the colour of its subject, euphemisms for euphemisms. Compton Mackenzie's Nanny thought pee-pee and wee-wee too near the knuckle and invented 'tee-tee'. Compton Mackenzie thought this was spelt 'teety' and was baffled that he could never find it in dictionaries. Nanny Ellis never allowed peeing on grass, but carried a pot with her everywhere. The disgust a euphemism implies imprinted itself deeply on the Nannied children. When he was three, Alexander Weymouth's father used to take him to a T.A. camp. His father, himself the product of a strict Nanny upbringing, has never been able to touch anything to do with excreta, at least not without enormous reluctance. He couldn't bring himself to wipe Alexander's bottom, so he gave the job to the Second Footman, Donald Marks. There was the Nanny terror of nakedness—the incredible skill with which they could undress without revealing an inch of flesh, creating great tents out of their nighties under which to unbuckle their 'bombazine armour' and slip off petticoats, knickers and skirts. An absurd terror which they often transmitted to their charges. Mary Clive, a highly intelligent and sophisticated woman, could never understand why Arthur Rackham's Peter Pan was naked "when the statue in Kensington Gardens shows that he was a decent size and decently dressed".

When it came to masturbation Nannies often felt their intervention should go beyond the mere emanation of disapproval. Sometimes, unknowingly, they actually encouraged it. As we have seen, Dr. D. W.

Winnicott noted that Nannies did sometimes masturbate little boys to produce a soothing sleep and he found that an early pattern of this sort can 'fix' an outlet and can persist. Suppositories will fire an anus to desire further stimulation; the need to be masturbated may reappear in later life. Also girls on the whole were left alone, though hints might be dropped.

> I remember masturbating [writes Bridget Tisdall], but never felt guilty as I was never caught. I also remember my dear grandmother telling me to go to sleep lying on my side, with my arms crossed and folded against my potential bosom. This seemed to me weird and very uncomfortable. However, I was always anxious to placate the adult loony bin, and did as I was told. I remember the rest of my body feeling very 'left out' lying in the 'safe' position. But there I would lie, longing to scratch my toes, spiritually truncated from the animal half of myself.

But on the whole the Nanny attitude was repressive and directed against little boys. To stop sexuality in very little children (boys) Acton had suggested exercise, showers, washing and bathing—though he issued a word of warning here. "The habit of remaining long in the water may be as great a source of evil as anything." But chiefly, he says, parents and nurses must "watch their children". Masturbation and related activities *must be stopped.* Fingering, mutual exploration, indecent questions, the whole dangerous rag-bag must be ruthlessly stamped out. Watch, watch, watch— so often is the admonition repeated that one feels the home turning into a sort of sexual concentration camp with eyes, fearful, avid and avenging, ever at the peephole.

And certainly Nannies kept their eyes peeled. Mark Culme-Seymour can remember (pre-1920) that when he was five he had his hands tied behind his head to the bed rail to prevent him masturbating, though he hadn't the faintest idea what masturbating was. His hands used to get very cold. Once, when he had managed to get them free and was holding them between his legs warming them, his Nanny hurried in and stripped off the bedclothes. "Aha! At it again Master Mark!" One informant (*c.* 1905) told me he can still remember, not the details, but the feeling of something dreadful, truly appalling, which would result, his Nanny told him, if he 'touched himself'. Simon T (1925) can remember being slapped every time his hand so much as strayed in the direction of his genitals and once, when he and his sister were aged four and six, they were caught examining each other and soundly thrashed. And so on and so on.

These repressive and overstrict measures had one or two unlooked for consequences. Mussen, Conger and Kagen note that practically all children discover that manipulating their genitals produces pleasurable sensations. Most of them therefore develop masturbating activities (and these are not only quite harmless, they are often beneficial, comforting and educative. Only very rarely, when they become incessant, do they denote anxiety and need to be dealt with.) On the generalising principle, this leads to an interest in other children's genitals. Yet for these harmless and pleasurable activities they are punished and spanked. The genitals then become a focus for conflict; on the one hand they cause pleasure, on the other they provoke punishment and therefore anxiety. "The combination of pleasure and anxiety over an object or activity, which is a definition of conflict, often leads to heightened preoccupation with the source of the conflict." This reaction no doubt partly explains the obsessive quality often found in English attitudes to sex during this period—in public reactions to moral lapses, in censorship, and conversely, in the ever rising tide of pornography and occasional relentless pursuit of sexual experience. Again, since hundreds of thousands of boys and girls masturbated without any of the dire results promised from their earliest years, these added to that dual standard, that hypocrisy of feeling, which we have seen Nannies quite unwittingly contribute to already. Geoffrey Gorer suggests a third result, that the omnipresent authority overlooking these primary pleasures— whether on the pot or in the cot—from an early age, and either, in the one case, forcing it on or, in the other, forbidding it all together, is one reason the English upper classes have such a passionate desire for privacy. Pleasure is something that can only be experienced alone. Immured in their clubs, safe behind ramparts of newspaper, silent in the corners of first class railway carriages, they are free at last from Nanny.

But the principal result of course was to strengthen that tendency to rigidity, conformity and inhibition which over-strict Nanny disciplines generally inculcated. Strengthen it, and extend it to sexual life. The precise scope of the damage is impossible to estimate. Often no doubt very minor, sometimes severe. All one can say is that where there existed sexual fears, confusions and inhibitions then, throughout our period, the Nanny must often bear a large share of the responsibility.

I say throughout our period, but it must be remembered that there were liberal and more enlightened movements growing during the first forty years of the twentieth century which did no doubt mitigate some of the Nanny effects (you could find one or two prep schools in the late 1930s, for instance, willing to admit that masturbation wasn't medically and psychologically fatal). Also, as the Nanny system slowly broke down, as more riff-raff tended to enter the ranks, a slight dilution did take place.

Nevertheless my own impression is that in this sphere the Nanny strictness was effectively constant. It may have become physically less severe, the religious overtones diminished, but in the quite numerous examples I have of this attitude, or of reactions clearly deriving from it, they are spread evenly. As many come from the 1930s as from pre-1914. And, with the proviso just made, they are the same attitudes. A man of sixty-five told me that of course, since a single act of sexual intercourse was the equivalent of a two-mile run, he couldn't do it very often now. But a comparatively young Nannied man (thirty-eight) told me he too found it increasingly exhausting to have sexual intercourse, though of course since it was equivalent to a nine-mile run, that wasn't surprising. (I suppose the energy put into sexual activity varies considerably. Kinsey suggests an average equivalent to a fifty yard sprint.) Fears about masturbation, euphemisms, forbidden activities—they seem to diminish hardly at all. As late as the mid-'30s Nanny Marks always referred to urinating as being 'a clean boy'. When Alexander Weymouth went to his prep school he always referred to his penis as his 'clean boy'. He can remember he and his brother Christopher Thynne fiddling with each other's penises in the bath, perhaps the 'cleanest' place to do it. Nanny Marks said sharply, "You're not being dirty, are you?" The outlook is still, essentially, Acton's.

CHAPTER NINE

The Cruel Nanny

I can remember when I was three and I was naughty my Nanny, Nanny Palmer, used to put me in a sack with the top sewn up and put me in the cellar. I can remember the appalling terror to this day. I couldn't see, or hardly breathe, the blackness—I screamed and screamed. She wouldn't let me out. She said. "You'll come out when you stop screaming." But I couldn't stop screaming.

Informant (male) who wished to remain anonymous. Married in the late 1930s, Ada Palmer died when he was twelve. I asked him what he felt. He said, "I laughed and laughed and laughed."

Practically everyone who is in charge of children secretly fears that one day they will lose control of them. Suddenly—it will be 1789: the children will storm the barricades, hurl fire-fenders or blackboards to the floor, Nanny or teacher or mother will be flat on their backs, buried, pinioned beneath upturned pots or desks, the receding sound of smashing furniture resounding in their ears.

This fear is another root of the absolute power the Nanny wielded. But to most people the exercise of power, the imposing of their will, is a pleasure in itself—a pleasure which, in the case of children, is no doubt partly based on the reversal of that inner fear. Mrs. Thrale wrote to tell Dr. Johnson how she had overruled her nurses and how angry they had been. He wrote back, "That the nurses fretted, will supply me during life with an additional motive to keep every child, as far as possible, out of a nurse's power. A nurse made of common mould will have pride in overpowering a child's reluctance. There are few minds to which tyranny is not delightful; power is nothing but as it is felt, and the delight of superiority is proportionate to the resistance overcome."

The step from enjoying power, from rejoicing in the collapse of resistance, to the enjoyment of suffering is, for some people, a small one. We have seen Nannies take it at various times in this book and there is no need to dwell on it. But, partly because it has some curious aspects which repay study, and partly because without it our picture of the British Nanny would be incomplete, it is this last, sombre corner of the nursery I propose to look at now.

The sufferings which Nannies caused their charges—resulting once or twice in actual death—were sometimes the result of ignorance. A prime example of this is their use of gas. Daphne Fielding describes how one of her Nannies was sacked for putting her brother Tony to sleep with a tube leading from the gas fire. Lady Diana Cooper told me it was quite common to hear of Nannies using ether to calm their charges. But the classic story is that told by Andrew Graham in *Mostly Nasty*.

The narrator was sitting in Hyde Park by the Albert Memorial one Saturday morning in July when two Nannies came and sat beside him. He listened intermittently and vaguely, when all at once one of them, a large, red-faced Somerset girl, said something that so amazed and appalled him he felt he had to follow her home and report it to her mistress. He followed her to 4A, Pytchley Gardens, S.W.7 where a Mr. and Mrs. John Maitland lived. Mrs. Maitland took him up to the drawing-room but when she learnt that he had come because he had overheard her Nanny say something about her children she began to look very upset. When he told her what the Nanny had said, she turned white and then fell into a chair sobbing and shaking. She was eventually able to explain that a few months before her beloved two-year-old daughter had died quite inexplicably. She had just faded away. And now the new baby, Julia, had begun to have the same symptom, just gradually growing weaker every day.

What the narrator had overheard, of course, was the Nanny describing how she put her little charge to sleep. "If mine won't go to sleep, I just hold the gas ring over her dear little face and give her a whiff." It transpired that the Nanny, after gas at the dentist, had assumed that all gas, whether from an anaesthetist or a fire, was the same. His fortunate eavesdropping had saved Julia's life. (Andrew Graham invented this story after hearing two Nannies discuss using a few whiffs of gas to get their babies asleep, but it seems to have become an archetype in the collective unconscious of Nannied children. No less than three people told it to me in various forms as though it had happened to close friends or relations of theirs.)

wished to remain anonymous, told me that his brother and sister-in-law (I got the impression he was really talking about himself and his wife) had hired a very young temporary Nanny to look after their daughter, aged eight months (this was in 1932), while the proper Nanny was away ill. They noticed that the baby, hitherto gay, became silent and unresponsive, as well as becoming prone to fits of screaming, heard even in the drawing-room. One afternoon the mother, greatly daring, picked the baby from her pram in the garden and was appalled to find its arms and legs covered in bruises. The Nanny was sacked, the doctor called, and the little girl was subsequently found to have a broken collar bone, fractures in both legs as well as multiple bruising. This was almost certainly an example of what today is called a battered baby. I know of two similar examples, both involving temporary Nannies, and I think it possible that the Nanny profession may have occasionally attracted potential baby batterers. (It cannot have been very common, though such occurrences are often hushed up by the guilty parents.) Research shows that women of this sort are usually of two kinds. Either they live over-isolated lives, the stress of which drives them to sudden violence against their children, or else (and often they are both) they are emotionally defective or retarded and, though they cannot face the idea of having a family, want to have a little living doll. When the living doll begins screaming and crying (screams which often raise echoes of their own probably deprived and ill-treated past) and generally stops behaving like a doll at all, they become infuriated and beat it. Such women would be more likely to become temporary Nannies, both because they could not possibly sustain the role of proper Nanny and because they would eventually be found out—either by especially vigilant parents or by the death or severe injury of their charge.

But too often one is driven to the conclusion that Nannies vented upon their little children, under the guise of discipline, not spoiling and the rest, emotions generated by their dissatisfied, frustrated, neurotic or downright sadistic temperaments. They had, of course, ample scope. For one thing, the ancient idea that very little children should be beaten persisted, though it steadily diminished, throughout our period. Daphne Fielding, in one of her amusing and light-hearted autobiographies *Mercury Presides*, describes a childhood of almost incessant smackings and beatings until she was seven. She bears to this day a white scar on her collar bone where a Nanny struck out with a spoon previously heated, by immersion in the saucepan, to the temperature of boiling Benger's food. Another Nanny used to whip her with nettles and cram her brother Tony's mouth with soap. He'd scream and yell, and Daphne Fielding used to watch bubbles flow from his mouth and nose. A third Nanny used to smack her continually and painfully with the back of a Mason and Pearson hairbrush. Indeed, so much was beating a part of her upbringing that when her father said he was going to marry again, a Miss Rose, her instinctive reaction was, "It *will* be nice to be smacked by such a pretty person."

Not everyone was able to remember so calmly. Some of the letters I received still seethed, quite justifiably, with remembered resentment and impotent fury. Miss W. V., born in 1925, had a Nanny who used to beat her and her brother so ferociously that their screams were often heard by the neighbours. Nothing was exempt from a beating. This Nanny even taught W.V. to ride a bicycle by rushing along beside her and slashing at her legs each time she fell off. Sheer pain forced her to cling on. She described, too, the hideous delay between a 'crime' and its punishment. When she was five she was given some embroidered handkerchiefs for Christmas. They were put away in her drawer, but a few mornings later, at six o'clock, she had a sudden longing to look at them. They were embroidered with Dutch scenes of windmills and skating on canals. She got up and carried them back into bed with her. Nothing was said about this crime (it had been detected and instantly reported by a maid noticing the light shining beneath the door) until eight hours later. After lunch, she saw Nanny ominously, and with her peculiar 'punishment' expression, unscrewing the long wooden rod, with a knob at its end, which kept the baby in his large high chair. Nanny ordered her upstairs to the nursery, and then set to beating her with concentrated rage, not just on her bottom but all over her back. "Nanny left in January, 1933, when I was just over seven years old. I remember the day well. We were not told until the morning she was due to leave, which was a pity because it would have been enjoyable looking forward to the day. I could hardly disguise my delight."

Cruelty was not always so overt. More common is the sort or thing we have seen with Compton Mackenzie; an absurd strictness, combined with the desire to make everything as unpleasant, uncomfortable and frustrating as possible—a desire to frustrate whose descent into minutiae reveals the relish behind it. Even the kindly prose of F. Anstey cannot disguise how wretched babyhood and childhood under such tyrants must have been. This is taken from *A Long Retrospect*.

We were under the despotic rule of a nurse whose name was Fanny Channer—a dark, sallow, hard-featured woman of about thirty. We were fond of her and, after her peculiar fashion, she was fond of us—but she led us a hard life. Before she came to us she had been a nurse at an orphan asylum, and she never outgrew an impression that stern discipline was what we required. At breakfast, our porridge, for which I conceived an incurable dislike, was served with nothing to make it more palatable, and I was compelled to swallow it, protest and bellow as I might. She also issued an edict that any crusts we had left overnight were to be eaten before we touched our bread and butter, and we obeyed until our father accidentally discovered this prohibition and put an end to it.

We had plenty of wooden bricks but Fanny, for no particular reason, made a rule that only six long bricks and twelve short ones were to be permitted, which did not give us much scope for architecture. . . . In 1865 and for some summers following, my father took a house, then called Colwell Cottage between Totland and Colwell Bays in the Isle of Wight. There was sea-bathing, of course, though as we had this Spartan nurse with a theory that to make children accustomed to the sea there is nothing like ducking them in it without warning, I rather disliked that part of the morning. For use on Sundays—though I think we were allowed no toys of any kind on that day—there were 'Scripture bricks', small oblong pieces of wood with a Biblical incident on one side and a text of wood on the other.

Anstey says he didn't hate his Nurse, but each time she is mentioned it is in connection with some prohibition, humiliation, crime or punishment—doses, blows or deprivations. By the time he was eight he was prey to periods of deep depression.

Anstey is interesting, as I mentioned earlier, because he wrote the classic novel of revenge on a Victorian childhood in *Vice Versa* (though the novel is a more penetrating study than this alone implies). Both his parents were kind and concerned themselves with the children (he adored his mother); his prep school, Crighton House, where *Vice Versa* was set, was relatively mild; it seems reasonable to suggest, therefore, that Nurse Channer provided the initial motive force for wanting to stand his childhood on its head.

Yet one can be sorry for figures like Fanny Channer. Often plain, and unlikely for other reasons to get married or even form close friendships, usually alone, always poor, they had been forced to take a job for which they were totally unsuited and which, if you are unsuited to it, can be the most exasperating in the world. Ever more alone, they watched their lives slip steadily away, unfulfilled and unloved. No wonder they became bitter, neurotic, frustrated, no wonder, really, if they vented their feelings on those around them. It was just unfortunate that these happened to be small, defenceless children.

Frequently they took to drink. Stories of heavy drinking Nannies are innumerable (less numerous, but by no means unknown, are cases of Nannies feeding their charges drink to shut them up). Nanny Spalding, the Nanny of Felicity, Iris and Viola Tree, kept gin in the pram. Nanny Smithson was found to have sherry in her teapot and not tea. Compton Mackenzie's Nanny drank, both in fact and in *Sinister Street*:

. . . lately he had always woken up when she came to bed. This was not his fault, because Nanny always bumped into his cot as she came into the room, shaking it so violently that no one could have stayed asleep. She used to look at him in a funny way with angry staring eyes, and when he sometimes spoke she would blow cheese-scented breath at him and turn away and bump into the washstand.

One night, after a nightmare, he creeps downstairs and peeps through the kitchen door.

> There was Nurse with a very red face in a heap on a chair, shaking her fore-finger at Mrs. Frith, who with an equally red face was talking very indistinctly to Nurse.

She is eventually found dead drunk in a kitchen chair by Miss Carthew the governess, and sacked.

One can laugh at these unhappy, misanthropic women, but it is not really laughable. They suffered terribly, and caused immense suffering to others. One of the most complete and brilliant portraits, as brilliant in its way as Compton Mackenzie's (though the Nanny doesn't drink), occurs in a book I have already quoted—*Goodbye For the Present* by Eleanor Acland. Though details of it are now fairly familiar to us—medicine as weapon and so on—I should like to quote some passages from it because Eleanor Acland faces issues—the effect on herself as a little girl, the attitude of her mother—in a way which Compton Mackenzie cannot really bring himself to do.

Barley, her nurse, was tall, thin, with a yellow face. She came when Milly (that is Eleanor Acland) was two and a half and her brother George was just over twelve months. It was 1880.

> To this day I cannot say exactly what was wrong with her. Perhaps it was simply that she was cursed with a superfluity of bile, mental and physical. She suffered at frequent intervals from what were known as 'me sikkedakes', and so did we. We could tell at breakfast it was going to be one of her dreaded 'sikkedake' days, because her complexion was a dingier cream than usual, and the brown pupils of her eyes were fixed opaque discs in their yellow whites, her lips more tightly compressed than ever, and she could 'touch nothing' but a large cup of very strong tea. How mum we sat, each with our left hand placed flat, palm downwards, on the table (according to one of her mysterious rules of nice behaviour at meals); how hushed we tried to keep our play . . . But in the end one, or all, would have been 'stood in the corner'.

The need to vent her spleen was endless. Therefore crimes had to be end-less.

I cannot remember many detailed incidents in our relations with Barley, but only the general sense that somehow she made naughtiness, and its accompaniment of scolding and punishment, a constant element in our lives. They seemed to interest her more than anything else, except illness and funerals. And the worst of it was that there seemed to be no way of knowing what was naughty and what good behaviour.

Why, for instance, if you looked up from eating your breakfast egg and said "Please, Barley, one day will you take us to see a hen laying an egg?" were you met with "Be quiet, Miss Milly. If I have any more of that sort of talk you'll be slapped and stood in the corner."

Eleanor Acland then gives examples which show that, if Barley wanted it, there was nothing that could not be a crime.

Crime was followed by punishment.

The punishments that were the sequel to naughtiness made no attempt at rationality so far as we could discern, not even the pooh-bah rationality of making the punishment fit the crime.

They were of three sorts—ostracism, physical hurt, and doses of medicine. Ostracism, which varied from being stood in the corner to banishment in the night nursery or being sent early to bed, was the most tolerable. Unless in the grip of some acute sense, either of guilt or injustice, you could readily find consolation in some form of make believe. Corporal punishment, on the other hand, besides its unpleasant painfulness was personal violation. It was worse than useless to retaliate, so we just had to cringe and submit to the slapping or (still more humiliating) the shaking of our small persons. It quite often happened that we admitted that justice was being done when we were put in the corner, but I doubt if we, or any child, ever admitted the justice of being hurt, since that offends against a prime canon of nursery law—namely that it is wicked to hit anybody smaller than oneself. The oddest sanction in our nursery penal code was the dose of medicine. It is arguable that if children are cross and sulky a suitable dose will put them to rights. But that was not how the case was presented to us. So far as we could make out, the choice between the three varieties of punishment was a toss-up, depending mainly on the state of Barley's liver and nerves. Moreover, though a dose of liquorice powder may be the right cure for bad temper, can anyone say why the graver sins of lying and persistent disobedience should have been met by the threat, and occasionally the administration of Gregory powder, abominable in taste and colour and after results?

There was one other punishment, meted out to George. He was a submissive, aloof little person, who would put up with a good deal more nagging and snubbing than Milly. But once his gentleness snapped, it snapped altogether, and he would kick out at Barley's shins with all his might and main.

"Very well, Master George," Barley would say. "You'll wear your card when we go for our walk."

Upon which George would beseech her. "No, no, Barley. Not my card. Oh, I'm sorry. I will be good. Please not my card."

But Barley with her sore shins would not be in a relenting mood, so when we set forth on our nursery walk there would be tied round George's neck a card bearing the inscription:

GEORGINA
SHE KICKS

The humiliating change of sex is a refinement on this particular punishment. Even Miss Paraman didn't think of that.

Barley reigned for twenty years—until the youngest member of the family reached schoolroom age and the kingdom of the nursery was no more. As a consequence Milly's childhood, and to a much lesser but still distorting extent, her adult life, was tortured by fears and guilts. She had nightmares. Her greatest burden, not surprisingly, was a permanent sense of sin; trifling misdemeanours lay in her mind for months. She was sure she would go to hell. She felt unloved and unwanted to such a degree that she felt she must be a changeling.

Unfortunately her queer mistrustful little soul had already been visited now and again by the notion that she did not really belong to the family, that she was a naughty child from somewhere else whom nobody wanted. So she left Fear to answer its own questions. "There is a plot against you," said Fear. "They swear to do away with you!"

The changeling is one of the most enduring and universal myths of mankind (Freud has an interesting paper on it) and no doubt it usually arises from similar circumstances. Indeed one wonders how many of mankind's myths spring from the nursery, since childhood, what is done to us then, our reaction to it, is the thing we have most in common. The myth that one parent is divine, for instance, and that therefore the child is a hero or also divine, does that not stem from idealisation of one parent? There are dozens of examples: Perseus, whose father Zeus seduced Danae in a shower of gold, is one (idealisation of the father); Jesus (idealisation of the mother) another. Again, the fact that women in myth and legend are so often portrayed as witches, enchantresses, whose feminine power is a threat to the hero, probably comes from the same nursery source. Partly it is an expression of the fear all men retain for the imprisoning sexual love they felt for their first mother—whether the real one or a Nurse. Partly the more simple memory of the all-pervading power of that early mentor.

> The question may very naturally arise [writes Eleanor Acland], "Why did your mother apparently never notice that Barley was a sort of evil genius in your childhood?" Or did she notice and decide it didn't matter or couldn't be helped, that the woman's obvious merits outweighed her defects, or that it would be a bother and upset to change nurses? I cannot say; but one must remember that the vogue for intensive child-study had not set in, that the nurseries of those days were a quite separate compartment in the life of the household and that we children were very seldom in Barley's and Mother's company simultaneously. When Mother came up to the nursery, Barley retired into a background of obsequious gentility—unless one of us were ill, when she came to the fore, a model of devoted efficiency. When we went downstairs we shook off all thought of Barley and her doleful views of life, and gave ourselves over to the enjoyment of Mother's company . . . I doubt if we ever entertained the idea that Barley could possibly be uprooted from the ground of our life. . . .

Now this is quite true. And one can make further excuses for mothers. Children respect and look up to adults. If things go wrong they tend to blame themselves. And they accept their world unquestioningly. Whatever is, is right. For both these reasons children very seldom told anyone about a cruel Nanny and it was extremely difficult for mothers to find out exactly what went on in the nursery.

Nevertheless, one can't help feeling they should have found out more. Some of that suffering was avoidable. After all, it isn't as though the parents knew nothing about Nannies. They had been brought up by them themselves. If they had been fortunate enough to have a kind one, which was no doubt usually the case, then they undoubtedly knew that cruel Nannies existed, that they were something to watch out for. Nor was the evidence always that hidden. If Miss W.V.'s screams could be heard by the neighbours they could be heard in the drawing-room. Again, if you hire an oafish Somerset girl of nineteen you might expect something stupid to happen. Why didn't Mrs. Maitland go and check that things were all right? No Englishman or woman at any time during our period would have dreamt of employing anyone untrained or unintelligent to look after their horses, yet time and again fools or sadists or incompetents were allowed to bring up their children. "Parents were aware that the child could be a nuisance," wrote Osbert Sitwell in *Left Hand, Right Hand*, "and a whole bevy of servants was necessary, not so much to aid the infant, as to screen him off from his father and mother except on such occasions as he could be used by them as adjuncts, toys or decoration." Nannies were a way of getting rid of children as well as a way of looking after them. Cruel and foolish mothers there will always be because there will always be cruel and foolish women and, as I pointed out earlier, people don't have children because they are suited to it. But when you could *choose* who brought up your children, then it should have been elementary that someone was chosen who was good and kind and knowledgeable. That there was *one* cruel Nanny is an indictment of the entire system.

TERROR BY STORY-TELLING:
THE NANNY AS BARD

Isobel Strachey told me that her family had a Nanny who had been a hospital nurse. She had a fund of gruesome stories. One was about a tiny boy so ill that he wasn't allowed to eat anything at all. He could just have a little soup. If he ate anything solid he would die. It was Christmas and the boy's father and mother came to see him. They had managed to smuggle in a tiny piece of Christmas cake, a crumb, so that he could have a bit of Christmas. He ate the tiny crumb of Christmas cake—and died instantly.

Nannies terrified their charges with the spoken word—and many of them seemed to have been equipped with strangely morbid and violent imaginations to do it. One wrote to me from America and said her Nanny's favourite walk, like that of Robert Louis Stevenson's Nanny, had been round the cemetery. They used to dwell on the graves. Her Nanny would read out the inscriptions in a mournful voice and interpret the tombstones. A pillar cut off at the top, for instance, meant a life that hadn't run its full span.

Nor is there anything more powerfully impressing than the spoken word, particularly that invented by the narrator and directed personally at a small audience, except perhaps television. Certainly many of the Nanny tales stayed in their charges' minds for the rest of their lives—sometimes even in the form of gibberish. I was having dinner with my parents-in-law one night and discussing Nannies with Count Friedrich Ledebur. He told me a number of things about English Nannies in Austria and in particular about his own English Nanny. Count Ledebur was then seventy, but he is about six feet four tall, with the figure of a guardsman, a thick lion's mane of grey hair and a powerful, handsome, aquiline face. He told me he could still remember the final sentences—or stanzas is it?—

of one of her stories. He then stood up, immense in the candlelight, and in a deep, swift, guttural and dramatic voice recited the following lines:

> "The Devon men wet though but desperet, HA! HA! The Coneor yet today— by night the right to the olemair and slink them underworth. Then we shall make a song of it men then shall come again to the throne."

The most enthralled and celebrated listener to Nurses' tales was of course Charles Dickens. Nurses in Dickens's writing itself cannot in fact add a great deal to our story. The glorious figure of Mrs. Gamp is a midwife and general monthly nurse and never holds a position approaching that of Nanny. One aspect she does perhaps reveal—one often hidden but sometimes still present. Mrs. Gamp, as Angus Wilson shows in his admirable *The World of Charles Dickens,* despite her squalor, greed and brutality, remains fundamentally in communion with the mysteries of birth and of death in birth; and since birth is due to sexual union, close to that mystery too. She is a repository therefore of that secret learning which was peculiar to women and around which, over the ages a great deal had accumulated, so that when she arrives— "a peculiar fragrance was borne upon the breeze, as if a passing fairy had hiccoughed, and had previously been to a wine vault"—she brings with her, as well as the scents of the cellar, that primitive folk and feminine knowledge which was to some Nannies a source of their power.

But it is in his experience with his own Nurse that Dickens is most interesting. In *The Uncommercial Traveller* he describes a nursemaid Mercy (who was without mercy) who had taken him to "utterly impossible places—people but none the less alarmingly real—that I found I had been introduced to by my nurse before I was six years old, and used to be forced to go back to at night without at all wanting to. If we all knew our own minds . . . I suspect we should find our nurses responsible for most of the dark corners we are forced to go back to against our wills." This nurse-maid, I assume, was his Nurse Mary Weller (though he may have had two. He writes on the same subject in *Nurse's Stories,* which appeared in *All the Year Round* in 1860). Whoever she was, she was a "sallow woman with a fishy eye, an aquiline nose and a green gown". She delighted to frighten him, having "a fiendish enjoyment of my terrors, and used to begin, I remember—as a sort of introductory overture—by clawing the air with both hands and uttering a long hollow groan." The stories she told were truly terrifying.

There was Captain Murderer, who forced his brides to make the pastry for the pies into which he put their bodies, sliced up and seasoned. This story was told endlessly. There were stories of rats and ghosts and rattling bones. The little Dickens did his best to avoid these stories, but Mary Weller (or Mercy) held him by saying that these terrible events had happened to her own relations. Sometimes she even seems to have played the heroine's role herself. She spoke of

> a brave and lovely servant-maid married to the landlord of a country inn; which landlord had this remarkable characteristic, that he always wore a silk nightcap and never would on any consideration take it off. At last, one night, when he was fast asleep, the brave and lovely woman lifted up his silk nightcap on the right side, and found he had no ear there; upon which she sagaciously perceived that he was the clipped housekeeper (a notorious burglar who had lost an ear in commission of his brutal crime), who had married her with the intention of putting her to death. She immediately heated the poker and terminated his career, for which she was taken to King George upon his throne and received the compliments of royalty on her great discretion and valour.

No doubt such dreadful happenings did frighten little Dickens. And the effects continued—there is a murderer in every single one of Dickens's books. Yet Angus Wilson points out how Dickens in fact hugely enjoys the absurd and improbable tales of his Nurse. Wilson goes on:

> The same relish seems to attach to his own telling of some of the more extravagant sinister events in his novels. But he is also evidently delighted by the sheer accumulation of gory detail in these remembered nurse's stories. His reference to his nurse's 'fiendish enjoyment' is a strange compound of admiration, accusation and complicity in the infliction of terror upon his childhood self. He would not, he must have known, have wished to have been without those nightmares, which were to prove so fruitful to him . . . in the early work, when Squeers is bullying the boys at Dotheboys Hall or Quilp is teasing his wife or his mother-in-law, it would be hard to say which is most gleefully tormenting— the fictional characters or their author. . . . This is not to say that there was any pronounced sadistic quality in Dickens' writing, only a certain fiendish enjoyment, like his nurse's, in the effect he knows he can produce; that, and in emulation no doubt of the success of the story 'Captain Murderer', an extraordinary, almost childishly delighted surprise at the badness of his own villains . . . Dickens retained a sort of comic, admiring amazement at the black horrors he could draw out of 'the dark corners' of his mind that is much like his shocked but laughing attitude to his flesh-creeping nurse.

Now there are two observations here. One is that Dickens's writing was directly influenced in certain respects by the tales of his Nurse. And we have seen this before. We saw it, for instance, with Stevenson. There is an indication in Mrs. Gaskell that the same may have been true of the Brontë family. Their self-appointed Nurse, Tabitha Aykroyd, a shrewd, strong and practical woman, was also possessed of a powerful and sombre imagination. While the winds whistled through the rooms of the gloomy parsonage and the rain beat off the moors and on to the windows, she told the children long stories of the squires of Yorkshire and their wild lives.

The second observation is about Dickens's enjoyment, as well as fear, of the gruesome tales. This, too, is common; indeed almost universal. Isobel Strachey and her family pestered their Nanny for stories about death and disaster in the hospital. The woman who wrote to me from America said that she left the cemetery each time with a delicious feeling of noble and uplifted sorrow. I can remember making my mother read a simplified but graphic story of the Crucifixion to me, with tears pouring down my cheeks, again and again and again.

Children seem to need violence and terror in their stories, or how else can one explain the overwhelming preponderance of these characteristics in children's literature throughout the ages and on television now? And though no doubt they quite often went unnecessarily far, Nannies satisfied this need. As to how far they went, or should have gone (and as to how far children's television should go), there is evidence from recent studies that provided it is not too close to their own selves, to reality as they know it, children can take a great deal without coming to any harm. Violence and terror must be insulated and removed, whether by improbability, by exaggeration, by symbolism, by humour, by time, by fantasy or by any of the other different methods one does in fact usually find in children's stories either as told by Nannies or in books.

Nor is the need itself surprising. A child's life is full of fears: fears and anxiety about the outside world, fears about figures in it, fears about forces dimly felt within himself, powerful aggressions, hatreds, loves. And there are still deeper, stranger fears. One psychiatrist told me, with surprise, that sometimes the images and events that turn up in analysis are so extraordinary, so monstrous, the creatures stalking the imagination so bizarre, that they defy any rational explanation. Forces appeared to be working in people which seemed to come from another place so that he was forced, reluctantly, to speculate about something very like the Jungian Collective Unconscious. Yet I do not know why he was surprised. There is a shot at the beginning of Stanley Kubrick's great film *2001—A Space Odyssey* where the figures of our remote ancestors, little more than apes, are huddled beneath a rock for the night. They cling to each other for warmth, but also out of terror. Because the night is alive. It is alive with predators seeking food, grunting, baying to each other, silently threading the darkness. At one moment a lioness leaps on to the very rock the ape-like creatures are sheltering under, and roars, so that they tremble and shrink and look at each other. For millions of years our species lived under conditions like this. It is hardly surprising that a tremendous premium was put on the development of an extraordinary and deep-rooted apprehension of the night and its terrors. Anyone straying from shelter, leaving the group, was doomed. The stronger and more vivid the fear of the outside world (during the day as well), the more likely he was to stay. Many of the monsters that are in our minds were once real.

Stories introduce children to the mystery of death, to the polarities of good and evil, they express and so exorcise the multifarious fears of childhood; and not only exorcise, they also show these fears can be handled and used. Such is the beginning of art.

To assist them, Nannies often seem to have been endowed with a quality of imagination very like that possessed by children themselves: direct in a physical way, concrete, vivid, fantastic, a queer mad logic obtaining. You can see this from the lore and the superstitions they invented, which they did in dozens. Mrs. Goriely's Nurse Binfield said that swallowed sewing cotton wrapped itself round the heart, causing death (Mrs. Goriely continued to believe this till she was forty). My grandmother used to describe how her Nurse Peattie used to say, "Never smell roses close to your nose like that. There was a lady who smelt roses like that and all the little insects ran up her nose. She screamed for a week and then she died. They opened her head and there were the caterpillars eating her brain." Noël Oakeshott's Nanny had an appalling fear of bulls; at the same time she knew how to deal with them.

> The best hope was to get behind a tree, should there be one in reach and in the direct line of the bull's advance. The creature would be careering at such a speed that it would impale its horns on the trunk and be held fast. Failing a tree, one should drop articles of clothing in one's flight, hat, gloves, jacket, etc. The bull would undoubtedly stop briefly to examine these articles, pawing the ground, thus allowing time for escape. It was of course fatal to be wearing or carrying anything red. There was a theory that the most favourable choice of attire was blue and white stripes, as the bull might mistake one for the butcher.

Like children, Nannies often enjoyed mystification for its own sake, embroidering events instantly with the patterns of their fantasy; and again like children this fantasy often took the form of their own romantic and mysterious past. This aspect of the Nanny as Bard is perhaps particularly applicable to nursery-maids, and a fine example occurs in *Parents and Children* by Ivy Compton-Burnett. The mother of the children is about to marry again with amazing swiftness after the apparent death of their father. The children ask the nursery-maid Mullet if anything like this had ever happened in her family. Mullet indicates that it did.

"Well what happened?" said Honor.

"It is a little hard to describe," said Mullet, with a natural hesitation, as she did not yet know what it was. "I was never at close quarters with it. It was one of those things that cast their shadows before and aft, and no one could escape the repercussions of it. Well, after my Aunt's bereavement there ensued a period of calm. My Aunt was disconsolate, of course, but she maintained the even tenor of her life. And then the change came. The man destined to be my uncle loomed into view." Mullet's voice deepened at the mention of this destiny. "A tall, sinister-looking man he was, with thin lips and a scar stretching across his face, and twisting in an odd way round his mouth. Handsome in a way, of course, with a kind of sinister charm, but a man whose very presence seemed to cast some primitive spell."

"How did he get the scar?" said Gavin.

"It was never spoken of, Master Gavin. There seemed to be a sort of unwritten law that no word of it should pass human lips," said Mullet, her voice gaining confidence. "And none ever crossed my father's or mine. I daresay he thought it was hardly a subject for my ears."

"He knew about it then," said Honor.

"Well, Miss Honor, these things pass from men to men. I suspect he had his shrewd suspicions. He was a shrewd man in his way."

"Well, what happened to the family?"

"In a way nothing, in a way everything. That is the best way to put it."

"But what was it?" said Honor, not taking this view.

"A strange, uncanny atmosphere brooded over that house. Laughter never seemed to sound, and the sun never to shine in those rooms. . . ."

There is a fine picture, in Hatton, of the Nanny-as-Mother in this book but to get her flavour would require very lengthy quotation. Oddly enough, since late Victorian and Edwardian family life was her field, I cannot recollect any other Nannies or nursery-maids playing so substantial a role in a Compton-Burnett novel.

Finally, Nannies could quite simply, without additional elaborations of fear or fantasy, introduce their children into the world of literature and speculation.

My nurse [wrote Leonard Woolf in *Sowing*], who was with us for many years and brought us all up, had much less education than our governesses, but she was the first person to interest me in books and in the strange and fascinating workings of the human mind. She was a Somersetshire woman, born and bred on a farm, a rigid and puritanical Baptist. She read a Baptist paper every week from end to end and somehow or other she had got hold of de Quincey's *Confessions of an English Opium Eater*. This book entranced her; she read it again and again. I find it difficult to believe my memory when it distinctly tells me that Nurse Vicary used to give me a detailed account of what she read in the *Baptist Times* and often read aloud de Quincey to me, and that at the age of four or five I was quite an authority on the politics and polemics of the Baptist sect and often fell asleep rocked, not in the cradle, but on the voluptuous rhythm of de Quincey's interminable sentences whose baroque ornamentations must have been embellished by nurse's mispronunciations and her Somerset accent. But I had the deepest affection for her and for the opium eater, and she was the first person to teach me the pleasure of fear and thrill over public events, the horrors and iniquities of the great world of society and politics as recorded in the *Baptist Times* about the year 1885.

SOME CONSEQUENCES OF NANNY CRUELTY

In this sphere, therefore, it would seem that Nannies did less harm than might have been expected; even the terrors they evoked were often not wholly unpleasant or useless; and where they did not terrify, they stimulated, enriched and entertained.

But the problem of the cruel Nanny remains. How large a proportion were they? It is of course impossible to say. Comparatively, I imagine, not enormously numerous; though while it is true that Nannies, if sometimes irritable and neurotic, were not very often actively and deliberately cruel, it should be remembered that when bringing up little children it is often possible to be cruel, through ignorance or stupidity, without meaning to be. Nevertheless, cruel Nannies certainly existed, and though I have the impression that there was a more self-righteous severity, a callousness and brutality in the unkind Victorian Nanny which one does not find so often later on, they existed throughout our period. Whenever it occurred their cruelty and suppression often acted to intensify that tendency to insecurity, conformity and inhibition that we have already charted.

They provoked other reactions. Frequently one comes across a longing to be adult, to escape the unpleasant world of childhood. "Nurse he had never learnt to endure," wrote Compton Mackenzie in *Sinister Street*. "She charged ferociously into his fancies, shattering them with her fussy

interference . . . But, at any rate, he would have to grow up. He could not
always be the same size. That was a consolation. It was jolly to dream of
being grown-up, to plan one's behaviour and think of freedom." The same
feeling is echoed in his autobiography. "Oh to be grown up and free from
this endless purgatory of childhood."

At the same time it seems to have been difficult, indeed almost impossible, for the children of cruel Nannies to admit that they hated them.
The hatred shines through the description; it cannot be faced. "I would
have been justified in hating my old nurse, but I did not hate her," writes
Compton Mackenzie. Frederick Anstey even says he was fond of his Fanny,
though he gives no single instance of kindness or consideration from her.
Curzon went to Miss Paraman's funeral.

And the reason for this is quite plain. It is one we have already discussed.
So great is a little child's need for love, so much does it need to love
someone, that it is almost more than it can bear to realise that neither of
these two things are possible. Desperately, it alters and falsifies and denies
reality. And this process continues on, and extends itself, in later years.
So much so that I would speculate that we have here the root explanation
of nostalgia—that strange alchemy by which humanity transforms the
past. In connection with the Nanny leaving I quoted some passages from
Enter A Child by Dormer Creston. It will be remembered that her beloved
Mary was secretly snatched away from her when she was seven. "Why,
don't you know, Miss Dolly? She's never coming back! She's gone for good,
she has!" In addition Dormer Creston had a brutal father and an indifferent mother. At the age of eight she wanted to commit suicide.

But the description of her childhood and home, which is vivid and
harrowing in the extreme, occupies only a relatively small part of the book.
For the curious thing about *Enter A Child* is that it isn't in fact a story of a
childhood at all. It is really only about those moments of her childhood
which were happy. And since these only occurred when she left her home
and went for a holiday to her uncle's house Hilldrop, the whole of the
rest of the book, the final three-quarters, is taken up by a lyrical, somewhat
over-lyrical, amalgam of these holiday moments. It is in fact plain that her
childhood was too painful, particularly after her Nanny had been ripped
away from her, to face again. So she manages to create, out of what must
have been numerically a tiny proportion of her childhood months, the
illusion that she had a perfect, radiant, sunny Edwardian girlhood. It is
of a type—with happy, kindly servants, grand houses, eccentric but happy
aunts and uncles and cousins in floppy hats and bustles, with gay games and
outings in early cars, huge picnics and even huger Christmases. There is in

fact a very definite, specific, late Victorian and Edwardian nostalgia. It has been created partly by those young in Edwardian and Victorian times themselves, in their memoirs, biographies and autobiographies. And partly by an uncritical acceptance by everyone born after 1914 that times *must* have been better before that war. Surely then there was leisure, peace, stability, wealth, etc., if only for a few. Yet the odd thing is that if you read a large number of these memoirs, it is plain that many of their childhoods were, frankly, appalling; how and in what ways will have been indicated when I have used them to illustrate various themes in this book. Brian Reade in an interesting lecture—*The Beardsley Foreground*—to the Art Historians of Southern California points out that this unhappiness and tension is reflected in the writings of the *fin de siècle*. Themes are nearly always tragic: betrayed women, abandoned men, death, madness, suicide, revenge, murder. Edwardians, he says, were either stoical or distracted. Yet either by drenching the events themselves or their later lives with that glowing Edwardian light, as Dormer Creston does, or else, as for instance does Compton Mackenzie, by simply denying that any of their childhood experiences had any later effect at all, most of the autobiographies of the time manage to preserve an illusion of Edwardian perfection. They describe often hideous events but remove their sting. The retrospective need for love on a personal level begins, as time passes, to operate on a general social one, to become a total view of the historic past.

The restrictions, the severity, the deprivation and instability in the upbringing of numbers of upper class English people are sometimes so reminiscent of the home backgrounds of delinquents that one wonders why they weren't all criminals. And in fact of course a great many of them virtually were. Since Regency days and before, right up till now, the English upper classes have habitually relieved the stresses caused by the restrictions and severities of their upbringing by behaviour which, had they been lower class and unprotected by wealth and privilege, would have landed them instantly in gaol and even, in earlier days, resulted in their execution.

Here is Jessica Mitford in *Hons and Rebels*:

We not only egged each other on to even greater baiting and acts of outrage against the class we had left, but delighted in matching wits with the world generally; in fact it was our way of life. Years later Philip Toynbee reminded me of the time we had stolen a car-load of top hats from the cloakroom of the Eton Chapel, and of the time we had pilfered the curtains at a rich country house where we were staying to embellish the Rotherhithe Street windows.

"Don't you remember?" he kept saying. When I confessed that I remembered only the barest outline of these particular incidents, Philip rejoined sadly, "It all made an enormous impression on me, but I suppose that to you and Esmond it was just another day's work."

The reactions were therefore different. And there were others. Mrs. Anne Turner sent me a truly appalling account of her Nannied childhood. She was left, like Kipling, with a false 'aunt' and 'uncle' when she was two and a half while her parents went to India. There were two other children of the aunt and uncle ; the Nanny, a small, shrivelled and sadistic woman, therefore concentrated her passion for discipline on Anne. She was beaten, locked up for hours in solitary confinement, subjected to furious tirades. She had rice pudding twice a day. Once a day there should have been fruit, but this her Nanny omitted. If she ate the rice pudding quickly, she was given another helping for being greedy, if slowly, which was more usual since not unnaturally she quickly came to loathe rice pudding, she was given a second helping for being a naughty obstinate little girl. On Fridays there was treacle pudding, very thick and heavy. This, too, came covered in rice pudding. This familiar but still horrifying treatment continued for three years "when at last I left my prison". Yet, said Mrs. Turner, it had given her an indomitable character. Nothing in life had ever afterwards daunted her. She had overcome all obstacles. Even now, past middle age at the time of writing to me, she had just successfully resisted a compulsory purchase order.

Rebellion, nostalgia, delinquency, repression, timidity—it is impossible to be certain how human beings will respond to events, even to events in their early childhood. I would finally, as an antidote to dogmatism, like to look briefly at two episodes involving savage Nannies where the reactions were so strange, so dramatic, as to almost defy belief.

THE NANNY AS MURDERESS

On the night of July 29, 1860, there occurred in the village of Road, near the river Frome in the West Country, a murder so brutal and at the same time so apparently motiveless that its mystery has continued to reverberate down to today. This murder, its mystery, its violence and its most likely solution all derive directly from the habit Mr. Samuel Saville Kent had contracted of sleeping with the Nurses he engaged to look after his children.

But to understand this event, and more especially what happened subsequent to it, which is what I am primarily interested in, it is necessary to go back to 1829. It was then that Mr. Kent married his first wife, Mary, and they began at once to have a number of children. Mr. Kent was now twenty-eight, a man fundamentally weak, but of considerable charm, hot temper, and ravenous sexual appetite. Children followed in quick succession, wearing Mrs. Kent down. We need concern ourselves only with Edward, the eldest, William, and Constance Emilie—who was born in 1843. At her birth, Mr. Kent engaged Mary Pratt. She was twenty-one years old, possibly a mill girl, but of superior intelligence, powerful character, and, everyone agrees, of great vitality and attraction.

Mr. Kent seems to have become immediately enslaved—and there is little doubt he began sleeping with her almost at once. At all events, Mary Pratt was soon ruling the house. Mrs. Kent, exhausted by childbirth, retired more and more into the background and Constance, from birth, had Mary Pratt as the dominant figure in the household. In fact so flagrant was Mary Pratt's behaviour, so plain the liaison between her and Mr. Kent and absolute her sway over the children, that scandal broke out. The Kents were compelled to move to Walton Manor, near Clevedon in Somerset. Quite soon, the nature of their ménage became plain here too. Once more local gossips were outraged. Before long the Kents were forced to move again, this time to Baynton House.

But by now Mr. Kent, a man imperious by nature and in appetite, was impatient of even the thinnest subterfuge. Six weeks after their arrival at Baynton House, Mary Pratt, "who had never been absent from their house for a single day", left to visit some friends in Devonshire. The next day Mrs. Kent, who had been in perfect health, was suddenly attacked without warning by the most excruciating pains. The nearest doctor, a complete stranger, was called in, but, vomiting and contorted with agony, Mrs. Kent died on the fifth day. Mr. Kent had been present throughout. Mary Pratt returned immediately.

When the news seeped back to the various places the Kents and Mary Pratt had lived before, it was said openly that "those two had brought about her end". No investigation was made, however, and when in August 1853 the period of mourning was over, Kent and Mary Pratt were married.

Years passed. Mr. Kent was always chronically short of money, and this now dictated moves hitherto forced by scandal. In 1860 they have moved to Road-Hill House in the village of Road near the river Frome. The new Mrs. Kent has three children living and is expecting a fourth. Her favourite is her four-year-old son Francis Saville, a big, lively boy, high-spirited and noisy. He in turn adores his half-sister Constance, who has grown to be a kind and lively girl of sixteen with a particular ability with children. A new nurse, Elizabeth Gough, has just been engaged, a not particularly intelligent girl, but striking in an animal, sexy way.

The situation has parallels, therefore, with that existing some years before when Mrs. Pratt, the second Mrs. Kent, was engaged. In fact so striking are these parallels that I would like to reproduce the analysis Yseult Bridges gives in her *Saint—With Red Hands?*—a revolutionary account of this case and one which, except at the end, I follow throughout, and from which I will occasionally quote (or quote her use of trial transcripts).

(A) 1. In 1844, when Mary Pratt was engaged as Nurse, the first Mrs. Kent was thirty-seven years old and expecting a baby.
   2. She—the first Mrs. Kent—had three children living: two girls and a boy.
   3. She had been married to Mr. Kent for sixteen years.
   4. Mary Pratt was twenty-one.

(B) 1. In 1860, when Elizabeth Gough was engaged as Nurse, the second Mrs. Kent was thirty-seven years old and was expecting a baby.
   2. She—the second Mrs. Kent—had three children living: two girls and a boy.
   3. She had been sleeping with Mr. Kent for sixteen years.
   4. Elizabeth Gough was twenty-one.

The first group of events was to end in violent death. So did the second. It seems plain that Mr. Kent had already begun his affair with the new young Nurse, a baker's daughter. It had become a recognised custom that he did the rounds late at night, and that the last room he visited was the nursery. This was across the corridor from his own and his wife's bedroom. In it slept Elizabeth Gough and Saville, the four-year-old favourite. The 'other family' slept on the floor above.

The crime was committed during the night of June 29 and early morning of Saturday, June 30. Murder is unique among human events. It plays a ritual part, exorcising the one desire we keep most deeply hidden. However distant, it can always evoke that curious combination of horror, disgust and temptation which is our response to violent death. Over that sleeping house during that long hot summer night there hangs in the imagination the same peculiar stench of squalor and remembered fear that hangs around a building newly gutted by fire.

At seven-fifteen on the Saturday morning Mrs. Kent woke up and was putting on her dressing gown, when there came a knock at the door. It was Nurse Gough.

"Well, Nurse, what is it?" asked Mrs. Kent. "Are the children awake?"

"Neither of them," the Nurse said.

"What? Neither of them?"

"Master Saville," the Nurse said awkwardly. "Is he with you?"

"With me?" Mrs. Kent cried. "Certainly not."

"He's not in his bed."

Brushing past her, Mr. Kent went straight to Saville's cot.

No bed, comments Yseult Bridges with justice, in which a child had slept normally could have presented the appearance which his did: the pillow bore an unnaturally deep indentation made by his head, the mattress a similar impression made by his body; yet the upper sheet and the counterpane were carefully smoothed, turned down and tucked in.

The sides of the cot were too high to allow the child to climb out of it unaided, and Mrs. Kent asked, "Did you put the chair near the cot?"

"No, Ma'am."

"When did you miss him?"

"At five o'clock."

"*At five o'clock!* Why didn't you come and tell me at once?"

"I thought perhaps you had heard him cry and had come and fetched him."

"You wicked girl, how dare you say so! You know perfectly well he is too heavy for me to carry—only yesterday when you brought him to me I told you to put him down because he was too heavy for me. I have always told you to come to me at once if there is anything wrong with the children. Go upstairs to his sisters' room and see if he is there."

So the saga began. Within an hour the body of the little boy had been found wedged half-way down the outside privy. The neck had been cut, back to the very vertebrae; at the post mortem that afternoon another wound was found—a stab which had entered "just below the left nipple and had been delivered with such force as to pierce the blanket [in which the boy was wrapped], night shirt and flannel vest, sever the cartilage of two ribs and extend three quarters across the chest. It had passed below the pericardium and diaphragm. . . ." And so on. A mighty blow. It had also been withdrawn with great force. Yet no blood had flowed from either wound. Nor was there more than an ounce or two of blood upon the privy floor. Dr. Parsons who conducted the post mortem said "that had the throat been cut while the heart was still beating its pulsations would have caused the blood to spurt out in such powerful jets through the severed arteries that, in so confined a space, the walls and seat would have been sprayed with it. I should have expected to find no less than three pints from so large a child." Either, therefore, the murder had taken place elsewhere, or those appalling wounds had been inflicted after death. In fact the last seemed to be the most likely, because, as well as the knife wounds, the mouth was bruised and blackened, the tongue livid and protruding and Dr. Parson's conclusion was that the child had been suffocated and the two wounds inflicted later.

Now, though it is a fascinating story, it is not relevant to my purpose to follow all the ramifications of this extraordinary case. To anyone interested I can heartily recommend Yseult Bridge's account—it is scrupulous, highly intelligent and completely gripping. Nevertheless, before proceeding to the end, a number of facts must be known and borne in mind.

It was plain from the start that the murder could only have been committed by someone in the house. It also seems likely that within a quarter of an hour Mrs. Kent, a woman of immensely strong character, had wrenched out most of the details of the crime and guessed the rest. At any event, evidence began to disappear almost at once, and in a systematic way which suggests a cool planner. After Saville's body had been found, Mrs. Kent went back to her bedroom and shut herself up alone with her husband. No one knows what passed, but after their conversation Mr. Kent hurried from the house and galloped off into the countryside, ostensibly to get a ludicrously distant doctor. Considering his state of mind, it was certainly where a cool planner would have sent him.

Because Mr. Kent's behaviour and attitude to the investigation were incredible. He was immediately—and for the next five years—consumed with terror. He was evasive, furious, told lie upon lie, and was frequently on the point of collapse. He and Nurse Gough contradicted each other's statements at every turn. They made blunder upon blunder. As to the efforts of the police, Mr. Kent obstructed them whenever he could. He seemed to have no interest at all in finding the murderer of his son (nor indeed did Mrs. Kent). Quite the contrary—he made it impossible.

There were, for example, only two concrete pieces of evidence. One of these was a night shift. It was discovered, wrapped in brown paper, far up the boiler store chimney, where it had obviously been hastily shoved. Too hastily, because it had been pushed so far up that it had escaped the flames when the fire was lit. It was "in a coarse material like a servant would wear". It was covered in recent large splashes of blood. All who saw it (there were not many), realised that it must have been worn by the murderer or an accomplice.

Even Mr. Kent realised this (he had been asserting all the time that the murder had been done by some outside maniac). He made desperate but unavailing efforts to get hold of it. When it was refused him he suggested an ingenious plan. The shift should be replaced that night in the chimney by two police constables, who should then leave ostentatiously, talking and banging the doors. The murderer would then creep down and retrieve the nightdress, at which two other policemen, secretly let in and concealed by Mr. Kent in the kitchen, would leap out and capture him. All went almost according to plan. The nightdress was concealed. The murderer did creep down and remove it. But the police did not leap out and catch him. They had been locked in the kitchen by Mr. Kent.

The nightdress was never found again. The second piece of evidence was a 'female breast flannel'—a prototype of the modern brassiere—which was found in the privy. It was soaked in blood. Every woman in the house—Mrs. Kent, Constance, her sisters and the servants—had to try it on. The only person it fitted, and it fitted perfectly, was Elizabeth Gough.

The conduct of the investigation was also fantastically inept. The police felt so foolish about being locked in the kitchen that they suppressed all information about the existence and disappearance of the nightdress. Whenever Mr. Kent forbade them some part of the house, they kowtowed. The numerous Inquests were hopelessly mishandled—neither Nurse Gough nor Mr. Kent being required to give evidence for instance. Eventually the state of muddle became so chronic, public concern so aroused, that Chief Inspector Whicker was sent down from Scotland Yard. He was Sergeant Cuff in *The Moonstone* by Wilkie Collins; and Dickens wrote about him as Whichum in *Household Words*. But on this occasion he too seems to have lost his head. Rumours had begun to leak out that a nightdress was concerned in the case: that it had been found or not found or lost. Inspector Whicker fastened on this. He ordered all clothes to be checked. One of Constance Kent's nightdresses was found to be missing from the washing bag. On this evidence alone she was arrested.

Constance Kent at this time was a warm, lively girl, intelligent and with a peculiar capacity for inspiring love and protectiveness. She had, as I have said, a particular gift with children. The day before his murder Saville had been fractious and difficult. It was Constance who had soothed and comforted him. At her school she was popular and successful. Under the appalling strain of imprisonment and trial she remained calm and brave. She resolutely maintained her innocence. And indeed no defence was needed or called. It was proved that her nightdress had still been there after the crime. That if it had subsequently been taken from the laundry it could scarcely have been taken by her. In fact no circumstance in the case pointed to her; all pointed away. She was freed on the evidence of the Prosecution alone.

Delay and muddle, incompetence and evasion now once more succeeded each other. Eventually public outcry, and the suspicions of more influential figures against Mr. Kent and Nurse Gough led to a new trial against the latter. But by now months had passed, all evidence had been destroyed, and an endless series of contradictory statements made. It was found too difficult to prove anything and the Nurse was acquitted.

Yseult Bridges more than fully establishes that it was Elizabeth Gough and Mr. Kent who committed the crime together. Her reconstruction is as follows: after his rounds on that Friday night Mr. Kent finished, as usual, in bed with the new young Nurse. Unfortunately Saville, usually a heavy sleeper, was restless from the Calomel pill which Mrs. Kent, thinking he needed a laxative to ease his fretfulness, had given him earlier. He awoke at the sounds made by Mr. Kent and Nurse Gough, saw something going on which frightened him, and began to cry out. Mr. Kent sprang up, seized the breast flannel, rushed over and pressed it down hard over the boy's face. Saville struggled and kicked, and Nurse Gough had to hold down his legs (hence the deep indentations in pillow and mattress). Panicked, they listened intently for sounds of anyone having been woken (Mrs. Kent was sleeping just across the passage). When Mr. Kent finally removed his hand, Saville was dead. They took the body wrapped in the blanket, in which the breast flannel had become entangled, down to the privy. There had been a number of motiveless murders by throat-cutting in the district at that time, so Mr. Kent now inflicted the wounds found later. The blood ran and oozed, not spurting, soaking the blanket and the night shift and some probably going into the privy, which was very deep.

This account, including much detail relevant to the crime I haven't space to go into, covers all the known facts, it accords with the characters involved and their subsequent behaviour. It all fits—except for one thing. Five years after the crime, Constance Kent confessed that she had committed the murder. She was sentenced to death, the sentence commuted and she served twenty years in Millbank Prison and later at Parkhurst.

Why? Yseult Bridges' brilliant deductions have created a second problem almost as difficult as the one she has solved. Why, if she was innocent, did Constance Kent confess? And innocent she undoubtedly was. The detailed confession she afterwards dictated of how she had committed the crime is, given the known facts, quite simply, and almost point for point, impossible. To take just two of the instances which I have followed through in the account, the blood and the wounds. She says she cut her brother's throat in the privy with a razor while he lay peacefully sleeping in her arms (peacefully sleeping, incidentally, after being pulled out of his cot in the middle of the night and carried through the house and out into the garden). She remembered thinking that the blood would never come—this from a large, living boy with heart pumping and neck slashed to the vertebrae, jugular severed. She then, this slight adolescent girl, thrust the razor, with its blunt and folding blade, three quarters of the way through the body. The other particulars are as absurd. Had the case ever been presented she would, as before, been freed on the evidence of the Prosecution. And her innocence was recognised. Victorian courts of law were not gentle places, yet in her trial there is the extraordinary picture of everyone, Prosecution, Defence, Judge, almost trying to force her to plead not guilty. When she refused and Mr. Justice Willes, not himself a particularly gentle man, had to pronounce sentence on this cold-blooded, deliberate and revolting crime, not only he, but most of the court, broke down and openly wept.

Why? Yseult Bridges' explanation is that the treatment Constance Kent subsequently suffered forced her to confess. Certainly this would seem partly true. Soon after the murder and her own trial, when she was freed from prison, Constance left home and entered the Convent de La Sagesse at Dinant in Brittany. She was entered as Emilie Kent, but her real identity leaked out. People used to gather and stare. The pressure had begun. Nevertheless, she did well at the convent. She was popular and loved, and was particularly noted for her gift with and tenderness towards young children.

In 1863 she seems to have decided that she would have a proper training in the care of infants and young children and then emigrate to Canada. To this end she entered St. Mary's Convent, No. 2 Queen's Square, Brighton. This had been founded by the Reverend Arthur Douglas Wagner and had attached to it a school, a lying-in hospital for 'fallen women', an infirmary, etc., which could teach her all she needed to know.

The Reverend Mr. Wagner was a pillar of the Oxford Movement. He was very rich, theatrical, intensely ambitious and eager for any sort of publicity. The Mother Superior was Miss Caroline Anne Greame, a strong, relentless character, fanatical, eager for the true welfare of her charges' souls, and more particularly the welfare of Mr. Wagner.

Here, Constance Kent's life rapidly became appalling. The convent was a strict, lonely, gloomy place, brooded over by that peculiarly masochistic spirit of Victorian holiness. Quite soon her real identity leaked out again and once more covert glances, staring faces, the whole weight of silent notoriety fell upon her. Totally alone, she was refused the sacraments since she still lay under the ban of murder, her innocence never having been fully confirmed. This isolation continued for many months— and must be seen in the context of, as the culmination of, years of pressure. And gradually this pressure became more overt. It seems that Mr. Wagner and Miss Greame began to see they had a possible religious scoop on their hands. Constance Kent might well know the identity of the murderer. If she revealed it to them—what a timely saving of a young girl's soul! What publicity for Mr. Wagner! Hints were dropped. The pressure mounted. Finally, at the end of Lent 1864, with its prolonged fasting and endless prayer, Constance was summoned to a series of long interviews, interrogations, with the Mother Superior. She was asked how the crime was committed, asked if she had anything, anything at all, however small, on her conscience. If she had then she was exhorted to tell all for the sake of the Lord, for the sake of her soul, for the Church. It was now, at last, five years later, that Constance Kent finally cracked. She must almost certainly have guessed that it was her father who had committed the crime. She had either to reveal this, or take the guilt on herself. And so she confessed. Only by doing this, writes Yseult Bridges, could she escape from the crime that had hung over her for so long; "only through the process of self-annihilation could she attain spiritual re-birth".

Now there is certainly great force in this. The only words, apart from her dictated 'confession', that Constance Kent ever uttered about the crime were when her father visited her in prison. Weeping, she flung her arms round his neck and cried, "My cause is due to you and God." Yet, if she had guessed the guilt of her father, she must have done so some years before. If she had wanted to help him, the time to have done so was then, when he was virtually one of the accused, not now when the scandal was dying, even dead. Also, to a religious person a false confession is worse than no confession; it is a lie in the face of God, a mortal sin. No Confessor's urgings can hide that. Furthermore, in innocence is enormous strength. To know you are innocent, to know that God knows it, those two things are enough. And Constance Kent was religious and she was innocent. She was also a woman of quite exceptional strength of character. She had showed this abundantly before. She was to show it to an even greater degree during her long harsh years of imprisonment. I do not think Yseult Bridges' explanation is by any means wholly wrong, but I do think that additional, and it will turn out stranger, forces are needed to explain what happened. They can be found, I believe, in two places. First we must return to the early infancy of Constance Kent, to her babyhood and childhood. After her trial there were rumours in the neighbourhood that the motive for the crime was revenge against her stepmother for the cruel treatment she had received at her hands. Constance Kent issued a statement that "this is entirely false. I have received the greatest kindness from both persons [her father and Mrs. Kent] accused of subjecting me to it." In point of fact this was not true. At one time Mrs. Kent had not just been cruel to Constance. She had been savage.

It will be remembered that Mrs. Kent, then Mary Pratt, had been engaged as Nurse just before Constance was born. Hers was the dominant presence in the home and, as the first Mrs. Kent grew weaker, one can assume in Constance's baby and infant life. And Mary Pratt was a tyrant. Dr. Stapleton, the local doctor who knew her well, said "she ruled with a severe hand all beneath her sway". She punished the little children with violent blows, striking them across the shoulders and boxing their ears. She would banish them to the hall at meal times. Another favourite punishment of hers was to lock them up for long periods alone in a room. As they grew older Mary Pratt's brutality became less and less restrained, and once she was mistress of the house it knew no bounds. William, Constance's brother, was weak and easily cowed, but Constance herself had a very strong will and would not flinch. This enraged Mary Pratt. She would heap punishments on her, not because of any crimes but to break her spirit. This she could not do, but Constance's health collapsed and, on doctor's advice, she was boarded out at a school in Bath. Some months later she returned, healthy and strong. But now, for the first time in her life, she had something to set conditions in her home against. The comparison horrified her. Taking little William with her, she fled, with a childish plan of reaching her elder brother Edward, who had always disliked Mary Pratt, and who was now serving as a sailor abroad. The children were soon missed. They were chased, caught and brought home to face the rage of Mr. Kent and their stepmother.

It was not pleasant. Rumours of the children's ill-treatment had been abroad in the neighbourhood. These grew when it was learnt they had tried to run away.

The Kents had managed [writes Yseult Bridges] to live down the domestic scandals of the past, so now, threatened with a new one, their united fury knew no bounds and descended like an avalanche upon the heads of the strained and exhausted culprits. William broke down completely under the thrashing he received: Constance, her cheeks smarting and her ears ringing from blows, was thrust into the cellars and the key turned upon her. Here, in the dark darkness, among rats, black beetles and festoons of cobwebs, she was kept for two days and nights—local legend says for even longer, and that it was by no means the first time she had been subjected to this form of punishment.

And Mary Pratt's cruelty continued when she came to teach Constance. John Rhode, who also wrote a book about the case, received an anonymous document from Australia. It contains such details of this period in the family life as to almost suggest it was written by Constance Kent herself. Rhode had it compared by an expert to a specimen of Constance Kent's known handwriting. He said they were not the same, yet one wonders what twenty-years in a Victorian prison would do to handwriting. Certainly it has a curiously autobiographical ring. Here is a passage on being taught by Mary Pratt.

> When words were to be mastered punishments became more severe. Days were spent shut up in a room with dry bread and milk and water for tea. At other times she would be stood in a corner of the hall sobbing "I want to be good, I do, I do," till she came to the conclusion that goodness was impossible for a child and that she could only hope to grow up as quickly as possible as grownups were never naughty. At times she gave way to furious fits of temper and was locked away in a distant room and sometimes in a cellar that her noise might not annoy people.

Now if you treat very little children in the way Mary Pratt treated Constance Kent, if you beat them and hit them and terrify them, you create, among other things, feelings of furious resentment. They will have fantasies of revenge; and a revenge not just of equal retaliation but of murder. They will want to kill you. At the same time they depend on you for love. They don't wish to hate you. And they will also have quickly learnt that any retaliation at all, much less murder, is wrong. They feel a guilt about their desire to kill almost as strong as the desire itself. The wish therefore becomes deeply repressed. And though it may manifest itself much later in guilts and aggressions over other things it is likely to remain repressed for ever, unless quite complicated processes should bring it to the surface.

In recent years a great deal has been discovered—particularly as a result of the communist freedom trials—about what happens psychologically to prisoners who are subjected to long and intensive interrogation. It is now understood why strong men confess to crimes they have not in fact committed. The terrible loneliness, the hours of talk, the alternation of kindness and threat, all produce some curious results. Apparently a situation arises very similar, in some cases almost identical, with that which takes place in analysis. This is particularly so after long periods of isolation and when the prisoner has been under continuous and powerful pressure. Transference takes place—that is to say the prisoner will transfer on to his interrogator the personality of a person in his very remote past. And this distant past—that of his childhood and infancy—will suddenly reawaken, as it does in analysis, and be re-enacted. And it has been found that those most likely to 'confess', those whose reaction most nearly corresponded to the analytic one, were the most convinced communists. They had the additional spur that if they confessed it would be for the good of the party, for the good, as it were, of their communist souls. In the end, the fact that they were really confessing because of, and about, guilts far in their past became completely blurred.

If Constance Kent had ever wanted to harm her Nurse, if she had ever wished her dead, and it seems reasonable to suppose that she did, then St. Mary's Convent, Brighton, was the one place where these feelings might have returned—and with them the guilt they had aroused. She had suffered prolonged isolation and been under intense pressure. She was subjected to interrogation in which one can be sure kindness and sternness alternated. And the Christian religion, especially in Victorian times, was particularly amenable to this kind of confusion. If you were guilty in your thoughts, if you had ever even wanted to harm your stepmother, then you were as guilty as though you had done it. That was the sin which compounded sin. I would suggest that when she cracked it was this primeval guilt that Constance Kent was finally atoning for.

No one will ever know. As Boswell wrote of another matter, "The world must vibrate in a state of uncertainty as to what was the truth." But it is undoubtedly one of the most tragic and sombre passages in the annals of the Nanny.

CURZON

In her savage moments she was a brutal and vindictive tyrant; and I have often thought since that she must have been insane. She persecuted and beat us in the most cruel way and established over us a system of terrorism so complete that not one of us ever mustered up the courage to walk upstairs to tell our father or mother. She spanked us with the sole of her slipper on the bare back, beat us with her brushes, tied us up for long hours to chairs in uncomfortable positions with our hands holding a pole or a blackboard behind our backs, shut us up in darkness. . . .

The words with which I began this book were found at Keddleston the country house of Lord George Curzon. They were on various sheets of paper, scribbled in faded pencil; notes for some autobiographical work which Curzon never had time to write. Here are some more which I didn't quote.

> She made me write a letter to the butler asking him to make a birch for me with which I was to be punished for lying, and requesting him to read it out in the servants' hall. When he came round one day with a letter and saw me standing in my red petticoat with my face to the wall on a chair outside the schoolroom and said, "My you look like a Cardinal", I could have died of shame. . . .
> At meal times she took all the dainties for herself and gave us nothing but tapioca and rice pudding which we detested and which we used to drop into our caps when she was not looking and carry away and hide in chinks in the wall where she was not likely to discover them. She taught us good manners— economy, neatness, method. . . .
> I suppose no children well-born and well placed [runs the final note] ever cried so much or so justly.

There is some doubt as to when Miss Paraman came into Curzon's life, but it would seem probable it was when he was between five and six. Her duties developed as he got older into those of a governess, but since at first her role was that of Nanny (no one else looked after them), and since she is a good example of the multiple effects such women could have, she is relevant to this study. Curzon bore her mark to the end of his life, often showing it in quite small ways. The unending stream of tapioca pouring from Miss Paraman left him with a perpetual anxiety over food. Chefs tried to drown him in "elaborate and costly slushes with incomprehensible names". All through his life he seems to have sat down to table with an apprehension which was usually fulfilled.

> Ever since you left [he wrote to his second wife], I have swallowed (or refused to swallow) the horrid little mould of jelly or yellow blancmange with a bisected apricot or pear swimming at its base. The chef gets worse daily and I will give him notice before the end of the week. He has given me one ice three times in five days and a second twice in two. Chicken five days running.

Again, at a later period: "The kitchen maid gives me everything that I detest and on this chill horrible day proposed mayonnaise of lobster and cold rabbit pie for lunch."

The parsimony of Miss Paraman, her meanness, her insistence on economy, all this too remained with him till the end of his life. At thirteen he wrote to his father, "When I got to Paddington I gave the cabman 1/–. He grumbled and said he ought to have 1/6 as it was over two miles but I said that I had given only 1/– in the morning and that I wouldn't give any more and while he was grumbling I walked away." The incident could have occurred at any time during the next fifty years. He would pay ten thousand pounds for a picture (his aesthetic pursuits and the claims of hospitality were alone exempt from his austerity), but would grudge the price of a dressing-gown. He fussed endlessly over tradesmen's bills. And he married money—an immensely wealthy American heiress, in 1895. There can be no question that he loved his wife dearly. Yet when a man marries, especially a Victorian aged thirty-seven, all things are taken into account, not the least of them being money. All his life he hoarded: every scrap of paper, every letter, tickets, objects, anything that could seem remotely interesting. His biographer puts it down to a sense of history. To me it smacks of strict toilet training.

However, Miss Paraman did not come until he was five. There is evidence that before then his childhood had been happier. As a young man he was attractive and attracted to girls and had various 'affairs'—totally chaste of course, we don't even have a word for what they were now; once it would have been flirtations, or *amitié amoureuse*—principally at Glen in Peeblesshire, which Sir Charles Tennant had bought with a fortune made in railway development and Australian land, and where he had produced four lovely daughters. Curzon also formed strong and lasting friendships, though towards the end of his life, when Miss Paraman seems to have finally surfaced in him, these all collapsed. One of his early friends, though not a very close one, was Oscar Wilde. Curzon defended him from attack once in the Oxford Union, and a few years later when Curzon was beginning his political career, Wilde sought his help in becoming an Inspector of Schools. "I know how the party think of you," he wrote, "you brilliant young Coningsby." "Curzon seems to have done his best," comments his biographer, in one of many felicitous touches, "but it was not as an Inspector of Schools that Wilde eventually won renown."

Nevertheless there can be no doubt that Miss Paraman was the architect of the fundamental shape of Curzon's life. Her harsh hand can be seen active right through it and towards the end, it can be argued, became as dominant as it had been when he was a little boy.

Because she arrived when he was five, Curzon was strong enough to fight her (and fight her he did) and at the same time, uncrushed, was eager to please her. Resentment and rage at her brutality bred in him a furious desire to overcome authority—to flout it and defeat it. Yet at the same time, both placating Miss Paraman and because it had seemed the only way, he had to defeat authority on its own terms. This element of doing what authority wanted in defiance of it reappears throughout his life.

Here he is at Eton:

> The masters with one or two rare exceptions (the principal was Oscar Browning, who always gave me encouragement and inspiration hence my lifelong attachment to him) would not regard me as a serious personage or at least not as thoroughly serious as I was. I accordingly experienced a sweet revenge in 'scoring off' them with their own weapons. I was a fierce worker and used to sit up half the night over my books. I have frequently at Wolley Dod's heard the morning birds begin to sing and I remember that it used to be invariably at about 4.15 a.m. in the summer.
>
> The two French masters (Frank and Harry Tarver) regarded me as an impossible pupil, and I determined to win the Prince Consort's French prize in independence of them. I did so, winning by a larger percentage of marks and at an earlier age than had ever been done before.
>
> Then I resolved to win the Italian prize. The Italian master was a long-bearded and ridiculous old personage named Volpe. I soon came to loggerheads with him over some irreverent pun on his name. I accordingly left his class and did all my work myself with the aid of an excellent edition of Dante containing a prose translation of one Carlyle. I became a master of the first twelve cantos of the *Inferno* and a very passable writer and translator of Italian. Anyhow, to Volpe's surprise and indignation I won the prize, beating his favourite pupil, a boy named Magnay, who was half of Italian extraction and had been brought up in Florence.
>
> I can recall a similar adventure as regards the History prize. The lecturer for this was Cornish—a charming man and afterwards one of my greatest friends, but with a querulous despairing manner that was vexatious. He was dissatisfied with my work and said I would come to nothing. From that moment I resolved to win the prize in spite of him. I left his class that next term, did all my reading by myself in out-of-school hours, entered for the prize much to his and the general astonishment and won it with consummate ease.

To succeed over authority you need power, and the power of a country resides in its government. The evolution of Curzon's ambition towards politics was swift and early.

If Miss Paraman can be seen at work influencing the ends, she also contributed to the means of Curzon's ambitions. Her relentless driving in his childhood tasks, the long hours she compelled him to work, developed in him a capacity for work which is comparable only to Napoleon's. He could absorb, almost without pause, working eighteen or nineteen hours a day for months, years on end, whole mountains of facts, libraries of books, cartloads of departmental reports, digest them, and then spin them effortlessly forth in books, or in governmental memoranda, directives and instruction. He was a Titan of work, a god. While a very busy and ambitious Member of Parliament in 1890, soon to become a junior minister, he wrote, in his spare time as it were, an enormous book on Persia, thirteen hundred pages and half a million words long. It has been judged logical, luminous and one of the most remarkable literary achievements of the nineteenth century.

And Curzon succeeded. He was Parliamentary Under-Secretary of State for India from 1891 to 1892, then Parliamentary Under-Secretary of State for Foreign Affairs, Privy Councillor from 1895 to 1898, Viceroy of India from 1898 to 1905. Honours, if sometimes late, were shovelled on to him: the Garter, an Earldom, Lord Privy Seal. He was Foreign Secretary in the Governments of Lloyd George, Bonar Law and Baldwin.

Yet Curzon died embittered, frustrated and unsatisfied, having lost every single one of his friends, and consumed by the feeling that he had not fully achieved his ambition. Why?

Although Curzon's capacity for work was prodigious, he laid upon it loads which no human being, no ten human beings, could have supported. The plain fact is, he could not delegate and he was obsessed by detail.

He was [to quote from his biography] incapable of appreciating that in great offices of State such habits of administration (delegation and ignoring of petty detail) were virtues rather than faults. Curzon perpetually immersed himself in needless trivia to the detriment both of his health and of his judgement. Throughout his life he wrote in his own hand not only a voluminous private correspondence but also the vast bulk of official documents. He hardly ever dictated. . . . Night after night through the long years of his public career, he chained himself to his desk until the early hours of the morning. If copies of letters had to be kept, they would be taken down by a clerk from the interminable sheets of his flowing script. And because he could trust nobody to meet his own standards of perfection, he would even draft acknowledgements and other purely formal papers for his secretaries to sign and send out under their own names. . . . As a Cabinet Minister he would correct and sometimes entirely redraft the memoranda of civil servants.

Often the corrections were only of grammar or language.

As an infant and child minute attention to detail, an intense punctilious-ness, an absurd sense of personal duty had been savagely beaten into him. All his life Miss Paraman brooded over him, daring him to let others do what he should do himself. He never dared. And, as one would expect, this attitude spread out into other departments of his life, adding to his burdens. He was fanatically tidy and clean. He did all his own filing, packed his own trunks, posted his own letters, spent much time dusting and cleaning and striding around doing odd repairs and fastening pieces of cork on to the backs of chairs. When he was Viceroy of India, where the volume of important and necessary official work in ruling three hundred million subjects was in itself enormous, the total burden began to get out of control. In addition to tidying, packing, dusting, he spent precious hours trying to trap a dishonest cook. "We caught him red-handed," he eventually wrote in triumph to Pam McDonnell. "He returned 596 chickens as having been consumed within a single month. We went to the tradesman who had the account and found the figures were 290."

He wrote up all his own accounts in colossal ledgers, corrected proofs while at dinner parties; he was wracked by ill-temper, insomnia and pain. There can be no doubt that the exhaustion and frustrations induced by these labours, many of them ludicrous, contributed largely to the final rows which drove him to resign.

There is yet another side to Curzon's ambition and energy. Men of outstanding abilities, who have early learned that satisfaction and reward can be earned from the use of these abilities, will always seek the maximum outlets for them. They will be ambitious. If they do not find these outlets, or for some reason fail, they will become depressed. But if they secure adequate outlets then they will be relatively calm and satisfied. But there is a sort of ambitious man—Curzon would seem to have been one, so are most modern industrialists—whose ambition is insatiable. It is a furious, nagging, gnawing ambition which can never be calmed. It would seem that this sort of ambition is sometimes due to very deep early resentment and frustration at cruel treatment. The resentment finds expression in a *perpetual* desire for revenge, an endless need to overcome.

The tragedy of Curzon's life is that in his own eyes he always enjoyed the appearance of power and never the reality. When he was Secretary of State in 1895, Salisbury retained too much control of foreign policy. When he was Viceroy, his Secretary of State could overrule him. When he rose still higher and became Foreign Secretary he was frustrated by Lloyd George and Baldwin. He had always been inclined to arrogance. "I can never leave his presence without a disagreeable feeling that he has made me appear a fool," said Cecil Spring Rice. As the years passed, years of almost indescribable work, made intolerably heavy by the myriad tiring and unnecessary duties he continued to impose on himself, and still he did not attain the power he needed, the power to overcome, Curzon's character was gradually scraped down to the essential forces which were driving him. The fury with which he reacted to frustration became less and less temperate.

By 1904 Sir Arthur Godley could write:

> He seems almost to have lost sight of the merits of the various questions in which he has differed from the Cabinet or from our Council (or they from him) and to be absorbed in a struggle for prerogative, control, independence. In any of these disputed matters, the thought that seems to rise in his mind is not "I will prove to the Cabinet, or to the Council of India, that they are wrong about this and that I am right," but "I have given my opinion, I have even reiterated it in two or more dispatches, I am Viceroy of India, and, confound you, how do you dare to set your opinion against mine?"

He quarrelled one by one with all his friends and became impossible to approach. In the end, he lost the one position where he might at last have been satisfied. In 1923 his claims to succeed Bonar Law—as regards experience and intellectual ability—were overwhelming in comparison with Baldwin. He was in the House of Lords, but there is little doubt this could have been got round. It was his character more than anything else which finally prevented him from becoming Prime Minister.

One must be careful not to exaggerate the effect of Miss Paraman. She came to him, compared with most of the Nannies we have studied, quite late. Yet she provides the single most consistent clue to his life. It was her viciousness which lashed the torpid, latent talents of his Derbyshire line into frenzied activity. It was her fierce disciplines which, as well as teaching him to work, had instilled into him the compulsive attention to detail, the need to do endless chores, which immeasurably increased his burdens. And it was her influence that in the end, after a glittering career, made him feel a failure and prevented him, ultimately, from being a happy man. It is enough for one woman to accomplish.

CHAPTER TEN

The Nanny in Perspective

And so we come full circle, from Churchill to Curzon, having moved through almost the entire spectrum of human behaviour on the way, from the blood-red violence of Miss Paraman at one end to the violet tenderness of Mrs. Everest at the other.

I dealt in the introduction with the possibility and validity of drawing the sort of general conclusions I have tried to draw. If you don't agree with them, or find them insufficiently argued, it is possible to take this study, with a proviso I shall make later in this chapter, simply as a description of a rather curious way of bringing up children, founded on economic wealth and privilege, which flowered in British society approximately between the years 1850 and 1939, and then virtually disappeared.

Those conclusions themselves have, I hope, been clearly enough set forth through the course of the book for a summary of them to be unnecessary. But before leaving the British Nanny forever I would like to make some last comments on these conclusions, and at the same time to draw back a little, to try to bring about some altering of perspectives.

Perhaps first I should explain why there were some aspects of the subject I came to no conclusions about. I decided not to go into the Nanny and male homosexuality. The causes of homosexuality are not fully understood. One very good American study suggests that if two elements in upbringing are present then you are likely to get a homosexual boy. These are a very dominant mother/mother figure who kisses and fondles and excessively stimulates her son physically and to whom the son becomes very strongly attached, and at the same time an absent or weak father/father figure. No doubt this situation often occurred in a Nanny environment. Certainly, quite a number of the examples in this book were homosexual. But this particular situation does not always produce homosexuality. Also I think there was quite often something in the calm, overtly unemotional, physically restrained behaviour of Nannies which considerably mitigated a system which otherwise might seem to be designed to produce homosexuals. Furthermore, the more you read about homosexuality the more complex it becomes. There are conflicting views. A spate of very recent (1972) but challenged evidence suggests once again that the endocrine glands may play a decisive part. I did not think the situation was clear enough to warrant coming to any general, or even particular conclusions.

Again, there is more and more evidence today that very early visual and auditory stimulation and 'education' of small babies during the first twelve months is of considerable importance. It is even possible (though this is still speculative) that if they are not adequately stimulated at the right time certain portions of the brain actually develop less fully than they otherwise might. And the importance of interesting and stimulating children continues throughout their early years. But here it wasn't possible to discern any particular trend in Nanny behaviour.

I was much tempted by flagellation.

"Is it possible," said Mrs. Trimmer, pulling his breeches down to his heels, "that your mistress suffered this tyrannical gentleman to insult her in the manner she was represented?"

"No indeed, ma'am, I never insulted my mamma upon my honour, I did not," roared the youth.

"Indeed Mrs. Trimmer," replied the Nurse, "there's not so bold a boy in the parish."

"So, so, so, so, so, so, so I understand!" said the mistress (making him caper as high as young Vestris at every stroke of the rod). "Yes, yes, yes, yes, I can see you are a wicked young rascal!"

"Oh, dear mistress, I'm not indeed! for pity's sake! Oh mistress! mistress! I'll never offend my mamma! Oh my arse! my arse! Oh, my dear Nurse, beg me off!"

"No, no, Sir, I'm desired to see you well whipped, and I think you never got into such excellent hands before."

"Try me this once, my dearest mistress! Oh, gracious! try me! Oh, I'm killed! Let me down! let me down! let me down! Nurse! Nurse! Nurse!"

In the literature of flagellation (which was immense right through our period), and the brothels where the perversion was practised, the Nanny, or Nurse, appears at first to be central. The scene is most often a nursery. The person to be whipped is accused of some nursery crime—disobedience, answering back, wetting the bed, an act of childish sexual misbehaviour. There is a formal accusation, defence, pleading—then punishment. In this fantasy, the Nanny frequently administers the beating. But it is a Nanny gradually transformed. Her figure swells and becomes huge, her bosom becomes monstrous, turbulent, her eyes flash, in her hand she holds a great birch, her weapon, her engine.

"With this weapon in her hand, how terrible she appeared! Juno deprived of the apple might have looked like her. Her splendid arms and neck were bare, her cheeks flamed, her huge breasts were heaving. Speech was too weak, the graces of the birching were ignored, nothing short of a savage beating could satisfy her present need of vengeance."

Not only does the Nanny play a dominant role, but there is a peculiarly Nanny snobbery about the literature. We are continually told of the great who have loved to be whipped—Voltaire, Charles II, Rousseau, etc. And it is the great who tell us—Lady Termagant Flaybum, Lady Bumtickler, the Duchess of Picklerod, Madame Birchini. Distinguished company.

For a fortnight, absorbed, my senses tingling, I read into the subject: Freud, Anthony Storr, a two-volume German work whose name I noted but now cannot find, Steven Marcus again, several volumes of flagellant pornography. The more I read the more it seemed to me that no one really understood flagellation. The explanations were either inadequate, contradictory or absurd. But whatever the truth, I reluctantly came to one conclusion; the Nanny could not be held responsible.

The fourth subject I felt reluctant to be too sweeping about was the influence of the British Nanny abroad. At various times they were quite numerous among foreign upper class families. There were a good many in Russia around 1900. Between the wars they were fashionable in France (and still are, as we saw, in Paris). Up to the Civil War, I am told, most Spanish aristocrats had a British Nanny. Even now they are not uncommon around Seville and Madrid. The doyen of them is the one who looks after Franco's grandchild and is known as Nanny Franco. There are other bastions where the Nanny holds out. The Suvretta Hotel above St. Moritz flourishes today as it did in late Victorian and Edwardian times. Five years ago Robin Fedden visited it and found that one entire floor was given over to British Nannies and their charges. But none of the employers were English—they were South American, Swiss, Austrian, French and Italian. Count Ledebur said that in Austria before the First World War to be English was to be everything. Their laws were modelled on English laws. They drove on the left. All their clothes came from England. That was why, when the war came, it was so upsetting to Austrians. And the cornerstone of this Englishness was the English Nanny. Every household that could afford one had one—and that was a lot. Even now, as I said earlier, there are a hundred or so English Nannies in Austria, around Vienna particularly, pensioned off, visiting each other.

It is a pleasing picture. One could go on and say that this subtle fifth column, influencing first the leaders and so gradually the masses, was responsible for that mingled dread and admiration with which the Continent used to regard this country; above all for that feeling they had of our stability, wisdom, and *rightness*. Perhaps, even, a deep but unconscious feeling that we were invincible. I think it would be quite spurious. British Nannies abroad have furnished numerous excellent examples of particular themes; there is evidence for no more than that.

SOME COMMENTS ON CONCLUSIONS

It is possible that exception may be taken to the Nanny Block, the phrase I used to describe those areas (alienation of the mother, leaving, etc.) where Nanny behaviour did not, in my view, change significantly from 1850 to 1939.

One of the problems about writing a book like this is to discern (or create) a pattern. This is true of writing any history, but it was particularly true in this case because most of the material was bound to be fragmented and anecdotal: bits of autobiography, dozens of little nursery events, vague, minute flashes of family memory, a few significant facts in otherwise useless interviews. There was a danger (and often the sensation) of being buried under a mountain of incident—a danger that some of my predecessors in the field have not altogether avoided.

I decided that chronology would provide the frame. Before even starting the research, I had several chapter headings—'1900–1914—The High Noon of the Nanny', '1918–1939—The Silver Years', '1945–1973—We're All Nannies Now'. Chronology—the conventional method of imposing shape on a history—has its own dangers of course. The fundamentals of life change slowly, but the historian can tend to exaggerate change to give his book momentum and significance; an effect augmented because as he gets closer to his period he assumes its sense of proportion.

Yet the more I studied the more I became struck by correspondences rather than differences. Nanny Robertson echoed Simpson who echoed Nanny Everest; Bridget Tisdall and Compton Mackenzie had suffered under creatures of the same sort; the disciplines imposed in 1860 were being enforced in 1929; Donleavy described a situation not totally dissimilar from Byron's. Nor perhaps was this surprising. I have said how of all things the pressures resisting change are greatest on methods of bringing up children. And we recognise this instinctively. It would surprise us to be told, say, that styles of clothing or methods of land tenure did not change significantly between 1550 and 1650. It does not surprise us to learn that child care stayed the same. The book therefore resolved itself into a series of themes.

These themes themselves I have treated chronologically, and I do not want to minimise the changes that took place. Despite an occasional feeling of stagnation, there were numerous and fundamental developments during our period and I hope I have brought them out. As I described in chapter 8, my original chronology was not totally at sea. There was certainly a period in the years before 1914 when families were richer and larger, when Nannies stayed longer, and when their sway over their charges was more absolute. After the First World War the green baize doors slowly broke up. Nannies left earlier and more frequently. There were closer contacts with parents, though the resulting rivalries meant this was not necessarily beneficial. Perhaps the Nanny Block should be viewed more as a mountain of ice which grew during the 1830s, '40s and '50s, reached its height between 1890 and 1914, and then slowly melted and crumbled, but was still very sizeable in 1939, still recognisably the same shape, and which after the Second World War finally and swiftly disappeared. But, and this is the fundamental point, the upbringing of upper-class children has more in common at any time during this period, in all significant areas, than it has with upbringing now or with the way children were brought up in the centuries before.

There are a few other short comments to be made about our conclusions. I explained in the Introduction that of necessity they could only be extremely tentative. Number, the study of a significantly large sample of good quality, could radically alter any one of them. It is possible, for instance, that there was a built-in bias in my research towards mitigating the undesirable effects of a Nanny. The vast majority of my correspondents described kind, sweet, dear, adorable, cosy Nannies. Now this may be because most Nannies were dear, adorable, cosy, etc. But it could be that those with less kind Nannies didn't want to revive the memory of them. Similarly, on the whole, the evidence I obtained from reading was either in books about those successful in one sphere or other, since only they had biographers; or it was from autobiographies. Now just to write an autobiography requires a certain sense of one's own worth, a certain self-confidence. That is to say, the literary sources were all from or about people who, if they had had cruel Nannies, had in varying degrees got over the damaging effects of them. About the many thousands who did not get over those effects, who were permanently maimed or silenced, I heard much less.

I said that those features of conformity, inhibition, diffidence, difficulty in forming relationships which one can often detect in the English upper classes of our period almost certainly owed a great deal to the over-strict and depriving upbringing of their Nannies. But this was a complicated development, brought about by many pressures. Some were religious. It was enormously reinforced by repressive prep and public schools. Nevertheless, as the first, the Nanny was the most important influence.

Was it a bad development? It is certainly fashionable to think so and in some respects of course it was. But there is another side to the argument. Is there not something embarrassing, almost revolting, about great, beaming, bellowing, self-confident Italians or Spaniards, lathered in mother love, who rush up and smile and touch you and pump your hand? Or the gross, almost indiscriminate, sexual confidence of some Americans? The inhibition of the English has a peculiar charm, and also a certain significance. After all they did, and do, as Antonia Duffy pointed out when we were discussing this, make contact. But, as a consequence of the difficulty they have doing it, they do it in more subtle, complex and, in some sense, more profound ways. They take longer to do it, but once achieved it lasts longer. They do it verbally rather than physically. They do it through and with shared pasts and shared experiences—the army, their public schools, their prep schools, their parties and deb dances, their Nannies. Because it is done verbally, they get to know each other better. Foreigners rush up and kiss each other and barely know each other at all. For this reason friendship is a peculiarly English thing and one we make much of. We have the best novels, particularly the best novels of manners and relationships; and for several hundred years, Britain (and Ireland) have produced the best conversationalists. And, despite what I said earlier in this chapter, there seems to run through all the English upper classes of the Nannied period, however apparently normal, a vein of more or less deeply repressed homosexuality. It is this which gives a complexity and interest to their characters, adds a tension to their friendships, and charges what would otherwise be the torpid air of their clubs, their First Class carriages, their city offices with, in Evelyn Waugh's phrase, bat squeaks of sexuality.

Much weight has been laid on the Nanny. Would the mothers, who after all shared many of their views about child upbringing, have done any better? I do not think this is really worth discussing, simply because given the economic circumstances and class assumptions that had developed in the nineteenth and early twentieth century it is inconceivable that upper class mothers would have looked after their children. It is arguable, for instance, that Nannies were even more snobbish than their mistresses; or that they were less susceptible (or less in touch with) new ideas and therefore a conservative force. It is not really relevant. But I think there is one valid point to be made in this connection. If mothers had for some extraordinary reason found themselves looking after their children they would also have tried to lead social lives, see their husbands, do their paintings, etc. The fact that the Nanny had time, endless time, was certainly a major factor in making her elaborate, and insist on, the multifarious rules, the pot-training, the routines we studied. Because the mothers of today don't have time it means that, even if they are often less patient and sometimes neglectful, it is physically impossible for them to impose such rigid patterns of upbringing. Their children are inevitably freer. No doubt something similar would have happened to the mothers of our period had they looked after their children.

THE NANNY AS A STUDY OF LOWER CLASS UPBRINGING

For most of this book we have been in the nursery. It can be a stifling, claustrophobic, trivial place. I would like now to draw back, to rise above it.

It is a cliché that today class has replaced sex as an obscene subject, in which case a book devoted entirely to the upbringing of the upper classes might be considered as little less than pornographic. But of course this book hasn't only been about that at all. I was at pains to stress two things earlier: first that Nannies were lower class, and second that they taught each other. This means that many of the attitudes they brought to, and disciplines they inflicted on, their charges were lower class ones. That is to say that, setting aside effects like alienation from the mother which were due to their peculiar position and relationship, in studying Nannies we have in fact been studying attitudes which were prevalent among a far larger section of British society—namely the labouring lower classes. And this rarely happens in history. All the aspirations and aims of the inarticulate masses are usually lost without trace. Here, for a brief stretch of time, using as a vehicle the early childhood of a privileged and literate élite, some of them have been preserved.

That this has also been the subject of our study is strongly supported by Geoffrey Gorer's mammoth survey of English attitudes, *Exploring English Character* (1955). In this, many of the ideas about child upbringing and the effects they produce, which we have been discussing, were found to be *still* inherent in the English character—and to be different from those found in other European countries. The accent was (and is?) on discipline.

It can be summed up like this: "The formation of a good English character depends on imposing suitable disciplines as long as possible; the child's character will be spoiled if the discipline is insufficient or not applied soon enough." Lower class permissiveness was a myth. And Gorer showed how many of the attitudes typical of Nannies were typical of the lower classes generally at that time. Strict pot-training and cleanliness for instance (he says that the Music Hall concentration on bottoms was due to this rather than beating). Pleasure was not a child's right but something granted to it while it was good. The Nanny prudery about undressing was a general lower class one. And this correspondence between Nanny and lower class attitudes showed up in specific correspondences between lower and upper class attitudes. For example, the upper and lower classes allowed considerable authority to women in the matter of disciplining children whereas the intermediate classes did not, ascribing it more to the father.

Instead, therefore, of limiting ourselves to the top five per cent or so of English Society after 1850, we have to a degree been studying something much closer to seventy per cent.*

THE NANNY AND SOME COMPARATIVE STUDIES IN CHILD UPBRINGING

I would, finally, like to put the Nanny into an even wider context than English Social History.

I think the best way to do this is via the breast. Despite exceptions, there does seem on the whole often to have been something anaemic, a lack of full-bloodedness about many Nannies. Talking to Nanny B about breast-feeding, I asked if she approved of it and if she had encouraged her mistresses to feed their children by breast. Oh yes, she said, she certainly approved, she always encouraged it. She'd had one, Lady E, who was particularly good at it, she was remarkable, really remarkable. In fact, as far as breast-feeding went, Lady E had been well-nigh incredible. Interested, I asked for how long Lady E had fed her children at the breast. "A month," said Nanny B.

The Lepcha of India feed their children at the breast until they are three; the Chenchu tribe of India wean at five or six, though the last child is often fed until puberty; in fact in a study of different cultures done by Whiting and Child only one society out of fifty-two weaned their children within the first year as we do, and that was the Marquesans of Polynesia.

* Because of the difficulty of definition, it is extremely hard to be accurate about class figures in English population divisions.

The average age of weaning was two and a half years. Now this may seem of academic interest only. But quite a large number of child psychiatrists regard breast-feeding, and more precisely the close early relationship between baby and mother which it particularly exemplifies, as by far the most important and far-reaching experience in human life. A very brilliant exponent of this point of view was Dr. D. W. Winnicott, whose books, especially *The Child, The Family, and The Outside World*, I would recommend to anyone interested in child upbringing.

Let me briefly try to give you the flavour of Winnicott. He says, first of all, that too many people have the idea that they have got to mould babies and infants, to train them. 'Train' them—what an unpleasant word. This is quite wrong. Babies are alive and independent; they grow on their own like any living thing. All they need is a suitable environment, particularly a loving environment, in which to grow. But as well as this a baby is a person. He can't exist alone. It is always a baby and someone. A baby is essentially a relationship.

This loving environment and this relationship is first and best formed, or founded on, breast-feeding. When the baby is hungry, the breast is there. When he is full, it goes. He quickly comes to love the breast, and therefore the person who provides it. Later, love will allow authority, because a baby wants to please someone he loves. But more complex attitudes are learnt and expressed while breast-feeding. Babies aren't stupid, they have ideas, ideas which are feelings as well. The baby attacks the breast. He is eating it, destroying it. Then, to his surprise, he sees the breast belongs to, is in fact, his mother. And though he has just eaten it, the breast and his mother are still there, and are there again and again. The world is a safe and reliable place. Similarly, the breast comes (more or less) when he wants it. And the mother adjusts to him. She shifts the nipple. She gets to know his habits, how he likes to be held, when he needs to be picked up, and so he learns that the outside world will adapt to him. Having enjoyed the breast, the baby is able to form an image of it; he imagines it, wants it, it comes. So he begins to learn something more about the world. He learns that things of the imagination can relate to things in the world of reality. And he can see, also, how they are different. At the same time he is learning the difference between himself and his imagination and the outside world. You cannot teach a baby anything until it has understood this difference and come to terms with it. And all this is greatly reinforced by the strength of feeling involved in breast-feeding. Though you may not easily believe this (and if you don't, Winnicott says, at least consider that it is possible) it is probably the most powerful of all human relationships. He calls it the breast-feeding orgy. Only, much later, will sexual feelings rival it and will in fact on analysis be found to have derived characteristics and peculiarities from those early patterns.

But above all breast-feeding becomes a relationship. The child feels guilty over his aggressive acts towards his mother, his attacks on the breast, but he knows that the attack can be repaired, because the breast returns, love is still there. The mother provides the stable environment where he can fuse guilt and love, can feel both towards the same person. And, just as he imagined the breast, so he imagines his mother, he builds—and after guilt rebuilds—an image of her in his mind. Guilt leads to rebuilding and reparation—the best form of guilt.

And of course the relationship spreads swiftly out. The child who is treated as a separate person early, at once, more easily develops as a person. He soon loves playing with his mother. And she with him. They make each other laugh—and cry. And the mother is the best person (though Winnicott recognises not the only possible person) for the baby to form a relationship with. Not just because it is founded on the enormous intimacy of the breast; but because she carried and bore him, because from the start she will have a deep interest in his point of view and because it is in her best interests that the baby does well. The mother, too, because these early adaptations and reactions to the baby—holding, picking up, shifting the breast, cuddling—are not a matter of training or conscious thought, they are beyond that: they are a matter of love. Only someone who *loves* a child can make these intuitive reactions. Such love comes most easily to a mother. And it should be the mother because it is good for her. It is by getting to know her child, trusting her judgment, doing what she knows and feels is right that a woman grows. She becomes at her best. If she has to take advice, follow a Nanny's rule, she loses confidence and dwindles. It is satisfying to have a child and bring it up; unsatisfying and meaningless if someone else does.

It would take too long to follow the immensely subtle and persuasive way in which Winnicott expands and qualifies the value of a close early relationship between mother and child. He recognises it can lead to intenser difficulties and stranger tensions later. But it also leads to an incomparably greater richness and depth of character, to the ability later to form deep, rich and satisfying relationships. And he raises the importance of this early relationship with the mother into a general statement about the human condition. Anyone who is sane, anyone who feels he is a proper person in the world, owes an immense debt to a woman. This debt should be recognised and faced, not because it will lead to gratitude but because it will lead to a lessening of fear. Not to admit this love dependence, this debt, means that a man continues to fear he is dependent. This fear can express itself in a fear of women in general, or of a particular woman, or just a general fear of domination and dependence. But, again paradoxically, this fear—born of the earlier fear—expresses itself by seeking out someone (or some state, some body) to dominate us. By choosing a specific dominator—or dictator—we hope to exclude the one we really fear. We look to him, with his strength to protect us. So it is that the health of our very civilisation depends on the understanding and right ordering of our and other people's childhoods.

We can approach what I mean to say from another angle. During my conversations with Dr. Storr he mentioned some letters he had received from an anthropologist, Richard J. de Boer, who was investigating Eskimos in the central Canadian Arctic. The letters might interest me, he said. They did; and Richard de Boer has kindly allowed me to take from them what follows.

In Eskimo society a baby is almost as close to its mother after birth as before. It is carried about on its mother's back all day and sleeps with her all night. Eskimo couples sleep in separate sleeping bags, the baby with the mother. When they make love, the wife climbs into her husband's sleeping bag returning to her own later. Because the child is in constant contact with the mother it is never frustrated. Its needs, usually feeding, are answered immediately. And in fact Eskimos regard crying as an indication that something is wrong which must be seen to. The Eskimo baby is not taught, by the mechanics of repetition, to suppress his crying. He is prevented from crying by the immediate removal of whatever it is that is making him cry. This instant response to infant needs is continued either until he can crawl (at about nine months) or until 'cognition'—that is until he knows himself sufficiently well to help himself or make his needs known in a precise and explicit way. The pattern of minimum frustration in teaching continues through childhood.

The most striking thing about Eskimo culture is the total lack of aggression. This does not mean that an Eskimo lacks initiative or is inactive or cannot respond to hostility. They are intensely individual and possessed of enormous skill and decision in dealing with the emergencies of a hostile environment. If they are attacked they will defend themselves with energy; if a man attacks the group he will if possible be restrained, if necessary he will be killed. They are expert hunters. But an aggressive act is an act of hostility which comes first. It of necessity presupposes hostile and aggressive motives, emotions. Eskimos don't have these. They feel no anger when they kill a bear. Nor have Eskimos ever gone to war. They did not know what it was and when it was explained to them were horrified and amazed. There are many other facets to Eskimo culture. It is communist. They share everything: food, territory (they have no territorial feelings), wives, husbands, children, food, tools. There is no jealousy or adultery, for example, because if a wife or husband wants another person's partner he (or she) can have them ('use them' is the Eskimo expression). But these factors are all underpinned by the lack of aggression. There are of course Eskimos who are stronger than their fellows and Eskimos who are cleverer and Eskimos who are both together, but they don't 'dominate' their companions because they have no wish to do so. De Boer describes how he watched in amazement while a superior hunter with five children distributed all the catch he didn't need to those less skilful. The Eskimo social system, which has endured unchanged and entirely successful for five thousand years, is almost totally anarchic.

Is there any connection between the method of upbringing and the cultural pattern? Obviously one would need to know a lot more about both to say—full details of subsequent training and its effects, the reason certain aberrant Eskimos spring up and so on. Obviously in small, closed, independent, far-spaced groups situated in a very tough environment there is a strong evolutionary premium put upon co-operative developments of the sort outlined above. But I think that de Boer would say there was a connection and a very close one. Certainly such comparative evidence as I have come across in a rather cursory study of this subject does suggest the two are related. For instance the Italuk in the South Seas carry and sleep with their babies, never let them cry, never leave them alone and are completely ruled by them until the children are three or four. To isolate a baby, to let it cry, is to commit a major atrocity, for if the baby is left alone "by and by dies, no more people". Similar patterns are found in fourteen other societies, including the Arapesh, the Lepcha, the Muria, Murngin, Kwana and the Reindeer Chukchee. All these societies are noted in varying degrees either for their lack of aggression or their ease in personal relationships and often for both.

De Boer would argue, I think, that there is a causal link between, among other things, the lack of aggression and the sort of upbringing he describes. He says in one of his letters to Dr. Storr (treading controversial ground here) that the desire to dominate, and create societies with dominance hierarchies, is not innate in man. For it to exist at all men have to be able to appreciate their own status in relation to those of other people. They can either do this through phylogenetically determined signals and

responses—that is through automatic responses which have become bred
into the species, rather as a male peacock, say, will always give way to one
with a superior sized and coloured tail. Or they can *learn* the significance
of status. Now man has no phylogenetic responses as regard status or
dominance bred into him at all. Therefore they must be learnt. Next he
points out that before birth three things are common to mankind: the
environment in the womb; the relationship with the mother, which is one
of total dependence; and finally the behaviour of the foetus. The reflex
actions and movements of unborn babies are the same everywhere. After
birth (and oddly enough for about the same period of nine months) these
three factors—dependence on the mother, the environment, the responses
of the child—remain all important. But they begin to change. The
dependence on the mother remains total. But reflex responses give way to
learned responses, which is in fact why this period of growth is spent
outside the womb. Also the environment alters. This is the moment when
human beings begin to diverge. Implicit in de Boer's argument (though
not stated by him in the letters I read) is the idea that it is the frustrations
and corresponding aggressions engendered in helpless babies during this
period by the frustrating way of treating them that leads later (much
reinforced by subsequent and similar training) to what he would regard
as the pathological developments of aggression, societies based on
dominance hierarchies, competition and so on. The point is that in human
beings (as with all primates) gestation does not end with birth; it continues after it. It was when it ceased to realise and act on this that the
human species ceased to be human. De Boer dates the event eight thousand
years ago.

Now I don't know if it has been evident in this book, but I find the sort
of attitude exemplified by Winnicott and de Boer inherently sympathetic.
For instance, I have always found the crying of little babies so piercing in
its anguish, arousing so immediately and violently the instinct to protect,
that to read of societies where this instinct is allowed immediate expression
just confirms what I have always felt. I was always interfering in the upbringing of my own children. It may be thought that, feeling this, I
could not help coming to the Nanny somewhat biased against her. After
all, compared to the spontaneous, easy and instinctive Eskimo, her child
permanently next to her skin, swinging it round every ten minutes to
stuff in a hot, dangling breast, the Nanny with her routines, her disciplines,
her warmth and love, though genuine, reserved, conditional and extremely
un-animal, the Nanny becomes a somewhat cold and inadequate figure as a
mother substitute. Alternatively, any hard-pressed, would-be liberated,

modern mother reading this, will think that if I expect her (and she will think this—because it is impossible to read any book about child rearing without applying what is said to oneself), if I expect her to stumble round her home, doing the housework, the cooking, her part-time job, with one child strapped to her back and the other one hanging from her breasts, then I just don't know what it's all about and am not fit to write about the upbringing of children even in an historical context. However, though the principal figure in my early life was my mother, I had a Nanny until I was five whom I remember dimly but with fondness. And I do in fact know a great deal (too much) about the practical effort of bringing up little children. But over and above this, there are stranger things, to our Western way of thinking, to be learnt about the upbringing of children than the methods of the Eskimos, and it was these, as well as the contrast between my background and my present life, which helped to bring a certain detachment to this study.

During the Second World War six German-Jewish children, all with different histories, arrived together at a concentration camp. They were all a few months old and their parents had been killed in gas ovens. For three years they remained as a group in the same concentration camp, then when they were between three and four they were taken to a country house in England—Bulldog's Bank, West Hoathly, Sussex. It is perhaps impossible to imagine a background more terrible, more deprived, more injurious to character and mental health. From their earliest months no single person had looked after them consistently for more than a few weeks at a time; no one had loved them or nurtured them; they had lived in the appalling atmosphere of a concentration camp (Terezzin), a transit camp on the way to an extermination camp. The following passages are taken from a study made of these children by Anna Freud and S. Dann.

> The children's positive feelings were centred exclusively on their own group. It was evident they cared greatly for each other and not at all for anybody or anything else. They had no wish other than to be together and became upset when they were separated from each other, even for short moments. No child would consent to remain downstairs, or vice versa, and no child would be taken for a walk or on an errand without the others. . . . If anything of the kind happened, the single child would constantly ask for the other children while the group would fret for the missing child.
>
> The children's unusual emotional dependence on each other was borne out further by the almost complete absence of jealousy, rivalry, and competition, such as normally develops between brothers and sisters or in a group of contempories who come from normal families. There was no occasion to urge the

children to 'take turns'; they did it spontaneously since they were eager that everyone should have their share. Since the adults played no part in their emotional lives at the time, they did not compete with each other for favours or recognition. They did not tell on each other and they stood up for each other automatically whenever they felt that a member of the group was unjustly treated or otherwise threatened by an outsider. They were extremely considerate of each other's feelings. They did not grudge each other their possessions . . . on the contrary lending them to each other with pleasure. When one of them received a present from a shopkeeper, they demanded the same for each of the other children, even in their absence. On walks they were concerned for each other's safety in traffic, looked after children who lagged behind, helped each other over ditches, turned aside branches for each other to clear the passage in woods, and carried each other's coats. In the nursery they picked up each other's toys. After they had learned to play, they assisted each other silently in building and admired each other's productions. At meal times handing food to the neighbour was of greater importance than eating oneself.

Anna Freud and S. Dann gave hundreds of examples of this group sympathy. Here is one (the names are false): "November 1945—John refuses to get up in the morning, lies in his bed, screams and kicks. Ruth brings his clothes and asks '*Willst du anziehen?*' (Don't you want to put them on?) Miriam offers him her doll with a very sweet smile. John calms down at once and gets up."

It is plain what had happened. Out of their need, these babies had created their own parents. The group was at once the mother and her children. But the astonishing thing about it was that it worked. I found it difficult to get full information about the subsequent development of these children, but it seems to have been normal. They were difficult when young, aggressive to outsiders, hypersensitive and difficult to handle. But they were not deficient, delinquent or psychotic. They grew up, married and had children. Only one of the girls had a history of disturbances.

What is one to make of this? It has become axiomatic, both in traditional psychoanalytic theory and in such of it as has seeped through to become one of the many *idées reçues* of our (Western) times, that three factors are disastrous in child upbringing: (i) No chance to form a close relationship with the mother or mother substitute in the first three years. (ii) Maternal deprivation or separation for limited periods. (iii) Changes of mother figure in the early years. Certainly, much criticism of the Nanny as a system would be based on these assumptions. Are they then untrue? The answer, tentatively and within fairly severe limits, would seem to be yes—in certain circumstances, separation, maternal deprivation and the rest do not matter.

One of the most extraordinary experiments in child upbringing ever carried out is that of the Kibbutz system in Israel. A very brief account (mostly taken from Bruno Bettelheim's brilliant *The Children of the Dream*) is highly relevant here.

In a Kibbutz a baby is taken from its mother at the age of four days and looked after by a metapelet (nurse) with five or six of approximately its own age group. It will not leave this group for the next eighteen years, though the group will be enlarged by the addition of other groups. Between one and two he moves to a toddler's house. Here there are one or two more groups and another metapelet. Between three and four these children, with the addition if necessary of a final group to bring the numbers to eighteen, go to the kindergarten house, where there is a new metapelet and a teacher. They move again at seven to the children's house, and to a new metapelet and new teacher. Finally, at around twelve or thirteen, they move into a youth home until they are eighteen. These are self-governing but are guided by a youth leader. Thus the child will have, in addition to parents and teachers, at least four metapelets looking after him (in practice usually more, as metapelets leave, get married, become ill and so on); and these changes of metapelet occur at crucial moments in his development—eighteen months, three and a half, seven and for the last time at the onset of adolescence. In addition night, often a time when babies and children particularly need love and security, is spent apart from his parents and regular metapelet. Different people look after him at that time, 'night watchers', strangers. If he is ill, he is ill in the children's house.

This system grew up for two reasons. First, the early Kibbutzim were small agricultural communities living in incredibly tough conditions. They had to work very hard indeed. There was no time to look after children. But it was also, says Bettelheim, a perfectly conscious reaction to ghetto life. There the family ties had been too strong, religion too dominant, women too motherly and subservient, property too important. The Kibbutz would have no religion, no property (everything is held in common) above all, no family. Women and children would never again mutually burden each other. Women would be free and equal. They would get their satisfaction from their comrades and the community. The Kibbutz system, like the Nanny, is a way of getting rid of children.

This shows in their relations with their children. Weaning is automatic and compulsory at six months, to lessen, in effect, a child's dependence on its mother. From then until a year, they see their children for half an hour a day. After that for two hours a day. But parents see their children at the end of the day, when they are tired. They are often eager to be off. They are noticeably on their best behaviour, a little unnatural. They give things, objects, not emotions. And though fond of their children in a distant way, they revealed by many small examples how they did not want their freedom interfered with. Sometimes, for instance, parents refused to take their turn sleeping in the children's home. If a child flees to his parents' house at night, he is taken back. The metapelet, even a bad one, is always deferred to. No very strong ties develop, and children very early learn that love will not come from their parents. But they also learn little about love from their metapelets. Some are not particularly nice or are too busy. But even the nice ones are whisked away before anything fundamental can grow. The only constant is the peer group and it will come as no surprise to learn, after reading about the concentration camp children, that quite swiftly it is to this that all the strongest feelings accrue.

The peer group is the first thing they see in the morning; at night it is to each other they turn for comfort. Their position in the group, the pecking order, is established early and thereafter there is no bullying and little competition. (This lack of competitiveness is later reinforced by the realisation that, however bad or good, each person will eventually be a full member of the Kibbutz.) A group spirit develops which begins to influence the child. They often teach themselves. For instance toilet-training is done by the group, which is the reason, not neuroses, why there is more bed-wetting than normal in a Kibbutz. When the group decides that bed-wetting is bad, the practice stops at once. Later, this group loyalty and obedience becomes absolute. Kibbutzniks (people in a Kibbutz) cannot go against the views of the group. If someone does—in the way, say, of not doing his or her share of the work—then the group becomes savage. One group who had a girl in this situation were "ready literally to tear her to pieces". They had had to be restrained by the youth leaders. If someone leaves the Kibbutz to join the outside world, as a few do, the group rejects him. Hence a Kibbutz is a very conforming, conservative, un-original place.

What are the other results of this strange way of bringing up children? Perhaps one should first say that the oddest is that there are none of those which pyschoanalytic theory would have confidently predicted. Members of a Kibbutz are not neurotic (oedipal conflicts, for instance, are either very weak or non-existent), not delinquent, not individually over-aggressive, not sexually disturbed, there is no breakdown of personality. But psychoanalytic theory can help us discuss some of the things which do happen to Kibbutzniks.

The theory postulates (or has discovered) the *Introject*. If a single person is deeply loved or needed by a little child then this person's loss is dreaded. When its loved figure is absent the child misses him. As a result he creates in himself a mental image, a picture, of his loved person. Energy and emotion flow round this image; the child can dwell on it and comfort himself. Later on, the existence of this image, the fact that the child has developed a skill and been able to create it, lead to two things. First, the ability to enter the feelings of others, that is to say re-create them inside ourselves, in imagination; second, to independence. The inner figure confronts us as 'other'; we see ourselves in relation to it. It is to this interior person that we inwardly talk. Kibbutz children and later adults are much less able to do this. So many people have brought them up (the system is in effect a form of multiple mothering) that no clear inner figure develops. Kibbutzniks are not independent; in war, for instance, they are inflexible and bad at taking independent decisions. They cannot see other people's points of view and Bruno Bettelheim found it quite impossible for them even to imagine there could be criticisms of the Kibbutz system.

But, more important, because they have never learnt to do so, they cannot form deep attachments to individuals. There is a flatness of emotion between single people, a physical and psychical distance. The Kibbutz has stuck at the Youth Society stage. Like Youth Societies, intimacy, comradely friendship, is praised in theory and dreaded in practice. The group is always together, without privacy, to protect them from intimacy. (Bettelheim says he could not be sure, without deep analysis, whether Kibbutzniks repressed a craving for intimacy, or whether they had not developed it. It was possible they had eliminated the need altogether.)

Not that Kibbutzniks don't feel strong emotions. Their group-centred feelings are very strong indeed, and rewarding. They dwell lovingly on the things they have done together when young, on the shared joys and adventures. Their group love continues all their lives, and the most poignant of the sufferings described by those who leave a Kibbutz is their longing to return to the group, and the pain they feel, on visits, to find they have been rejected.

Sexual behaviour appears to be more strongly influenced by things other than the Kibbutz system. Despite the lax toilet-training and apparent freedom there is in fact a good deal of suppression. The first Kibbutz settlers were deliberately, even relentlessly, promiscuous; but this had such an unsettling and disruptive effect on the communities that now adolescent and other pre- or extra-marital sex is discouraged. Children and adolescents are supposed not to have sexual feelings. Also the close physical proximity in the Youth homes, when four or six of both sexes sleep in a room, mean that sexual feelings often have to be repressed in the interests of harmony. All this must be assisted by the difficulty Kibbutzniks have in forming single relationships. On the whole they are cold, repressed and puritan about sexual matters.

Flattened emotions, uncompetitive, unoriginal, no strong individual ties—no doubt we can feel superior. Yet is our competitiveness creating an ideal society? How many of us have truly deep and intimate relationships? How many of us are original and have opinions of our own? And how many of us would not welcome solace from grief or sharing of joy in the love and support and warmth of a close-knit group?

CONCLUSION

This is all interesting enough, but of course it is extremely rough and ready. A complete study, even a complete précis, of Kibbutz upbringing would need to be a great deal more subtle and extended. Dr. Winnicott is an unabashed proselytiser—he is determined to persuade women to breast-feed their children (one gets the impression sometimes he would like to breast-feed them himself). What I read, and relayed to you, of de Boer's ideas were really only an outline of what now exists on the subject. In the absence of support, you could easily reject his suggestions. I haven't really even scratched the surface; only indicated where it is. But I did so because I wanted to make, in conclusion, two final observations about child upbringing and the Nanny.

There is a sense in which we duplicate collectively, the reluctance most of us have personally to admit and to face up to the implications of the overwhelming importance of early upbringing. In the last fifty years the mechanisms by which we develop have begun to be understood. And if they show anything at all, it is this: so crucial are the first five to seven years of our life that attempts to change human nature—whether made by Christ, by Buddha, by Freud—are virtually useless. They can palliate, comfort, they can attempt, and usually fail, to redirect energies. They can do nothing more. They arrive on the scene long after the fundamental mould has irretrievably set. And the reason that has always been given is that you can't change human nature. In fact of course nothing could be further from the truth. It is possible to change human nature completely. What impressed Bruno Bettelheim about the children of the dream was that they showed that it was possible to create a *radical* new personality for a people in a generation. From, in their case, over-emotional, property-hungry, tight, ghetto Jews to under-emotional, non-property-owning, open, rational Israeli farmers.

I said we have only begun to understand the mechanisms and of course that is true. But even now things have been learnt that could be used. There may be something to question or regret about a Kibbutz upbringing, but there can be no doubt at all that it produces adults infinitely more stable, happier, able to live fuller and richer lives than, say, many children from broken families in the slums of Glasgow or New York or children brought up among the intense conflicts of a disintegrating middle class family in an isolating suburb. If there are really women who wish to have children and only look after them for one or two hours a day while they pursue other goals, then there exists a perfectly sound model for them to copy.

But we can go deeper than this. You may have reservations about Winnicott and de Boer, but even if they are only half right, if they are even one quarter right—is this not of vital importance? While the world thunders onward driven by fears, aggressions and competitiveness in a direction which seems ever crazier and more dangerous, should we not explore the only avenue which can bring about the only change fundamental enough to make any difference? Yet even the little we do know is not taught in our schools. Nursery schools instead of having the most public money have the least. Yet at nursery school it is still just possible, in a way it will not be three years later or ever again, not only to teach people how to learn but how to live. The amount of money spent in research on this subject is negligible. Advice or facts or help in child upbringing features on no foreign aid programme anywhere.

And the last observation I want to make is that it is on this level and in this context that the Nanny must be judged. This is the final shift in perspective I would like to bring about. Because, arising fortuitously as a result of economic wealth, influenced by puritanism, echoes of the dynastic family, customs which had developed as a result of natural exasperation and all the rest, that is what the Nanny was—an experiment in child upbringing. Nor was it at all a dishonourable one. There are factors which, were it possible to revive the system *in toto*, which of course it is not, would lead one to reject it: disciplines and routines deriving from mistaken views about human nature, the fact that the Nanny left, the danger of employing and then not detecting someone unfit to look after children, the ease with which mother and Nanny could become rivals and so on. But when judging a system of child upbringing, as with a political system, or an artist or indeed a human being, it is charitable to judge it at its best. Note is taken of the slave foundation of fifth-century Athens; but she is remembered for her drama, philosophy, and architecture, for Socrates and Plato. And at its best the Nanny was very good indeed. Either when mother and Nanny shared—when you could say it fell somewhere between Winnicott and the Kibbutz; or where the Nanny took upon herself the burdens of the mother and was worthy of them. And just because the architecture of this book dictated that we should end our study with fiends, with Barley, Nurse Pratt, and Miss Paraman, it would be unjust to leave them as the final picture. It is much fairer to remember Gibson disappearing without a thought into the smoke and flames in Moscow, returning minutes later, her grey hair scorched, carrying her baby. Or Nanny Everest chiding Churchill for having a wet coat when he came to see her on her deathbed. Or the image of Simpson sitting beside the bed of her sick boy through the night. To remember all those thousands, hundreds of thousands, of devoted, caring, selfless, single women about whom A. P. Herbert wrote and who, if not its whole subject, must in the end be allowed to be the heroines of this book.

> Alas! The twig becomes a bough:
> We do not need a Nanny now;
> Forgetting her who showed us how,
> We walk to death or glory;
> And whether fate blows hot or cold,
> Whatever woman shapes our lot
> It's safe to say a Nurse will not
> Be mentioned in the story.
> Some other baby far away
> Is hers to soothe or slap.
> Some Nelson's in the bath today,
> Some Shelley in her lap;
> And when I think on this small star
> How many mighty men there are,
> I call for wine and drain a jar
> To England's noble Nannies.

Some Nanny Sayings and Practices

Nothing illustrates certain sides of Nannies so well as the things they say: kindness, sharpness, both individual and proverbial folk wisdom, humour, their soothing quality, playfulness, superstition, patience, love. . . . Here are some of the things I have extracted from the letters I received. The categories are very rough and ready.

Reactions to comments, requests, questions

"Play with me Nanny."
"I've a bone in my leg."

When asked how old they were:
"A little older than my teeth and as old as my tongue."
"Twenty-one and a bit."
"Ninety-eight and a half."

"Why Nanny?"
"Z darling." Or "Why don't table legs have knees?" Or "Don't ask me, ask your mother."

A child comes in with a bit of news Nanny knows already, that they are going to the seaside or Cook is sick.
Child: Cook's ill!
Nanny: Queen Anne's dead.

To a question that irritated Nanny—probably about her age again:
"Ask no questions and you'll hear no lies."
"I'll thank you not to use that tone of voice to me, Miss."

Child refusing to answer:
"Has the cat got your tongue?"

Nanny teased for being small:
"All the best goods come in small parcels."

Manners, instructions or advice on behaviour, wisdom

"Never go upstairs empty handed, never go downstairs empty handed."

"There's no such word as can't."

"Elbows off the table."

"God helps those who help themselves."

"Children should be seen and not heard."

"If you want your hair to curl you must eat fried bread behind the door."

"Save your breath to cool your porridge." (That is, don't talk so much.)

"It's rude to point."

"Patience and perseverance brought the snail to Jerusalem."

"Don't let them run, it's bad for their hearts."

"'What's' dead long ago and 'Pardon' took his place."

"It takes two to make a quarrel."

"There's a time and a place for everything."

> "Don't care was made to care
> Don't care was hung
> Don't care was put in a pot
> And boiled till he was done."

"There are three sorts of sin: little sins, bigger ones, AND TAKING OFF YOUR SHOES WITHOUT UNDOING THE LACES."

Definition of the word 'please': "A little word and a bonny word."

"If at first you don't succeed, try, try, try again."

"There's a place for everything and everything in its place."

"Fine feathers don't make fine birds."

> "The other side of every cloud
> The sun is shining.
> I therefore turn my clouds about
> And always wear them inside out
> To show the silver lining."

"Laugh before breakfast, cry before bed-time."

"I'm not going to have answering back/argufying/such goings on in *my* nursery."

If 'please' was forgotten: "I don't quite hear you, dear."

> "Never hurry, never worry, never fret or fume;
> But when the Devil comes in sight just bid him leave the room."

"Never trouble trouble till trouble troubles you."

"Better to wear out than to rust out."

"Two wrongs don't make a right."

Food

"Hot grows cold while greedy waits."

A correspondent described how his Nanny "made us touch our cake onto our own plate before eating it and not eat it straight off the cake plate, which looked greedy."

"Bread and butter before cake."

"Bread and butter before bread and butter and jam."

"Don't eat with your eyes."

"Waste not want not."

"Eat up—you'll be glad of it some day."

"We always say—nasty first, nice afterwards."

"Your eyes are bigger than your stomach." (If someone has taken a helping they can't finish.)

"Everyone's got to eat a peck of dirt before they die." (Child fussing over some sand, say, in the salad.)

Child hovering over plate of cakes or biscuits to find the best: "Now, no pickings or choosings—just you take the first that comes."

"Eat your crusts and it'll make your hair curl." (This is to get crusts eaten, and differs from the fried bread injunction, which was genuine advice.)

One Nanny used to scrape bananas before they were eaten. Unscraped bananas gave you appendicitis.

Too hot food: "It came from a hot place so what do you expect?"

"Always pick blackberries *above* dog-lifting-leg height."

Ian Parsons' Nanny: "You have made your bed, Master Ian, and now you must eat it." (Presumably Master Ian had asked for an overlarge helping of kedgeree or the like—or perhaps just crossed some more general rubicon.)

Food left on plate: "That's a saucy plate."

"Leave a bit for Miss Manners."

Child: "What's for dinner, Nanny?"
Nanny: "Not dinner, dear, lunch."
Child: "What's for lunch, Nanny?"
Nanny: "Wait-and-see pudding."

If it were cold mutton or rice pudding: "You just finish it all up. Yes, fat and all—I want to see a clean plate, please."

On the other hand, if it were birthday cake or Queen of Puddings: "What's happened to Mr. Manners? Doesn't he live in this house any more? He'll want a bit left for him, poor man."

> "Dearly beloved brethren, is it not a sin
> To eat a boiled potato and throw away the skin?
> The skin feeds the pigs and the pigs feed us,
> Dearly beloved brethren, is it not thus?"

Some Nanny practices, children's reactions

"When Nanny fixed her outdoor hat with two long hatpins, we were convinced she put the pins through her head and thought she was some kind of God for being able to do so. She never disillusioned us."

Michael Macarthy said good night to his six-month-old son. As he went away, Nanny said to the baby, "I wonder if somebody's daddy is going to forget to shut the door tonight."

Mrs. Clauson's Nanny never punished them. She gave them 'reminders'. You were stood in the corner, not as a punishment, but as a reminder. It was somehow less aggressive. It was also pleasant to say to other children that you were never punished.

"Why can't you leave your poor little brother alone, Miss Mary? You know he's on a chalk line today—wot with his cold and all, poor little chap."

Before a journey: "Have you made yourselves comfortable? Off you go then, round the corner—quick as you can. No you can't 'go' on the train. You never know if there won't be a man lurking in one of them places." (To this day Mrs. Somerset dreads using a station or train lavatory.)

To the nursery-maid about potting: "Now Kate, you just take the two little girls and sit them down nicely."

To the baby: "Come on, my lamb, let Nan hear you make a nice rattle. Oh Lor' he's starting to do number two. All right, my duck—eh—ha-ha-ha-ha."

Mrs. Mary Somerset gave me nearly twenty of these practices and sayings from Edwardian Nannies from 1900 to 1906. There were seven children and they had five Nannies. She didn't dislike any of them but can't remember a single kind thing any of them did. Their mother was very close to them all and it's possible she made the Nannies jealous.

"Master Rex and Miss Ena, they never wanted to be always running off to their Mama—quite happy in the nursery with poor old Nana, they was." (Rex and Ena were past charges.)

Christopher Kininmonth had a temporary Nanny in the mid-1920s who was about sixty. If they were naughty she would say: "Boney will get you." A tribute to the immense fear Napoleon had inspired.

> Tick, tack, toe
> My first go
> Ten jolly nigger boys all in a row.
> Put one up,
> Put one down,
> Put one in the old man's crown.
>
> Edward (or any child's Christian name)
> Tedward
> Rix tix tedward
> Boo ba binx
> And a big-toed Edward.
>
> *Jennifer*
> *Ennifer*
> *Rix tix tennifer*
> *Boo Ba Binx*
> And a big-*Toed Jennifer*.

My correspondent, Mrs. Pooley, did not say, but I presume this rhyme accompanied the counting of toes, each toe being counted where I have indicated the stress in the third example, ending with one of the big toes.

Words	Action
DOWN by the station	
EARLY in the morning	
SEE the puffing billies all in a row.	
See the engine DRIVER	
A stoking up his engine—	Nanny does vigorous miming of
Poo poo poop	stoking
Chuff chuff chuff	
AND AWAY WE GO!	
Eensie weensie spider	Nanny makes spider movements
Climbing up the spout	with her fingers.
DOWN comes the rain	Shakes head

Washes POOR spider out.	sadly
OUT comes the sunshine	Flings arms wide.
DRIES up all the rain.	HUGE smiles.
Eeensie weensie spider	
Goes climbing up again.	Spider movements.

Miscellaneous comments

Frosted windows on a winter morning: "Jack Frost's been at work."

"I know you, you'll go right through the orchard and never pick a crab." (That is, you'll never marry.)

"You're one of Pharaoh's lean kine." (Too thin.)

"What a nice snap that would make for the *Tatler*."

('Words' meant disputes.) "I don't want to have words with her." "I had words with him." Or "It came to words."

Blowing nose: "There! Big blow! That's better."

"Good riddance to bad rubbish."

"If wishes were horses beggars could ride."

Victorian Nanny at three p.m. on a rainy afternoon in a seaside lodging: "I don't 'old with it being so early."

"I took her from the month." Many Nannies took charge of their children after a month; till then the monthly nurse had looked after it. (This, incidentally, must have been the last distant echo of the wet nurse.)

"You're so sharp you'll cut yourself."

"Those who ask don't get; those who don't ask don't want."

Taking medicine: "Upsie daisy, hold your nose. Swallow hard and down she goes."

Going to sleep: "The Sandman's on his way." Or "Up the little wooden stairs to Bedfordshire." Or "Up the wooden hill and down sheet lane."

Or
> "Good night
> Sweet repose
> Lie on your back
> And not on your nose."

"Somebody got out of bed the wrong side today."

"You know what'll happen if the wind changes while you're making that face." (When child looks cross. The angry expression is fixed for ever.)

"It's enough to try the patience of a saint."

"Patience is a virtue, virtue is a grace, hope the cat don't scratch your face." Alternative: "Patience is a virtue, virtue is a grace, both of them together make a very pretty face."

"Cry on your birthday, cry every day of the year."

"If you tell fibs you'll get pimples on your tongue."

"Want must be your master."

"If you ask me, too much book-learning never did nobody any good." (Arrival of a governess.)

Dirty finger nails: "In mourning for the cat?"

Child swallows a cherry stone: "A cherry tree will grow out of your head."

> "Friday night's dream, Saturday told
> Will surely come true, however old."

"What can't be cured must be endured."

"He'd be late for his own funeral."

APPENDIX B

Comparative Values of the Pound

Comparing the purchasing power of the pound is notoriously difficult. However, some rough approximations may be obtained from the table below. It should only be regarded, warn the Central Statistical Office from whose figures it is derived, as impressionistic. It is based on the value of the pound in February 1993.

Year	Value	Year	Value
1830	£42.17	1915	£39.88
1835	£46.88	1920	£19.31
1840	£37.52	1925	£27.53
1845	£44.95	1930	£31.05
1850	£49.89	1935	£36.20
1855	£39.24	1939–45	No figures
1860	£44.95	1946	£18.86
1865	£46.89	1950	£15.57
1870	£44.22	1955	£12.51
1875	£44.25	1960	£10.97
1880	£46.89	1965	£ 9.42
1885	£52.30	1970	£ 7.62
1890	£54.94	1975	£ 4.38
1895	£60.06	1980	£ 2.19
1900	£56.36	1985	£ 1.48
1905	£54.63	1990	£ 1.10
1910	£51.09	1993	£ 1.00

BIBLIOGRAPHY

This is not the complete list of books I consulted. I read a fairly large number of books which yielded little or nothing. I have not, for example, included *Scoop* by Evelyn Waugh, or *The Odd Women* by Gissing. I also developed a technique I called Memoir Skimming. This entailed sitting in the stacks at the London Library and skimming through the early chapters of autobiographies and biographies—stopping whenever I saw the word Nurse or Nanny. I obtained or confirmed many small items of information in this way, but only recorded the source if I discovered something substantial.

Abbot, Eleanor Hallowell, *Being Little in Cambridge, When Everyone Else Was Big*, D. Appleton-Century Co., New York

Aberconway, Lady Christabel, *A Wiser Woman?* Hutchinson

Acland, Eleanor, *Goodbye for the Present*, Hodder and Stoughton

Almedingen, E. M., *Fanny*, O.U.P.

Anstey, F., *A Long Retrospect*, O.U.P.

Ariès, Philippe, *Centuries of Childhood*, Cape

Baring, Maurice, *The Puppet Show of Memory*, Heinemann

Barrie, James, *Peter Pan*, Hodder and Stoughton

Bennett, Alan, *Forty Years On*, Faber and Faber

Bessborough, Earl of, ed., *Georgiana*, Extracts from the Correspondence of the Duchess of Devonshire, John Murray

Bettelheim, Bruno, *The Children of the Dream*, Thames and Hudson

Boswell, James, *Life of Johnson*, O.U.P.

Brenan, Gerald, *A Life of One's Own*, Hamish Hamilton

Bridges, Yseult, *Saint—With Red Hands?*, Jarrolds

Brooke, Harold and Kay Bannerman, *All For Mary*, A Farce in Three Acts, Evans Bros.

Butterfield, Herbert, *Man on His Past*, C.U.P.

Cecil, Lord David, *The Young Melbourne*, Constable

Cecil, Robert, *Life in Edwardian England*, Batsford

Chesney, Kellow, *The Victorian Underworld*, Maurice Temple Smith

Churchill, Randolph S., *Winston S. Churchill*, Vol. I: *Youth, 1874–1900*, Heinemann

Churchill, Sir Winston S., *My Early Life, 1874–1908*, Collins

Clephane, Irene and Alan Bolt, *Our Mothers*, Gollancz

Clive, Mary, *Christmas with the Savages*, Macmillan
——*The Day of Reckoning*, Macmillan
Comfort, Alex, *The Anxiety Makers*, Nelson
Compton-Burnett, Ivy, *Parents and Children*, Gollancz
Creston, Dormer, *Enter a Child*, Macmillan
Dickens, Charles, *The Uncommercial Traveller*, O.U.P.
——*Nurse's Stories*, in *All the Year Round*, 1860
Donleavy, J. P., *The Beastly Beatitudes of Balthazar B*, Eyre and Spottiswoode
Eager, *Six Years at the Russian Court*, Hurst and Blackett
Evelyn, John, *The Diary*, ed. E. S. de Beer, O.U.P.
Fane, Julian, *Memoir in the Middle of the Journey*, Hamish Hamilton
——*Morning*, John Murray
Fielding, Daphne, *Mercury Presides*, Eyre and Spottiswoode
Finley, M. I., *The Ancient Greeks*, Chatto and Windus
Freud, S., *A Child is Being Beaten*
Gibbs, Mary Ann, *The Years of the Nannies*, Hutchinson
Godrey, Elizabeth, *English Children in the Olden Time*, Methuen
Gore, Betsy, *The Gore Family*, memoir privately printed
Gorer, Geoffrey, *Exploring English Character*, The Cresset Press
Gorer, Geoffrey and John Rickman, *The People of Great Russia*, The Cresset Press
Graham, Andrew, *Mostly Nasty*, Geoffrey Bles
Halsband, Robert, *Life of Lady Mary Wortley Montagu*, O.U.P.
Hare, Humphrey, *Swinburne*, H. F. and G. Witherby
Howe, Bea, *A Galaxy of Governesses*, D. Verschoyle
King-Hall, Magdalen, *The Story of the Nursery*, Routledge and Kegan Paul
Kipling, Rudyard, *From Under the Deodars and Other Stories*, S. Low, 1890
——*A Diversity of Creatures*, Macmillan
Lane, Margaret, *The Tale of Beatrix Potter*, Frederick Warne
Lawrence, Evelyn, *Friedrich Froebel and English Education*, Routledge and Kegan
    Paul
Linklater, Eric, *Juan in America*, Cape
Locke, John, *Thoughts Concerning Education*, ed. F. W. Garforth, Heinemann Educ.
Mackenzie, Sir Compton, *Sinister Street*, Macdonald and Co.
——*My Life and Times, Octave I*, Chatto and Windus
Marchand, Leslie A., *Lord Byron: Biography*, John Murray
Marcus, Steven, *The Other Victorians*, Weidenfeld and Nicolson
Mitford, Jessica, *Hons and Rebels*, Gollancz
Mitford, Nancy, *The Blessing*, Hamish Hamilton
Moran, Lord, *Winston Churchill: The Struggle for Survival*, Constable
Mussen, P. H., J. J. Conger and J. Kagan, *Child Development anersod Pnality*,
    Harper and Row
Nabokov, Vladimir, *Speak, Memory*, Weidenfeld and Nicolson
Nicolson, Harold, *Some People*, Constable

Pearson, Hesketh, *Bernard Shaw*, Methuen

Peter II, King, of Yugoslavia, *A King's Heritage*, Cassell

Pinchbeck, J. and M. Hewitt, *Children in English Society*, Routledge and Kegan Paul

Psychoanalytic Study of the Child, The, ed. A. Freud and others, Hogarth Press

Reade, Brian, *The Beardsley Foreground*—Lecture to Art Historians of Southern California

Rose, Kenneth, *Superior Person*, biography of Lord Curzon, Weidenfeld and Nicolson

Ross, J. B. and M. M. McLaughlin, *A Portable Medieval Reader*, Viking Press, New York

Sackville-West, Edward, *Simpson*, Weidenfeld and Nicolson

Sinclair, Catherine, *Holiday House*, Longman

Sitwell, Osbert, *Left Hand, Right Hand*, Macmillan

Stephens, William N., *The Family in Cross-cultural Perspective*, Holt, Rinehart and Winston

Stewart, J. I. M., *Rudyard Kipling*, Gollancz

Storr, Dr. Anthony, A. J. P. Taylor and others, *Churchill: Four Faces and the Man*, Alan Lane

The History of The Times, Vols. II and III, The Times Publishing Co.

Waugh, Evelyn, *Brideshead Revisited*, Chapman and Hall

Wilson, Angus, *The World of Charles Dickens*, Secker and Warburg

Winnicott, D. W., *The Child, the Family and the Outside World*, Tavistock Publications

Wolfe, Tom, *The Kandy-Kolored Tangerine-Flake Streamline Baby*, Cape

Woolf, Leonard, *Sowing*, Hogarth Press

Index